W9-BZF-547

INTO LAOS

INTO LAOS
The Story of Dewey Canyon II/Lam Son 719;
Vietnam 1971

Keith William Nolan

PRESIDIO

Map of Lam Son 719 by Shelby Stanton copyright by Shelby Stanton 1985
Used with permission from *Rise and Fall of an American Army, U.S. Ground
Forces, Vietnam 1965-1973*, published by Presidio Press, Novato, CA.

Printed in the United States of America

This book is for all those
who soldiered in Vietnam
especially those
who in the demoralized last days
still looked out for
the man to their right
and the man to their left

...and for April

What makes people rebel against suffering is not really suffering itself, but the senselessness of suffering. Man, the most courageous animal, and the most inured to trouble, does not deny suffering per se; he wants it, he seeks it out, provided that it can be given meaning.

Friedrich Nietzsche
The Genealogy of Morals

CONTENTS

PART FOUR: A RENEWED EFFORT

Preface

The return of our Vietnam veterans was not greeted with a parade or handshake, but with a magazine article which warned the parents and wives of ex-soldiers, "If you avoid argument because he's been trained to killing and to anger, and you are afraid of his releasing them on you—another common problem—you've got to talk about it. Chances are he has been afraid about this, too."

It was just such glib and abhorrent generalizations about those young Americans who went to Vietnam—all the old tales of psycho killers, human time bombs, and drug addicts—that first prompted my interest in the subject. My main concern is, and has always been, not so much the tactics of the campaigns, but the personalities, motivations, and behavior of the individual American soldier. For this reason I sought out the veterans themselves; men, it turned out, who, despite the ominous warning cited above, were usually willing to talk, encouraging, and well settled back into civilian life. Or they were as well settled as any man who has seen war, especially an unpopular war, can be.

My initial efforts were met by overwhelming support from the Vietnam veterans with whom I had the honor of communicating. The result was a history of the U.S. Marines in the Battle of Hue City. That was the story of young men who were all volunteers and who fought in early 1968, a time when even though the nation was divided, there were at least no major outcries against the warriors themselves. But what about the latter stages of the war when draftees filled the ranks. Incidents like

My Lai warped the nation's attitudes towards its fighting men, and dark stories of drug addiction, murder, and mutiny in the U.S. Army made the headlines.

The last major operation the Americans fought in Vietnam was the invasion of Laos in 1971, when the crisis in morale was at its peak. It was a sad, confusing time; a time when American politicians declared, while young Americans were dying on the Vietnam battlefield, that the true heroes of the Vietnam War were those who protested; a time when the media inferred that the American soldier was no match for the North Vietnamese; a time when returning veterans were physically and mentally attacked by their own countrymen.

Just how bad were things on the battlefield of 1971? To attempt an answer, the invasion of Laos seemed a natural focal point as it was the last major campaign that the U.S. Army mounted in Vietnam, involving in combat infantry, aviation, armor, artillery, and support units. There is no denying that morale was bad but not as bad as reported. My main concern is to explore the reasons things had soured. Hopefully this book will illustrate the frustration which drove morale down, and how this change in attitude manifested itself in the day-to-day performance of the U.S. Army in Vietnam.

The veterans of the Laos campaign who helped in preparing this book were: Lt. Gen. Sidney Berry, USA (Ret.); Lt. Gen. Donn Robertson, USMC, (Ret.); Lt. Gen. Donald Rosenblum, USA (Ret.); Lt. Gen. James Sutherland, USA (Ret.); Maj. Gen. Ben Harrison, USA (Ret.); Maj. Gen. Robert Molinelli, USA; Brig. Gen. Phan Hoa Hiep, ARVN, (Ret.); Brig. Gen. Richard Morton, USA (Ret.); Brig. Gen. Charles Pitman, USMC; Col. Ray Battreall, USA (Ret.); Col. George Chase, USA (Ret.); Col. William Dabney, USMC; Col. Edward Davis, USA (Ret.); Col. Joseph Ganahl, USA (Ret.); Col. Gerald Kirklighter, USA (Ret.); Col. John Klose, USA (Ret.); Col. Richard Meyer, USA (Ret.) Col. John Miller, USMC; Lt. Col. Tom Stewart, USA (Ret.); Majors Philip Bodenhorn, John Christian, John Dewing, USAR; Majors David Ferrell, Charles Garwood, John Mercadante, Steve Overstreet, and Euell White, USA (Ret.); ex-Capt. Gerald Downey, USA; Capt. Rich Johnson, USA; ex-Capt. Ken Lord, USA; Capt. Drayton Markle, USAR; Capt. Harold Spurgeon, ARNG; ex-Capt. Bruce Updyke; ex-Lt. Don Malmstrom; Lt. Philip Smith, ARNG; Lt. Harry Walters, ARNG; ex-Lt. Don Stephen; CW4 Chuck Hawk, USA; ex-WO Lyle Borders, USA; ex-WO Harold

Smith, USA; Sgt. Maj. Roy Nelson, USA (Ret.); 1st Sgt. Roy Hatfield, USA, (Ret.); M. Sgt. Guy Shelley, USA; T. Sgt. Charles Barnett, USAF, (Ret.); ex-Sergeants James Brock, Frank Burnett, Michael Daugherty, Ray Keefer, John Kucera, Jim McCormack, Charles McKenzie, John Michalak, and Larry White, USA; ex-Sp5s John Carney, Dennis Fujii, Dennis Lundstrom, and Bill Wilder, USA; ex-Cpl. Carson Bartels, USMC; ex-Sp4s Mike Castro, John Coleman, Mike Davis, Mike DeAngelis, Mike Fitzmaurice, Pat Hallman, Jim Keeney, Russ Morse, Steve Rhodes, Ron Smith, and William Warren, USA; and John Saar of Time-Life, Inc.

A special note of thanks also goes to Mr. and Mrs. William Stahl whose son, Roger, was killed during the Laotian operation while with the 101st Airborne Division. They contacted me and provided valuable information. In the same vein, a heartfelt thanks goes to Mr. John Palm whose son was killed while a platoon leader with the 101st Airborne in the Ripcord operation. He was most helpful. And another thank you for the information provided by Mrs. John Cope Pence; her husband participated in Operation Lamson 719 and I wrote to his address, not realizing he'd passed away.

There were numerous other veterans whom I interviewed who were not in the Laotian campaign; their help is much appreciated. Those whose thoughts or commentary were specifically used in this book include: Col. William Hauser, USA (Ret.); Maj. Charles Hawkins, USAR; Dr. Jim Bannon; ex-Lt. John Bayers, USA; ex-Sgt. Larry Moss, USA; ex-Sgt. Kim Rider, USA; ex-Sp5 John Weller, USA; ex-Cpl. Lewis Lawhorn, USMC; and a veteran who requested anonymity and who is described in the prologue.

Numerous official agencies helped in the research, including: Administrative Service, Veterans Administration, Washington, D.C.; Association of Graduates, and the Library, U.S. Military Academy; Chief of Military History and the Center of Military History, Washington, D.C.; Fort Polk Military Museum, Louisiana; Naval Historical Center, Washington Navy Yard; Office of the Adjutant General, Alexandria, Virginia; U.S. Army Enlisted Records and Evaluation Center, Fort Benjamin Harrison, Indiana; U.S. Army Transportation Technical Information and Research Center, Fort Eustis, Virginia; and the U.S. Marine Corps History and Museums Division, Washington Navy Yard.

This then is the story of those Americans fighting the country's last major operation in Vietnam. Few generalizations can be made about them, as in the confusion of the time they responded as individuals, not members of a united effort. Perhaps the only generalization that can be made is that, whatever their beliefs and motives, most of the men depicted in these pages were brave.

For that alone, they deserve America's recognition.

Prologue

T he Green Berets of the 5th Special Forces Group were the best trained American soldiers in Vietnam, and the college professor had been one of them. He spent eighteen months in Nam, coming in-country in 1968 when he was twenty-three and newly married. He was a staff sergeant, tattooed and tough, but he was also an educated man. When his reconnaissance teams crossed the border for operations along the Ho Chi Minh Trail in Laos, he thought of the line from Corneille: "Deeds of great courage were done in the darkness and never seen or recorded." Cross-border ops in Laos were not publicly authorized and therefore did not happen; most of the sergeant's friends would not discuss the matter with outsiders (reporters), and he emphasized that his statements were merely guesses.

What he guessed was detailed and immersed in the incredibly euphemistic language of Vietnam. The Special Forces units that raided Laos were designated SOG (Studies and Observation Group). They were ostensibly in Vietnam to study the tactics of the forces fighting the war. The teams were issued maps without international border lines. After-action reports were couched in a bizarre language: Laos was "denied and enemy-controlled territory," the U.S. recon teams were FGUs or "Friendly Guerrilla Units," casualties were recorded as having been incurred inside South Vietnam. The reconnaissance teams didn't go out with U.S. weapons, carrying instead "sterile" ones, communist-made Ak-47 automatic rifles or Swedish K submachineguns, keeping their ammunition in

North Vietnamese pouches slung across their chests. They even wore modified jungle boots, the cleated soles having been replaced with tire rubber so the prints resembled those of the enemy's Ho Chi Minh sandals. The sergeant and his team of U.S. soldiers and Montagnard mercenaries crossed the border on a variety of missions: recon, prisoner snatch, trail watch, truck counting, bomb-damage assessment from the B52 Arc Lights, and harassment of NVA supply columns coming down the Ho Chi Minh Trail. Whenever they went in big, up to twenty-four men, with the purpose of raising hell, they were met punch for punch by the many North Vietnamese Army units bunkered along the Trail. The NVA probably loved hunting down the small commando teams, the sergeant thought, after having endured numerous U.S. airstrikes where they could only shake a fist skyward in helpless rage. Using air and artillery to cut the Trail usually met with disaster; the NVA, realizing that someone must be in the hills adjusting the fire, would sweep the high ground. They usually flushed out the recon teams and bitter firefights ensued with the woefully outnumbered Americans and Montagnards calling in close air support while they scrambled aboard extraction helicopters under fire. Sometimes entire teams vanished in the Laotian mountains, overrun, the few survivors captured. Nearly everyone, including the young sergeant, ended up with some kind of wound.

The only time they came through unscathed was when they worked small, two Americans and two to four Montagnards (primitive hill tribesmen, suspicious of Saigon but fiercely loyal to the Green Berets). They wore tigerstripe fatigues and went out loaded down with ammunition, gear, medical supplies, and demolitions. They moved silently through the jungles of Laos, gear fastened so it didn't rattle, the point-man not hacking at the brush with a machete but only pushing the bramble aside, the last man in line pushing it back in place. Sometimes they reached a deserted point on the Trail and took intelligence photos, installed electronic listening devices, or pulled dirty tricks like booby trapping ammunition caches with exploding mortar rounds and AK-47 magazines.

The sergeant could only marvel at the Ho Chi Minh Trail. It was not a single road, but a tangle of trails woven and interconnected; and anything but a trail. It was more a high-speed, two-lane highway of laterite clay, with bunkers along the side and living vines and palms thatched overhead to hide it from U.S. planes. All the constructions were well planned, underground, sturdy. Even the individual spider-holes for the NVA soldiers were perfectly dug, all sides squared off and reinforced with lashed bamboo. Hundreds of them dotted the branches of the Trail, all exactly the same. The sergeant had heard that the Communists copied the foxhole dimensions from French manuals and never deviated a millimeter from the textbook examples. Ants, the enemy soldiers were called. Even down under the sweating triple-canopy jungle, amid wreckage from airstrikes, political indoctrination classrooms were found equipped with chalk boards, benches, and stacks of mimeographed communist doctrine.

Fighting the North Vietnamese was like battling an army of robots; an indoctrinated mass, without imagination or individuality, who blindly kept fighting despite horrendous losses. Regardless of motives, they were brave and disciplined and the sergeant had a lot of respect for them.

Khe Sanh Area and Lam Son 719 Offensive

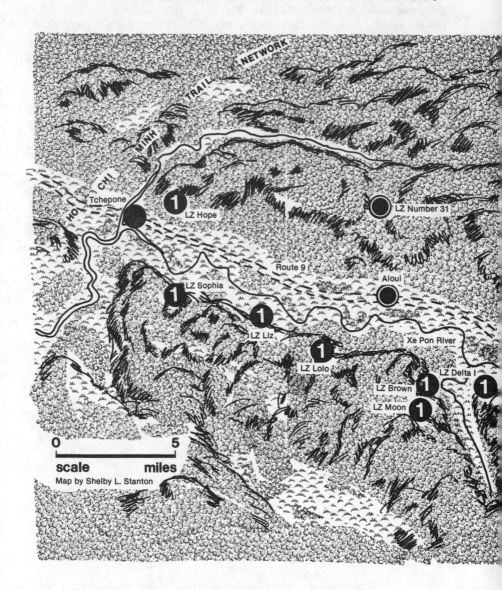

Map by Shelby L. Stanton

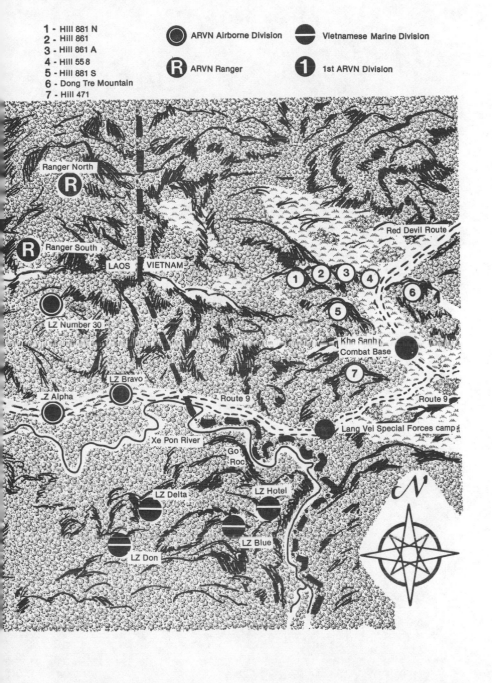

1 - Hill 881 N
2 - Hill 861
3 - Hill 861 A
4 - Hill 558
5 - Hill 881 S
6 - Dong Tre Mountain
7 - Hill 471

ARVN Airborne Division

Vietnamese Marine Division

R ARVN Ranger

1 1st ARVN Division

Ranger North
R

R Ranger South
LAOS VIETNAM

LZ Number 30

Red Devil Route

1 2 3 4

6

5

Khe Sanh
Combat Base

7

LZ Bravo

Z Alpha   Route 9   Route 9

Lang Vei Special Forces camp

Xe Pon River
Go
Roc

LZ Delta   LZ Hotel

LZ Blue

LZ Don

N

PART ONE: Operation Dewey Canyon II

CHAPTER ONE: The Cambodian Prelude

The grunts of D Company, 6th Battalion, 31st Infantry, 9th Division were nervous. Two days before, they'd been airlifted from an operation in the Plain of Reeds in the Mekong Delta and deposited at an abandoned sugar mill in the jungle near the Cambodian border. There was no word on why they were there. One of the officers, Lt. John Bayer, the company's artillery forward observer, was as uneasy as the young infantrymen. He was a thin man with eyeglasses and a toothbrush mustache, cajoled into the service after graduate school. A world apart in age and education from most of the grunts in Delta Company, Bayer shared at least two things with them; he wanted nothing to do with Vietnam and was there because, even though he thought it a nonsensical war, his sense of duty would not allow him to rationalize an excuse by which he could shirk his way out.

On the company's second day of rumor-filled waiting, Bayer and the four platoon leaders joined their company commander in the gutted mill building, sitting casually on their cots as the captain explained that the battalion was going to be part of an offensive into the North-Vietnamese-Army sanctuaries in the Parrot's Beak.

They were invading Cambodia.

The next day, the entire battalion boarded UH1 Hueys, troop-carrying helicopters nicknamed slicks because they had only two door-gunners in the cabins for protection. They crossed the invisible line separating the South Vietnamese and Cambodian jungles and made an airmobile combat assault (CA'd) into an NVA basecamp. It was a cold insertion—free of enemy fire—and, as the infantrymen fanned out, they found no enemy soldiers but did uncover bunkers and caches of food provisions in the sweltering patchwork of bamboo groves and rice paddies. From that jumping-off point, Delta Company was detached from the main body of the battalion and humped (patrolled) a few kilometers deeper into the jungle. The company commander established his command post amid the weeds and began sending platoon patrols out to hunt for the North Vietnamese and their supply caches.

One of the platoons was ordered to patrol near a beautiful Cambodian village called Chantrea and, although Lieutenant Bayer's FO team was not assigned to go, his radio-telephone operator, a blond kid named Lonsdale, asked to go with him. Bayer told him he didn't have to but Lonsdale grinned and said he wanted to; he loved to go out and hump, playing John Wayne with the grunts. The company had not had a serious contact for a long time and this still seemed much like a war game. They moved out, Lonsdale took the point and, on the outskirts of Chantrea, an NVA blew him away with a burst of AK-47 automatic rifle fire. The radio reports crackled back to the CP that the platoon was pinned down in a dry rice paddy. Bayer grabbed his helmet and M-16 rifle with a vengeance, absolutely boiling for revenge: Lonsdale had been a rock-steady kid. He clambered aboard the slicks which had come to whisk the remainder of Delta Company to the firefight, feeling the desire to kill for the first time in his life.

They sailed in over the treetops and CA'd into the parched paddy field, the door-gunners firing madly toward the village, the grunts jumping out and hitting the ground at a run. It was a hot LZ, under enemy fire. Bayer threw himself to the ground scrunched against a one-foot-high paddy dike, GIs on line beside him the length of the berm, pouring fire back at the far treeline. A grunt next to him held up his M-16 to fire blindly over the dike, and a GI crouching nearby broke into snarled obscenities when his weapon jammed in his hands. The North Vietnamese fire relentlessly tore holes in the air around them sounding, Bayer thought like bees, AK rounds zipping over his head and thunking loudly into the paddy behind them. His whole body tensed up in anticipation of a bullet hitting him. Finally he relaxed a bit and got on the radio to the artillery battery which had been airlifted into Cambodia to support them. He requested white phosphorus shells be fired on the bamboo grove between them and the ville, hoping to burn it down and expose the NVA. A half-dozen rounds slammed into the treeline, burning white and smokey against the green before the artilleryman on the other end of the radio said they only had three Willy Peter rounds left. Jesus Christ, Bayer cursed inwardly, typical, fucking typical. He started calling in high explosive shot and the village of Chantrea shuddered under the shrapnel-spewing explosions. But, for all that, the NVA kept up their fire and Delta Company was stuck in the rice field. Finally as the sun went down, the enemy fire slacked off enough for the company commander to order them north to set up for the night behind a network of higher paddy dikes.

That night five mortar rounds exploded in the space they had vacated.

In the morning, Delta Company swept forward on foot. The NVA were gone. The grunts shared their C rations with the Cambodians in the village, then told them to leave. The company commander ordered Chantrea burned. The young grunts loved it, finding it a catharsis for the memory of their buddies who'd been killed or wounded the day before. They dragged torches through the thatch hootches, gunning down pigs and water buffalos, rock'n'rolling from the hip. Bayer thought of William Calley, under investigation at the time for My Lai; before long he and the other officers were shouting to get the worked-up infantrymen back under control.

The next day, they were back on the move, Bayer humping along with the company commander in the broiling sun as they patrolled down a dirt road in the jungle. Coming upon a deserted bamboo village, it was gut-tightening to see food and NVA gear stacked beside the hootches. The company kept moving, everyone a little more tense and alert. The platoon off on the right flank began to get disorganized in the bramble of vines, trees, and bushes—then the NVA hit. AK-47 fire erupted from the front and Bayer jumped flat into a ditch alongside the foot-path. NVA mortar shells began thunking from their tubes and exploding among the trees. Bayer could see a small concrete building tucked in the vegetation up the road and was sure the NVA had a forward observer sitting in there with a radio.

With NVA fire slashing around them, the captain got on the horn to call for air support. AH1G Cobra gunships came on station and began circling and strafing; the jungle shook in the blizzard from 7.62mm mini-guns screaming at two thousand rounds a minute and 2.75-inch flechette rockets pumping down with white trails. Bayer could see figures among the trees on the other side of the trail. He got up to run to them but hesitated, and instead, a tall, mustached GI named Macomber ran onto the path—just as one of the Cobras plunged down in a strafing run and fired two more rockets. The pilot pressed the button a moment too soon and the rockets exploded amid Delta Company. Bayer curled up in the dirt, clutching his helmet, shrapnel and dirt clods blowing over him, a piece of U.S. steel stinging in his hip.

In seconds the dust and roar was settling and then he could hear screams from the platoon across the path. AK rounds continued to punch past. There was a moment of hesitation, but then the young grunts ran like hell towards the carnage. It was all chaos and blood. Macomber was sprawled on the road, his chest peppered with shrapnel. Bayer crouched next to him as he gave a long sigh and then was dead. Another grunt ran up, clutching his weapon, blood running down his arms, dripping from his fingers. The kid stumbled about in shock, screaming at people to get up and help the wounded, then he blew off his M-16 magazine into the dirt and collapsed. Bayer started helping with the casualties, then saw the platoon leader sitting dazed in the grass. He was a big friendly man from Georgia who'd been in the company since Bayer had transferred in. The back of his head was ragged with shrapnel and streaming blood. He turned to his platoon sergeant, told him he was in charge, then slumped mortally wounded in the undergrowth.

The NVA fire kept up, most of it coming from a bunker twenty yards away. If if wasn't silenced, the wounded might be pinned down and die. Bayer began crawling towards it, firing his M-16 nonstop until he realized he had only two magazines left from the fourteen he'd been carrying. Two more grunts ran up to fire on the bunker; then a fair-haired kid named Walker stood up in the brush across the road, and as Bayer watched, amazed at his cool, he just walked through the AK bursts, firing his M-16 and lobbing fragmentation grenades. With an M-79 grenade launcher he popped rounds right into the bunker aperture.

The North Vietnamese fire stopped.

They rushed back to carry the dead and wounded down the path, and medevacs—medical evacuation helicopters—came in. The captain got back on the radio to call in F4 Phantom jets splashing napalm canisters. The grunts crouched down while eighty feet ahead, the jungle turned into a black and yellow fireball, flames rolling up in thick streamers, heat shimmering back. The jets banked off, the captain said to saddle up, and

Delta Company started forward again. Bayer found a book on the path that had fallen out of the thigh pocket of his jungle fatigues. It was a collection of readings from western philosophy and was burnt from the napalm. He thought it a morbid symbol.

They overran the NVA bunkers, but the enemy had fallen back, disappeared. Delta set up in a tight night position and Bayer sat there, getting more and more spooked as he stared at the lumpy body bag of Macomber lying inside the perimeter with them. The next day, Bayer got his reprieve; he was choppered out of Cambodia to attend the memorial service for his dead radioman at their battalion basecamp. He was still numb from his first and last heavy contact, not caring much when the captain said he was up for the Silver Star. The only things on his mind were guilt and waste; guilt because Lonsdale had been eighteen when he died, a solid young man, and it had been Bayer who had allowed him to accompany the patrol; waste because he could find no good coming out of the deaths he'd just seen.

Lieutenant Bayer and Delta Company had crossed the border into Cambodia on 1 May 1970 as part of Operation Toan Thang (Total Victory) 43. It was a major attack along the border aimed at destroying the NVA basecamps and supply caches which had long been in the area, safe as a sanctuary because of Cambodia's previous neutrality. The invasion force included ground elements of the 1st Air Cavalry Division, the 4th, 9th, and 25th Infantry Divisions, the 101st Airborne Division, the 11th Armored Cavalry Regiment, and a host of ARVN (Army of the Republic of Vietnam) units. President Richard Nixon's decision to launch the incursion into Cambodia was a radical departure from the policies of the Johnson administration, and a dramatic indication of the aggressive methods the new president was willing to pursue in the fight against the North Vietnamese invasion of South Vietnam. It was a politically divisive move, but a military imperative if "Vietnamization" was to be given the breathing room to grow and mature.

Cambodia and its northern neighbor, Laos, had long been thorns in the side of the U.S. war effort in Vietnam. The Communists, taking advantage of the weakness of the leaders and armies of the two nations, moved in force to occupy the sparsely-populated border regions. There they constructed elaborate roadways for infiltration into South Vietnam, supply depots, basecamps for the rest and refitting of units, artillery emplacements to shell across the border, and the like. Cambodia and Laos gave the North Vietnamese sanctuaries from which to launch attacks and for retreat when bloodied in battle.

Before Nixon, President Johnson had followed a policy of essentially ignoring the sanctuaries and instructing the military to do the same. Gen. William Westmoreland, Commander of U.S. forces in Vietnam from 1964 to 1968 (his official title was Commander, U.S. Military Assistance Command—Vietnam) had always suspected the importance of the sanctuaries. As early as 1965, Westmoreland's intelligence chief had compiled evidence of seven major NVA bases in Cambodia (including the Parrot's Beak, a bulge less than thirty miles from Saigon) and of the Cambodian port town of Sihanoukville being used to bring arms and supplies which were then infiltrated into South Vietnam. By 1966 the continued investigations by MACV Intelligence showed that the NVA was using Laos and Cambodia as major infiltration routes, converging into South Vietnam from the north by the Ho Chi Minh Trail and from the south by the Sihanouk Trail.

The evidence was duly reported to the Johnson administration, with the weight of the reports falling on Cambodia. The government's response was to try to court the Cambodian premier, Prince Norodom Sihanouk, and usher him into the allies' circle ("... which seemed to us in Saigon to be naive," General Westmoreland wrote in his memoirs, "unless we should demonstrate unmistakably that we were going to succeed in South Vietnam, for Sihanouk clearly was out to play the winner."). The administration was timid about responding openly and forcefully to the Communist presence in Laos and Cambodia, afraid that too strong a flexing of muscle would drive Sihanouk into open collusion with Hanoi. Therefore, Westmoreland was forbidden to reveal the presence of sanctuaries to the world press. There came as a result, some embarrassing moments such as a lieutenant general telling reporters his units would engage the NVA on the border and then they "disappeared to the west." Did this mean the enemy was operating within Cambodia? "One can draw no other conclusion." A journalist pursued the point with Secretary of Defense Robert McNamara who answered that there was insufficient evidence to support the general's comment. Asked to clarify this disagreement, the lieutenant general smiled, "I stand corrected."

The Cambodian and Laotian sanctuaries were major assets to the Communist invasion effort, and U.S. commanders chafed with frustration at their inability to do anything; their stated mission was to hunt down the Communists and destroy them, but they were not only denied access to North Vietnam but also to the border regions. General Westmoreland shared that bitterness. Starting in 1965, he requested permission to launch counter-measures in Cambodia which included air and ground reconnaissance across the border, hot pursuit against NVA units retreating into the sanctuary, and B52 bombing missions against confirmed enemy basecamp. The Joint Chiefs of Staff approved most of his ideas; the State Department vetoed them. Westmoreland bitterly wrote, " . . . all we could do to the enemy in Cambodia was drop propaganda leaflets on our side of the border whenever the wind was right to blow them across."

In 1966 President Johnson acquiesced slightly to the general's requests. Permission was granted to conduct air and artillery strikes in Cambodia against NVA units firing from across the border. In rare cases, usually when the survival of an allied unit was at stake, hot pursuit was permitted. Later, permission was granted to conduct limited air reconnaissance over Cambodia, but the pilots were not allowed to return fire. Still later, ground recon patrols were authorized. Most were organized by MACV-SOG and their covert form of war was given a free hand in Laos. However, in Cambodia, they were only allowed to fight in self defense. Such measures were small and did little to upset the Communists' continued use of sanctuaries. It wasn't until late 1967 that Johnson even admitted their presence, and that was forced upon him after reporters visited an NVA camp in Cambodia. Still, no major actions were mounted. Westmoreland's contingency plans of multi-division invasions of Laos and Cambodia only collected dust at MACV Headquarters. Even in 1968, when the North Vietnamese Army and Viet Cong were crippled and on the verge of collapse after their disastrous Tet Offensive, President Johnson would not allow the military to press home a meaningful victory by cleaning out the sanctuaries.

As history would have it, it fell to Gen. Creighton Abrams (Westmoreland's successor as COMUSMACV) to launch the Cambodian and Laotian incursions. The change in policy was instigated by President Nixon who, in 1969, soon after taking office, authorized secret B52 bombing raids on the NVA in Cambodia. In March 1970, Prince Sihanouk was overthrown by Gen. Lon Nol, the anti-Vietnamese prime minister. Lon Nol closed the Sihanoukville port to communist ships and ordered the NVA and VC to remove themselves from Cambodia. The NVA responded by pummeling the Cambodian's "palace-guard" army, Lon Nol requested U.S. support. With this impetus, Secretary of State Henry Kissinger brought up the idea of finally moving into Cambodia to neutralize the sanctuaries. Nixon gave the go-ahead.

When the U.S. and ARVN divisions crossed the border they were limited to a thirty-kilometer penetration. Antiwar protests quickly broke out, the most tragic being at Kent State where panicky National Guardsmen killed four students during a riot.

Yielding to the antiwar outcry, Nixon ordered all U.S. troops out of Cambodia by 30 June 1970. The ARVN stayed behind to continue operations against NVA still holding in the area. The results of the two-month American intervention were impressive. The Communists put up several bitter fights against the invasion force (over two thousand NVA were reported killed), but most had retreated in disorder, abandoning basecamps and supply caches. To put the number of captured or destroyed NVA gear into understandable terms, one analysis computed that the U.S./ARVN incursion had denied the NVA enough weapons to equip fifty-five battalions, enough crew-served weapons for eighty-five to ninety battalions, and enough small-arms ammunition to provide the basic combat load to fifty-two thousand soldiers. Also captured were ninety-five thousand tons of foodstuffs and twenty-eight tons of medical supplies. The blow had been severe (but not permanent because of the short duration of the invasion) and enemy activity in the South Vietnamese provinces bordering Cambodia dropped dramatically.

Impressive intelligence data was collected in Cambodia, much of it adding detail to what Westmoreland's intelligence officers had been saying since 1965. It was learned that Prince Sihanouk had sided with Hanoi in March 1965 (not so much out of ideological agreement, but because he felt they would be the side to emerge victorious from the long war) and had geared his policies accordingly. For example, the Cambodian army did not interfere with the NVA on their soil and the government itself sold fifty-five thousand tons of rice annually to the Communists (another hundred thousand tons came every year directly from Cambodian farmers).

The Cambodian incursion shut down the Sihanoukville port, Phnom Penh airfield, the Sihanouk Trail, and the North Vietnamese sanctuaries. It was a crippling setback for the Communists. From that point on, the NVA had to depend solely on their Laotian basecamps and the Ho Chi Minh

Trail. Following the logic which had set in motion the spoiling attack against Cambodia, the natural corollary would be similarly to disrupt the Laotian sanctuaries. As it turned out, seven months separated the two invasions;* the U.S./ARVN drive into Laos was launched in February 1971.

The communist response to the Cambodian invasion was typical of their tactics throughout the war—tenacious. With the Cambodian mainland closed to them and the coast actively patrolled by the U.S. Navy, the NVA worked feverishly to improve and expand the Ho Chi Minh Trail in Laos. Their ultimate goal was to use Laos as a springboard for an offensive back into Cambodia and east into the northern regions of South Vietnam. Directly east of the Laotian border were four South Vietnamese provinces (Quang Tri Province, furthest north and facing the DMZ border between the two Vietnams, followed by Thua Thien, Quang Nam, and Quang Ngai). They were what the U.S. called Military Region 1, and the ARVN called I Corps. The American command in the area was XXIV Corps (Lt. Gen. James W. Sutherland) and the ARVN was I Corps Headquarters (Lt. Gen. Hoang Xuan Lam). XXIV Corps controlled three major combat elements in MR1: 1st Brigade, 5th Infantry Division (Mechanized) (Brig. Gen. John G. Hill); 23d Infantry Division (Americal) (Maj. Gen. James L. Baldwin); and the 101st Airborne Division (Airmobile) (Maj. Gen. John J. Hennessey).

The first stage of the North Vietnamese counterattack in the wake of Cambodia was to strike from Laos towards the cities in MR1. One branch

---

*Invasion was the term used by the media and in popular history. It was not favored by the military, as Col. John Miller, a U.S. Marine advisor during Cambodia and Laos explained: "Those of us who had participated in the earlier cross-border thrust into Cambodia were both amused and irritated by the eagerness of the media—once again—to slap the hyped-up, pejorative label of 'invasion' (with its ponderous and chilling WWII connotations) on these relatively limited operations. Instead of wallowing in self-inflicted guilt, Americans should have been cheering about the long-delayed disruption of North Vietnam's sanctuaries along the Ho Chi Minh Trail and along the Cambodian border. We knew that the fight was not with the Laotians; it was with the NVA which had long before seized Laotian turf for its own use. Hysteria about so-called 'invasions' only further muddied the water, which had never been quite clear to begin with." The U.S. military described the operations as limited incursions or preemptive defensive raids.

of the Ho Chi Minh Trail diverted into South Vietnam through the A Shau Valley of Thua Thien Province; it was a major infiltration route to Hue City and the various military installations in the coastal lowlands. The A Shau/Hue area of operations was under (as supervised by XXIV Corps and I Corps) the U.S. 101st Airborne Division and the ARVN 1st Infantry Division. To meet the build-up in the A Shau Valley in July 1970, the 101st "Screaming Eagles" mounted operations from Fire Support Base Ripcord, and the 1st Division from Fire Support Base O'Reilly. Fighting was so intense that FSB Ripcord was evacuated under fire before July was over, and the ARVN withdrew from O'Reilly in early October before the onset of the rainy season further complicated defense of the firebase. The Ripcord/O'Reilly campaign did not drive the NVA from the A Shau Valley, but it did blunt their aim of an offensive against Hue City.

Despite the initial stalemate, the NVA continued their Laotian buildup and it soon became disturbingly obvious to intelligence officers that serious trouble was brewing across the border.

On 8 December 1970, Gen. Creighton Abrams (COMUSMACV) convened a special meeting of selected MACV staff members and field commanders to discuss countermeasures against the NVA buildup in Laos. The conference was top secret and only six officers were called to attend: Gen. Fred Weyand (DEPCOMUSMACV); Lt. Gen. Welborn Dolvin (Chief of Staff, MACV); Lt. Gen. Michael Davison (CG, 11 Field Force); Lt. Gen. James Sutherland (CG, XXIV Corps); Maj. Gen. Donald Cowles (G3, MACV), and Maj. Gen. Petts (G2, MACV).

It was General Petts who presented the estimates of the situation in Laos to the group. Following the Cambodian incursion, the enemy had conducted a massive buildup in the A Shau Valley and although their plans had been stunted, the foe was still concentrating on efforts to strike at the vulnerable city of Hue. Intelligence data from August and September indicated the NVA was preparing a full-scale logistical effort on the Ho Chi Minh Trail; logic indicated that the communist effort would begin in earnest when the Laotian dry season began in early October.

The Trail was not a single highway cutting from North Vietnam, but a twisting maze ranging from foot paths to two lane roads; it had started as a small trail during the war against the French and had grown haphazardly to thirty-five hundred miles of roadways contained in a thirty-mile corridor. A Laotian coolie labor force and an estimated thirty thousand

NVA of the 559th Transportation Group were assigned to maintain the network. Located along the intermingling branches were military relay stations, Binh Trams, with permanent complements of engineers, transportation soldiers, and antiaircraft crews. Each Binh Tram was independent and responsible for their section of the Trail; this included maintaining land-line telephones, local patrolling against the occasional MACV-SOG raid, and constant engineer work to repair what the weather and the U.S. Air Force did their best to crumble. To avoid the USAF, the NVA truck drivers on the Trail worked almost exclusively at night with headlights dimmed or off; drivers were only assigned a twenty-mile portion of road so they could learn to navigate it in the pitch black night. Material was stored in bunkers and caves at each twenty-mile point, then reloaded to continue the trek. The estimated time for transporting, from North to South Vietnam, each load of weapons, ammunition, and medical gear was two months.

U.S. efforts to interdict the Trail were in full swing with the USAF's Operation Igloo White. Electronic surveillance devices were dropped to monitor vehicle-and-troop movement in Laos, and a constant orbit of manned and drone planes relayed the signals from under the jungle blanket to the Infiltration Surveillance Center in Thailand. There, two computers processed high-speed printouts showing which sensors had been activated, how often, and when. Other computers fed this information to an Airborne Battlefield Command & Control aircraft which then called in appropriate air power. A typical day over Laos saw the Ho Chi Minh Trail hit by thirty B52 bomber strikes and three hundred USAF, USN, and USMC aircraft. C130 transport planes, mounted with Gatling miniguns, flew night and day to strafe convoys and troop marches. Bombs mounted with lasers and televisions were sent against cave entrances. Cluster bombs were sowed over Binh Trams. Mines and booby-traps were airdropped, some designed to demolish trucks, others to mangle a man's foot so he became a burden to his comrades. The destruction was staggering; but the Soviet Union, East Germany, Czechoslovakia, and Red China continued to funnel war material to North Vietnam, the engineers on the Trail kept constructing new branches amid the wreckage, and contingent after contingent of NVA willingly marched down those paths. Firepower alone could not stop the flow.

And, thus, came Abram's meeting to discuss the alternatives.

Turning to the map, General Petts indicated the main areas of communist concentration in Laos, which MACV had labelled Base Areas 604 and 611. Running generally east—west, a French colonial road called Route 9 extended from South Vietnam through the Laotian mountains; sixty kilometers into Laos along this dirt highway was Tchepone, a small village which was now only a deserted and bombed-out section in the jungle. All branches of the Ho Chi Minh Trail passed through the Tchepone area, and BA 604 was the encompassing NVA group. Southeast of this grouping, and closer to the border, was BA 611, another major storage area along the Trail.

As predicted, in the five weeks since the advent of the October dry season, the Communists had greatly increased their activity, particularly around BA 604. NVA efforts had been numerous: repair and rebuilding of the Ho Chi Minh Trail where it had been destroyed by the rainy season and the USAF bombing campaign; construction of new roads to accommodate the increased flow of supplies; improvement of a river channel from the western tip of the DMZ to Tchepone which would permit the floating of supply containers; extension of a POL (Petroleum-Oil-Lubricants) pipeline from the western DMZ southward; improvement and enlargement of basecamps. Such activities had been spied upon by the electronic sensors and the daily USAF aerial photography flights.

To counter this buildup, Petts explained, the air force had intensified its interdiction effort. Despite the increased use of firepower, though, the sensors in BA 604, BA 611, and the A Shau Valley noted increased truck movement. In BA 604, more trucks were counted entering from the north than were leaving for the south toward BA 611 and the A Shau, indicating a particularly heavy buildup around Tchepone. One intelligence report indicated that 90 percent of the material coming down the Trail was being funnelled into MR1. These factors led MACV to predict a four-part NVA offensive as soon as their efforts in Laos came to a conclusion:

1. A multi-division invasion of various targets in Quang Tri and Thua Thien Provinces with BA 604 as the launching pad into Quang Tri City, and BA 611 using the adjacent A Shau Valley as a channel pointing at Hue City
2. A renewed attack in Cambodia, aimed primarily at the capitol of Phnom Penh to overthrow the pro-American Lon Nol Government
3. A rebuilding operation along the Cambodian-South Vietnamese frontier to reclaim their vanquished sanctuaries

4. A continued buildup in southern Laos throughout the dry season (October to April) with obvious results for MRl

The first phase of this strategy, as MACV understood it, would be the attacks in Quang Tri and Thua Thien. To sit and wait for the Communists to take the initiative was a dangerous prospect, since they grew stronger by the week and the U.S. Army grew weaker with troop withdrawals continuing at a steady pace. To attack into Laos was also a dangerous gambit; the Laotian border and the Ho Chi Minh Trail belonged to the NVA. There had been no allied ground operations there and in the past twenty years, the NVA had built elaborate defensive positions. The jungled mountains and river valleys in Laos contained thousands of mutually-supporting anti-aircraft positions, bunker systems, and machine-gun emplacements. Any foray into Laos would be costly.

General Abrams, however, was a boldly aggressive commander. Hulking, cigar chewing, and gruffly brilliant, he had been a tank hero at the Battle of the Bulge and was in his fourth year in Vietnam.

His commentary revolved around only one concept—attack.

But any offensive planning at that stage had a major stumbling block imposed by the U.S. Congress. The Cooper-Church amendment, born from the antiwar hysteria following Cambodia, prohibited U.S. ground troops from entering Laos. American infantrymen could be employed as support along the border, and aviation units could actually attack Laos, but only the ARVN could mount the necessary search and destroy campaign in Laos. Not even the U.S. advisors could accompany the ARVN. This was a major departure from procedure, for every South Vietnamese unit had Americans with them to help coordinate support fire and logistics from U.S. sources, and to offer guidance on the waging of war. Command of the ARVN invasion force would go to the local commander, General Lam of I Corps, but because of the top-secret nature of General Abram's conference, Lam had not yet been notified.

With the weather dictating the amount of supplies coming down the Trail, movement would be greatest in February and March (the peak of the dry season); Abrams, accordingly, wanted the invasion to take place in February 1971, when the finds would be the greatest. The offensive, as they conceived it in the airconditioned conference room, would not be a takeover of Laos, but a spoiling attack toward Tchepone to destroy the stockpiling in BA 604 and 611, and thus stunt the coming NVA offensive.

U.S. troops were to pave the way to the border along Route 9. U.S. aviation would ferry the ARVN across into Laos where the ARVN were to wreak damage for as long as possible, hopefully up to the advent of the rainy season in April.

Simultaneously, it was hoped, the ARVN could launch a second offensive in Cambodia to halt the stirrings-up there. Two days later, on 10 December, the seven generals met again at MACV Headquarters. The topic this time was detailed analysis of precisely how to carry out the spoiling attack, covering the number of U.S. and ARM troops required, the numbers actually available, the timing of the planned campaign, and the area of operation. On that day, the unnamed Laotion operation was no longer a broad concept but a reality becoming more and more clearly defined.

A frontier of approximately fifty kilometers faced the DMZ at the end of South Vietnam, and the terrain ranged from low sandy areas on the South China Sea, to rolling grasslands, and finally great mountains which stretched into Laos. Militarily, the center of MRl was the coastal city of Da Nang which housed the headquarters of both XXIV Corps and I Corps, as well as the vital logistical base maintained by U.S. Army Support Command, Da Nang, USARV (Brig. Gen. Arthur Sweeney). The main highway was Route 1, a paved all-weather strip which ran along the coast all the way from Saigon to beyond Da Nang. From there it continued past a succession of military bases and cities, including Hue and Quang Tri, and finally ended its northern trek at a village called Dong Ha below the DMZ. Route 9 began at Dong Ha and extended all the way to Tchepone, running west. It was a paved highway until halfway to the border from Dong Ha at an abandoned U.S. Marine combat base (Vandegrift); here Route 9 turned into a narrow dirt path. It cut through the mountains there, past Khe Sanh and Lang Vei which had been made famous during the 1968 Tet Offensive but which had been abandoned for nearly three years. Since Tet no major operations had been launched west of Vandegrift and the deserted mountains belonged to the North Vietnamese Army.

As commanding general of XXIV Corps, the responsibility of on-scene American command for the Laotian campaign fell to Lieutenant General Sutherland. His duties were divided into three main areas:

1. To provide complete support for the ARVN in Laos, including logistics, helicopters, engineers, artillery and opening and securing a main line of communications (LOC) along Route 9

2. To reopen the Khe Sanh airfield to support the operation
3. To coordinate air support for the invasion as provided by the U.S. Air Force, Navy, and Marine Corps

Roughly speaking, Sutherland's mammoth undertaking had several simultaneous components. Drawing from the ground assets of the 101st Airborne and the 1/5 Mechanized Brigade, Route 9 was to be secured physically and patrolled to ensure the ARVN a bloodless entry into Laos. Engineers were to upgrade the dirt highway and reopen the Khe Sanh airstrip. Artillery units were to establish firebases along the border to lend support fire. Aviation units would then have the mission of transportation, support, medical evacuation, and withdrawal of ARVN troops in Laos.

The operational concepts they were developing were classified top secret. General Sutherland, for example was forbidden to discuss the plan with his XXIV Corps staff or subordinate commanders. He could not even mention it to his Vietnamese counterpart, General Lam, whose I Corps troops would be the ones entering Laos. All messages relating to the plan were to be passed by military courier, none by electronic means.

With such a premium on security, Sutherland discussed a problem with Abrams which had occured in MR1. The monsoon storms of October and November had wreaked havoc on the river ports at Hue and Dong Ha (most supplies to these forward bases came via boat from the Da Nang Support Command) and ammunition, food rations, and fuel stockpiles were far below desired levels. When informed of this situation by General Sweeney and the XXIV Corps G4, Sutherland ordered an all-out effort to fill the ammunition and fuel depots to capacity. Then came the call to Saigon. Abrams told Sutherland to continue the resupply effort in MR1 so that the NVA in the area would view the logistics as the natural follow-up to the monsoon, and not as the prelude to an impending invasion.

At the end of the 10 December meeting, the assembled generals agreed on the broad concepts of the operation. General Abrams said he would send the proposals for the joint Laos-Cambodia drives to the JCS in Washington, D.C., whose approval would allow the development of a detailed plan. From that day on, the invasion of Laos and the Ho Chi Minh Trail was merely a matter of time.

Response from Washington over Abram's secret message did not come immediately. They were still in waiting stage when General Sutherland was told of a situation that may have drastically affected all their hopes. On 22 December 1970, Vice President Nguyen Cao Ky and Bob Hope's troupe were scheduled to arrive at Camp Eagle, the home of the 101st Airborne between Da Nang and Hue on Route 1. Generals Sutherland and Lam flew in from Da Nang to meet Ky at the adjacent Phu Bai airfield. With them was Brig. Gen. Pham Van Phu, newly appointed commander of the ARVN 1st Infantry Division, and a colonel who was his senior U.S. advisor.

As they waited in the VIP lounge of the airport, Lam and Phu began conversing in Vietnamese. Their talk lasted twenty minutes and Sutherland and the colonel could only stare uncomprehendingly, not understanding Vietnamese, their counterparts choosing not to include them in talk. Ky arrived as scheduled, the entourage watched the last half of the Bob Hope show, then they visited various field units and wound up their inspection tour at Da Nang by late afternoon. At nine that night, the colonel telephoned Sutherland and asked if Lam had revealed the subject of the conversation in the VIP lounge. He had not. The colonel insisted that it was imperative that he see Sutherland as soon as possible. Since the XXIV Corps commander was scheduled to visit wounded soldiers the next morning at nine, they arranged to meet at the Phu Bai hospital.

There, the colonel explained to Sutherland that after Ky had departed, he and Phu had returned to their division headquarters in Hue. In the privacy of Phu's office, he had told the American that he and Lam had been discussing the possibility of an operation in Laos. Lam wanted a plan worked up, and Phu wanted his advisors to help develop it. Sutherland feigned ignorance of the subject, but told the colonel he had no authorization to work in any such plans. He also ordered him not to discuss the content of Lam and Phu's conversation with anyone. Back at Da Nang, Sutherland quickly dispatched a military courier to COMUS-MACV in Saigon to report the possible breach of security. The VIP lounge, where Lam and Phu had openly discussed the idea of a Laos campaign, could have been easily monitored by communist agents.

Six days later, on 29 December Sutherland met with Lam at I Corps HQ. For the first time, Lam told him that the ARVN were disturbed by the NVA buildup in Laos and were working on invasion plans. Sutherland had no choice but to again feign ignorance, but he was deeply worried and reported this second incident to Abrams. As evidenced by the open discussion in the airport, the South Vietnamese had little patience for secrecy in their military planning. Sutherland knew, for example, that officers at I Corps, including General Lam, often used telephones to discuss tactical matters with Saigon. Such methods of communication were easily tapped by the Communists, but most ARVN refused to shake their naive assumption that speaking English was a sufficient countermeasure against any NVA eavesdropping.

Sutherland's reports caused grave concern among Generals Abrams and Weyand at MACV: it was entirely possible that the North Vietnamese were now aware that an invasion was at least being planned.

CHAPTER TWO:
The Soldiers

The American fighting man who was to face the North Vietnamese along the Laotian front in 1971 was perhaps the least motivated in U.S. history.

It had not always been that way; in fact the decay had been a slow (and predictable) progression from best to poor, brought on not by events on the battlefield but by the politics in the United States. To examine the extent of the problems and what effect they had, it is necessary to look at the evolution of the U.S. Army in Vietnam. General Westmoreland remarked, "Having fought in three wars, I am convinced the United States never fielded a more professional force than in South Vietnam during the years 1966-69." In short, morale and performance were excellent. The average infantryman was nineteen and was generally athletic, intelligent, and patriotic. On the battlefield, every major action ended in an American victory. This is not to imply that the soldiers were spoiling for a fight or that they were not miserable, homesick, and scared like the mud-slogging grunts have always been. But it does mean that the majority were willing to set aside their fear and discomfort to get the job done. It was a time when two-thirds of the troops had enlisted (compared to two-thirds having been drafted in WWII) and when 150,000 men volunteered to extend their one year tour of duty in Vietnam.

Mainly it was a time when they felt they had the backing of the nation and that victory was not far off. Cpl. John Musgrave, wounded four times along the DMZ as a marine rifleman in 1967, graphically described the combat grunt's view of the war, "There was no withdrawal. We were still bombing the living shit out of the North, and we were literally waiting for the orders that would let us cross the Ben Hai River and get into North Vietnam and start kicking their ass. Take Uncle Ho by his inscrutable balls and lead him down the streets of Hanoi."

But those orders to attack Hanoi—to, in effect, fight aggressively without political restraints—never came and therein lay the first seeds of decay. The nature of the war as decreed by Washington called for search and destroy, for units to patrol repeatedly through the same patch of ground, measuring success not by positions taken—and held—but by the all-important Body Count. Search and destroy could wear down even the most willing. Sgt. Larry Moss had not resisted when he was drafted out of college, and he believed in the war when they sent him to a tank battalion, but, "We were fighting to stay alive. No other reason. You did not accomplish anything in the field. Wasn't any territory taken. Honest to God, when I was going over I left a map with my wife and said, 'Here, I'll let you know all the places I've been and you can follow me on the map.' Well, goddamn, I didn't do anything. It was totally alien to what we were taught. I was still fighting the way Patton used to fight—I wanted to anyway. It was very frustrating mentally. When I joined my platoon, it was in War Zone C. When I left, we were still there trying to do the same goddamned thing."

It produced a cycle of frustration: no matter how much firepower and bravery were thrust into the jungle, no matter how many body counts were racked up, nothing changed because the war was not taken home to North Vietnam, because the land was not developed, because the communist leadership was willing to absorb horrific losses in their patient wait for the U.S. war effort to burn itself out. The gung-ho zeal which had buoyed the American soldier was drastically deflated in 1969 when President Nixon ushered in Vietnamization (turning the ground war back to the ARVN) and the scheduled withdrawal of U.S. troops. Politicians began saying the war was over, protesters screamed for the other side, the president said the ARVN were shouldering the fighting—but, as any grunt would acidly note, those Americans in Vietnam were still out there. The fact that the war was supposed to be over meant nothing to a grunt walking point in the jungle with a hundred pound pack on his back and bands around his trouser legs to keep the leeches out of his crotch.

Politicians pointed with reassurance that the U.S. weekly death toll, after the withdrawals began, was only 81 or 49, instead of 460 or 300 as it had been previously. Cold comfort to the man left to trundle a dead buddy into a body bag in a forgotten war.

No military victory was called for, no speedy withdrawal could occur, and it wasn't long before the average draftee in Vietnam thought himself the expendable rear guard at the butt-end of a war no one wanted anymore. Said a medic in the 1st Air Cav in late 1970, "The first time I was here in 1968, we were more aggressive. Then people felt if we really went at it, we could finish the war. Now we know it will go on after we leave, so why get killed?" Such sentiments found an echo up the line; said a 25th Division lieutenant, "The men see very small returns for their accomplishments. . . . They kill a few Viet Cong, but more will be there next time. They know the army will be leaving and that the job is not going to be finished. Six months or a year from now, Vietnam won't be much different from today."

Finally, the U.S. Army in Vietnam was composed of combat units, swollen to 80 percent with draftees, who saw little purpose in the war—and were increasingly unwilling to fight it. In late 1970, British correspondent John Saar spent time with Alpha Company, 1st Battalion, 8th Cavalry Division, conducting ground patrols in the sweltering jungles along the Cambodian border. Saar's portrayal of Alpha Company was representative of most infantry units at the time. The men continued to function not out of any commitment to the war, but because of the able leadership of their young West Point captain, whom they respected for his abilities and common sense. Combat was rare for the company, most of their two-week patrols being hot walks in the sun; most of the GIs were glad about that, as one said in reviewing their last operation. "It was all right. Main thing was we got through without anyone hurt. We didn't get anything done, but I don't care." There were some discipline problems (for example, a young private refusing to go on a night ambush patrol because he thought his comrades were too inexperienced to pull it off correctly), but the company commander handled them mildly, allowing troubles to fade away because "military justice has no answer to the grunt's ironic question: What can they do to me, send me to Vietnam?" There was no drug use in the field for safety's sake, but at their firebase between missions the grunts split into the juicers (beer) and the rollers or heads (marijuana). "We pass the pipe around," said a squad leader, "and

ask what the hell are we doing here." It was a baffling army to the
veterans. One old first sergeant, wounded with the unit in 1966 then sent
back in 1970, had to be transferred out because he couldn't deal with the
new crop of draftees. As the sergeant said, "Things have changed. Before, everyone was gung-ho and wanted to mix it with Charlie. Now it
seems everyone's trying to avoid him."

The reporter, Saar, concluded about the unit:

> Virtually no draftee wants to be fighting in Vietnam anyway,
> and in return for his reluctant participation he demands, and gets,
> personal freedoms that would have driven a MacArthur or a Patton
> apoplectic. It is an Army in which all questions—including
> "Why?"—are permissible. Alpha Company seethes with problems,
> but it has not fallen into chaos . . . the company commander's con-
> tinuing problem is to find an effective compromise between his own
> professional dedication and his draftees' frank disinterest in any-
> thing that might cost an American life. . . . Grunt logic argues that
> since the U.S. has decided not to go out and win the war, there's no
> sense in being the last one to die.

Soldiers were less willing to take risks in an ending war, and such
sentiments sometimes resulted in the grunts simply refusing to fight.
Usually such instances were without drama and Col. Ben Harrison, a brigade commander in the 101st Airborne in 1970, thought most resulted
from poor leadership. By then most of the veteran NCOs he saw had already done one or two combat tours, no longer wanted to hump up and
down the mountains with reluctant draftees, and wangled rear area jobs.
Consequently the small-unit leadership in his brigade was left to young
draftee lieutenants who were fresh from the turmoil of the campuses and
unsure about the war, and young draftee sergeants who had been sent to
instant "shake'n'bake" NCO academies. Mostly they were inexperienced and shared the bitterness of the grunts they were supposed to lead.
"When we can get away with it," a lieutenant said in 1970, "we radio the
Old Man that we are moving our platoon forward into the bush to search
for the enemy. But if there is any risk of getting shot at, we just stay
where we are until the choppers come to pick us up."

The fact that the intensity of the Vietnam ground war was waning by
1970 and 1971 also contributed to poor morale in the field. Too much

combat can drain a unit but no action can, contrariwise, turn an infantry unit into a mob. For example, in March of '71, the 1st Battalion, 46th Infantry, Americal Division saw little of the NVA around their basecamp, FSB Mary Ann. The men became bored and sloppy and the officers decided recon patrols weren't even worth the effort anymore—until the night the NVA sappers hit. Fifty North Vietnamese overran Mary Ann in the middle of the night, killed thirty-three Americans and wounded seventy-six out of a two-hundred-man company on the hill, and faded into the black before the company could get organized. The NVA left behind only twelve bodies. Disciplinary action was taken against the commanding general and five other officers.

And yet, most combat units continued to function. Debacles like Mary Ann were rare. Albeit, the effort was at half-step compared to 1965-69, but the American soldier did fight well when combat was forced on him. The men were not cowards; Sp4 Mark Jury, an Army photographer in 1969–70, described that unique mix of courage and hopelessness in poignant detail, "The fact that they wear love beads and peace medallions doesn't mean they can't fight. The kids learn quickly that the best way to stay alive is to kill the guy trying to kill you. And in combat they're ferocious. But once the firefight is over, it's back to being peace and pot lovers. Often their opposition to the military has nothing to do with the moral aspects of Vietnam. It's just that they pick up a battered copy of *Life* magazine and see everybody else skinny-dipping at Woodstock, and that's a hell of a lot better than *'greasing gooks,'* fighting malaria, and maybe going home in a plastic bag."

In more conventional terms, Col. William Hauser, a battalion commander wrote, "What kept them going, in spite of a pervasive sense that the war served no real purpose and the country didn't care, was a combination of pride, mutual interest, and loyalty to good leadership."

Those three ingredients were missing in the rear-echelon support units of the U.S. Army, Vietnam, and that was where the morale problems exploded. Menial jobs in rear outfits were almost always performed without pride, but with a big dose of boredom, bitterness at the privileges of the officers, and frustration at the petty disciplines of the military. Such lobotomized routines were endured when there seemed a worthwhile goal to be reached; take away the mission, and morale hit rock bottom. Adding to the problem of bored, sullen draftees, was the fact that combat units often transferred their drug abusers and malcontents to the rear. By 1970 the combination had turned the Vietnam rear areas into hotbeds of discontent between the career "lifers" and draftees, and between blacks and whites. Drug use flourished and macabre talk of "fragging" was always in the air.

As Lieutenant Bayer commented after he'd been rotated to a desk job with the 4th Division, "They just cruised around, there was no discipline. When I was with the grunts, they called them REMFs— Rear Echelon Motherfuckers. They had nothing to do and their lives weren't on the line. They didn't do anything except sit around and smoke dope and get in trouble. It was real flaky. I thought, Jesus, what kind of place is this? You drive around the perimeter and look at the defenses, bunkers and wire, and it was not very tight. Wire falling down, a few claymores scattered around. The impression was just a general lax attitude."

Added an Americal grunt, "We had tremendous comradeship in the bush, and didn't really like coming to the rear. The dope and race problems were crazy."

The most widespread problem in the rear was drug abuse. In 1965 the Army arrested or investigated forty-five servicemen in Vietnam for using drugs; in 1970 the number was eleven thousand. Marijuana had always been present; even during the gung-ho days of the war, it was not unknown for a young soldier to smoke grass out of curiosity or to relax between operations. But by '70, the drug problem in the U.S. was rampant, many young draftees arrived in Vietnam already having experienced narcotics, and others turned to them to escape the insanity of their situation. There was some drug use in the field by combat units, but most followed the credo explained by an Americal grunt in 1971, "When we got there the first sergeant said, '90 percent of the company are probably heads, but don't smoke in the field because you might get killed or get someone else hurt.' I never saw anyone smoke in the field." Most combat officers would not tolerate drug use in the field, but ignored it in basecamp.

In the rear, though, there was no danger, only restless boredom and rebellion, and when inexpensive but potent heroin (known as skag or smack) appeared on the Vietnamese black market in mid-1970, the problem spread like wildfire. In short order, horror stories were circulating. Said a first sergeant, "The drug situation is horrible, really horrible. . . . In my unit, some of the medics were on heroin, using needles from their

own stores. You could see the punctures right up and down their arms."
In one four-month period in 1970, seventy-five GIs died of heroin over-
dose in Vietnam.

By 1971 it was estimated that 10 to 15 percent of the soldiers in Vietnam used heroin and an additional 40 percent smoked marijuana. The
army, displaying a certain practicality, ignored pot as a mild problem and
concentrated on heroin addiction. Amnesty houses were opened where an
addict could turn himself in for medical and psychological treatment
without fear of court-martial. The program was ineffective: veteran sergeants considered it a five-day vacation for the malcontent junkies in
their units and let their feelings be known when the trooper returned, and
it was hard to shake the habit when the frustrations that had spawned it
were still present and when the drug was always close at hand. One
draftee, who had a history of drug abuse as a civilian and became a heroin addict while with a supply unit in the Mekong Delta, described it: "I
lasted a week out of the amnesty house when a buddy talked me into
smoking some smack with him behind the barracks. I thought this time I
know what I'm doing, I can handle it. But you don't. I saw so many
young kids messed up."

The army found no solution to the drug problem. Nor could it remedy another social ill that was carried to Vietnam—racial conflict. As
with drugs, there were only rare problems in the infantry; the stress of
combat transcended the color of one's skin and it was common for black
and white grunts to be the best of friends. But in the rear, there was no
bond of fire and the races tended voluntarily to segregate. The problem
was not helped by black soldiers who, displaying the racial pride of the
time, took to wearing clenched fist amulets, slave bracelets, and greeting
other blacks with an elaborate handshake ritual known as the dap. In rear
units, intense peer pressure developed among young blacks to ostracize
"brothers" who became too friendly with white soldiers. Racial tension
was heated by the widespread but mistaken belief that blacks were dying
in a higher proportion in relation to their numbers in society. This was not
true, but virtually every black draftee believed it and many arrived in
Vietnam already convinced they were objects of discrimination.

The average black GI had been as gung-ho as his white counterpart in
he beginning, but by 1969, Black Panther and Mau Mau groups were
:landestinely organized in some units, and there was much bitter talk
ibout the White Man's War. Unfortunately, for some blacks the solution

to their dissatisfaction and racial pride was to strike blindly at their white comrades. In 1969 the crime rate in the U.S. Army, Vietnam, went up, with half of those in the stockade being black. It is important to note that reviews of court-martial decisions show no prejudice; nevertheless, cases of black attacks on white victims accounted for 19.2 percent of murders, 50 percent of attempted murders, 43 percent of aggravated assaults, and 71 percent of robberies.

The military instituted discussion groups for blacks and whites to talk out their gripes, and most strife simmered down to segregation in the mess halls and barracks, a few sullen looks, and relatively peaceful coexistence. But no viable remedy was found and—like back home—there were occasional outbreaks of violence. In August 1968, black inmates at the Long Binh stockade rioted and beat a white inmate to death. In October 1970, at the Americal Division Headquarters in Chu Lai, a fight broke out between the races at an EM Club, turned into a four-hundred-man melee, and left a white soldier shot to death by a black GI. In March, 1971, a white GI killed a black GI in a brawl at Camp Baxter. At the memorial service, black soldiers turned their backs on the chaplain and the American flag and raised their own banner, a red field with a clenched fist and the legend BLACK POWER.

Then there were fraggings—deliberate attempts to kill officers and NCOs by enlisted men. Every war has had such murders, usually the result of a commander callously endangering the lives of his men and the troops responding in kind. In Vietnam, a near-ritual method developed: first a smoke grenade in the officer's tent to warn him; then a tear gas grenade if no reforms had been made; and then as a last resort, a lethal fragmentation grenade. There is no evidence, however, that the rate of fragging in infantry units in Vietnam was any different from WWII or Korea.

But fraggings did make a dramatic rise in rear units. With the initial breakdown of morale in 1969, there were one hundred and twenty-six cases; in '70 the count was 271; and in '71 it had increased to 333 incidents. Certainly every officer or sergeant was not in fear for his life, but there was an air of distrust between the lifers and draftees which caused men to proceed with caution even if there was no immediate threat. All the loose talk about fragging often intimidated officers to the point where just the rumor of such a threat would cause them to change attitudes. In 1969, when fraggings first made an upsurge, the 126 cases resulted in thirty-seven deaths, but in 1971, when the officers realized the enlisted men were serious, the 333 cases resulted in only 12 deaths.

Some fraggings were committed by soldiers especially bitter against abusive commanders or those who did not see the withdrawals as a signal to be more cautious in sacrificing lives for pieces of ground; some happened because innocent officers became symbols of the situation to heroin addicts, black militants, and malcontents, because the loosening of morale and discipline set the stage for criminals in uniform to settle personal vendettas with a grenade. One theory pointed to age as a key factor; the average soldier in WWII was in his late twenties with a wife and a job, whereas the average GI in Vietnam was nineteen, the type more likely to use violence rather than discussion to solve a problem. As reporter Eugene Linden noted, ". . . it seems as though the commanding officer of every unit leads what in any other war would be singled out as a rare 'trouble' unit. . . . A drug counselor with the 101st Airborne told me that for many GIs fighting a war in Vietnam is so confusing and unassimilable that when they are there they feel as though they are in a dream, that they are not really themselves. Because life there is not real, it becomes acceptable to snort skag and frag the sarge."

On one hand, the officer in the rear was expected to accomplish the mission; on the other hand he had to deal with social problems no expert in America could solve. Unlike WWII, where an officer's veteran sergeants associated man-to-man with the enlisted men and were a buffer and personal link between command and troops, the sergeants in the Vietnam rear usually avoided the junkies and draftees below them. Linden wrote, "The overall futility and senselessness of the war makes hollow all the individual acts that constitute it. The Army is stalled in Vietnam; there is no front on which to advance, no cause to fight for that can be convincingly argued, and not even any real sense of withdrawal as we withdraw. . . . The frustrations that spawn fraggings have to do with the collision of a people who don't accept our mission in Vietnam and those who do. We are still killing people in Vietnam; yet, there are no convincing arguments to continue doing so. If you can kill Vietnamese without convincing arguments, you can kill officers too because to the battle-weary grunt the gung-ho, nit-picking officer is as inhuman and remote as the gook."

There were rare counter-fraggings in which career NCOs, discouraged because no hard evidence could bring a young fragger to justice, took matters into their own hands.

Somehow, the U.S. Army continued on in Vietnam, running combat operations with reluctant warriors, trying to keep the rear functioning despite drug, racial, and fragging incidents. Little could be done because the roots of the problems were in the soldiers' weariness with the war itself. The only redeeming factor was that the individual soldier on the frontlines still exhibited a strong bond of loyalty with his comrades. Cpl. Lewis Lawhorn, a black grunt, described it from the heart, "I know that there was problems in the rear, racial incidents back in the rear. But we didn't have time for stuff like that. We were too busy ducking and dodging and trying to stay alive. The North Vietnamese didn't care what color you was when he shot. My outfit—we had people from down south, deep south, we had people from New York, we had people from Massachusetts, different places, different accents—but we all was together as a team. We had blacks, Puerto Ricans, Indians, whites. We had no problems. The white brothers, the blue-eyed brothers we called them. We got along great because, for one thing, we were Marines; we were all there to do our tour and go home. Another thing, we had to depend on each other. That's one thing about being in the infantry, when you're a grunt. You live with each other, you sleep with each other, you cry with each other, you pray with each other. I was friends with everybody in the platoon. We were all friends."

CHAPTER THREE:
Background, Planning, and Mobilization

On 7 January 1971, Lieutenant General Sutherland was in his office at XXIV Corps Headquarters, Da Nang, when Major General Cowles walked in to deliver a sealed letter from Saigon. It was from COMUS-MACV. The directive instructed Sutherland and Lam to go ahead with detailed planning for an attack against Base Areas 604 and 611 in Laos. Abrams's letter said the Laotian operation should commence in February, just after the Tet Lunar New Year holiday. As soon as possible, but no later than 16 January, Sutherland and Lam were to submit their plans for the approval of Abrams and his ARVN counterpart, Gen. Cao Van Vien, Chief of the RVNAF Joint General Staff. That gave them nine days.

After reading the letter, Sutherland immediately met with Lam, who had been informed by an ARVN colonel from the JGS. They decided to include only two more officers, one U.S. and one ARVN, in the immediate planning circle at corps level. They would use a secure area at XXIV Corps HQ for the planning conferences, and all maps, written scenarios, and similar material would remain in that area. Later that day Sutherland called Major Hennessey and Brigadier General Hill to his headquarters. He described the concept of the operation, gave them authority to assemble small planning groups, and detailed their specific responsibilities.

General Hill's 1st Brigade, 5th Mechanized Infantry Division would be the lead element with four main areas of responsibility:

1. To launch a ground attack from the brigade basecamp at Quang Tri north along Route 1 to Dong Ha, then west along Route 9 to the Laotian border
2. To secure Route 9 as the main line of communications to the operation, and to protect the engineer units assigned to upgrade the highway
3. To physically secure Vandegrift, Khe Sanh, and Lang Vei and conduct intensive patrolling in these areas and along Route 9 to keep an NVA counterattack from disrupting the South Vietnamese side of the campaign
4. To construct a pioneer road to Khe Sanh as an alternate LOC in case the NVA severed Route 9 (as they had done during the Siege of Khe Sanh in 1968 against the 26th Marines)

The 101st Airborne was to have an equally vital role in the operation, although in different areas, as Sutherland dictated five jobs to Hennessey:

1. To provide command and control for all U.S. Army Aviation units in the operation, including maintenance support (this to include not only the helicopter, maintenance, and repair units organic to the 101st, but also attached aviation units from the Americal Division, 1st Aviation Brigade, and 1st Marine Air Wing, which would more than double the number of helicopters available to the division)
2. To take over responsibility for the AO of the ARVN 1st Infantry Division (Thua Thien and Quang Tri Provinces) when they moved into Laos
3. To attach the required units to the 5th Mech ground task force
4. To help secure the stretch of Route 9 from Dong Ha to Vandegrift
5. To provide helicopter support for all U.S. and ARVN units committed to the operation, on both sides of the border

From 7 January on, the activity among the senior American and South Vietnamese commanders in MRl was furious; "With each passing day," Sutherland wrote, "the tempo of planning increased and with it more personnel were added to the combined planning staff. With more people having knowledge of the plans the risk for leaks and compromises increased. A list was maintained of all persons having knowledge of the plan."

Basic concepts began taking detailed form. It was decided that the supply buildup in northern MR1 (Quang Tri and Dong Ha before commencement of the operation; Vandegrift and Khe Sanh after D day) would be initially handled by U.S. logistics exclusively. They would be responsible for the ARVN's supply needs for the first ten days of the operation, thus delaying the need to bring ARVN supply officers into the planning group and avoiding that security mess. As it was, the efforts of General Sweeney's Da Nang Support Command were sufficient to get the needed material in place (Sweeney was informed of the operation on 13 January and assigned to provide all logistical support on the RVN side of the border).

On 8 January Sutherland brought the engineers into the planning. They were to play a vital role in the first stage of the campaign, reopening Route 9 to wheeled traffic to the border, rebuilding the Khe Sanh airstrip for C130 transport aircraft, and constructing the pioneer road. Except for small engineer units assigned to combat divisions, all engineers in Vietnam were under the centralized control of the U.S. Army Engineer Command, Vietnam, in Saigon. Missions were assigned to various units through the Command. Sutherland thought undue strain would be put on security if all echelons of the Engineer Command were made aware of the impending operation so he requested operational control of the engineers headquartered in Da Nang (the 45th Engineer Group, 18th Engineer Brigade); this was granted (effective 19 January), meaning the headquarters elements of the 18th Brigade and Engineer Command were not to question the activities of the 45th Group or request status reports.

Security again hampered the engineers. An on-the-ground inspection of Route 9 and Khe Sanh by the 45th Group commander would alert the NVA, so the engineer colonel could only study aerial photographs. Every bridge on Route 9 from Vandegrift to Khe Sanh was either destroyed or damaged, and over thirty new bridges and culverts would have to be installed. The highway itself was merely a narrow path, overgrown from disuse in many areas. After an aerial recon and two days of planning, the colonel returned with his report that it would take a week to reopen Route 9. Sutherland rejected that answer. He wanted the highway operational within twenty-four hours of D day and envisioned not repairing bridge-by-bridge as they proceeded down the road, but placing the engineer teams and required material at their work sites as the 5th Mech task force pushed through, then simultaneously airlifting in prefabricated bridges and culverts by CH47 Chinook and CH54 Sky Crane helicopters.

The engineers went back to the drawing board and worked up a one-day scheme. On 13 January agreement was reached on placing the main supply base at Quang Tri and of the need for two forward bases—one at Ca Lu (Vietnamese name for Vandegrift) and the other at Khe Sanh.

By then the Laotian campaign was basically described as a four-phase effort. Phase I was the U.S. ground attack to the border and the securing of the LOC and airhead to pave the way for the ARVN border crossing in Phase II. Following this, Phase III called for the ARVN to search and destroy in BA 604 and the simultaneous continuation of the U.S. ground effort to keep the supply lines open. Phase IV was the withdrawal sequence which had two options, one in which they would simply pull back after BA 604 had been razed, and the other, which Abrams favored, a fighting withdrawal through BA 611 to wreak more destruction on the NVA sanctuary. As sketched by ARVN I Corps, the South Vietnamese invasion called for an armor element to strike west on Route 9, while infantry units were airmobiled on the northern and southern flanks of the highway to leapfrog to Tchepone in a series of successive and mutually supporting firebase. The key was mobility as provided by U.S. Army aviation.

There were no delusions among the planners that it would not be a costly campaign. In Cambodia the NVA had been hit by surprise and had retreated; in Laos, however, they had before established elaborate defensive positions and they would be fighting with their backs to the wall—the wall being North Vietnam. To lose Laos would be to lose their last buffer between the allies and their homeland. To prevent the Communists from rushing reinforcements to Laos, several cover-and-deception operations were envisioned to confuse Hanoi as to allied intentions. A fifteen-hundred-man U.S. Marine task force and the 7th Fleet were to go station off the coast of North Vietnam, and ARVN units were to assemble along the eastern DMZ to give a show of preparing for an invasion of the North. At the same time, elements of 101st Airborne were to move into the A Shau Valley as a supposed spearhead for further U.S. attacks against those basecamps (these plans were employed and, according to U.S. intelligence, proved highly successful in keeping NVA forces in the A Shau and DMZ from being repositioned to reinforce their comrades in Laos).

On the following day, 14 January, the campaign was given its official operational titles. Phase I, the exclusively American effort, was dubbed Operation Dewey Canyon II. The original Dewey Canyon had been a 1969 U.S. Marine drive in the Khe Sanh area, directed to the south, not the west; this was hoped to have some deception value. The Marine operation also had a dramatic sense of history because during it a regimental commander, who later became Commandant of the Marine Corps, without authorization from higher command, sent one of his companies on a highly successful ambush raid into Laos. The second half of the Dewey Campaign II was named Operation Lam Son 719; Lam Son was the birthplace of a famous Vietnamese patriot who defeated an invading Chinese army in 1427 A.D., and the numerical designation came from combining the year, '71, with the main highway to be used, Route 9.

Two days later, Generals Sutherland and Lam flew to Saigon with the plans from U.S. XXIV Corps and ARVN I Corps, and presented them to Generals Abrams and Vien. They were approved. That night, U.S. officers left Saigon for Honolulu and Washington to obtain final authorization for Operation Dewey Canyon II/Lam Son 719. Sutherland and Lam, in the meantime, were directed to continue building up their forces on the assumption they would get the go-ahead.

The submitted plans fit General Abrams's wishes almost exactly. The ARVN, though, were not overly enthused. General Vien had supported an invasion all along, but wanted a short hit-and-run raid. His plan called for an airborne attack to Tchepone and an armor push down Route 9; after link-up, they would exit via BA 611, destroying targets along the way. When he saw the more ambitious plans endorsed by MACV, he feared that his objections would interfere with obtaining necessary U.S. fire support, so he did not discuss them with Abrams. President Nguyen Van Thieu, meanwhile, privately concluded that if three thousand ARVN were killed in Laos, he would cancel the operation at that point. The Americans were not informed of these reservations and restrictions.

While XXIV Corps pieced together the big picture, the subordinate units were also organizing for Laos. In the 101st Airborne Headquarters at Camp Eagle, the initial planning group consisted of Major General Hennessey, Col. Don Siebert (Chief of Staff), and Lt. Col. John Bard (G3). It soon became apparent, though, that further planning would have to include officers adept in aviation and logistics. The next meeting included at least four more key officers: Brig. Gen. Sidney B. Berry (Assistant Division Commander for Operations), Brig. Gen. Olin P. Smith (ADC for Support), Col. Edward Davis (CO, 101st Aviation Group), and

Lt. Col. Donald E. Rosenblum (CO, Division Support Command). General Hennessey was not present at this meeting; he had rotated home on 15 January. His replacement (Maj. Gen. Thomas Tarpley) was not due until 1 February, leaving Berry in temporary command.

Following the routine briefing that night, Lieutenant Colonel Rosenblum was walking back to his quarters when Lieutenant Colonel Bard called him aside. Bard looked around to ensure that no one was in listening distance, then whispered that several officers in the division were to be made aware of an operation code-named Lam Son 719. A secret meeting was to be held that night. Rosenblum was to tell no one, but was to start thinking about how to support a large ARVN force.

"What is a 'large' ARVN force?" he asked Bard.

"Think about five divisions."

Rosenblum was worried; the 101st Division Support Command did not have such capabilities.

At the meeting, Rosenblum first heard of the plan to disrupt the Ho Chi Minh Trail in Laos. General Berry and Colonel Davis were assigned the monumental task of providing the aviation support. The only word about Rosenblum's DISCOM was some vague talk about "supporting the operation." He tried to pin it down, but no one was really sure what responsibility DISCOM would have. One officer suggested that they would be called to handle setting up of refuel/rearm stations for the helicopters. With that mission in mind Rosenblum bent security to talk with Lt. Col. Ken Jacobs, commander of DISCOM's 426th Support & Service Battalion. He asked what material would be needed to establish helo points for a multi-division force, swearing Jacobs to secrecy and indicating he thought the division was going to conduct a test operation. The list was astronomical.

Rosenblum travelled to XXIV Corps HQ in Da Nang to talk with someone in the logistical or operational field to find out just what was happening. The Corps G4 said he was not up on DISCOM's capabilities, and suggested he see General Sweeney of the Da Nang SUPCOM. He made an appointment with Sweeney that same day and showed him the list. He also mentioned the name Lam Son 719.

Sweeney's eyes widened and he said, "Are you cleared for all this?"

"Yes, I am."

Sweeney rose from his desk and shut all the windows and doors, saying it was all top secret.

"General, the only way I know of to get this equipment is to come to you direct. I have a handwritten list. I have one other copy in my safe back at Camp Eagle. And you and I and one other are the only ones who know about it, but I need this equipment in order to set up these refuel points and rearm points that I think I'm responsible for setting up."

Sweeney said he would do the best he could, and directed Rosenblum to contact Col. Emil Konopnicki, CO, 26th General Support Group, Da Nang SUPCOM.

And so it went. Responsibilities of commanders and units were slowly pieced together. General Berry and Colonel Davis were to control the aviation aspects of the operation (over six hundred helicopters were involved initially) and these helicopter units organic to the 101st Airborne were to be employed:

101st Aviation Group
101st Aviation Battalion
158th Aviation Battalion
159th Aviation Battalion
2d Squadron, 17th Air Cavalry
4th Battalion, 77th Aerial Field Artillery

A large number of aviation units were to be attached to their command, most of them from the 1st Aviation Brigade unless otherwise noted:

14th Aviation Battalion
212th Combat Aviation Battalion
223d Combat Aviation Battalion
71st Assault Helicopter Company
116th Assault Helicopter Company (opcon from the Americal Division)
174th Assault Helicopter Company (opcon from the Americal Division)
132nd Assault Support Helicopter Company
Troop B, 7th Squadron, 1st Air Cavalry
Troop F, 8th Air Cavalry
Troop C, 7th Squadron, 17th Air Cavalry
HMH-463 (opcon from the 1st Marine Air Wing)
HML-367 (opcon from the 1st Marine Air Wing)

To provide fuel and ammunition to these helicopter units, Lieutenant Colonel Rosenblum was assigned construction of five depots, using DISCOM's organic assets:

426th Supply & Service Battalion
801st Maintenance Battalion
326th Medical Battalion
5th Transportation Battalion

In conjunction with these efforts, the 101st Airborne was taxed to provide a ground force to take up the AO of the ARVN 1st Infantry Division and to move on the feint operation into the A Shau Valley. Headed by Col. Paul F. Gorman (CO, 1st Brigade, 101st Airborne), this task force included four infantry battalions.

The men of the 101st Airborne who were saddling up for Laos were mostly experienced veterans. Even during the withdrawals, the Screaming Eagles conducted aggressive operations and made sporadic contact regularly with the NVA. Their combat spirit was embodied in Sid Berry, a key player in the new operation. He was lean, athletic, his white hair closely cropped, coolly professional, personally brave, a man of old-fashioned ways and values. A graduate of West Point, class of 1948, he was an infantry officer throughout his career: platoon and company commander with the 25th Division in Korea, 1950–51; a senior advisor to the ARVN 7th Division, 1965–66; brigade commander with the 1st Infantry Division in Vietnam, 1966–67. From lieutenant to general, Berry always led from the front. He had been wounded twice and had received four Silver Stars. He arrived for his third Vietnam tour as Assistant Division Commander on 2 July 1970. He was just in time to take charge of the division's FSB Ripcord operation in the mountains between the A Shau and the coastal plains.

The battle for Firebase Ripcord was the most costly U.S. campaign during the time between the Cambodian and the Laotian incursions. It pitted one infantry battalion of the 101st Airborne against the NVA F4 Division, and evolved from the allied response to the NVA buildup in the A Shau Valley following Cambodia. Recon patrols had discovered fabulous bunker systems under the triple-canopy jungle, including complexes carved several stories underground with hospitals, supply depots, and troop bunkers. At the time, Division Intelligence placed several NVA companies in the area, the forerunners, they thought, of enemy divisions who could attack Hue from the developing basecamps. General Hennessey decided to hit them first.

Perhaps the biggest plus regarding Ripcord was the performance of General Berry. Berry had arrived after Ripcord had already commenced but, as Assistant Division Commander, found himself commanding the entire division (General Hennessey, after two years in Vietnam, had taken three weeks' leave).

As it became obvious that Ripcord was going under, Berry was constantly overhead in his C&C ship. While some commanders were more of a nuisance than an asset during combat, breaking in on radios, asking questions, and generally distracting the lieutenants and captains who were trying to fight the war, Berry was too professional for that. He had the deftness to simply listen and calculate ahead, to understand what was happening on the ground, because he'd been in similar circumstances, and to be ready to bring in whatever support was requested by the ground commander. The men appreciated his efforts, even if they were sometimes surprised by them. Three days before the evacuation, Berry spent an hour on Ripcord. After a few mortar rounds dropped in, he knelt beside a young GI who was sitting on the ground in the artillery berm, cleaning a 155mm breechlock. He stuck out his hand and said, "I'm General Berry. What's your name?" The artilleryman looked up astonished, shook the offered hand with an oily one, and exclaimed, "Jesus, what's a general doing here? I thought you'd be back at headquarters or some shit like that!"

Ripcord was just the first action in which Berry proved himself to the Screaming Eagles. He often accompanied infantry companies in the field and his reputation was almost legendary among senior officers, although precious few chose to copy it. Capt. Charles F. Hawkins was proud that it was Berry who pinned on his Silver Star for Ripcord, and he spoke with admiration: "General Berry is one of the few generals I know with any real guts. Once, after Ripcord, when we were working in the FSB Kathryn AO, General Berry landed his C&C ship in the midst of a CA I was conducting. His aide kicked out a ruck and an M-16 and took off with the ship. Berry told me he would be spending the night and not to worry about him, he would join my CP after the dust had settled. He spent the next four hours talking to and working with the troops. He helped them assign sectors of fire, construct foxholes, fire in defensive targets, debriefed recon patrols, you name it. Then he and my RTO dug his foxhole at the CP and we settled in for an evening of discussion. Our big bitch was radio call signs for forward observers, which remained the same and allowed the NVA to identify the units after listening to the FO for a few minutes. Three days later, Berry had the Signal Security Instructions/Signal Operating Instructions completely revamped."

General Berry's professionalism was complemented in kind by the performance of the entire division. By the time of the Laotian incursion, the 101st Airborne Screaming Eagles was arguably the best combat unit still in Vietnam. This stemmed from the generally high quality of its commanders and because it operated in an area where, despite the withdrawals and the toning down of the war, contact was still made on a regular basis. The grunts had no opportunity to get flaky.

Another reason for the relatively good morale was that the 101st was one of the few units which could see progress in their war effort. When they had moved to MRI during the 1968 Tet Offensive, the outskirts of Camp Eagle were hotly contested; by 1971 Eagle was a rear base with spit-shined jungle boots and starched fatigues. As Hawkins explained, "Tet 1968 saw the NVA in the city of Hue. Okay, so they're tough guys who can mount an offensive. Where were they in the spring and summer of '68? Kicked back some five to ten kilometers from the population centers. Where were they in '69? Some fifteen to thirty kilometers back in the A Shau Valley where, incidentally, the 101st conducted a brilliant operation culminating in the successful assault on Dong Ap Bia-Hamburger Hill. By the time Lam Son 719 kicked off, we had to strike into Laos to find them and cut supply lines. The point is that each time the infantry grunt took to the bush he believed he would win—maybe not the war, that was someone else's job, but he could and would win his little part of it."

This positive thinking, however, was not enough to sustain even the Screaming Eagles through the withdrawals. As Hawkins continued, "The war wasn't won. But, in my opinion, it wasn't the rifle squads, platoon, company, or battalion that lost it. I've had guys, draftees, come to me just prior to DEROS back to the world and unequivocally state that if they thought the U.S. wanted to win the war, really win it, that they would be happy to stay and fight. They'd be on the first combat assault into Hanoi if they thought it would be won." The point, of course, is that there would never be any attack on Hanoi and, deep down, even the proudest soldiers came to realize their efforts were futile. Morale could not help but be eroded. Sometimes the men sardonically referred to the division as the One-Oh-Worst, and the 1971 issue of the division's yearbook, *Rendezvous With Destiny,* was an underground classic. The cover was a watercolor of several GIs slingloading artillery rounds to a hovering helicopter; a closer examination shows that the young sergeant who painted it had put peace signs on the artillery fuses and had twisted the tree branches in the background to spell FTA—Fuck The Army—the draftees' celebrated phrase.

Yet, the 101st Airborne was still a fine field unit. The NVA gave them no chance to grow rusty from inactivity and most of the men accepted as fact that the best way to survive was to hunt and kill the enemy before they could do likewise to you.

"How did I lead men like this?" asked Captain Hawkins. "By listening to their ideas, incorporating their thinking into my tactical planning, letting them know what we were doing each day and why. By taking weak platoon leaders and putting them where they could do the least harm until they matured. By walking point on a night move. By showing a rifleman how to throw grenades at an NVA bunker and assaulting it with him. By recognizing performance and knowing that each man performs as an individual part of the whole. By making sure the medevac got there or by holding the man in my arms if I knew he wouldn't make it. And a lot more. I think I fit in well with the men. They called me Charlie Oscar, short for CO, I called them by their nicknames and surnames. There were no titles. When I screwed up, one of the NCOs would tell me. My radio operators and I would share food packages from home. The Kit Carson Scout take me by the hand and show me where positions needed more camouflage or where the likely avenues of enemy approach would be. I recall few discipline problems that weren't handled man-to-man."*

Morale and performance in the 101st Airborne were such that even Pfc Bill Warren, an unenthusiastic draftee destined to fight in the Laotian incursion, couldn't help but be impressed, "I would say morale was high and everyone had pride in the 101st. I don't think the 101st was ever disgraced like other units were. Like disobeying orders, retreating, fraggings, and so forth. The drugs were not widespread and never used in the field. The racial problem that other units had was nonexistent, for

---

*From a letter to author, 1984.

everyone knew the next day you would be covering him and he would be covering you. The morale of the men was high because we had USO shows, good food, and what we used to call no Mickey Mouse Bullshit, which means we were not harassed with typical Army waste-your-time nonsense. The leadership was good. We were not asked to do stupid things in or out of the field, or take unnecessary chances. We never stayed in a safe position or faked our coordinates. We never avoided contact and always fought our hardest when we encountered the enemy. As a matter of fact, we had a lot of men who were gung-ho and loved a good fight. I am still proud to this day that I served in this unit and with its gallant men."

The 1st Brigade, 5th Mechanized Infantry Division—the other major American ground unit in the operation—did its planning at its headquarters at the Quang Tri Combat Base (between Hue City and Dong Ha on Route 1). The brigade was equipped with M48A3 main battle tanks, M551 Sheridan armored reconnaissance assault vehicles, and M113 armored personnel carriers.

The brigade commander, Brigadier General Hill, was a fine leader, an infantry officer who had won the Distinguished Service Cross and Silver Star in Korea and Vietnam combat. He was respected by men throughout the ranks, including General Sutherland who commented that Hill was "a very effective and low-key commander; he went about his job, didn't cry wolf, and carried out all assigned missions." Hill's brigade was to be the lead element in Operation Lam Son 719, charged with securing the area along the border and then holding it. His task force was tailored primarily around ground-combat elements, both organic and attached:

2d Battalion, 1st Infantry (opcon from the Americal Division)
4th Battalion, 3d Infantry (opcon from the Americal Division)
1st Battalion, 11th Infantry
1st Battalion, 61st Infantry (Mechanized)
P Company, 75th Infantry (Rangers)
3d Battalion, 187th Infantry (opcon from the 101st Airborne)
1st Squadron, 1st Cavalry (opcon from the Americal Division)
E Troop, 1st Cavalry, 11th LIB (opcon from the Americal Division)
3d Squadron, 5th Cavalry (assigned to the 9th Division but permanently opconned to the 1/5 Mech)

A Troop, 4th Squadron, 12th Cavalry
H Troop, 17th Cavalry (opcon from the Americal Division)
C Battery, 6th Battalion, 11th Artillery (opcon from the Americal Division)
5th Battalion, 4th Artillery
C Battery, 1st Battalion, 82d Artillery (opcon from the Americal Division)
A Battery, 3d Battalion, 82d Artillery (opcon from the Americal Division)
A Company, 7th Engineer Battalion
C Company, 26th Engineer Battalion (opcon from the Americal Division)
11th Support Battalion (Provisional)
75th Support Battalion
298th Signal Company
B Company, 23d Medical Battalion (opcon from Americal)

It was an impressive force in numbers, Hill was a good commander—but the troops were mostly combat green. The brigade AO was northern MR1 and the NVA in the area generally had been content to remain elusive. To the grunts of the 5th Mech, the war consisted of endless patrolling where they rarely if ever saw a "gook," but were sometimes made bloody by booby traps, rockets, and quick ambushes. By the time Hill took command in August 1970, he inherited a brigade chafing with frustration, bitter over unavenged casualties, abounding with problems. The rear areas at Dong Ha and Quang Tri had become hotbeds of drug use and racial conflict, many of the blacks organizing into bullying cliques, and fraggings were not unknown. The grunts had pinned a cynical label to the brigade—"The Worst of the Fifth."

The brigade was significantly beefed up with components of the Americal Division, a unit also growing rusty by 1971. The Americal had become the hard-luck outfit of Vietnam, one which had more than its share of incompetent officers and confusing operations, which had the worst fragging and drug-abuse rates, which had been rubbed raw by the booby-trap war. The massacre at My Lai and the case of an Americal general charged with shooting civilians from his helicopter cast a shadow over the entire division.

The men of the 5th Mech and the Americal were not cowards. They were generally unenthusiastic because of the withdrawals, demoralized and bitter because their patrols seemed to produce nothing but amputees. When the shooting war was finally forced upon them during Operation Lam Son 719, it brought out the worst in some, but the best in most.

With the initial planning and confirmation completed in mid-January, the tempo of activity in northern MR1 increased to the point that, despite the emphasis on security, it was obvious something big was coming. Thousands of troops from various commands were alerted: MACV, USARV, XXIV Corps, the 101st Airborne, 5th Mech, Americal, 1st Aviation Brigade, 1st Marine Air Wing, 1st Signal Brigade, the Support Commands, Transportation Command, Engineer Command. Men and materiel from all quarters of Vietnam converged north by road, sea, and air.

Many of the Americans caught up in the operation were support troops who had virtually no combat experience. Their reaction to the confusion and secrecy of the movements around them was a mixture of dread and nervous excitement. The one common trait among most of these support units was that they were, in a word, flaky. One such unit saddling up was the 39th Transportation Battalion, 26th General Support Group, Da Nang Support Command, USARV. And one soldier typical of the flaky attitude was Sp4 John J. Carney, the battalion mail clerk. The first word he had that something big was coming was a remark from his Vietnamese hootch maid; then three truck companies arrived to augment the battalion, they moved from Camp Eagle to Quang Tri, and the rumors started flying.

The general consensus among the enlisted men was that they were getting ready to invade North Vietnam. For the first time, Carney thought, things got tight and a sense of esprit de corps actually gripped the battalion. For the first time there seemed to be a purpose—no carting truckloads of soda anymore but hitting the enemy where it hurt. Carney was amazed at the transformation among the GIs at such a prospect; short-timers, guys who didn't care, dudes whose major concern previously had been to have enough dope to pass the time, all seemed suddenly motivated.

It was the only time Carney saw such high morale in his battalion, for he was not a model soldier and the 39th Transportation was not a model component of the U.S. Army. Carney, who was twenty, came to the Army unwillingly. He'd grown up poor in a Massachusetts housing project, with a laborer father who moved from job to job and a mother who spent her nights playing bingo. His draft notice had come right after high-school graduation but, troubled over the war, his thoughts honed down to one issue: could he think of any reason to die for South Vietnam? He couldn't and when a favorite relative asked him to come live with her in Nova Scotia, he decided he would. He tried to talk to his father about it, but was quickly cut off with, "If you go to Canada, you can't step back in my house." Carney was surprised at such an outburst. His father was not a stern man; he usually just went to work, came home drunk, and didn't talk to him. The only other alternative would have been a college defer-ment but lack of money and poor grades made that impossible, so he fi-nally did what he hated: he enlisted in the army. Carney was sent to medics school but did not last. The army said it was because he failed an examination; Carney said that he and several others who had signed an antiwar petition were all eventually kicked out on one pretense or another.

The army retrained Carney as a clerk and in July 1970 shipped him to Vietnam. During processing at Tan Son Nhut, the NCO behind the counter rattled off a regulation that clerk-typists were supposed to be cross-trained as drivers, and assigned him as a truck driver with the 666th Truck Company of the 39th Transportation Battalion. Carney was much too sensitive and insecure for Vietnam and it wasn't long before he was devastated. On his first day in the company, the first sergeant tore the strand of beads from around his neck (a gift from his sister), then shouted at him to shine his jungle boots.

That first night with the 666th, he was assigned a cot inside a hootch occupied by several southern NCOs. Carney lay there, thoroughly miser-able, as the old sergeants drank whiskey and listened to country and west-ern tapes, until he finally had to get out and talk with someone. He ran into some of the company truckers and fell in with their talking and laughing. They were passing weed; Carney didn't know if it was peer pressure or what, but it just seemed natural, and he got high for the first time in his life. It mellowed out all his fears and anxieties. Before long, he was getting stoned every day. After a few lessons with the trucks, he started with the convoys. He lasted a week. He didn't know how to han-dle a big truck, was overwhelmed by the whole depressing atmosphere of lifer sergeants and abundant drugs and, when a convoy he was on took sniper fire, he cracked. The company commander sent him back to Camp Eagle to rest. While there, he heard that, if you broke your eyeglasses, it took a month for replacements to arrive, so he smashed his and hung around battalion showing how well he could type and do paperwork. He was finally cut orders to Headquarters & Headquarters Company.

Three days in-country, Carney had been sitting with his company on benches at an outdoor movie. There was a sudden explosion and Carney jerked around to see a hootch blowing up. He dove under the benches, but everyone else just began hooting and laughing, telling him, "Don't worry, it's just the first sergeant's hootch." The sergeant wasn't in it that time; but later some men in the 666th got him with a frag. They heard that the old sergeant went home with one leg.

For Carney, the worst of the lifers was the battalion commander. One incident in particular earned for the colonel hatred of the draftees. The scuttlebutt was this: a convoy was out in a monsoon storm that winter and had stopped on one side of a flooded river near Quang Tri because the convoy commander did not trust the bridge in the weather. Since they were only carrying soda and PX goods, he radioed the CO for permission to turn back. But the colonel gave him a direct order to keep moving. Some of the jeeps made it, but the first truck on the rain-slicked bridge slid off into the swollen river and two soldiers were drowned. The colonel was just trying to play the tough commander again, Carney thought, and the story, true or not, was widely believed by the enlisted men.

Things grew ugly in the battalion. The group Carney smoked dope with decided to frag the colonel. They planned to wire a claymore mine to the commo wires outside the battalion operations hootch so that when he picked up the field phone it would set off the claymore and send seven hundred steel balls exploding through the plywood wall and into him. They stole a claymore. They never used it. Perhaps they were afraid, but Carney said it was because they could never catch the colonel alone and they didn't want to kill an innocent bystander.

Carney was amazed that the colonel survived his tour in Vietnam but, even when the battalion was in formation for his change-of-command ceremony, the draftees stamped one more mark of rebellion on him. During the night, someone painted a peace symbol on the helo pad so it would be the first thing the new commander saw when he choppered in. He boarded the helicopter and left, Carney noted, "looking like a tired, sick old man. He was shaking."

But such disputes were temporarily forgotten when they headed for

Quang Tri. They set up in the noisy tent cities that were going up to accommodate the influx of troops, and prepared for what they thought was to be the invasion of North Vietnam. They were rear-echelon troops about to experience their first taste of the shooting war in Vietnam.

In January 1971, the ARVN launched a second offensive in Cambodia. On 19 January the Department of the Army authorized the detailed plans for Operation Dewey Canyon II/Lam Son 719.

On 20 January, XXIV and I Corps completed the draft of the operations order.

On 21 January, XXIV and I Corps received approval of their plan.

On 22 January, XXIV and I Corps revised and finalized the operations order.

On 23 January, rumors began circulating in earnest throughout Da Nang and Hue that a major allied push was coming sometime after the Tet Lunar New Year.

On 25 January, information was received by MACV that the Communists had some knowledge of the impending operation; also that day, a XXIV Corps Forward Staff (twenty officers and fifteen enlisted men) was selected and briefed.

On 26 January, Generals Abrams and Vien, with Ambassador Ellsworth Bunker, presented the plan to President Thieu for his final approval. A former infantry division commander, Thieu gave his consent.

On 28 January, intelligence reported the NVA were reinforcing their units in Laos. At that time, the U.S. had approximately nine thousand, and the ARVN twenty thousand combat and support troops slated for the operation. MACV estimates, at the time, put ten thousand NVA combat troops in BA 604, with the ability to reinforce with thirty thousand more. A five-day news embargo was imposed by Abrams as a security measure.

The campaign was to begin on the next day, 29 January 1971.

CHAPTER FOUR:
The Road to Khe Sanh

Sgt. Raymond C. Keefer had been fighting for a long time. In a sense, his entire life had been a struggle. He was born on a chicken farm in Maryland. His father died when he was three, and Keefer dropped out of school, hitting the streets when he was fifteen. He was on his second tour in Vietnam, all of it with A Troop, 1st Squadron, 1st Cavalry, Americal Division; and now he was twenty-one, a long-haired, mustached, and cynical veteran.

His first tour had been back in '68 and '69, a grotesquely bloody experience when he was still a gung-ho kid. The cav was the division's fire brigade, dispatched from firefight to firefight, sometimes finishing one battle only to be immediately sent to another unit in trouble. In those situations, they would break jungle back to Route 1, block off the highway to civilian traffic with their tanks and APC tracks, and Chinooks would drop cargo nets of ammunition and blivets of diesel fuel. Then they'd hit the throttles, pass a joint, and haul ass down the road toward the sound of shooting. When friends were killed, the grunts wanted revenge and Keefer could remember actually being enthused going on a search-and-destroy mission, the tracks on line, jets shrieking low to tumble napalm canisters on the treeline and village ahead, the colonel buzzing over in his C&C, the adrenaline pumping as they swept forward, firing on line, lighting up anything that moved.

That had all changed by the time Keefer returned to Alpha Troop in

1970. There were no more bloody firefights. The patrols were all routine, lackadaisical meanderings through villes and aimless foot patrols through treelines. They spent the days simply moving from one point on the map to the next, half-heartedly poking around for the enemy, and rarely finding anything. The withdrawals were well under way and procedures were becoming so garrison-like it was almost a joke: they received an order to use their .50-caliber machine guns only on enemy bunkers and concentrations, not to waste the expensive ammunition on lone individuals. Keefer thought, man, I don't even want to hear that. You see a dink, you burn him with anything you have.

He quickly noticed, though, that few of the men had the desire to "kill gooks" anymore. It didn't seem that they minded being in Vietnam, that much (it was, after all, interesting), but with the way things were going, nobody seemed interested in getting shot at for any reason. It wasn't long before Keefer began seeing things the same way; sometimes, on patrol, he'd just halt the column in a brushy grove, radio the captain that they were on the move without finding anything, and sit down to smoke grass and snort smack. Why go looking for a booby trap, was the rationale, when we're all going home soon? He thought the enemy had a corresponding outlook; they knew the Americans were pulling out, and Alpha Troop was not hit constantly as it was on his first tour.

In that environment, Keefer found his own officers to be the biggest threat. One platoon leader was resented because his gung-ho zeal to kill Communists was much greater than his willingness to take personal risks. He couldn't read a map or figure out a compass so the platoon was constantly getting lost in the coastal sand dunes or in the jungle. Even the captain seemed nervous about his abilities. Keefer thought, he's kind of like a colonel in his own right, in his own little world buzzing around. As the most combat-experienced soldier in the platoon, Keefer felt he was running things. It finally evolved to the point where the lieutenant took him aside before each patrol and asked him to come up with the plan. Keefer carried his own set of maps and the lieutenant usually agreed with his recommendations; sometimes when they disagreed, the lieutenant would shout, "Okay, then fuck it, you spoiled brat." Sometimes the platoon leader would come up with something needlessly dangerous and would not budge; then Keefer and the grunts would politely tell him to go to hell. The lieutenant would threaten to court-martial them for it and finally just go away.

The situation finally came to a heated confrontation one blistering day when the platoon was working a dismounted foot patrol through some parched, listless villes outside Da Nang. Keefer was talking with a friend of his, Pfc Ollie from Baltimore, when the lieutenant walked up. He gave Ollie an order—something so idiotic, Keefer thought, that he couldn't even remember what it was—and Ollie said no way. The lieutenant got pissed and, to show who was boss, told Ollie to take the point. Ollie, a platoon old-timer, a wild man with his front teeth knocked out, said he wouldn't go.

The lieutenant said it was a direct order.

Pfc Ollie looked at him. "Fuck you, I ain't taking point."

The lieutenant turned to Keefer, "You heard him refuse a direct order," then screamed at Ollie that he was going to bring him up on court-martial charges when they returned to basecamp—and Ollie, suddenly levelling his M-16 at the lieutenant's chest, snapped, "You ain't back yet, motherfucker! I wouldn't do too much talking if I was you!"

The lieutenant stepped back, eyes wide, babbling that Keefer would be a witness at the court-martial. Keefer smiled and said he hadn't seen a damn thing.

The next day, as they continued the foot patrols down a stream in a ville, Ollie called Keefer up. He had found an M-79 grenade-launcher round in the dirt. It didn't look booby-trapped, but Keefer prepared to wire it with explosives anyway—destroying it if it was a trap, denying its use to the enemy if it wasn't. Before he had a chance, the lieutenant came up asking what the delay was. Ollie pointed to the grenade and said they were getting ready to blow it in place. The lieutenant glanced at the M-79 round, then at the grunts gathered around, and said, "That's ridiculous. That's not booby-trapped." With that he snatched it up and threw it into the stream. Keefer instantly boiled with anger—if it had been rigged, the lieutenant's impatience would have made casualties of them all—and he swung up his M-16, snarling, "Look. If you ever do something that stupid again, I'll blow your head off. You won't have to worry about having any hassles with Ollie or anybody else in the platoon. There ain't no way in the world I'm going to put up with having some stupid sonuvabitch like you getting me killed over here."

The platoon had barely simmered down from the two hot-headed fragging threats when the captain recalled them to Da Nang. Once there, they were told they would be going up north for an unidentified operation, and to clean out their vehicles, pick up ammunition, and repair weapons and engines. The GIs milled around, talking with friends from other units, but no one knew what was going on. They finally got down to sweating as they loaded their APCs and Sheridan tanks with crates of ammo. They were finally getting ready to move out when Keefer noticed that the lieutenant was nowhere to be found. He asked around and found that the lieutenant had previously been slotted for an R&R leave out of Vietnam. If he gave a damn about his men, Keefer thought, he would have stayed for the operation up north. Bastard weaseled out of it. But then Keefer caught himself: Well, why shouldn't he? We really don't take orders from him and he's afraid of half of us. The platoon was to be led by its platoon sergeant.

Noisy confusion abounded as the 1/1 Cav headed for the U.S. Navy docks where they boarded transport ships. The flotilla, crammed with men and vehicles, steamed into the deep blue glitter of the South China Sea and headed north along the coast. After four hot, cramped days at sea, the transport ships followed the Perfume River to the U.S. Navy boat ramp detachment at Hue City. The cavalry squadron was put ashore, reorganized, and then it hit Route 1. They drove nonstop. The grunts knew of only one target this far north, and their talk was: "We're going to invade North Vietnam."

On 28 January, General Hill held the operational briefing for Dewey Canyon II. His battalion commanders and a few select company commanders gathered in the 1/5 Mech TOC at Quang Tri and, for the first time, received solid information on what the growing tempo in the area meant. The operation was ultrasecret, Hill cautioned, and subordinates were only to be briefed the next day, after the task force had left Quang Tri where the GIs had contact with the locals.

Hill explained that their brigade was to secure Route 9 all the way to the Laotian border so an ARVN force could roll down and invade Laos from that beachhead. They were to depart after midnight, 29 January, leaving Quang Tri on Route 1, obtaining additional units at Dong Ha, then advance west on Route 9. At a mountain nicknamed the Rockpile, where the highway took a southern turn, Vandegrift Combat Base was to be secured, followed by Khe Sanh, Lang Vei, and, finally, the border. Vandegrift and Khe Sanh were abandoned U.S. Marine firebases with nothing left but overgrown bunkers. As a security measure, the halfway point to Vandegrift was to be referred to as Ca Lu, a nearby village. Radio silence was to be maintained until the lead elements passed Mai Loc (between Dong Ha and the Rockpile) or made contact with the enemy, so the NVA would not immediately know the location of the mechanized column. The road march to Vandegrift would resemble, it was hoped, a routine artillery raid (as in the past, when 5th Mech ground units had secured areas near Vandegrift, brought in artillery batteries, shelled suspected NVA supply trails around Khe Sanh, then returned to Quang Tri); after the size of the buildup became obvious, it was hoped the enemy would suspect a thrust into the DMZ, not Laos.

Hill assigned the 1/77 Armor as lead element to Vandegrift, where the tank battalion would reestablish the firebase, while the 1/1 and 3/5 Cav would continue the push to Khe Sanh. Since Route 9 turned into a dirt trail at Vandegrift, engineer units were attached to the cav to widen the road and install bridges. In addition, three infantry battalions were to be airmobiled along Route 9 between Vandegrift and Khe Sanh to secure the road's flanks: 1/11 on the Khe Sanh plateau itself, 4/3 in the middle, and 3/187 furthest east, up to the western edge of the new 1/77 AO. Simultaneously, the 3/5 Cav was to begin constructing the pioneer road from the Rockpile to Khe Sanh.

When General Hill and his staff concluded the briefing, the commanders quickly caught jeeps and helicopters back to their units. They had only a few hours to organize: D day was set for 0400 hours on 29 January, 1971. The weather had turned unexpectedly foul. Heavy fighting was expected.

Under Hill's plan, the point went to an armor-infantry task force organized around the 1st Battalion, 77th Armor, and commanded by Lt. Col. Richard Meyer. Meyer's battalion was the only one in Vietnam still equipped with the heavy and sturdy M48 tanks. He was to proceed north on Route 1 with B and C Companies in the lead, followed by the Scout Platoon, Mortar Platoon, and Hq&Hq. Continuing west on Route 9 from Dong Ha, other units already in the field were to link up under Meyer's command to secure Vandegrift. These units included: A and C Companies 1/61 Mech Infantry; A Troop 4/12 Cav; B Battery 5/4 Artillery; and various Vietnamese Regional Force units to patrol the flanks of the road. Such an organization was in keeping with the artillery raid cover concept, of the type 1/77 Armor had executed a month before.

Meyer prepared his tankers for the move, organizing and coordinating with his Executive Officer, Maj. Dan Wilson, and his Operations

Officer, Maj. Bill Murphy. Meyer was an ex-staff sergeant from River Rouge, Michigan, a family man in his forties on his fourth tour of duty in Vietnam. He'd seen action in that time with MACV and the 5th, 9th, and Americal Divisions, but it had all been in staff positions. Except for brief periods as an acting commander, the tank battalion was his first combat command and he was proud that General Hill, whom he greatly respected, had picked him to spearhead the operation.

Mostly, though, he simply wanted to get his men in the field on a viable combat operation. The battalion had been growing restless at Quang Tri; the bitterness of the patrols, the despair brought on by the withdrawals, and the abundance of heroin and marijuana at Quang Tri had presented Meyer with a volatile situation. His XO and S3 were brand new to him because their predecessors had been attacked only two weeks before. It had happened on another depressing, do-nothing night at Quang Tri. Several blacks in the Radar Section of Hq&Hq Company refused to turn down their stereo in the maintenance hootch at two or three in the morning. A disgruntled and sleepy GI fetched Maj. Mike Davis, the XO, and Maj. Bob Degen, the S3. They ordered the soldiers to turn down the stereo, were obeyed, then told two of the blacks from another unit to leave. In defiance, they turned the stereo back up; an angry major yanked the cord out—and suddenly one brother, Sp4 Alfred Flint, drew a .22 pistol and opened fire. He shot them both in the head, killing Degen, a West Pointer, and seriously wounding Davis. In minutes, xenon searchlights were trained on the troop barracks, the soldiers were ordered to fall out in formation while MPs searched for Flint and the murder weapon. The battalion was convulsed with turmoil, and Flint eventually got thirty years hard labor.

The withdrawals had taken away a goal for the GIs of 1/77 Armor and the boredom of Quang Tri was robbing them of whatever discipline they might still have mustered. Meyer was sick of such problems. He wanted his battalion in a major combat operation that would give the men a chance to act like American soldiers. He knew they had the capability to win but, in a place like Quang Tri, all they did was boil with frustration.

In the 1/77 area of Quang Tri, the sniper section of Hq&Hq Company was indulging in late night revelries in their private hootch. The eight volunteers for sniper duty were downing beers and trading war stories when the leader of the battalion Scout Platoon, a Lieutenant Revelak, walked in. He was obviously keyed up and in a hurry. He told the snipers to be prepared to move out by 0300 hours atop the Scout's tracks.

Sp4 Harold Spurgeon pointed to all their gear. "Everything?"

"Just your fighting loads," Revelak answered, "enough to sustain yourselves for awhile."

The snipers were impressed. There had been a number of rumors that the brigade was going to be pulled out of Vietnam and the lieutenant's urgency confirmed their suspicions. They couldn't think of anything else this important so late in the game.

"We're always getting screwed on transportation," Spurgeon continued. "Just exactly which armored personnel carriers do you want us to ride on so we don't have to argue with your Scouts?"

Lieutenant Revelak made a quick head count and said someone would meet them and direct them onto the last three APCs of the Scout Platoon. Then he was gone as quickly as he'd come. The snipers packed their gear into rucksacks with aluminum frames. Then the ones still buzzed from the party slept it off, crashed on their cots, and the rest waited nervously. At around three in the morning, a GI stuck his head into their hootch and told them it was time to go. They hefted their rucks and filed to an adjacent conex box where a supply sergeant, using a flashlight to check serial numbers, issued them their M-14 rifles, sniper scopes, and boxes of match ammunition.

The vehicles were forming up several hundred yards away, the Scout tracks parked in single file; the snipers climbed aboard, Spurgeon sitting on the back of the last APC. He looked around. The whole camp was in motion, vehicles moving, dust flying in the headlights. They slowly clanked forward a hundred yards towards the edge of the perimeter and then sat idling in the dark, the GIs repeating the old joke of hurry-up-and-wait, but not too harshly because it was obvious that something big was on its way. And it did not look like any withdrawal. Most of the men nestled among their packs on the vehicles, trying to snatch a bit of sleep, but Spurgeon could only stare with excitement. He couldn't believe the volume of the engine noise around him. To his front, all he could see was a line of red taillights, and behind him, more vehicles had moved up, forming a line of white headlights. There seemed to be no end to the column, and Spurgeon shook his partners awake in glee.

Hal Spurgeon had come to Vietnam for combat and it looked as if he was going to get his chance. The oldest son born to a career U.S. Navy man and a Japanese mother, he was a handsome mixture of races, thick black hair, strong features, a thin mustache, and cold, flinty eyes. He was a gung-ho, nineteen-year-old kid without any responsibilities back home, and to him the war was an adventure. He had thrived on the television combat footage, had decided to join the army because they had the highest weekly casualty figure in the papers, and three days out of high school, he had signed his enlistment papers. He didn't care about the political or moral questions. Vietnam was simply the place to let loose the energies that got him in trouble back home. He loved it. Us against them in the bush, he thought, us against us in the rear; all problems solved with an M-16.

Yet, even though he'd been in-country for fifteen months and had been in the Cambodian invasion, he wasn't satisfied. By a draftee's definition, Spurgeon had already done enough, winning an Army Commendation Medal for Valor for blowing apart a wounded VC with an M-60 during a five-minute skirmish in the Mekong Delta, and picking up a Purple Heart from a minor booby-trap wound. Mostly, though, he'd just been bored. He'd never been in a heavy firefight or seen a living, fighting enemy soldier. He wanted more out of Vietnam and was willing to take nonsensical risks in the field for a little excitement; some of his comrades found him downright dangerous to be with. Most of all, he wanted to line up a "dink's" head in the crosshairs of his rifle and squeeze the trigger.

That's why he'd extended his tour, why he'd volunteered for the battalion snipers, and that's why he was enthused to see the battalion gearing up for a major combat operation. Spurgeon didn't think it was to be an historical event—even as he sat atop the APC, he couldn't help but reflect that the American public didn't care about them—but it was a moment of personal glory. He stared at the tremendous armor column, thinking it was like the Roman army on the march, or like a scene from Gettysburg; it was the glory part of war, standing and looking invincible, preparing to attack. For all their griping and reluctance, Spurgeon thought most of the soldiers felt as he did: "Men say that they didn't like battles or the war, but at those exact moments you would have had to physically remove many of them from their vehicles if you told them they couldn't go. It appeared, on that particular morning, that others were not immune to adventure either."

By 0400 hours, the tanks and armored personnel carriers of 1/77 Armor were on line at the north gate of the Quang Tri Combat Base. Previously, Lieutenant Colonel Meyer had assembled the men in the mess hall; he had told them they were heading into likely heavy combat and that he saw it as his job to get as many back alive as possible. To do that, he said, they would have to cooperate; to not shed helmets and flak jackets because it gets hot; to follow orders. With the battalion ready to go, he climbed into a jeep and the lead tanks rolled onto the hard surface of Route 1.

It was still dark and a heavy ground fog blanketed the road; Meyer thought it looked like a WWII newsreel. They drove with only their blackout lights on, maintaining radio silence as they reached Dong Ha and rendezvoused with the 3/5 Cavalry. They left the gates, making a left onto Route 9, as the attached units began rolling out of the fog of the Cam Lo River valley to link up with the convoy. Shortly after dawn, as they were travelling in the hill country east of Mai Loc, Meyer left his jeep to take his place in the fifty hatch of the lead tank. They had passed the Rockpile and were on the southern leg of Route 9 when he began receiving calls from General Hill. There had been no encounters with the NVA and Meyer had no intention of breaking radio silence.

By mid-morning, Meyer's tank was crashing through the brush of Vandegrift, nestled in a lush green valley surrounded by jungled ridges. Soon General Hill helicoptered in and shouted at Meyer for ignoring his radio calls; the general had just been naturally nervous, and soon began asking about the tactical situation. Hill and Meyer enjoyed a good rapport.

By noon 1/77 Armor was digging in at Vandegrift.

The armor left Quang Tri at intervals to avoid bunching up on the roads, and it was well after daybreak before the Scout Platoon and the hitchhiking sniper team rolled out of Quang Tri. The sun was up by then, burning away the fog, and Sp4 Spurgeon sat enjoying the ride and listening to the radio inside the track. The talk was not of combat, but of maintaining distance between units on the highways to avoid traffic jams.

By around two in the afternoon, the Scouts clanked down the southern dip of Route 9, and Lieutenant Revelak radioed to pull into a roadside dirt clearing a few yards to their left. They sat idling for about twenty minutes and Spurgeon soaked up the scenery, feeling good in the sun, content with being back in the field. To their right rear, the Rockpile rose like a volcanic island from the brushy flatlands between it and the road. Craters and tread marks scarred the flatlands from operations long past. To their left down the road, Spurgeon was surprised to see literally an anthill of GIs: tanks, tracks, jeeps, vehicles of every description, self-propelled artillery pieces, engineer equipment, tents going up, soldiers hustling back and forth.

They were still paused in the clearing when Spurgeon heard two shrieks begin a high whining descent from the direction of the Rockpile. The rush became louder. They stared over their shoulders into a vacant blue sky and, suddenly, two explosions boomed fifty yards to their front, raising mushroom clouds of dirt and debris. Spurgeon saw the GIs ahead instantly slam shut the hatches of their APCs, but he and the other snipers stayed topside, not catching on yet and feeling curious. Two more rounds exploded, one on each side. Spurgeon, astonished that they hadn't been touched, was grooving on the whole thing. Inside the APC, he could hear Lieutenant Revelak's voice screaming over the radio to the artillery support:

"Check fire, check fire, check fire!"

"All missions have stopped. Are you still taking fire? Over."

"Affirmative."

"Standby. . . . All friendlies have stopped firing. Must be bad guys. Over."

"Roger."

Lieutenant Revelak swung his APC back onto the highway and they hauled ass, one or two more rounds exploding behind them. Once inside the developing Vandegrift perimeter, the snipers dismounted, met up with the commander of Hq&Hq Company, and were shown to a hole in the ground that was to be their new home.

The armor spearhead had paved the way for the influx of troops, including the airmobile insertion of three infantry battalions to secure Route 9 from Vandegrift to Khe Sanh. The grunts were in the rear, at the time, and it was a truism that the U.S. Army infantry units that patrolled the Vietnamese countryside in '71 changed completely when they were pulled out of the field. The rests—standdowns—only lasted two or three days, sandwiched between weeks or months in the bush and, inside the safety of basecamp, even the sharpest field units unwound to the point of ill-discipline.

The 3d Battalion, 187th Infantry, 101st Airborne Division was a good combat outfit, but was no exception to the rebellion of standdown. The dramatic change that came over the men was a shock, at first, for Sp4 Michael E. Daugherty, the senior RTO in the Second Platoon of D Company. Daugherty was twenty-two, bright, a tough kid from Fall River,

Massachusetts, who was raised by his grandmother and had gotten out of school with a young bride and a factory job. The draft notice came in February 1970, and he was in Vietnam by August. His first assignment had been with the Triple Deuce, a mech infantry battalion of the 25th Division near Saigon. In October, the battalion stood down and the unit colors went home with the withdrawals, while the remaining men were reassigned to other units. Daugherty drew the Screaming Eagles, and was pinned with a routine Army Commendation Medal and Purple Heart in the mass ceremony prior to the dissolving of the unit. Actually, Daugherty had been wounded twice; the first time had been when the VC had turned around a U.S. claymore mine and he'd caught some light shrapnel in the snafu, and then again in October when his APC had hit a mine which peppered him with shrapnel and cracked several ribs.

The change that took over when they hit the rear, which Daugherty found most noticeable and shocking, was the stratification between black and white soldiers. He'd seen it first with the 25th, when they would come clanking into basecamp atop their dusty tracks. The blacks on the road would throw the clenched fist of Black Power, and their brothers on the APCs would shout and smile and throw power too; some of the white troopers would look with disgust and raise a clenched fist with the other hand curled over it—White Supremacy. Daugherty didn't do that, but was irritated when two brothers meeting each other would go through the elaborate dap ritual; he and a buddy took to mocking it by playing patty-cake when they saw blacks doing it. Daugherty's squad leader in the 25th was a black sergeant who was a great soldier in the field; back at basecamp, he wouldn't even talk to the whites in his squad, stayed with the brothers, and looked ashamed to be seen with whites.

The race problem existed with the 101st Airborne at Camp Evans also. The blacks in the 3d of the 187th were particularly militant, having been organized, by an angry black soldier, into a paramilitary clan, complete with a chain-of-command and identifying arm bands. In the battalion area, each company had a row of ramshackle hootches used as barracks and the blacks seized one of the shacks as their own, a place in which to smoke dope, listen to soul music, and talk about the burden of the "White Man's War." Blacks from the whole battalion gathered there, men from the rifle companies as well as clerks and supply people who would have been dismissed as REMFs if not for the allegiance of brotherhood. The white GIs called it the Ghetto of the Harlem Hootch and some, like Daugherty, thought it was a disgrace. For example, there were seven blacks in his platoon, four of whom were fine field soldiers. The other three were AWOL and hiding in the Harlem Hootch.

The Harlem Hootch did, in fact, become a haven for the malcontents and drug addicts. It was a constant irritant to the career men. On the battalion's Christmas 1970 standdown, the battalion executive officer got drunk in the Officer's Club and, together with the battalion sergeant major, stormed off to the Harlem Hootch. The major stood in the middle of the all-black shack, drunkenly ranting that they were all a bunch of niggers and revolutionaries, until the sergeant major, waking up to all the hostile stares coming back at them, managed to drag him out. The sergeant reported the incident to the battalion commander who had enough street-sense to have the major immediately sent to Division to keep out of harm's way. The next night, there was a fragging against an officer's hootch. It was unoccupied at the time but the message was clear. To defuse the tension, the colonel decided to break up the Harlem Hootch and transfer the men to other units. A black supply sergeant was sent in to mediate, and the young blacks were loaded aboard several trucks. As they were preparing to depart, their leader began shouting against the "conspiracy" and they bolted. MPs surrounded the hootch with V100 gun vehicles and got them to surrender only after many shouted threats.

Friction between the lifers and draftees was another manifestation of the basecamps. The GIs were on standdown to get high, get drunk, parlay with the local prostitutes, sleep without having to worry about guard duty, and generally to say FTA for three days. The lifers wanted haircuts, mustache trims, shined boots, and manpower to fill sandbags and dig new bunkers. The 3/187 sergeant major was a short, fat man. His office hootch overlooked the main battalion area and he would sit inside all day with the door open. When a grunt came by with his shirt unbuttoned, unshaven, his hair too long, his trousers not bloused correctly, or wearing a boonie hat which was unauthorized for basecamp use, the sergeant major would charge out, screaming madly for the trooper to square away. The blacks hated him over the Harlem Hootch incident; the rest resented the fact that he rarely made it to the field and, as Daugherty thought, who needs that kind of shit while fighting a war.

Another major change in basecamp behavior was considered a problem by the career men, but relished by Daugherty and about half the battalion. You could get stoned, get drunk, and no one cared. Daugherty never touched drugs in the field but, in the hootches and bunkers at Camp Evans, he and his buddies would light some candles and pass the grass. They have some damn fine dew in the Nam, he thought. For a certain percent of the battalion, the abuse did not stop with marijuana; some of the GIs were heroin addicts.

Delta Company 3/187 was helicoptered to Camp Evans in mid-January for another two-day standdown. Then they were given three days and the grunts loved it. They were given a fourth day and Daugherty started getting nervous; it seemed like the lifers were always nice to them before they were sent someplace rotten. Then it was five days, then six—and they were confined to the company area and ordered not to write home. Everyone was on edge. On the evening of 29 January, Delta Company was confined to its barracks. The grunts nervously sat around, trying to occupy their time, and Daugherty decided to attend the briefing on the upcoming mission they'd been told about. He walked into the operations hootch, nicknamed the War Room, and found his way through the crowd. All the company and platoon leaders in the battalion were there, along with platoon sergeants, RTOs, and the like. The officers sat in chairs or stood against the walls, while the enlisted men sat cross-legged on the plywood floor.

The battalion command group sat behind a desk in the back of the hootch. They were a professionally competent group, but there were very few similarities between the officers and men in the battalion. The warning order for the operation had been met with general enthusiasm by the commanders; career men or not, most saw the war as a job that had to be done and, if a battle was to be fought, they wanted the Screaming Eagles in the thick of it. Few could have been more willing to go than the battalion commander Lt. Col. Bryan Sutton, a small man, a former Green Beret, who often worked side-by-side with his men in the field. He was a gentleman of the old school, who rarely cursed, and drank only an occasional glass of wine, who had enough respect for his troopers to treat them each as individuals. He was also a good fighter; during a previous Vietnam tour, Sutton had been a Special Forces officer working in an area under the control of then-Colonel Hill. Hill, who had a general dislike for the mavericks in the SF, had nevertheless been impressed by Sutton; when Lam Son 719 was being planned, he specifically asked that it be Sutton's battalion attached to his brigade task force.

Sitting with Sutton at the battalion briefing were his Executive

Officer, Maj. Euell T. White, and his Operations Officer, Maj. Ron Scharnberg. All three officers had been professional friends during previous stints with the Special Forces. Major White was a mustang, the eighth child of a poor Alabama family, who had dropped out of high school at fifteen and had joined the army at seventeen, taken in by the allure of the paratroopers. In ten years he'd made it to sergeant first class, then was given a direct commission to second lieutenant. In the years since his commission, he'd spent fifteen months as an ARVN advisor, during which time he'd been twice wounded and twice decorated for bravery. He'd only recently arrived to the 3/187, replacing the previous exec who'd been transferred after the Harlem Hootch incident. The Op. Officer, Major Scharnberg, was young for his rank, a dedicated and enthusiastic officer always ready for a good fight; the grunts thought him a good soldier, but found him almost amusing in his shouted enthusiasm to mix it with Charlie.

The hootch fell silent as Lieutenant Colonel Sutton began the operational briefing. He went into detail about a big operation they were to participate in the next morning, then pulled down a map behind him—the roll-up kind, Daugherty noted, just like in school. He used a pointer to locate Khe Sanh on the map.

Daugherty blanked out the colonel's talk after that. Oh shit, he thought, that's where we're going. Khe Sanh! That's bad, bad, bad bush.

Daugherty didn't know it but his new platoon leader was also at the briefing. Lt. Donald E. Stephen had signed into the battalion only two hours before. He was twenty-four, drafted out of college within a month of divorcing his wife and losing that exemption; they'd sent him to OCS and now he was in Nam, willing to do his bit, but still green. After the briefing, Stephen packed his first combat rucksack and nervously entered the hootch housing Second Platoon. His lieutenant's bars were met by cold stares. He introduced himself, said he would do the best job he knew how, but that they were veterans and he'd be depending on their help. Then Stephen told them to get packed for the CA coming at four in the morning.

Daugherty was tentatively impressed; you couldn't ask for a better attitude from a brand new lieutenant. The man seemed to have common sense.

They spent the rest of the night preparing for combat, packing ammunition and C rations, cleaning weapons, testing the radios. When

Daugherty finally rolled into his cot, he could not sleep. The usual uneasiness before any operation was there, that terrible fear of the unknown. Khe Sanh. Jesus. His gut was tight all night and Daugherty just wanted to get moving. Let's go get this over!

The second of the three infantry battalions to be alerted for the Route 9 securing operation was the 4th Battalion, 3rd Infantry, 11th Light Infantry Brigade, Americal Division (Lt. Col. Albert F. Coast). The unit operated from a dot on the map called FSB San Juan Hill, with its rear at LZ Bronco—Viet Cong—booby-trap country down south in Quang Ngai Province. The 4/3 was in the field when the operations order came. In fact, Lt. John Dewing and the First Platoon of Alpha Company were in the middle of a contact.

The platoon was working through some treelines and paddies when they found a hole, and Pvt. Russel "Doc" Morse climbed in to check it out for false walls. There was a sudden eruption of shots. His buddy, Pfc Ary "Chip" Park, hauled him out and they ran to a paddy berm; six-hundred yards away, two VC were sprinting across an open rice field for the far trees. Pfc Tim Barnhart fired his M-16, Pfc Richard "Buddy-Fucker" Wessells his M-79, and Morse went to the prone, popping rounds from his M-14 rifle. Pfc Denny Able opened up with his M-60 pig gun. Morse saw the lead VC disappear in the brush, then watched enthused as the second VC went down in their flurry of tracers. He started to change magazines, when the Viet Cong suddenly jumped back up and made it to cover with tracers dancing all around him. Lieutenant Dewing called in artillery to block and the platoon swept forward on line.

They found nothing; not even a blood trail.

The grunts shot up a thatched hootch they found in the treeline. Then Dewing searched the inside while the men spilled over the U.S. and Chinese ammo cans filled with rice and corn. Denny and Chip found a tunnel and called for the lieutenant. Their shouts of "Chieu hoi!" went unanswered, so Morse handed his M-14 to a buddy and borrowed his lighter sixteen. Denny prepped the tunnel with a long burst from his pig, and Morse climbed in, holding a flashlight in his left hand and the M-16 on rock'n'roll in his right. The tunnel and bunker were empty. The platoon used their Zippo lighters to burn down the hootch. They kept moving, with Morse taking the point, following some footprints through a sandy area to a half-buried dud 155mm artillery round, which they gave a wide berth. After a while, they took five and Morse asked Buddy-Fucker why he hadn't used his M-79 grenade launcher more on the dinks in the paddy; they laughed when he said that they were out of range and the damn gun was only good for sound effects.

Lieutenant Dewing came over then to pass the word: they were going to be pulled out in the morning. He didn't know why their patrol was being cancelled.

A stream was there so the platoon knocked off, half on guard, the rest swimming and washing off. While Morse was in the water, an old Vietnamese woman wandered into their perimeter, and he hustled over to have a look. She seemed to be about seventy, mumbled and pointed to the mountains, and hungrily gulped down the C rations the GIs gave her. The platoon sergeant joined them and commented bitterly that they should shoot her. Morse was taken aback; the sergeant was fearless but scuttlebutt said he'd lost a good friend on his first tour and despised the Vietnamese. He was a lifer, but a good dude if you got to know him—and another Calley, Morse thought, if someone didn't watch him.

He said to tie the old woman up, but no one wanted to, so he said he'd do it himself. Morse was afraid he'd bind her too tight, so he stepped up and loosely tied her arms with some GI shoelaces. A helicopter came in and they lifted the terrified woman aboard. Morse could see the hate in the door-gunner's eyes and, when the pilot pulled up, the helo veered sharply and the old woman almost fell to her death. Morse didn't think twice about the few dead VC he'd seen, but civilians were another matter. The men were pissed at the sergeant. Buddy-Fucker tried to pull the pin on a CS tear-gas grenade hanging on the sergeant's ruck to give him some hell. He fended him off with a shout, everyone laughed, and things were back to normal.

They spent the night in the jungle, then were picked up by Hueys in the sandy area the next morning. At the 4/3 Rear at LZ Bronco, the company received replacements, plus new fatigues, air mattresses, and the like; that night, the grunts partied with steaks, beer, coke—and some marijuana. At eight the next morning, the company commander held a formation to tell them they had an important mission ahead of them. They spent the rest of the day cleaning weapons and packing gear, and welcoming more replacements. Spirits were high. The next day a warm rain swept LZ Bronco, more news arrived, more gear was issued, and an Australian band with the USO played rock music for the GIs in the battalion area. Midway through the concert, loudspeakers blared for the battalion to saddle up. They packed aboard C130 transport planes, everyone starting to get nervous when they learned their destination was Quang Tri on the DMZ. To break the depressed mood, Morse began running through some dirty jokes and things grew more relaxed; he finally stopped when he noticed the battalion chaplain laughing along and got embarrassed.

They landed at Da Nang, then sat on the runway, broiling under a savage noontime sun. They waited for hours, and it was dark by the time they got to Quang Tri. Lieutenant Dewing stared from the window at the runway lights glowing in the fog. It was an eerie sight. They disembarked from the back cargo ramps, carrying only their rifles and rucksacks, and were met by a chilling night mist. They were directed to a swamp field to spend the night. It was miserably wet and cold. People milled around in the dark, tripping over each other. There were no dry places to sleep. Nearby, the runway was a constant roar of departing and landing aircraft. Dewing couldn't understand why they were risking such flights in the fog. He looked around him; in the dark, there was no way to tell where the perimeter was. Things seemed confused, no one knew what was going to happen, and it was an uneasy night.

It was nearly midnight when Lt. Col. Raymond E. Farrar, commander of the 1st Battalion, 11th Infantry, 5th Division circulated the operations order to his subordinate commanders. Most of the battalion spent the night in their barracks at Quang Tri, but Alpha Company under Capt. Philip Bodenhorn was in the field at the time. They'd spent the last two months at Mai Loc, between Dong Ha and Vandegrift; it was near the NVA infiltration routes to Quang Tri and the company was constantly conducting airmobile and infantry sweeps in the flatland country. They had seen a smattering of action. Bodenhorn, himself, had been awarded four Purple Hearts in the last seven months as a result of his up-front style of command; shrapnel from two booby-trap incidents and a night mortar raid, and an RPG fired during a hasty ambush.

Captain Bodenhorn decoded the warning order battalion had sent over the radio; It said they would be combat—assaulting onto the Khe Sanh plateau in several hours. His first emotion was one of simple disbelief. As far as he was concerned, the area west of them belonged to the North Vietnamese. There were occasional air cav or ranger forays, but generally the foe was left undisturbed at Khe Sanh. It was "Indian Country." The name itself brought back vivid recollections to Bodenhorn of the news clippings he'd seen of the bloody Marine siege there when he was still a senior at the University of Arizona.

The captain gathered his company around his bunker that night, one hundred twenty men in four platoons: First under Lt. Blake Clark; Second under Staff Sgt. Terry LeGore; Third under Lt. William McConnell; and the Weapons Platoon under Lt. William Stremky. Bodenhorn gave them a sketchy outline of their upcoming CA to Khe Sanh. Morale was relatively high because of some previous successes, and it did not seem to waver at the bad news; but mumbles of, "Aw, Jesus," and "We're really going to be stepping into some shit," broke out among the young infantrymen.

It wasn't going to be a cakewalk, Bodenhorn told his men; it would probably be the most dramatic action they would see in Vietnam. To convey the danger of what they were getting into, and to try to reinforce the spirit of the infantry, Captain Bodenhorn sent his men to their positions only after having fixed a bayonet to his own M-16 rifle.

Waiting in the bush west of Vandegrift was Capt. Thomas Stewart, commander of Alpha Troop, 3rd Squadron, 5th Cavalry. His troop had been personally selected by General Hill to lead the second phase of the operation, the road march to secure Khe Sanh. Stewart had been one of the few captains at the operational briefing the day before, having helicoptered in from Dong Ha and returned immediately thereafter. Hill had taken him aside after the briefing to reiterate his mission to Khe Sanh and let him know he had broad latitude to carry it out as he saw fit.

When he informed his platoon lieutenants and sergeants, they joked that it was a mixed blessing, an honor to have been chosen over all the other units but still a risky prospect. Captain Stewart did not share such misgivings. He was a family man from Las Vegas who had decided to become a professional soldier after his first tour as an ARVN advisor, during which he'd been wounded twice. He volunteered for a second tour in March 1970, serving with the brigade staff and as S3 of the 3/5 Cav, until being happily "demoted" to command Alpha Troop in November. Stewart took much professional pride in his troop being selected as point, in light of the ill-disciplined state it had been in when he took over. One of the platoons had balked at a combat mission which had resulted in the troop commander being quietly transferred to a new post. Hill knew Stewart well from his staff assignments, so he placed him in command of the reluctant cavalrymen. In short order, he confirmed his suspicions about the platoon leaders: one was indecisive; one burnt out; the third too gung-ho. He transferred them all, and brought in three experienced lieutenants. He also beefed up the number of sergeants first class in the platoons to compensate for some staff sergeants considered to be lazy. After the revamping, Alpha Troop began to perform better (this being measured at a time of little combat, by meeting schedules of movement) and, in the two brief contacts they had before the Laos operation, they came out on top.

Alpha Troop's major problem in getting to Khe Sanh was that Route 9 was merely a narrow dirt trail, overgrown in some spots, all the bridges down. The road had not been travelled—not at least by U.S. troops— since 1968. Twelve major river crossings required bridges and a number of creeks needed culvert crossways. Stewart's primary mission, then, was to place engineers along Route 9 and guard them as the construction began. A platoon of bulldozers from the 59th Land Clearing Company and two companies from the 14th Engineer Battalion, 18th Engineer Brigade were to accompany the troop's road march. Captain Stewart decided to go down the road with the troops dismounted. They organized and checked their equipment outside the Vandegrift wire, only the drivers staying with the ACPs, two men per mortar track so they could fire illumination rounds if needed, two men per Sheridan so the main gun could be employed, the rest walking forward with the engineer teams.

By the time they began their slow march down Route 9 it was pitch black, around one in the morning of 30 January. The point was taken by Alpha Troop's best platoon leader, Lt. Jimmie Johnson of Second Platoon, with a small group of grunts, accompanied by an engineer minesweep team and a mine-dog team. As they walked into the blackness of the road a trio of vehicles followed them: a Sheridan tank using its infrared searchlight to scope out the trail for enemy movement; a mortar track for fast firepower; and a single bulldozer. Captain Stewart walked behind the armor with First Sgt. William Bradley, plus his forward observer and radiomen, the chief engineers of the two engineer companies, and the bulk of his dismounted troopers. The rear was brought up by the loudly rumbling procession of Sheridans and APCs, Armored Vehicle Launched Bridges and bulldozers, under Lt. Dave Boyd of First Platoon.

They were just moving out when the platoon sergeant in Third Platoon reported that one of his men was refusing to go. The man was a chronic complainer and, on the verge of what looked like a dangerous patrol, he claimed to be a drug addict who should be sent to the amnesty house in the rear. Stewart scoffed at such an attempt to avoid combat. The platoon sergeant, taking away the GI's M-16, chewed him out and forced him to go along.

Only a short way down Route 9, the lead Sheridan and APC both threw tracks on the rough road and had to be abandoned until daylight. The dozer driver said he couldn't effectively clear the road of brush without his headlights so Stewart said, "What the hell, turn 'em on." They proceeded then with headlights blazing and engines coughing. To deter NVA attacks, Stewart had his FO place artillery fire north of the road; the noise of their column was so loud and the hills so foggy that they could neither hear nor see the impacting rounds. The first bridge was already repaired, an AVLB having been launched from Vandegrift that afternoon. At the next downed bridge, a half-dozen cavalrymen and engineers were left with a radio and an M-60 machine gun. They radioed for the helicopter to bring in the span bridges which were being assembled and slingloaded at Quang Tri, and for another helicopter to transport the necessary equipment. They worked throughout the night. In all, six M4T6 dry-span bridges and five AVLB bridges were installed.

Trailing behind A/3/5 and the engineers was the 1st Squadron, 1st Cavalry. Sergeant Keefer sat hunkered behind his fifty shield in the cold mist, nervously eyeing the darkness around him. The long column came to a halt, rumbling idle in the mud, and someone came by and shouted to Keefer, "Hey, the Old Man wants to see you!"

At the command track, Capt. James W. Pierson had his map out and Keefer joined the other platoon lieutenants and sergeants gathered around him. In two hours, the captain told them, they would be pushing down Route 9 to the Laotian border for a major operation. Seven to eight thousand NVA were suspected of being in the area, and intelligence said they were fully equipped with artillery, tanks, trucks, heavy weapons, and maybe even jets. Keefer could feel his gut tighten when he heard that.

After the briefing, Captain Pierson called Sergeant Keefer over and told him the acting leader of First Platoon, a staff sergeant, had slipped off his Sheridan turret in the rain. He'd wrenched his back badly and had been sent back down the column for medevac. The captain wanted Keefer to assume command of First Platoon.

No way, Keefer said, there were two other E-5s in the platoon and he didn't want the responsibility.

That may be so, Pierson responded, but, since Keefer had pulled another combat tour, he was the most experienced and the best man for the job. Keefer knew the Old Man was right and finally relented. Like it or not, he figured, I am the best qualified. He didn't want to let Pierson down; the captain had always done right by his troops. Still, as Keefer trudged back to his APC, he almost shook with anger and fear. I'm not even supposed to be here, he cursed inwardly. Four Purple Hearts and they got me back in this shit. The thought of all those NVA in the Laotian border mountains, and the responsibility that was now his, forced him to squat in the roadside brush and defecate in raw terror.

After all he'd been through, he didn't want to die now.

Keefer had first arrived in Vietnam in September 1968, an unruly eighteen-year-old who had the notion that war was an adventure and the army would make a good career. By the time that first year with Alpha Troop was over, he'd been wounded four times, he'd been pinned with an end-of-tour Army Commendation Medal, and his mind had been shut down with an intense loathing of the army, the lifers, and the dinks. He'd joined the National Guard originally at sixteen because his family had always served. It was a proud tradition; his grandfather had been gassed and severely wounded in France during the Great War; his father had contracted a lung ailment aboard a burning ship in WWII which eventually killed him; his brother Frank had been wounded twice as a Marine in Nam. Keefer wanted his piece of the action. The dudes in the neighborhood said Nam was for suckers, but his working-class background upheld the ideals of duty to one's country and made him volunteer for the "Regular Army" and for Vietnam. It wasn't long before the hatred set in. It was as if the army didn't care; you're ready to give your life for your country, Keefer thought, but all you are is another number. Army don't care, officers are incompetent, grunts die. That's how he saw it.

His first sign that the military was not to be trusted came when he volunteered for Vietnam. Since his basic training had been geared for the National Guard, with obsolete weapons and classes in riot control, he requested to go through infantry training again to catch up on the new weapons and tactics. He was amazed that this permission was denied, that he was sent directly to Vietnam. They don't care what kind of combat soldier you make, Keefer thought. They don't care if you survive the war. They just want warm bodies to fill the ranks.

His hatred for army bureaucracy was crystallized by the fate of a soldier in his platoon back in '69. His name was Robert and he was a tall, gawky bookworm who'd been a mathematical genius in college.

Everyone liked him, but he had absolutely no common sense. A good kid, Keefer concluded, but he should have been a clerk-typist somewhere in the rear, not humping around with the infantry, and Keefer hated the Army for sending Robert to a place where it was obvious he wouldn't have the sense to survive. Robert was killed in May. The platoon received a letter from his father; a newspaper article was enclosed in which the father had said, "His death was a complete and tragic waste. His life has gone for nothing in a senseless military adventure." It was a humble letter from parents to the platoon, asking to hear from men who had known their son. It went on to say that they had sent their boy a package of candy and cookies the day he was killed; they hoped his friends had enjoyed them, and they were praying for all of them. The father said the Army had told him that Robert had been killed by an enemy rocket-propelled grenade while driving an APC. Keefer was furious at that. The kid had not been killed by the enemy. They'd been in a firefight when the genius, whom everyone liked but who knew nothing about the bush, had wandered forward, got lost in the tall grass between the two sides, and had been accidentally raked across the back by one of the track-mounted machine guns. You're just a number, Keefer thought over and over. They take a good kid, send him to the wrong job, then lie when he's predictably killed. They don't care who they hurt. He never wrote to the father; he was afraid of being court-martialled on some trumped-up charges.

Keefer despised the Vietnamese with an equal fury. When his brother had come back from Vietnam in '66, he'd told how they'd gone into villages with medical programs and had raised money for orphans. By '68, when Keefer had arrived, the Americal Division was no longer interested in civic action; the name of the game was S&D, free-fire zones, and body count—especially body count. He'd come over ready to help the Vietnamese people and had made good friends with an old woman and her two children who did the GI's laundry. They were nice people and he would write his mother to get tennis shoes and clothes for the little boy. But Keefer learned to hate the rest of them; they seemed so maddeningly indifferent to American deaths.

When they passed through villages, the people seemed to have ample amounts of rice, plus water buffalos, chickens, and gardens. But when a GI tossed a can of C rations from his truck, they would fight like dogs to get it. Men would pummel little children for a measly can of Cs. Greedy bastards, Keefer thought, no better'n animals. The platoon would take their revenge on the Vietnamese. If they'd been cheated buying beer, dope, or whores in the shantytowns around Da Nang and Chu Lai, they would roar through on the next time around, raising dust and pitching smoke and CS grenades. When they went through the hamlets, they had another nasty trick. They would punch a hole in a C ration meal can, then hold it with an asbestos glove over a flame of C4. They'd start tossing C rats, the people would fall into a kicking, screaming mob, then someone would toss in the scorched can. Keefer thought it was funny as hell to watch "the slant-eyed animals" keep grabbing at it and burning their fingers. The can would go through the whole village.

And, when they went through the tiny villes deep in the jungle, they killed the Vietnamese. Once Keefer watched a tank driver in his platoon simply swerve and crush to death three Vietnamese standing beside the road they were on. The ARVN interpreters with the troop were ruthless; at first Keefer couldn't believe what he saw. They threw babies down wells and hung women from trees. Keefer knew the Vietnamese were in a murderous bind; if they helped the Americans, the VC would butcher them and, if they did nothing, an angry GI might open fire. But, after a while, the circumstances meant nothing to him. They would hit a mine and the farmers nearby would act as if they hadn't seen a thing; they never pointed out the booby traps in their fields. Women and children in a paddy would suddenly start walking quickly for the woodline, and then the platoon would be ambushed; the people never warned the Americans of the NVA waiting for them. Keefer felt sick the first time he saw his buddies shoot at civilians in revenge, but soon he fell into the same brutal mindset. After seeing friends dismembered by mines, he found it easy . . . a catharsis. You forget about home, Keefer mused; you lived with death, could feel it in every hedgerow and villager's stare, and could see it every day they tallied the body count.

"Let's just kill everybody and go home," was the attitude.

It was the lifers' fault, he concluded, with their condoning and encouraging of anything to beef up the kill. They had turned him into something he did not like to ponder. They just wanted the glory and the medals, and didn't care who got killed or warped in the process. Half the time, it seemed as if they had to fight the lifers as much as the enemy. In '69 on Hawk Hill, they had a first sergeant they called Teddy Bear. One night, the platoon was getting stoned in a bunker when one of the guys went out to piss; he ran back in saying he'd seen men in front of the perimeter wire. Flares had popped in the distance, he said, and he'd just made out their shadows in the paddy water. They called Teddy Bear but, unable to see anything, he mocked them by standing at the wire and shouting, "If there's anybody out there, shoot me, I dare ya!" The sergeant laughed at his men and walked away. The grunts hustled back to the bunker, piled up ammo and grenades, and waited; twenty minutes later, a trip flare went off in the wire and they cut loose. The next morning they counted over a dozen dead NVA sappers in the wire. The shooting over, Teddy Bear reappeared and strutted around with a cigar in his mouth. He ordered the platoon to go count the bodies and patrol for the survivors, and Keefer complained that they'd been fighting all night; why not send another platoon. The sergeant laughed, "No, you guys started this battle, you're going to finish it." Keefer felt that they were being spit on for doing their jobs. The platoon left the perimeter, sat down out of sight in the brush, and radioed in a fake patrol report.

Keefer blamed the lifers for his being back in the combat infantry. After that year of heavy fighting, he'd finally rotated out in September 1969, and had ended up in Germany; but he couldn't get along with the spit-and-shine officers there and was shocked by the racial violence he saw. As a sergeant, he was told to put only whites on work details. When he complained, the battalion commander said that, they, at least, wouldn't revolt when given orders. One old first sergeant who didn't see it that way was manhandled into a wall locker by some blacks and heaved out of a second-floor window. After the camaraderie of Vietnam, it was saddening to see black and white GIs not only fist fighting, but pulling knives and chucking grenades into each other's clubs. He didn't want to be beaten to death by a gang of blacks who didn't even know him so he decided to get away by volunteering for a second Vietnam tour. He would get overseas and hazardous-duty pay, a drop in the time left on his enlistment, and (an officer in personnel told him) with four Purple Hearts, he could not be assigned to a combat unit.

When he came in-country again in December 1970, someone saw his combat experience and put him in exactly the same unit he'd survived before: A Troop, 1st Squadron, 1st Cavalry Americal Division. Keefer raised hell, showing a letter an officer had written saying he couldn't be sent back to combat, but the personnel staff said no such letter was in his file and that he must have forged it. Disgruntled, he reported for duty. When he showed the letter to the troop commander, Captain Pierson, and explained why he should be sent back to the rear, Pierson answered, "Boy, we sure need you. We can really use some experience."

Keefer developed an almost immediate rapport with Pierson; the CO seemed to be a good officer so Keefer dropped the whole issue at that point. As the weeks went by, Pierson, virtually alone among the officers, impressed Keefer as a trustworthy combat leader. He didn't like being in Vietnam any more than the grunts liked it; he just did his job, performed the mission with the least risks, and never told his troops to do anything he wouldn't do personally. And that night on Route 9, when Keefer found himself in command of a platoon, he shook away his fright thinking of the leadership he'd seen Pierson exhibit.

After the captain's roadside huddle, the lieutenants and sergeants returned to their vehicles and the column continued its bumpy passage along Route 9. Other vehicles appeared out of the black until no matter which way you looked, there were lines of road lights curving along. Keefer had never seen so much armor together before. At one point, he noticed, the road was carved almost directly into the side of the mountains, a sheer wall and above them a cliff. Keefer found himself cursing the Army again, "Stupid lifers got us on this road. All the dinks have to do is blow up the front and rear vehicles, and we're trapped."

As they rolled slowly on, Seargeant Keefer resolved one thing in his mind: his only duty was to keep his platoon alive. He didn't care about the success of the operation. All that mattered was that his friends should make it home in one piece from this insane war, and if that meant refusing an order or faking a patrol, so be it. He wasn't going to take any more chances. And he intended to keep himself alive too. By 1971 the grunts had a saying: "You owe it to yourself." After all he'd been through, Keefer figured he owed it to himself to survive.

By early morning, the men of 1/11 Infantry were crowded at the Quang Tri airfield. It was cold, wet, and overcast and the young grunts wore field jackets and towels like scarves. An air armada, including forty-five Hueys for the infantry, deposited them at Mai Loc, then picked them up again and sped towards Khe Sanh. Maj. Harlow Stevens, battalion operations officer, rode the lead slick. It was his second trip to Khe Sanh; as a young Green Beret in 1963, he had worked at the original SF outpost there.

The son of one of Stevens's commanders at Khe Sanh in '63 was riding the second Huey in. That was Lt. Charles Garwood, twenty-three, recently married, of the Pathfinder Platoon, 101st Aviation Group, 101st Airborne Division. With him were Cpls. Guy "Evergreen" Fearn and "Blinky" Collins; they had hooked up with 1/11 at Mai Loc to control aircraft into the LZ once the CA was completed. The Hueys flew in line down the river bordering Route 9, skids barely off the surface; Garwood, whose baptism of fire had been the Ripcord retreat, stared uneasily at the brushy banks whizzing behind them.

There was no shooting.

They CA'd onto the shell-pocked airstrip, and the grunts fanned out across the desolate plateau. There was no one in sight, and Major Stevens shouted, "This force will be dug in before dark!" The GIs, who'd been expecting a fight, put aside their rifles for picks and shovels, while Lieutenant Garwood's team set up in the elephant grass beside the strip and directed in the other helicopters.

The last company of the battalion into Khe Sanh was Captain Bodenhorn's Alpha, coming out of Mai Loc and overshooting the armor column on Route 9. Through the overcast Bodenhorn could see the jungled mountains; then the base appeared, helicopters circling above it, some lowering cargo nets of gear. The terrain brought back more vivid flashbacks of the full-color television footage he'd seen as a college student: the bombed hills; the low plateau in fog; the ravines running up to the base. They settled down on the strip and the company sat along the edge, helmets off, taking a cigarette break. Bodenhorn reported to Major Stevens who assigned Alpha the job of securing the east side of the strip, with a warning to beware of uncharted "friendly" minefields.

They moved out through the mud and overgrowth, Bodenhorn surveying the haunting landscape of old Marine trenches, abandoned gear, rusting pieces of a C130, three years destroyed strewn across the perimeter. Beyond the overgrown and dilapidated coils of concertina wire on the edge of what used to be the perimeter, they could see other collapsed trenches zig-zagging forward. They assumed those had been the NVA positions during the '68 siege. Eerie, Bodenhorn thought, eerie and haunting. The grunts began digging bunkers with interconnecting slit trenches, "very mindful," the company commander reported, "of the fighting positions that had been abandoned a few years earlier, their strength, their absolute screaming necessity. We had no problems constructing our positions. The materials were ample and the spirit was more than willing."

Alpha Company 4/3 Infantry was also on the Quang Tri strip. They were issued maps of their new AO and Lieutenant Dewing joined the company command group huddle. Capt. William Spinning, their reasonable and calm CO, was there with Lt. Jerry Cunningham, the artillery forward observer, Lt. Larry Walker of Second Platoon, Lt. John Sheridan of Third Platoon, and the RTOs. As leader of First Platoon of A Company, Dewing was to lead in the battalion CA and report back if the LZ was hot or cold. The landing zone was between Route 9 and the river.

Dewing's platoon broke into groups of seven or eight to board the Hueys, then jogged to them, ducking under the whirling blades. The ships flew high and took direction from the ribbon of road below them while the grunts, letting their legs dangle out the open cabin doors, endured the freezing wind. Below, Dewing could see some convoys on Route 9 and the raw mud splotch of Vandegrift, but he was more intent in the jungled mountains towards which he was being sped. Smoke drifted over the intended LZ and nervous chatter broke out on the headphones. As they slowed down and dipped lower, the door-gunner beside Dewing tapped him and shouted for the grunts to move their heads back. In the next second, he swivelled his M-60 around and opened fire. Dewing recoiled in shock as the muzzle flash exploded three feet from his face.

The slicks came in at a hover and the grunts jumped the six or eight feet from the skids into the brush of the landing zone. Dewing leaped from one side of the cabin, his RTO went out the other door, and they suddenly realized they'd been CA'd into a brush fire. There were artillery craters from the prep barrage in the area, and some of the elephant grass was ablaze. A few grunts laughed and stomped out the fire while Dewing radioed Captain Spinning that the LZ was cold. Before long, more slicks began to appear in the sky, smoke grenades were popped as guides, and the remainder of the battalion began disembarking.

With the LZ expanding, First Platoon moved out on its preassigned mission to find Route 9 and be at a particular point on the map by a particular time. The area was all thick brush, elephant grass, and rolling hills. Dewing told Private Morse to walk point. Morse was a favorite of his; he'd known him in a stateside unit and was surprised to see Morse already a vet in his platoon when Dewing arrived in Vietnam. They were friends, but Morse wasn't a model soldier. He was notorious for drug use back in the rear, and did not adapt well to military discipline. One of his bigger adventures had been during a standdown at LZ Bronco. Bored with the steam'n'cream massage parlors in the adjacent ville, he and three other grunts had gone AWOL to the Americal Division Headquarters at Chu Lai; they'd wanted a crack at the beaches, skivvy joints, and Donut Dollies about whom there were many tantalizing rumors. They hadn't gotten a Donut Dolly, but had found a sandbag with eight pounds of grass, and had hidden in a transit hootch full of new guys, rolling joints, and passing bamboo bowls and ivory pipes. The shack had filled with thick smoke and the few new guys who hadn't joined the pot party had gotten stoned just lying on their cots.

Morse was a different man in the field, though. He had joined the army at seventeen, wanting an escape from his impoverished beginnings and gung-ho over John Wayne movies. He'd earned his jump wings, had volunteered for Vietnam, and had taken a Purple Heart for a VC grenade. He was damned proud to be a grunt and consistently walked point. He moved expertly through the jungle, tight as a drum, ready to blow away anything that moved—which was exactly the attitude Lieutenant Dewing wanted.

Before long, Morse came upon a small trail in the brush. They gathered on it and scraped the surface with their boots, moving aside grass and vines. Underneath was a surface of packed earth and quarter-sized rocks from an engineer rock crusher (probably from the French days, Dewing reckoned). He checked his maps and realized that the little cart trail was Route 9. They organized on the road, then moved out, well spaced for fear of ambush. Morse on point moved along, slow and quiet, especially nervous about tripping a booby trap. He had led them perhaps a kilometer when something rustled to his left front and, throwing himself down in the brush, he emptied his M-14 rifle at it. The rest of the platoon dove into the bushes.

Morse slammed in another magazine to fire again as the platoon sergeant ran up, shouting "What the hell are you firing at?"

Morse suddenly noticed that no one else, U.S. or NVA, was shooting. The sergeant checked the riddled area and came back shaking his head. By the time Dewing worked his way up, Buddy-Fucker, Chip, and Denny were razzing an embarrassed Morse, calling him a farmer. A scrawny wild boar lay in the brush, shot across the belly.

By late afternoon, the platoon reached its position atop a hill on the northern side of the highway. They hacked away some bushes, laid out air mattresses, strung ponchos, and set out claymore mine booby traps on Route 9—devices the army euphemistically termed Mechanical Ambushes.

The 3/187 Infantry was on the Camp Evans airstrip before sunrise. Lieutenant Colonel Sutton and Majors White and Scharnberg were in a cluster, watching the line companies form up to wait for the lift birds. White could feel the apprehension in the air; everyone expected heavy contact and responded with a tight-lipped, no-nonsense demeanor.

As for Delta Company, they had been picked up by trucks at their barracks, deposited alongside the airstrip, and now stood in an expectant mass. They were to CA onto Route 9 to hold one of the damaged bridges for the mechanized engineer teams. Sp4 Daugherty looked with apprehensive wonder; he'd never seen so many helicopters and men in one place. The company commander conferred with his platoon leaders and Daugherty eyed him uneasily. The CO was new, inexperienced, and never seemed to catch on. A plump, noninfantry type, he was so gun-happy he'd traded his M-16 for a WWII style grease gun. That was really good for hitting the broad side of a barn, Daugherty thought, but not too cool if a dink popped up. The men called him Porky the Pig, and only stuck with him because he was willing to listen to advice. Besides, he reckoned, he'd seen worse officers and, if they let the captain down and he screwed up, he'd take a lot of grunts with him.

Waiting in the predawn darkness, Lieutenant Stephen was having his own worries. He knew only four of his men by sight—the platoon sergeant, the radioman, the medic, and a rifleman. The rest of them were anonymous in the dusk light. Within one day of getting to the battalion, he was heading for a major airmobile assault and it was extremely unsettling to Stephen that some of his men might die in a few hours and he didn't even know their names.

Finally, Delta Company was directed onto their Hueys. The sky was filled with formations of helicopters and, past Quang Tri, Daugherty's radio crackled with a helo pilot reporting ground fire. Daugherty couldn't hear or see a thing. There was no more shooting. By the time they started their descent into the hills astride Route 9, the armada that had taken off from Camp Evans had thinned down to the fifteen or so slicks carrying Delta. They came low into a brushy field that was their LZ, the door gunners blasting precautionary fire from their sixties into the treelines. The skids hit the ground and the grunts piled out the cabin doors, quickly jogging away from the birds.

The LZ was cold.

Lieutenant Colonel Sutton and Major Scharnberg were in their C&C

controlling the insertion of the battalion's four rifle companies and one recon platoon, while Major White monitored the action from Camp Evans. The infantrymen had successfully secured their various LZs around Khe Sanh and Route 9, but the expected enemy resistance had not materialized. The only reported casualties were sprains and bruises caused by men jumping out of helicopters that hadn't been low enough.

For Delta Company, the afternoon went methodically. They secured their position, sent out patrols which made no contact, and firmed up back to field discipline standards. Daugherty's nerves had calmed too. Out in the bush, with things to do and people depending on you, you just didn't have time to be scared.

Hours earlier, as dawn was just hazily breaking through the mountain fog, Captain Stewart's force took a break in place along Route 9. Everyone was dragged out from the sleepless night and long march. They got moving again, reached the next bridge by ten, were supposed to have a bridge brought in by chopper at eleven, but finally left the engineer team without the bridge at two in the afternoon. A bit further down the road, Stewart's dismounted grunts and CP linked up with Delta 3/187.

Sp4 Daugherty and his platoon were on patrol at that time, sweeping the high ground above Route 9. It was steep and tough going and, looking back down the forested slope, he couldn't even see the bridge they had come to secure. They scouted the ridgeline, found nothing, and humped back downhill. Daugherty had no idea about a rendezvous and was surprised to see bulldozers, tanks, and tracks on the road inside the company perimerter. Out of sight around a bend further down the road, they heard the shout, "Fire in the hole!" and the grunts dove into the grass as an explosion was followed by a shower of fragmented rocks. One thudded into Daugherty's back.

At the river bank, the engineers were working on the site. It was supposed to have been ready for a bridge to be dropped in place by AVLB, but first they had to blow big boulders which clogged the route. Stewart radioed for an AVLB to be driven up, but it could not make it down the road until all the other bridges had been put in place. There was no telling how long that might be, so the dozers cleared space in the roadside brush in case a night defensive position would have to be set up. The men took another break at around four in the afternoon, and the AVLB finally made it to the position at around six o'clock as dusk was coming.

By dusk Lieutenant Stephen's platoon was ordered back to the high ground overlooking the bridge to establish their NDP and watch for enemy movement. The grunts humped and sweated in the dim light and were still moving into position when night came and blackness enveloped the ridgeline. The men put some claymores around them, divided up the watch time, and tried to get to sleep on the jungle floor. There were no foxholes or wire. Daugherty looked back down the hill and could see APCs and Sheridans on the road. The tank cannons were trained into the brush. He was afraid that, if something went down, the tanks would accidentally hit them with their return fire. "Tankers are taking it easy tonight," he grinned, "with all us grunts up here protecting them."

Sitting atop the ridgeline with tank cannons pointed at them, with only a few claymores between them and the no-man's-land of black jungle, Daugherty was as nervous as common sense dictated. But he wasn't terrified. The men beside him were dependable, the problems of base-camp having disappeared as soon as they'd hit the bush. The blacks and whites again stuck together. The officers exhibited good leadership and even the colonels, Daugherty thought, had learned enough by '71 to have them not do stupid things. And the dope stayed stashed at Camp Evans. The general consensus was that you could get as stoned as you liked at camp but, when you boarded the helicopter in the morning, you'd better be straight: you couldn't trust somebody who was high watching the flank or walking point. Daugherty was sure that, somewhere along the line, somebody from Delta must have broken the rule. If anybody'd been caught, his buddies would have felt no guilt in beating the shit out of the offender. But Daugherty had never caught anyone.

They were tight, Daugherty thought. They stuck together and did their job. It wasn't because they believed in the war; from a grunt's point of view, he reckoned, it was all pretty hopeless. As far as he could see their efforts merely made a small percentage of Vietnamese black marketeers and businessmen rich while doing nothing for the average person. The rice farmers he saw did not care about democracy, capitalism, communism, or nationalism; they just wanted to be left alone to tend their rice and water buffalos, and to scratch a living out of the soil. If there had to be a war here, Daugherty didn't feel right in attacking his own government for it. The worst thing, to him, was that after they went to the trouble of waging a war, they never committed themselves. He could find no sense in coming and going, coming and going.

What kept Daugherty going was that the grunts in the bush had to stick together. There were the high points and the low points, he surmised; the lows were really low and the highs weren't all that great. No one wanted to be the last man to die in Vietnam—Daugherty heard that many times—but he dismissed it; no one wants to get killed—first, middle, or last—and if you were the last, you'd never know it. You were just there, he thought, you were drafted and in the Nam and you did your job with the least number of hassles. Just put one foot in front of the other and keep moving.

The AVLB at the bridge site was just preparing to turn on the road to face the bank when Captain Stewart noticed that four end-connectors were missing on the left side. He wasn't willing to take the chance of the AVLB breaking a track before it turned completely and blocked the road, and he shouted at the driver to stop. It took another couple of hours to repair the track. They finally crossed the river just before midnight, with the minesweeps still up front, and everyone else now back on their vehicles. They left the 3/187 AO and crossed the imaginary line into 4/3's area.

Around midnight, Lieutenant Dewing's platoon could hear all kinds of racket coming down the road, and got a radio call from the combat engineers. Dewing gave his position to them, sent a detail to pull in the MAs, and told the engineers he would meet them on the road. He was hesitant to send one of his grunts for fear, if the man were not careful enough, he might get blown away by a nervous engineer guard. He waved at the column as it approached and stepped into the glare of the lead dozer's headlights. Dismounted sweep teams were in front, the bulldozer using its light to illuminate the road for them and its blade to carve away the roadside tangle for the column following them.

As they passed, Dewing talked with some of the engineers who said they were clearing Route 9 all the way to Khe Sanh. He still didn't know what the whole operation was about, but for the first time his road security job made sense. The rest of the story would fall in place soon and, Dewing would reflect, the operation was the only one he'd been in which was clearly a campaign with specific objectives. The rest had been merely like a nine-to-five job to keep the VC off balance; "waltzing through the woods," he called it, "chasing the commies." It rarely made sense. But the new op was different and Dewing thought the change was for the better. After the tedium of their booby-trap war down south, where casualties were rarely avenged with even the sight of a live VC, the platoon appeared glad to be on the DMZ. They were doing something different and their depression was replaced by a state of nervous alertness and excitement.

Continuing down Route 9, Stewart's sweep teams stayed up front, followed by the line of combat vehicles from A/3/5 and the bulk of 1/1 Cav. Around two in the morning, the lead Sheridan of Alpha Troop—back behind the point, the minesweepers, the mine dog, and the bulldozer—hit a mine in the road. There were no casualties, but it blew off a tread and blocked Route 9. The whole column came to a halt in the mud and Stewart radioed the nearest infantry unit. He explained that he had a tank down and, if they were to continue at their set pace, he needed permission to bulldoze it off the cliff along the roadside. Otherwise, it would require several hours of hard labor to jockey the vehicle enough to the side to allow passage. The infantryman on the other end of the radio had no idea what he was talking about and gave him no answer. Stewart ordered the GIs to push the Sheridan to the side of the road.

It was not until the next morning that they finally moved again. Just then the lieutenant of the bulldozer platoon refused to go any further, claiming he had maintenance problems with his dozers and needed to work on them. Stewart suspected that the lieutenant was balking from fear of encroaching so deeply into NVA territory or from simple exhaustion, but he didn't know enough about dozers to say anything. He left the engineers and walked ahead only to find another problem: troopers from the 326th Engineer Battalion, 101st Airborne—who had airmobiled to Khe Sanh and were supposed to have installed the last bridge to the base—were still at work. The old bridge abutments were not usable so they had had to construct new ones a bit upstream. They said another two or three hours were needed. General Hill was there, his C&C helicopter sitting in the brush, and Stewart got clarification of his command over the engineer lieutenant. Hill told him to use his gun if that's what it took to get the man moving again.

By the time Stewart walked back, the lieutenant said his dozers were ready to go and they moved up to where the 326th Engineers were hard at work. Finally, a chopper hovered a slingloaded span bridge into place. Captain Stewart's task force went across, then churned through the mud and elephant grass to link up with 1/11 Infantry which was securing the Khe Sanh plateau. Mission completed, Route 9 was officially declared open to tracked vehicles that afternoon at 1130 hours, 31 January.

Earlier in the day, the 8th Battalion, 4th Artillery, XXIV Corps was alerted to move from its basecamp at Dong Ha to Vandegrift, to provide additional fire support to the task force. The soldier who took the phone call for the move was Sfc. Roy H. Hatfield, first sergeant of Headquarters and Headquarters Battery. He, for one, was extremely nervous at the prospect of heading into a hot area. In the argot of the draftees, he considered 8/4 Arty a flaky battalion. Hatfield was himself an experienced vet, a thirty-three-year-old family man on his twenty-first month in Vietnam; he'd been in field units the entire time, had been with the Marines during the Khe Sanh siege, was twice decorated for valor. With that experience behind him, he thought the outfit was not ready for action.

The problems started with the battalion commander who, Hatfield thought, was typical of the career officers at that stage in the War. Most of them had their six-month slots in the battalion and seemed only to want to promote their careers with a war record. One captain had told him he would be making major soon and that, if the war lasted long enough, he might get to be a lieutenant colonel.

The leadership problem affected his Hq&Hq battery also; Hatfield thought of their captain as a good-old-boy type, just there to get his ticket punched. He simply floated along, not too concerned about how things got done and not willing to be a bad guy to the troops by enforcing discipline. He thought the young sergeants were trying their best, but most had earned instant stripes in the shake'n'bake NCO schools and lacked the experience and deftness to effectively lead disaffected draftees. They would show up in Hatfield's orderly room, complaining that so-and-so wasn't doing this or that, then threaten to put the man on report. Very few GIs responded well to that type of threatening leadership.

It was the young artillerymen who were Sergeant Hatfield's biggest headache. Since he'd arrived in the battalion in October, things had been quiet in the area and virtually no one had any combat experience. They'd been leading the good life, he thought, and he worried about how they'd hold up under fire. In their boredom, they'd been mostly bitter and frustrated and the battalion had experienced a few fragging incidents. There were some subliminal racial problems, but Hatfield's major concern was drug abuse. He was never able to catch a single user or pusher, but it was obvious that more than one of the artillerymen were heroin addicts. He was convinced that some of the medics bought dope from the locals, hid it among their medical gear, then brought it back to the troopers.

Trying to pack away his apprehensions, Sergeant Hatfield joined the 8/4 Artillery road march. The trucks of Hq&Hq fell in behind another unit on Route 9, and the firing batteries strung out behind them aboard their self-propelled artillery pieces. It was nearly dark by the time they got to Vandegrift, and the base was so crowded with people and machinery, that someone just pointed to a patch of brush and told them to spend the night there. They dismounted from their vehicles but Hatfield told the men only to risk sleeping on the ground if they had cots—so the tanks and trucks rumbling through the grass would see them and not run them over.

The grunts of 1/1 Cav pulled perimeter security around Khe Sanh, while Stewart's A/3/5 immediately departed for their next objective. The bulk of 3/5 Cav, with A Company, 7th Engineers, had started the pioneer road through the mountains, from the Rockpile to Khe Sanh, the day before, and Alpha Troop was to secure the end point of the road north of Khe Sanh. That evening, they set up their NDP in the foothills, Stewart being damned careful to get his Sheridans and APCs in a tight wagon-train circle—command group in the center, RPG screens, claymores, and trips in place—and to having the FO call in protective artillery fire all around them in the dark. Stewart knew how vulnerable they were—the only U.S. unit so far north of Khe Sanh, in only spotty communication with arty, days before 3/5 could open the road and link up with them—but, surprisingly, the North Vietnamese didn't fire a single shot at them. In fact, by the end of the third day of Operation Dewey Canyon II, no fighting had been reported.

It was still early in the morning, 1 February, when 8/4 Artillery prepared to move out again, this time to Khe Sanh. They passed other artillery batteries already dug into the green elephant grass along the road, the troops waving and exchanging peace signs and throwing power. Sergeant Hatfield thought the men already in position looked damned happy to see the war going past them.

Hatfield was sitting in a truck near the front of the convoy, the rocky terrain and dirt road bringing back memories of the bad shellings and ambushes in the area when he'd been with the Marines in '68. It was a peaceful day and it could have been a nice ride in the country, but he couldn't shake his worries about snipers. He kept studying the beautiful terrain, thinking how easy it would be for the NVA to ambush them; all they would have to do was blow two of the newly-installed bridges on either end of the column and it would have been nearly impossible to maneuver effectively from the narrow road. Few of the young artillerymen seemed to share his concerns; they had never been shot at, had no feeling for the possible dangers around them, and looked almost awkward in their helmets and flak jackets.

When they reached Khe Sanh, the plateau was overcast but bustling with activity. Hatfield quickly went about pointing out places for the men to dig their bunkers and foxholes in case of shelling, then watched unhappily as they lazily pretended to dig in. They began finding abandoned gear on the edge of the perimeter, including old Marine grenades and ammunition, and a dud 500-pound bomb half-buried in the dirt. A engineer ordance disposal team was called up, and the artillerymen took cover as the ammo was blown in place. Hatfield ordered the men back to digging and a kid beside him began breaking earth with a pick. He swung, there was an explosion, and the artilleryman was suddenly on his butt, astonished and cut by shrapnel. He'd hit an old M-79 grenade round.

The first day of the operation, General Sutherland moved his XXIV Corps HQ into the TOC bunker of the displaced 5th Mech at Quang Tri. By the evening of 1 February, the reports coming to him indicated that the initial objectives of Operation Dewey Canyon II had been achieved. At that time, the whole of three infantry battalions, one mechanized infantry battalion, one armor battalion, two cavalry squadrons, three engineer battalions, three artillery battalions, and assets of other units were in position with no enemy-related casualties.

The fact that enemy resistance had been nonexistent in an area where the NVA had held sway for over two years was a surprise. Some sources, primarily the news media, ventured to propose that Dewey Canyon II was a failure because no impressive body count had been tallied, or that the NVA were swarming around Khe Sanh and were suckering the allies into a trap. General Sutherland responded that only the "unknowing and uninformed" would think that the area was teeming with North Vietnamese. With no allied presence in the area, the Communists did not need to maintain a large force at Khe Sanh. Dewey Canyon II was a race of sorts. Sutherland's intelligence officers suspected that the NVA may have been forewarned as early as 25 January and were probably converging on the area to delay opening of the road and airstrip. The 5th Mechanized Infantry Division won the race, and any North Vietnamese in the hills had little choice but to stay concealed and simply watch the enormous American buildup.

Sutherland was most impressed by the combat engineer effort along Route 9 which, in two labor-filled days, had made the whole operation possible. "One of the many parts of Dewey Canyon II and Lam Son 719 which I continue to recall with professional pride and admiration," Sutherland said, "was the performance of the 45th Engineer Group with its two battalions, the 14th and 27th. Other than I, there is probably no person who participated in the operation who can really appreciate the contribution of those engineers. It was the most outstanding performance that I observed in my thirty-four years of service. . . . the sight on D day was magnificent to behold—a steady stream of helicopters moving engineer equipment, culvert and bridge sections from the rear areas to the front."

CHAPTER FIVE:
The Buildup

In the week following the opening of the offensive, the Quang Tri front was a flurry of activity. The ground operations continued along Route 9, while 1/1 Cav and 1/11 Infantry continued the push to the Laotian border. In their wake, elements of the 7th and 14th Engineers performed several tasks: upgrading the highway; carving tank trails in the mountains; installing water points, rock crushers, and basecamp facilities. Meanwhile, Dong Ha filled with thousands of ARVN troops coming by sea and air and long convoys of ARVN trucks hit Route 9 to basecamp around Khe Sanh.

A Company, 14th Engineers began improving Vandegrift (Forward Support Area-I) with ammunition storage areas, fuel blivet berms, vehicle staging areas, and more. The rest of the battalion (with the 326th Engineers and a platoon from the 59th Engineer Company) upgraded Route 9 to Khe Sanh, while the 27th Engineers and the rest of the 59th continued the job to Laos. Khe Sanh (Forward Support Area-II) was simultaneously revamped. DISCOM, 101st Airborne handled the slingloading of heliborne materials and the Da Nang Support Command brought in supplies by convoy.

At Khe Sanh, the 27th and 326th Engineer teams worked on the airfield. Aerial photographs taken before the operation had not revealed the extent of damage to the original strip, thick brush covering the shell holes made in 1968. Much time had to be devoted to minesweeping the area, while EOD teams destroyed dud rounds and abandoned explosives, and the decision was made to begin simultaneous work on a second assault airstrip parallel to the original.

Things were falling behind schedule.

The day the op began, an allocation came down to the 24th Transportation Battalion, 124th Transportation Command, U.S. Army Support Command, Cam Ranh Bay, to detach two convoy officers to travel the four-hundred miles to Quang Tri. The battalion commander assigned the mission to Lieutenants John Doyle and Don Malmstrom of the 442d Truck Company. After the colonel called Malmstrom into his office and gave him his orders, he said apologetically, "We're sending you because you're the only unmarried officer." Malmstrom wasn't bothered by that, and the colonel told him to get his gear and meet up with Doyle.

Lieutenant Doyle had just transferred in from the 1/5 Mech, extending his Vietnam tour in a rear job in exchange for a drop in his Army commitment, and it gave Malmstrom some confidence to be going into an unknown area with an experienced veteran. His confidence faded when he talked with Doyle, who described the area as a quagmire of broken bridges and ambushes, with no secure areas. He was also angry that, after just getting a safe job with the transportation corps at Cam Ranh Bay, he was being sent right back to the Quang Tri bush. He said he was getting the shaft.

Malmstrom was also unhappy with the assignment. He was twenty-three, from Aberdeen, Washington, and had been cajoled into the Army by signing up for ROTC in college to avoid the draft. Reading the newspaper, he had been convinced that the American public would put an end to the war before it became a personal threat to him, but that was not to be. In August, 1970, he had found himself with orders to South Vietnam. Since his parents owned an automotive store, he'd been able to talk his way into the transportation corps and avoided the grunt's war. If it had been WWII, Malmstrom felt, he would have gone willingly, but Vietnam seemed nonsensical to him. He'd been in-country five months, but it had been in the security and lax discipline of Cam Ranh Bay and he felt inexperienced and unwilling to head to the war up north.

Lieutenants Doyle and Malmstrom took a plane to Da Nang, where they met with a Major Butler, a transportation officer from Saigon. He was a capable, friendly man and was to be their commander for the mission. They spent the night at the airbase, then signed out a jeep and started north on Route 1, a relatively secure stretch of road that only became noticeably dangerous in the Hai Van Pass area. They were coming out of the pass, going downhill, when they saw a ROK unit with VC prisoners along the roadside. The Koreans had just been through a firefight and were keyed up as they manhandled their black-pajama-clad prisoners out of the elephant grass and threw them down on the side of the road. The scene only made Malmstrom even more nervous about what they were getting into.

They passed Camps Eagle and Hue, stopped for lunch at Camp Evans, then finally pulled into Quang Tri, only to find hustle, bustle, and confusion. Major Butler immediately left for Vandegrift to coordinate what was becoming the major convoy staging area on the way to Khe Sanh. Malmstrom stayed at Quang Tri, sticking with Doyle, who seemed used to the confusion inherent in any major operation and who was in no rush to leave until their mission had been pinned down. They asked around, but got different stories from everyone, and finally hitched a ride to Dong Ha where they spent the night with some 5th Mech folks. In the morning, they were back at Quang Tri but were only told to go down the road, with no specific mission, so they again retired to Dong Ha. The next day, a colonel collared them and said, "Get your asses down that road!" which is exactly what they did, thumbing a ride in a five-ton troop truck. Before they left Quang Tri, Doyle pointed out something with partisan pride; a hootch with the sign 1/5 MECH INFANTRY DIVISION REAR HEADQUARTERS was next to another shack with the sign 101ST SCREAMING EAGLES FORWARD HEADQUARTERS.

Route 9 from Dong Ha was blacktop, and military vehicles rumbled back and forth at will. The weather was brisk, though, and the terrain a foreboding patchwork of elephant grass, hills, and treelines. Doyle tried to impress upon Malmstrom how easily the NVA could lay in ambush, that other units had had their asses kicked on Route 9, and to always keep alert. Malmstrom was nervous and the five or six GIs sharing the ride in the back of the truck were in helmets and flak jackets and had their M-16s trained towards the underbrush as they rolled along.

The two-way paved highway turned into a one-way dirt trail at Vandegrift. Major Butler met them there on the road and explained that one of them would stay there with him while the other went to Khe Sanh to coordinate the convoys there.

Lieutenant Doyle said he wanted to stay at Vandegrift.

"Well, Malmstrom," Butler said, "that leaves you to go to Khe Sanh."

"Hey, no problem."

He knew Doyle was unhappy to be there to begin with and, besides, a friend of his had been through the '68 seige at Khe Sanh so he was curious about the place. Butler gave him some instructions (which were vague because even he didn't know the whole picture yet) and told him to play it by ear, to do nothing drastic without consulting him. Malmstrom hitched a ride with the 300th MP Company, 18th MP Brigade, sitting in a jeep with a captain, a lieutenant, and several young military policemen. They had come straight out of Saigon and were excited, asking Malmstrom questions about being "up north." They did not seem to have any concept of the dangers of snipers and ambushes. They skirted around a few hills, made a final turn, and rolled into the southern rim of the Khe Sanh perimeter where several dirt roads made a juncture in the elephant grass and brush. The place looked dusty and raw, still in the process of going up, with helicopters and cargo nets overhead, tents being pitched, minesweep teams out. Someone met them and said not to wander off the roads for fear of the old Marine minefields. The main dirt trail went right to the airstrip and the 300th MPs camped alongside it, having had a bulldozer dig a large hole in the ground, putting up a troop tent and breaking out cots and C rations.

Lieutenant Malmstrom was assigned to establish a convoy checkpoint at the juncture to help organize truckers for the return trip to Vandegrift and to aid convoy commanders in finding places. He was assigned two Sp5 MPs and their checkpoint was simply the MP jeep parked on the road. The job was not as easy as it seemed; no helicopter was available for Malmstrom, so he could not recon the area and see what the dots and lines on his map really meant, and the radio line to Major Butler was spotty. Thus, no on-the-spot coordination could be made with the many convoys running on the one-way road between Vandegrift and Khe Sanh.

The situation was still new and confusing when a headquarters detachment wearing 101st shoulder patches pulled up. The major in the lead jeep pointed on his map to a spot along the main road to the runway. A large convoy had already rumbled past and was bottlenecked near the ammo dump so Malmstrom figured this new convoy would just fuel the chaos. He shrugged and laughed, "I have no idea where that is."

"Aren't you controlling the road?"

"Yeah, but I just got here and they won't let me look around."

The major craned his neck, looking around, and Malmstrom thought he looked so anxious that he wouldn't wait his turn around the ammo dump. So he checked the map again and said, "I think that's where you should be going, sir," pointing him in the direction of Lang Vei. By the time the convoy returned, the traffic jam into Khe Sanh had cleared up, but the major was furious. Malmstrom could see that, because of his lack of communication, he was hacking off a lot of convoy commanders (as well as the organizers at Vandegrift, who never knew when he would be sending an unloaded convoy to them).

Hundreds of trucks were coming and going every day but Malmstrom didn't have the acreage to form a convoy staging area—meaning whole convoys would have to pull to the shoulder on the one-way dirt trail while other convoys slowly squeezed past. He wanted an area where the truckers could do maintenance, wait for the road to clear, and organize for the trip back; he also wanted enough land cleared so three hundred trucks could spread out to minimize damage during a possible rocket attack. He headed up the road to the airfield and found a lieutenant colonel. He explained the situation but the colonel seemed unconcerned and Malmstrom blurted out in frustration, "Well if you don't need these trucks in a convoy staging area, then maybe we can put some of the trucks getting ready for the ammo dump, maybe we can put them right alongside your tent out here." The colonel stared at him as if to say he did not need such outbursts from a young lieutenant, then finally said he would try to get some dozers. When? In a couple of days. Malmstrom was worried about rocket attacks on the crowded trucks, but did not know how to press the issue with a colonel.

The next day he went to find help elsewhere. He'd been ordered to stay at the checkpoint but shrugged that off. The Sp5s were responsible for their jeep, but they recognized the problem and he appreciated their lending it to him. He headed down Route 9 and found a small engineer compound along the way to Vandegrift. A number of dozers were on the highway pushing away brush to widen the trail and grading the clay surface. Malmstrom explained the situation to the young lieutenant in charge, saying he needed three dozers to scrape away a three-hundred by two-hundred-foot area that the minesweepers had okayed. The lieutenant, knowing his business, said one cat could do that in an hour, and detailed one of his Sp4s to follow Malmstrom back. The kid cleared the area in the northwest corner of the checkpoint intersection.

The area proved to be too small and the next day Malmstrom called again on the engineers, who dispatched another dozer. Even two staging areas were not enough to accommodate all the convoys, and the trucks usually sat bumper-to-bumper in them—Malmstrom was thankful that no rockets were coming. It was mostly a boring routine of counting trucks. He still hadn't been able to scout the area, so when troops asked for directions he could only say, "Beats me, ask your convoy commander."

The ARVN literally descended like a plague out of the sky on Lieutenant Malmstrom's checkpoint, in the form of an infantry battalion helicoptering into his second convoy staging area. He had been given no notice so he rushed over to their MACV advisor, exchanging a few terse words with the captain. The ARVN were given the area as their camp, but friction soon developed between the allies. The South Vietnamese soldiers were seemingly undisciplined, wandering around outside their perimeter, so gunhappy that they tossed grenades and fired their rifles like toys, getting on everyone's nerves. Malmstrom complained to the MACV captain, who said he would take care of the problem; it seemed to Malmstrom that, the more he complained, the more he understood how little actual control an American officer had over Vietnamese troops.

The ARVN also made the mistake of wandering into the U.S. convoy areas. The GI truckers did not trust them, didn't like "gooks" anyway, and one night, having caught an ARVN snooping around their vehicles, they nonchalantly punched him silly. The man turned out to be a South Vietnamese officer. The next morning, a lieutenant colonel and a major cornered Malmstrom, looking for an MP officer and, finding none, blamed the problem on him. No, Malmstrom defended himself, he took orders from Major Butler at Vandegrift, was there to organize convoys and had no authority over the troops. They discussed it back and forth and, finally, the lieutenant colonel told him that he was in charge of all the transportation personnel who came into the area. Malmstrom balked. He didn't want to ride roughshod over the truckers, and said the individual company commanders should be in charge of their men. The colonel said no and left.

The friction with the ARVN continued unabated. A back-trail east of the checkpoint was cleared of mines and set up as a way station for the ARVN convoys beginning to arrive. The South Vietnamese truckers seemed to have no grasp of the organizational aspects of convoys, felt they could come and go as they pleased, and made no attempt to

coordinate their moves with the Americans. Malmstrom had no interpreters, but he tried to work the ARVN into the routine of waiting in the
staging areas and leaving on Route 9 only when permission was given.
He hoped they would imitate the American truckers; but they didn't. The
biggest problem was that they would run the checkpoint. Four or five
times a day, an ARVN convoy would come down the road; Malmstrom
and the two MPs would shout, "Slow, slow down! Dung lai, dung lai!"
and the ARVN would curve around them and keep going.

Since the road was one-way, coordination was essential and the
ARVN often found themselves head-to-head with U.S. convoys. The
bush was so thick along the side that convoys could barely pull over or
back up, turning the highway into dusty, shouting chaos as the two
columns jockeyed for position. Malmstrom knew it wouldn't be long before the angry GIs simply began manhandling the ARVN drivers out and
shoving the trucks off the side to make room, so he and the MPs adopted
a drastic tactic: when the South Vietnamese tried to run the checkpoint,
they shot out the tires of the lead truck and the fed-up young MPs levelled
their M-16s to quiet the now screaming ARVN. They had been hesitant
to build a barricade, since the U.S. convoys never ran the point and it
could cause accidents during the foggy nights, but they finally had to in
order to control the ARVN.

Other problems stemmed from the South Vietnamese's more casual
outlook in war. Sometimes, when Malmstrom drove the road with the
MPs they found ARVN convoys stopped on the road cooking rice in upturned helmets. If they played around too long, the direction of the road
would be switched on them and they would come up against some mean
GI truckers coming from the opposite direction. Malmstrom and the MPs
would hurry the ARVN along and the complaints went back and forth on
both sides. It ended up with another visit to Malmstrom from some
ARVN officers, an interpreter, and more U.S. brass. The discussion concluded with his being put in charge of not only the GIs, but also any
ARVN who came into the staging areas. The two MPs in the checkpoint
jeep joked with him about how he'd gone from a glorified truck counter
to the commander of a multi-national force.

CW3 Chuck Hawk, second-in-command of the Flight Check Section,
165th Aviation Group, 1st Aviation Brigade, was summoned to a classified briefing at 7th USAF HQ at Tan Son Nhut airbase when the operation began. Most of those at the meeting were air force officers; they

discussed the opening of the Khe Sanh runway and said they hoped to establish an almost continuous daisy-chain of C130s from Da Nang to Khe Sanh. Only one pass was to be allowed. If the C130 missed because of ground fire, weather, or damage to the runway, the pilot was to divert to Quang Tri, follow the coast back to Da Nang, and loop back into the daisy-chain. At peak efficiency, they hoped to have a C130 land every three minutes, slide off the supply pallets without even shutting off the engines, and have forklifts clear the taxiway for the next plane.

Hawk's section was to install the air-traffic-control tower at Khe Sanh; he jeeped back to his base at Long Binh, reported to the lieutenant colonel commanding the section, and they organized a crew of six master sergeants. They started off in a U21 turboprop plane with Hawk flying over four hundred miles to Khe Sanh, only to find the field socked in with fog and visibility at zero.

The next day, they departed Long Binh again, this time with a civilian tech rep who was a radar expert. Hawk circled Khe Sanh as engineers moved their equipment off the now dirt strip they were constructing. As soon as he landed and taxied to the side, the vehicles clanked back to work. Hawk was amazed at the scene around them. Rough-terrain forklifts raised dust as they noisily filled in old bunkers and cleared away rusting wire. Men were digging new positions, putting up tents. Minesweep teams moved slowly and methodically. Others worked on the old, shell-pocked strip. A swarm of helicopters came and went with supplies, raising great sheets of red dust. Hawk couldn't believe all the dust; everything and everyone was covered by the fine red clay and you couldn't tell a black man from a white man unless he rolled up his sleeve.

The airstrip ran east-west and the ATC tower was built north of it. A team from the 125th Air Traffic Control Company had arrived from Quang Tri the day before, and the engineers had already dug the support holes for the tower. Forklifts dropped in the thirty-foot-telephone-pole supports, and a Chinook, with a standard army ATC cab slingloaded underneath it, gingerly set the box atop the four poles. The civilian tech rep was an expert in his field and he schooled the young army specialists in getting the radar and radio equipment installed. After four hours, they had the FM, VHF, and UHF radios working, along with a GCA (Ground Control Approach) radar, and a non-directional beacon. Hawk then had to fly repetitive patterns in the area so they could make adjustments and work out the GCA glide path.

Hawk and two of the master sergeants got in the U21 and flew a pattern at fifteen hundred feet, going back and forth between Khe Sanh and Lang Vei. That was the part of the job he disliked; it could take up to twenty patterns over the same piece of ground to align the radar correctly, giving the enemy ample time to track the unarmed, slow, low-flying plane. Sure enough, as they passed by one of the Lang Vei hills, Hawk heard the distinctive crack of three or four AK-47 rounds going past his ship. It happened again on the next orbit and Hawk decided to call for an airstrike. But the two sergeants were nonplussed; they figured it was just some lone NVA popping off with his AK. They were crustier and older than Hawk, and just shrugged, "Aw, Mister Hawk, don't even call it in. If the Air Force blows him away, they'll just bring in someone who knows how to shoot." It took about twelve patterns to get the radar on target, and the sniper blasted away without hitting a thing.

A day or two later, on 4 February, after the engineers had finished grading the dirt strip, Hawk received a call from 7th USAF HQ at Tan Son Nhut. They wanted to know if the new strip would support C130 traffic; he said he doubted it, the ground was too soft. He was surprised when, a bit later, a C130 began its landing approach. It hit the sod strip, used reverse props to slow down, and then the nose tilted forward as the giant plane sunk in several inches. Hawk and his crew muttered, "Well, what did they expect?" Within a couple of hours, they had drained the bulk of the fuel and chained forklifts to the front landing gears; with the props going, they pulled the C130 out and to the end of strip. It turned around, the pilot hit high speed and they hurtled back down the twelve hundred feet of runway. The engineers began laying down pierced-steel matting, and the delays continued. With the airfield completion behind schedule and the terrain of Route 9 hindering the supply convoys, the buildup at Khe Sanh was below par. Fuel shortages were especially a problem.

The old marine minefields also continued to be a problem. One morning at Khe Sanh, Lieutenant Garwood and a Sergeant Crowle of the 101st Pathfinders monitored a radio request for medevacs for two men wounded on a perimeter patrol. They had walked into the mines outside the wire. Garwood radioed to sit tight, help was on the way, but they called back a minute later saying they had another casualty, and shouting, "Are you going to do anything?" Garwood and Crowle attached a couple of cargo slings to the underbelly of a Huey and hung onto them as the pilot sped to the patrol. The pilot hovered over them, and three wounded grunts could be seen—one with his toes blown off, one with his heel missing, another with a chunk blown out of the back of his leg. They'd stepped on U.S. antipersonnel mines; designed to maim, not kill. Garwood shouted to halt another patrol he could see filing towards the minefield, then they ferried the men out, two at a time on the slings. Garwood and Crowle jumped off, helped the wounded aboard, grabbed dropped gear, and came out last. A man in the second patrol elected to come out on the chopper rather than walk back; he lost his grip and fell to his death.

On 5 February, the first official U.S. deaths of the operation were recorded. A Cobra from D/3/5 Cav, lost in a pocket of fog, flew into a mountain northwest of Khe Sanh, and the two pilots were killed. The following evening, the next official casualty report indicated A/1/82 Artillery, Americal, was hit by 122mm rockets on Route 9 near the Rockpile; one American killed, four wounded. Gunships from the 2/17 Air Cav caught ten NVA on the Laotian border that morning and killed six.

While the 1/11 Infantry and 1/1 Cavalry secured the land route into Laos, the South Vietnamese began moving up their units which were to cross the border on Route 9. This task force consisted of two airborne battalions attached to the ARVN 1st Armor Brigade, commanded by Col. Nguyen Trong Luat. For security reasons, Luat had not been included in the planning of the operation and was only made aware of his role in it on 5 February, by a call to his headquarters in Da Nang. His orders were to take his command group and the 17th Cav and road-march to Dong Ha, where he would be joined by the 7th and 11th Cav. He was then to continue to the Laotian border and make camp adjacent to the U.S. 1/1 Cav until further orders.

The operation was Colonel Luat's first major campaign as a brigade commander, but he had already seen much war, earning prominence as a national hero during the '65 Plei Me battle and receiving high accolades from his U.S. advisors. General Sutherland, however, was an old armor officer who had not been impressed by his inspection of the brigade the past winter. He felt it necessary to visit Luat to impress his mission upon him. That evening he helicoptered from Quang Tri to Dong Ha, where the brigade was preparing to camp overnight, and spoke with Luat and his American advisor. Sutherland went into detail on the POL problem, namely that the delays in rebuilding the strip for C130 traffic meant that the only way to get fuel to the forward supply base at Khe Sanh was in rubber bladders slingloaded to CH47 and CH53 helicopters, or by fuel trucks on the highway. Both methods were precarious and allowed only a minimal amount to be stockpiled; Sutherland, therefore, had issued a general order that all U.S. vehicles and helicopters top off with fuel at Vandegrift so the fuel reserves at Khe Sanh could be used exclusively for the machinery in the area and for occasional emergencies. Sutherland emphasized the problem to Luat and his major, stating that they must top off their tanks and APCs at Vandegrift but as a U.S. commander, Sutherland could only suggest such an action to an ARVN officer.

In the morning, the brigade continued west. When they passed Vandegrift, Colonel Luat did not order a halt for refueling, but continued straight for Khe Sanh. Command relations between the Americans and Vietnamese were frequently baffling and usually frustrating for the U.S. officers involved. In this case, as in most, there was no way to know why the ARVN did not respond to a clear-cut and logical directive. Perhaps as Sutherland had detailed the problem, Luat, struggling to keep up with the English and failing that, had fallen back upon the maddening Vietnamese practice of politely smiling and nodding even though he understood nothing he was hearing. Perhaps, like most ARVN officers, Luat lacked sophisticated training in logistics and from that had developed a cavalier attitude towards the subject, always confident that the Americans would solve any problems that arose.

Either way, the 1st Armor was nearly out of fuel by the time they reached Khe Sanh and, as expected, the Americans did come up with the solution; they had to open their fuel reserves to the ARVN. General Sutherland was furious. When the reports reached him that Luat had not refueled at Vandegrift, but instead, at Khe Sanh, he made a point of discussing the problem with General Lam and expressed his doubts about Luat's abilities as a commander. He would have liked to relieve the colonel of command, but was again restrained because he had no operational control over any ARVN units.

By late afternoon, the 1st Armor was past Lang Vei and they simply pulled off Route 9 into the low hills and scrub brush to make camp. Settling in for the night with the lead force, the 11th Cav, were a half-dozen hitchhiking journalists. Among them were two Englishmen, both on assignment for *Life:* Larry Burrows, a frail-looking man with thick eyeglasses, an utterly noble and unassuming character, who had been covering the war since '62; and John Saar, an athletic blond, a paratrooper officer in the British reserves, who had been there since '69. This was their first day on the new Laotian front.

The reporters sat down for the evening at the command track of the 11th Cav which had a tent rigged like an awning behind it. The regimental commander, Lt. Col. Bui The Dung, knew enough English to greet them with a warm smile, and the entourage of U.S. advisors was relaxed and open as they ate dinner with their Vietnamese friends. It was a quaint scene, men in a grassy field on the way to war; as Saar noted, "Rice savored with onions and vegetables bubbles over dozens of fires, scalding tea in blue-and-white china bowls passes delicately from one hand to the next." The war seemed far away, its only reminder the jets dropping bombs in the distance.

Saar was standing and talking with Burrows about film shipments when the scream of a diving jet sounded too near. The next moment, two explosions erupted close by—and then suddenly, the space around them was all blast, noise, and confusion. His brain lurched at the abrupt impact of the explosions; for a freeze-framed microsecond he could see the horror and incredulity on the faces around him, and then everything was a scramble for cover. Saar jumped into a cooking trench, catching a blur from the corner of his eye of a body diving through mid-air for another slit trench. Two large fires and two boiling pots were inches away as Saar hugged the earth—thinking, Christ, I'm going to roast to death—too paralyzed with fear to move, afraid another salvo of what he thought had been mortars would land. He reached for his helmet, looked up to the din and confusion at ground level, and saw Burrows already up and running for the impact zone.

Without thinking, Saar followed him.

They were the first ones to the craters and Burrows hit the prone to photograph the scene. Saar stood shocked and sickened, his mind unable to accept what he was seeing. ARVN soldiers, dead and wounded, were strewn in the elephant grass and brush, screams of pain and cries for help coming amid the explosions. And things were still exploding, flashing red in the black. Patches of brush were on fire and an APC was ablaze, cooking off ammunition. All around was confusion and shock. One officer, an advisor major, sat hunched up, chin on his chest, momentarily too rattled to move. Others were galvanized with adrenaline; two officers quickly jumped to a radio to call for medevacs; and then the unshakable

Burrows was again at Saar's side, shouting, "Come and help me bring that chap in!"

There were no stretchers so Burrows and Saar awkardly picked up a wounded ARVN by his arms and legs. They stumbled back over the uneven ground, sweating hard, Saar feeling the blood soak into his shirt. The man was torn up by shrapnel, his chest, stomach, and head oozing life, and he suddenly gave a shuddering groan of terrible pain. Burrows answered with a groan of pity. They dragged the soldier into an old crater where ARVN medics were frantically setting up an aid station. Saar could hear the American advisors shouting back and forth and their talk was not of a mortar raid, but of a jet accidentally hitting them with cluster bombs. Three bombs had been dropped, each one splitting open in midair to disperse dozens of cluster bomblets over the field. They kept exploding at random points, spewing shrapnel.

Men still kept moving. Saar was crouched in the crater when a young ARVN medic raced in barefoot, wide-eyed but still clutching his aid bag. South Vietnamese soldiers ran amid the explosions to drag wounded comrades back. Two more times, Saar and Burrows ventured out into the chaos to drag men back and lay them at the edge of the crater. It was pandemonium around the aid station, the Americans excitedly calling out on the radios, men running into each other in the dark, the APC going up in a roar of exploding ammunition. The wounded kept piling in, few able to walk alone. Saar recoiled at the individual scenes. One ARVN rolled in the pool of his own blood, rocking to and fro with pain, until three medics tried to hold him down to change dressings and he bucked in anguish, ramming his head into a body sprawled beside him. Another man lifted his head to see his leg, reduced to bone and flayed flesh, with medics crouched above it scissoring away the trousers, and silently let his head fall back. An ARVN lying in the crucifix position inched across the dirt to the man beside him; they clasped hands tightly and talked in murmurs. Saar couldn't imagine what they were saying, couldn't imagine a worse scenario: two medics killed outright in the first explosions, the rest undermanned to handle such carnage. They worked on those who had a chance, abandoning the seriously wounded. Saar watched one man die, wishing to God he would die quickly, die peacefully—not as he did, heaving his chest, laboriously trying to suck air down a blood-filled throat, suddenly dying with his chest still expanded. He saw the first man he and Burrows had brought in, already dead, the other two they'd carried still unattended in the dirt.

Saar and Burrows finally left the wounded and moved about the perimeter, taking photographs, watchful of the cluster bombs nestled unexploded in the brush. Saar was terrified of them, having no idea what might set them off. At the command APC, they found Lieutenant Colonel Dung wearing a long coat and hunched over the radios. He was trying to coordinate the evacuation of the wounded, alerting his outer posts lest the NVA take advantage of the chaos with an attack. Among the advisors, the most assertive was a Major Todd, a Georgian with the ARVN paratroopers. He shouted at the Vietnamese in bastard English and French, getting them ready to evacuate the wounded when the choppers came.

The first helicopter circled over Route 9, came down cautiously through the night fog, then abruptly pulled up when clouds of red road dust whipped up.

"What's the problem?"

"He can't see to land!"

"Throw water to dampen the dust!"

The helicopter landed, still churning up considerable dust, and Major Todd shouted at his paratroopers, "Only the men! No stretchers 'cause so beaucoup many!" The red lights of the helo glowed eerily on the helmets of the ARVN as they ran forward with the most seriously wounded. Saar watched them, "forced to treat their commrades like so many carcasses, the paratroops shove wounded on top of one another until the cabin is a surreal slaughterhouse."

With the wounded gone, Saar could see the ARVN regain their confidence. He heard a man laugh; others began to talk and joke again, and shovels clanked in the dark as soldiers covered the bloodstains and bandages. Although it had been a U.S. jet that had caused the casualties, he detected no animosity among the South Vietnamese. They accepted it as an accident of war. The dead were wrapped in ponchos and tied to stretchers with bandages. One of the advisors suggested the helo pilots be called back to get the bodies without being told they were running risks for the dead, but Major Todd quickly axed that idea.

When the final reckoning was done, it was duly noted that at 1920 hours on 6 February 1971, one aircraft from the U.S.S. Ranger attacked a moving target on Route 9, accidentally hitting friendly forces and causing the deaths of six ARVN, the wounding of fifty-one, and the destruction of one APC. They were the first South Vietnamese casualties of Operation Lam Son 719. Four days later, the reporter who had behaved so courageously during the mishap, Larry Burrows, boarded an ARVN helicopter to cover the war in Laos. The helo was shot down. His body was never recovered.

On 7 February, Lieutenant Malmstrom was at his Khe Sanh checkpoint when a small column of empty five-thousand-gallon tanker trucks pulled up. They had come to field-test the large trucks on Route 9 and, although their captain seemed excited, the truckers were less than enthusiastic. They talked about maintenance problems that were sure to develop and that the turns were too tricky for their wide loads. It was about an hour before dawn the next morning when an MP radioman woke Malmstrom, saying, "You gotta be kidding me!" He couldn't understand why higher would send the vulnerable fuel trucks at night, when in the morning they could have air cover.

He could just think they were hurting for fuel worse than reported.

Sp4 Spurgeon was asleep in an APC of the 1/77 Scouts—he was suddenly startled awake by a big ball of fire illuminating the area. He stood up in the crew hatch to see what was happening. The track sentry was standing astonished on deck with a blanket hanging from his shoulders; to their west, around the Rockpile, there were shots and explosions. They cranked up their APC just as a lone track sped from the direction of the ambush. Lieutenant Revelak sat atop the open driver's hatch beside the fifty mount, yelling to follow him. They sped down the paved highway right up to three burning fuel trucks, one of which had crashed over the road embankment, and Spurgeon could see figures moving in the brush. He held his fire, unable to distinguish friend from foe. Revelak jumped onto his track, there were eight GIs on deck; Spurgeon grabbed an M-60, and they hauled ass further into the ambush area. A GI wearing a steel pot jogged alongside them for a second, screaming something, but they ignored him. Revelak shouted to fire, Spurgeon started to ask, "What about our guys?"—and sides of the road lit up with tracers.

They didn't fire straight ahead; there were more burning trucks there.

They crossed a bridge, passed the burning trucks, then saw a gun truck on fire down the highway. Spurgeon then saw a bareheaded man ten feet from his APC, crawling in a puddle of blood which reflected in the flames. He levelled his M-60 to blow the NVA away—then abruptly noticed the man was too big to be a Vietnamese, and that he looked black. The GI was painfully struggling to get up. Spurgeon pulled his gun away as they sped past. Another soldier appeared from the shadows, running in

a crouch beside their APC, shouting something they could not hear. They
stopped at the burning gun truck, its weapons hanging down, unmanned;
there was only darkness past that point. They did a pivot on the highway
and roared back, Revelak screaming to fire up the place again, Spurgeon
cradling the M-60 as they bumpily tore on, emptying a hundred-round
belt at the gun truck, grooving on the tracers and ricochets.

They stopped and dismounted at the ambush scene. Spurgeon could
see a burnt-out truck, four others parked, all of then riddled with AK bullet
holes. The truckers were gone, already evacuated. A jeep full of lifers arrived, all in helmets and flak jackets, and they stood in the headlight beam,
bullshitting, Spurgeon thought, like cops at a traffic accident. The next
morning, he talked with a GI who said the NVA had ambushed the lead of
the convoy with AK-47 and RPG fire; they had tried to stop traffic from
crossing the bridge, he said, but the gun-truck crew had shouted at them to
get out of the way and had barrelled towards the shooting. The North Vietnamese then blew them away. The two GIs who'd been yelling at the APC,
it turned out, had been trying to get them to turn back before it was too
late. APCs began clearing the wrecks off the highway and Spurgeon
thought it looked like some kind of graveyard, the burnt-out shells shoved
together down the road embankment. The official word was that one GI
was killed, eight wounded, and six tanker trucks destroyed.

Lieutenant Colonel Meyer arrived and directed the tank-infantry teams
of 1/77 Armor to conduct a search for the ambushers. An NVA RPG crew
tried to hit a tank, but the GIs gunned them down before they could get
their round off. They were still cleaning up the mess when a helicopter armada began beating overhead. This was the morning the ARVN had chosen to invade Laos.

PART TWO: Operation Lam Son 719

CHAPTER SIX: D Day into Laos

L ieutenant General Lam chose 8 February 1971, as the day the South Vietnamese would invade Laos. It was not a date he preferred but rather one which had been pressed upon him. The rainy weather and the unexploded ordnance on the Khe Sanh plateau had delayed construction of the airstrip and, thus, the fuel and ammunition reserves had not reached their peak. To wait, though, invited disaster as by now the NVA were well aware of the allies' intentions, and were moving to bolster their forces in Laos. Lam had little choice but to attack as soon as possible.

To carry out the spoiling operations, Lam had five major combat units assembled on the border: the 1st Infantry Division, 1st Airborne Division, Vietnamese Marine Corps Division, 1st Ranger Group, and 1st Armor Brigade. With Tchepone as the western objective of the attack and Route 9 the straight line to the target, Lam's plan called for his units to leapfrog to the objective through a series of firebases along the mountainous flanks of the road, while the armor headed straight down the dirt highway. Destroying as they went, they were eventually to reach Tchepone, then begin the withdrawal phase. It was hoped (especially by U.S. planners) that the ARVN could maintain the offensive until the advent of the rainy season in May and then withdraw through BA 611 and the A Shau Valley.

The battlefield from the border to Tchepone was split north/south by Route 9 and a branch of the Tchepone River which ran generally east/west.

The terrain was divided into three areas; mountain ranges to the north, flat brushy country in the river valley, and more rolling mountains to the south. The latter region was marked by two overpowering terrain features. A fifteen hundred foot escarpment ran thirty-five kilometers, from the border nearly all the way to Tchepone. There was also the Co Roc, a mountain range four kilometers long, which rose abruptly on the border, just inside Laos. The escarpment and the Co Roc dominated the battlefield. Lam's plan called for the 1st Infantry Division to secure these two vantage points while the main thrust occurred to the north. The 1st Armor was to slice down Route 9, while the 1st Airborne and 1st Rangers were airmobiled into the northern mountains to move on Tchepone. The Vietnamese Marines were to be the reserve force in the Khe Sanh area.

General Lam had never before commanded such a large-scale operation, a fact which did not particularly disturb his counterpart, General Sutherland; he considered Lam "a strong, positive leader who could be very decisive with his commanders in I Corps. I respected and trusted General Lam and I believe that he had the same feelings toward me." Others gave more mixed reviews. To them, Lam was a large, moonfaced man with a pompous air, who had been made the Corps commander because he'd kept his infantry division loyal to Saigon during the '66 Buddhist Rebellion. Like most ARVN corps commanders, he was an administrator who gave broad directives and left the tactical planning to his division and regimental commanders. He had no experience in actually controlling a major campaign, and the Vietnamese Marines gave him the nickname Old Bloody Hands after his manner of grandly sweeping his hands over tactical maps when discussing operational concepts, leaving the impression that the welfare of his men was not an overriding concern.

Lam's command was complicated by a host of petty jealousies and political jostling among his subordinate commanders. Except for the 1st Infantry Division, the other units assigned to the operation had never operated as complete divisions in the field; thus, brigade commanders were used to operating independently and division commanders were accustomed neither to exercising control nor to being controlled. For example, when the 1st Airborne Division set up its command post within three kilometers of the I Corps HQ on the Khe Sanh plateau, its commander, Lt. Gen. Du Quoc Dong, refused to leave his plush villa headquarters in Saigon. As an officer equal in rank to Lam, he was upset at being given a secondary role. He finally joined his CP, but still refused to go to I Corps briefings at FSB Kilo, I Corps HQ south of Khe Sanh, sending a staff major instead. To further complicate the matter, the Airborne Division was considered an elite unit by President Thieu and had previously been afforded special considerations, Dong was the type to flaunt his friendship with the president and to try to use governmental pressures to get what he wanted.

With a commander as weak as Dong, it was no wonder the paratroopers performed as they did. As the Deputy Commander of II Field Force during the Cambodian invasion, General Sutherland had been dismayed to watch an Airborne unit secure an LZ without opposition, then sit out the duration of the campaign. No amount of cajoling could persuade Dong to seek the sound of battle. Dong was placed in operational control of the 1st Armor Brigade for the Laos operation. After the armor set up a CP at FSB Kilo, little liaison was established between them and the Airborne CP; and Dong, an inexperienced commander with no expertise in armor, virtually ignored the brigade, giving them inadequate tactical guidance and logistical support.

Similar problems arose with the VNMC Division. The Commandant of the VNMC, Lt. Gen. Le Nguyen Khang, held a slight seniority edge over Lam but—either because he was miffed at being placed in a subordinate position, or because, realizing his own inexperience, he wanted to save face—Khang stayed in Saigon. His only visits to the Quang Tri front consisted of brief tours in the company of his political ally, Vice President Ky, and were more of a show to bully Lam than for any military value. Khang left the operational command of the marines to the assistant commandant, Col. Bui The Lan, who set up his CP in the general vicinity of Kilo. Fortunately, Lan was an intense, taciturn man, a field soldier who exercised firm control over the independent-minded brigade commanders. The Vietnamese Marines were, likewise, a tough, combat-proven bunch.

Perhaps Lam's best asset was the 1st Infantry Division. Its commander, Brigadier General Phu, was not a brilliant leader but he was a combat veteran, competent, and hard working. His division, alone in the invasion force, had often worked as a single force under his command in major operations. The division had seen much combat in MR1 and its troops were experienced men who had exhibited much bravery and tenacity. As things developed, Phu was the only major commander who followed Lam's orders.

The actual ARVN push across the border was wholly dependent on U.S. Army Aviation; helicopter units had been streaming north before, during, and after the opening of the operation. The largest aviation unit setting up for the invasion was the 223rd Combat Aviation Battalion under Lt. Col. Gerald W. Kirklighter, a gruff, blunt, and experienced pilot on his second Vietnam tour. He had taken command only a week before the operation began, and the 223rd CAB was itself a confusing hodgepodge of various helicopter companies thrown together solely for this campaign.

When the shift north began, Kirklighter had been a deputy group commander at Tuy Hoa in MR2; the deputy commander of the 1st Aviation Brigade flew in, had a private conversation with his group commander, and the two officers, who both knew him well, picked Kirklighter to command the 223rd during Laos. At the time, the battalion was in the process of standing down, its former CO and staff rotating home or being assigned to other units. The battalion command consisted of a mere hundred men in the Hq&Hq Company. Maj. "Banjo" Davis, a former enlisted man with a touch for administration, was assigned as executive officer. Maj. John A. G. Klose, ex-sergeant, an unassuming but dedicated aviator just arrived for his second combat tour, was made the operations officer.

The battalion was still getting back on its feet when Kirklighter was informed that Dong Ha was to be his new CP. He had no information on the upcoming mission when he and Major Klose hopped a U21 from Tuy Hoa to Camp Eagle. There they met with officers of the 101st Aviation Group and took a Huey for a quick recon of Dong Ha. They landed in a desolate area of the base; a lieutenant colonel gestured grandly at the bushy plain and said to Kirklighter and Klose, "This is yours. We have secured permission from the Vietnamese to make this your battalion headquarters."

The only structure in view was a tin-roofed hootch with no walls.

Within a few days, the 223d CAB received a list of its components (the 48th AHC, 173d AHC, 282nd AHC, 235th AWC, D/227th AWC, 179th ASHC, and the 75th Med), and Majors Davis and Klose worked from Tuy Hoa to get the companies up to Dong Ha via air, ship, and convoy. Kirklighter went first with the advance party of Hq&Hq Company. They took a C130 to Quang Tri, then begged, borrowed, and stole some trucks to get to Dong Ha. It was raining when they arrived and the abandoned airstrip was just as cold, wet, and miserable as everyone had feared. There was little left save some old Marine tent frames which the locals hadn't carried away for firewood. In short order, they moved in, throwing canvas over the frames to escape the weather, laying down C ration cardboard and ammo box wood on the dirt floors, setting up cots and commo gear. They lived in tents, ate C rats, and, by the end of that first day, were swept by freezing winds and rains. If it hadn't been so miserable, Kirklighter could have found it amusingly incongruous to see soldiers, in one of the hottest regions of the world, huddled around campfires, wearing flak jackets for warmth, with blankets wrapped around them.

One at a time, the helicopter companies began arriving at the 223rd CAB HQ. Kirklighter's major problem at Dong Ha was security. For the first time in his experiences in Vietnam, an aviation unit was in the field without infantry support. He was in contact with the 5th Mech but they had no units assigned to the airfield, and the mech units he saw passing through appeared ill-disciplined. There were jeeps full of ARVN roaring through the area, but he had no communications with their commanders and was leery of depending on them to move if anything happened. Kirklighter had no choice but to force his men to pull double duty. Door gunners, clerks, cooks, and mechanics began piling sandbags around the tents, stringing wire, standing night guard duty. The bitching doubled. Aviators don't lead a charmed life, Kirklighter mused, and he was taking no chances. Luckily, even though Dong Ha was in easy range of the NVA artillery in the DMZ, not a round was fired at them.

This made Kirklighter's next biggest headache the lack of information. He had no idea why his battalion had been dispatched to the DMZ. Security was tight.

The briefing for aviation support to Lam Son 719 was held by General Berry and Colonel Davis at Khe Sanh on the evening of 7 February, in the 101st Airborne Forward Headquarters. The CP was emplaced just south of the runway in an ingenious construction of four trailers lowered into giant trenches, in the shape of a Greek cross, with a connecting catwalk between them and sturdy overhead cover. The headquarters was virtually impregnable to enemy shelling. The helicopters of the various aviation commanders were parked on the runway, and the men assembled in one of the underground trailers. They sat in folding chairs, facing Berry and Davis, who stood before the map board under soft fluorescent light.

In his calm, professional tone, Berry announced the invasion of Laos.

"I'll be a son of a bitch," Kirklighter mumbled to himself, "I thought we were going into the A Shau."

Berry and Davis proceeded to detail the ARVN I Corps plan, and noted that no U.S. advisors were allowed in Laos. Therefore, U.S. ground rescue teams which could have been used to recover crews of shot-down helicopters, were also forbidden. Because of security, the LZs in Laos had not been reconned—a very sticky point. The attack was to begin in the morning with the armor brigade crossing the Tchepone River on Route 9. At 1000 hours, U.S. helicopters were to launch three simultaneous combat assaults; the Rangers and Airborne along the north flank, the Infantry on the escarpment.

The 101st Airborne Division and the 101st Aviation Group were to form the nucleus of command from Khe Sanh, and the duties of the divisional and attached units were detailed at the briefing as follows:

The 223d Combat Aviation Battalion, 1st Aviation Brigade (Lt. Col. Gerald Kirklighter) to support the 1st Infantry Division.

The 158th Aviation Battalion, 101st Airborne Division (Lt. Col. William Peachy) to support the 1st Airborne Division, 1st Ranger Group, and the 1st Armor Brigade.

The 14th Combat Aviation Battalion, 1st Aviation Brigade (Lt. Col. Joseph Rutkowski) to support the Vietnamese Marine Corps Division.

The 159th Support Aviation Battalion, 101st Airborne Division (Lt. Col. George Newton) to control all medium and heavy lift support to all U.S. and ARVN units on both sides of the border.

The 4th Battalion, 77th Aerial Field Artillery, 101st Airborne Division (Lt. Col. C. L. Nowalk) to provide Cobra gunship support for 101st ABD aviation missions in Laos and U.S. ground missions in South Vietnam.

The 2nd Squadron, 17th Air Cavalry, 101st Airborne Division (Lt. Col. Robert Molinelli) to control all air cav troops and to provide scouting and gunship support to the entire ARVN invasion force as personally dictated by the CG, ARVN I Corps.

When the briefing concluded, Kirklighter received permission from Berry to leave his aircraft at Dong Ha—he did not trust Khe Sanh's vulnerability to rocket attacks—then sent Major Klose and the company commanders back to Dong Ha to organize the battalion. Kirklighter spent the night at Khe Sanh to catch up on last minute details and to establish radio communications with Colonel Harrison—recently appointed as senior advisor, ARVN 1st Infantry Division, after commanding a brigade in the 101st Airborne—to coordinate the pickup and assault. The hectic procedure was being repeated by all the commanders involved; as Major Klose remarked, "It was like twelve football games going on at the same time."

General Sutherland had planned to put three days of airstrikes into Laos to soften up the numerous NVA AA positions, but the unexpectedly foul weather had grounded the jets for one of those days and had hampered them for the other two. The plans had been prepared in a rush and there was no chance for careful analysis. They were already behind schedule. Nevertheless, a spirit of easy victory pervaded the commanders as their units boiled along the border, waiting to be released. As the senior advisor to the Airborne wrote in his after-action report: "It was apparent at this time that United States intelligence felt that the operation would be lightly opposed and that a two-day preparation of the area prior to D day by tactical air would effectively neutralize the enemy antiaircraft capability although the enemy was credited with having one hundred seventy to two hundred antiaircraft weapons of mixed caliber in the operational area. The tank threat was considered minimal and the reinforcement capability was listed as fourteen days for two divisions from north of the DMZ." The ARVN were expected to be in Tchepone in about three days.

The official word put the ARVN 1st Armor Brigade crossing the border at 0700 hours, 8 February, 1971. The helicopter combat assaults followed shortly. The Dong Ha airstrip was alive and in motion as the 223rd Combat Aviation Battalion mounted up. Major Klose and the company commanders had briefed the aircraft commanders the evening before. The briefing reminded Klose of a football huddle, all conversations pared down to the essentials, everyone knowing the routine. It all depended on professionalism and teamwork. The facts were quickly outlined: time of departure, coordinates of the pick-up zones and landing zones, radio frequencies to be used, route of flight, coordination of gunship escort. "Any questions? Okay, go brief your flights." The night had been a nervous one, and busy, with crew chiefs and mechanics going over the helicopters by flashlight.

It was cold and brisk in the morning, steam coming from the breath, men putting on gloves and jungle fatigues over their flight suits for warmth. C ration coffee was sipped, cigarettes chain-smoked, maps re-checked, door guns mounted, rocket pods loaded. Word came to go and crews climbed aboard their machines. In moments the helicopters were vibrating, blades thumping and turbine-engines screaming. They lifted off the strip, circled, then assumed a trail formation. Major Klose piloted the battalion C&C and set the group down at FSB Kilo. There Kirklighter joined them and another quick briefing was held with General Phu and Colonel Harrison. The CA was to be made on the Co Roc ridgeline to secure the vantage point overlooking Route 9; the position was designated LZ Hotel and the ARVN 4/3 Infantry was slotted for the CA. The South Vietnamese infantrymen stood in long lines by the helo pad boarding the waiting choppers one squad to a bird.

They took off again. Kirklighter and Klose flew the C&C, the ARVN battalion commander and staff in the cabin with radio headsets. They crossed the border on schedule and reconned the Co Roc in the C&C. Two small clearings, about fifty feet by fifty feet and relatively flat, were visible in the jungled ridgeline and they pulled up after marking them with smoke. The slicks went in and the ARVN jumped out. There was no shooting. The CA continued with the helicopters shuttling back to Kilo for more troops while the Chinooks began coming in with slingloaded bulldozers, bunker material, and 105mm artillery pieces.

Lt. Philip Smith of the 48th Blue Stars hadn't been able to sleep the night before. The cold LZ made them all feel a lot better. They figured Laos would be no sweat.

The 158th Aviation Battalion took fire from the moment they crossed the border. One of the pilots, WO Harold Smith of A Company, was flying with an ARVN squad aboard his Huey. He would have preferred to have been anyplace else. Twenty-one years old, from South Mountain, Pennsylvania, Smith was on his second Vietnam tour. The first had been as a teenage marine at the siege of Khe Sanh; he'd joined the army, within months of his discharge, for their warrant officer pilot program—he'd always wanted to fly—and thinking his previous combat tour made it illegal to send him back to Vietnam. It didn't. His company, the Alpha Ghostriders, spent the night in the bunkers at Khe Sanh and awoke to the sight of two hundred helicopters on the sod strip. Their battalion, thirty slicks, crossed into Laos with Rangers aboard.

Once across the river, the tracers began floating up at them. A

12.7mm machine-gun position took them under fire from somewhere in the jungle blanket, strafing the whole trail formation. The third ship in formation, piloted by WO Paul Stewart and WO Tom Doody, took a burst in the tailboom. Stewart calmly reported on the radio, "Lead, chalk three has taken some hits. I've lost pedal control. Am returning to Khe Sanh."

A buddy shouted over the radio that he wanted to follow him as cover. Lieutenant Colonel Peachy screamed to stay in formation.

A few moments later, Stewart was again calmly on the radio, even as panicked shouts could be heard from the ARVN and maybe some of the crewmen on board, "Lead, chalk three is going inverted at this time." In the next moment, the ship crashed upside down in the treetops and exploded. There were no survivors.

There was a helpless, angry silence over the radios.

Smith's crew chief hollered on the intercom that he had a make on the 12.7mm, and requested permission to fire.

"Go ahead!"

The man's M-60 popped ineffectually at the trees far below.

All along the way, NVA fire poured up at them. This is fucking ridiculous, Smith thought, just glad his ship wasn't taking any hits. He made five more trips into Laos that afternoon, to ferry in ARVN infantrymen, taking more and more fire each time as the NVA prepared for them. Each mission was a story unto itself, he thought, but there were so many, his mind began to blur from exhaustion. Around noontime, WO Lyle Borders, a Cobra pilot with B/7/1 Air Cav, was screening west of the 1st Infantry Division insertions. His team of two Cobra gunships, two Loach scout ships, and a C&C Huey slick found nothing and was heading back to refuel at Khe Sanh. Another team from the Bravo Dutchmasters flew west past them to take over the air reconnaissance; and within minutes, the second team was urgently radioing that they were taking fire, that their C&C Huey was hit at four thousand feet and going in. It burned all the way to the ground. WO Borders and his team circled around and as they came in high; he took photographs through the plexiglass windshield. The C&C was crashed upside down in a field of tall elephant grass and bamboo, white smoke pouring from it. The Loaches buzzed low, throwing red smoke grenades at the sound of NVA weapons in the treelines. The smoke slowly filtered over the tops of two-hundred-foot trees, and Borders banked his Cobra down to rake the area with rockets and minigun bursts.

On the ground, the crew chief of the downed Huey, Sgt. John Seaman, had been hurled from the wreck. It was a cold morning and he wore a set of jungle fatigues over his fireproof nomex flight suit; the fatigues were on fire and he burned his hands as he frantically beat out the flames. He ran back to his helicopter. The copilot, Capt. David Fox, and the door-gunner, a young private, were dead. The pilot, Capt. Joseph Beardon, was hanging upside down, strapped in his seat. He was semiconscious and being burned by the fire, but when Seaman moved to get him, the blistering heat set his clothes afire again. He retreated. Seaman charged again into the flames and managed to drag Beardon out into the grass.

The Cobras continued pumping fire into the trees; Borders could see no bodies but the NVA fire ceased. A Loach landed about forty meters from the Huey and the door gunner ran to the wreck. Because of the thick bamboo and elephant grass, he had to run into the wall of vegetation and mash it down bit by bit before he could reach the badly burned Beardon and Seaman.

The troop's aero rifle platoon (Blue Team) was on alert at Lang Vei with the Hoc Bao Company, ARVN 1st Infantry Division. The Blues were perimeter security, the Hoc for pilot rescue, to conform to the ban on U.S. ground troops in Laos; but when the air mission commander requested the reaction force, the Blues shrugged with the attitude of, "If you didn't intend to use us, why'd you bring us up?" and climbed into their Hueys. They secured the crash site and medevacked Bearden and Seaman. The Blues were still on the ground in Laos—reportedly in contact with the NVA—when Lieutenant Colonel Molinelli, the cav commander, ordered in the Hoc Bao. The ARVN were inserted behind the Dutchmaster Blues and took their place in an orderly transition of lines under fire. Molinelli assembled the Blues back in South Vietnam, told them their CA had been a direct violation of presidential orders, and asked them not to discuss it with reporters. He then reported the incident to General Berry; it followed the chain of command to Nixon. Days later, he publicly changed policy and U.S. troops could now be inserted to evacuate downed airmen. The U.S. aero rifle platoons were, however, never again inserted into Laos.

The initial three-pronged airmobile assault into Laos was underway when the 223rd CAB was taxed to bring in another ARVN battalion. Their first move to LZ Hotel had been the only aviation operation of the day not taken under fire, and their next assignment was to CA the ARVN 1/3 and 2/3 Infantry to LZ Blue, several miles south of Hotel. Lieutenant

Colonel Kirklighter and Major Klose again dropped into Kilo, consulting with Colonel Harrison and the ARVN commanders. Several ARVN rode with them, including the battalion staff, an English-speaking radioman, and the deputy division commander, a Colonel Ghai. Kirklighter heard that Ghai had been nicknamed the John Wayne of the DMZ, and he appeared to be a tough customer, complete with a pair of pearl-handled revolvers worn Patton-style at the waist. The South Vietnamese troopers looked tough too, he thought; they appeared well disciplined and effective, each man with a helmet, rucksack, and modern U.S. weapons—a far cry from the ARVN he'd seen on his first tour four years earlier.

With Klose flying, the C&C circled the jungle at the coordinates designated for LZ Blue. It looked good, big and level without too many shrubs or trees in the way, and they made another pass to mark it with smoke for the Hueys following them. They sailed low, the crew chief holding a smoke grenade with the pin pulled and the spoon held tight; Kirklighter said, "Now," and the chief dropped it from the cabin door. It jetted below them, thick and bright. They were pulling up when the crack of small arms fire erupted. They gained altitude unscathed, Kirklighter got on the horn for air cav gunships and recon support, but word came that they were tied up with the airborne and recon insertions. In their place, Kirklighter ordered in the UH1C Huey gunships of the 48th Joker Guns, and they skimmed at treetop level around the intended LZ. The first shots had not been much, the recon did not draw any fire, and no enemy gun positions could be seen through the foliage. The ARVN commanders on board elected to continue the CA.

The slicks of the 48th led the approach into the LZ, Maj. Willis R. Bunting flying the lead Huey as he usually did, gunships shadowing them as security. Lieutenant Smith was piloting a slick five back from the major, when he suddenly saw so many black spots burst around chalk four that he thought his engine was malfunctioning. Then he was abruptly aware of the rattle of fire around him, of Major Bunting shouting into the radio that he was hit. He watched the major's slick trail smoke and make a crash landing on a sandbar in a river.

A rescue Huey quickly darted down to get the crew.

A quarter-mile from the LZ, they dropped low and Smith could see a bush shaking below them, fire coming from it. His door-gunners fired madly at it and Smith watched the stream, every fifth round a tracer, bounce harmlessly off the bush. Jesus, he thought, they must have a concrete or steel bunker in there. He piloted his ship into the LZ, the door-gunners still going hot, the five ARVN aboard scrambled out, and he quickly pulled pitch out of there, enemy fire cracking in all directions the entire time.

Several more Hueys were hit coming out of the LZ and Kirklighter began directing them in from different directions. It did no good; the NVA 12.7mm machine gun emplacements under the trees had the range to track the ships no matter which direction they came in from. The ninth chopper in and out of the LZ was strafed and it crashed in the brush. North Vietnamese soldiers began moving towards the wreck and the crew radioed their position while moving away. Kirklighter figured the best thing to do was simply to go on in and get them. He told Klose to bring them down. The crewmen were in a tangle of elephant grass and scrub brush and as the Huey skimmed low towards them, the door-gunner said over the helmet intercom that he could see NVA moving towards the crew. He opened fire with his M-60. As they came closer, some of the stranded men tried to wave them away because of the fire, but Klose took the ship down. They landed in the field of elephant grass, the rotor blades whacking noisily at it, more NVA fire cracking around them. Two rounds thudded into the Huey, jostling them like a car going over a bump, as the crew emerged from the brush and ran through the prop-blasted grass. They scrambled aboard, and Kirklighter and Klose worked the controls, building up rpm for the overcrowded Huey, then quickly lifted up and away from the NVA fire.

The caution-lights on the console had flashed the moment the two AK rounds had hit the bird, but it was still flyable so they headed for the border, radioing ahead for another C&C helicopter to be prepared for them. Lang Vei was the first safe haven across the border from Laos—if an injured helo managed to cross the border, the pilot could practically autorotate down to it—and they landed there at the refuel/rearm pad manned by the 101st DISCOM. The two bullets holes in the transmission were smoking. Colonel Ghai, who had been educated in the United States, joked to Kirklighter that he felt like Lee changing mounts as they climbed aboard a new ship and headed back into Laos.

When the day was finally over, the men of the 158th Aviation Battalion returned to Camp Evans, as they would every night during the campaign. Theirs was another world where the hell of the day was washed away with clean beds, free-flowing booze, and rock music in the Officer's Club.

Young and trying to bolster themselves through the horrors they were enduring, they would get drunk and sing, "Gory, gory, what a helluva way to die. . . . " The enlisted men of the battalion let off steam at night too; sometimes when the pilots walked past the EM barracks, the smell of marijuana was overpowering. The attitude of most of the officers was, "If the enlisted men do their job, don't hassle them about the grass."

The men of C Company were the most wrung out that night. The Huey that'd exploded had been from their Phoenix Birds and four of their comrades, including Stewart and Doody, were dead. They were most saddened about Stewart, who had previously earned the nickname Mr. Invincible for his cool courage and who had just extended his tour. Lt. Bruce Updyke, a twenty-three-year-old slick pilot from Ohio, was getting drunk in the O Club when someone said, "Wasn't that a bitch about Stewart getting wasted?"

"Yeah," Updyke said, "it really was."

"Fuck it," his friend mumbled, "better him than me."

The sad part, Updyke thought, was that they really meant that, even when a good friend was involved. One had to become calloused to carry on and, as the days wore on, he had buddies morbidly joke to him before he took off, "Hey, man, if something happens, can I have your stereo?" In spite of the banter they all knew they could rely on each other.

By the end of 8 February, the ARVN 1st Infantry Division had established two firebases in Laos south of Route 9: LZ Hotel held by 4/3 and LZ Blue held by 1/3 and 2/3. The ARVN 1st Airborne Division had two firebases north of Route 9: Hill 30, held by the 2nd and 7th Airborne Battalions; and Hill 31, held by the 3d Airborne Battalion. The ARVN 1st Ranger Group had established two firebases northeast of the paratroopers: Ranger North, held by the 39th Ranger Battalion; and Ranger South, held by the 21st Ranger Battalion. The ARVN 1st Armor Brigade had advanced nine kilometers into Laos on Route 9. While the air moves had been met with heavy fire (seven helos were recorded shot down on the first day), the ARVN foot patrols met virtually no resistance. There were no delusions that the Communists were not there. The next morning, bad weather cancelled all air moves, knocking the ARVN back another notch in their schedule and giving the NVA additional time to prepare.

CHAPTER SEVEN:
An Uneasy Start

T he foul weather, which hampered air moves on 9 February, did not tie down the armor spearhead. The 1st Armor Brigade continued the attack down Route 9 that day and Akihiko Okamura, a Japanese photojournalist who had briefly been a prisoner of the Viet Cong in 1964, smuggled himself aboard a supply truck.

The truck stopped at the head of the lst Armor column. They were nine kilometers inside Laos, and preparing to push deeper, when Okamura climbed aboard the third APC in line. Morale seemed high among the combat troops; he thought the paratroopers riding atop the vehicles looked sharp and disciplined and the APC crew was friendly. He was a non-smoker, but carried many cigarettes to give to the troops, and sat talking with them as they lurched forward. The dirt highway was narrow at that point, unused and overgrown, hemmed in by a wall of bamboo and vines. The tracks ground through the foilage corridor, occasionally cutting across narrow footpaths that crossed the highway. The paratroopers would hop from the vehicles each time, pointing and shouting enthusiastically, "Ho Chi Minh Trail!" They camped on Route 9 that night, the soldiers inviting Okamura to their dinner, boiled rice in bowls. The young ARVN loved his cameras and leather boots, and touched them, asking how much they cost. Okamura laughed with them, "If I'm killed, then you can have them. But now I need them." They slept under their APCs for protection, but the only noise that night was the thunder of their own artillery.

The next day, 10 February, they reached their objective, a spot on the map called Aloui, about twenty kilometers inside Laos. Helicopters lifted the 9th Airborne Battalion through heavy AA fire to the target, and they secured it in twenty minutes. Two hours later, at around seven that evening, the lead elements of the 1st Armor linked up with them. When Okamura drove in, the grassy field was still smoking from the Cobra prep strikes. He inspected a main branch of the Ho Chi Minh Trail which intersected Route 9 at Aloui, running south. The surface was crushed stone and it showed numerous tire marks. For two days, patrols worked the enemy trail but found neither NVA nor supplies. The troops seemed mightily disappointed.

The 1st Armor Brigade had already consolidated at Aloui when the senior Armor advisor, Col. Raymond R. Battreall, arrived at Khe Sanh. A crewcut, bespectacled man of forty-four, he was on his second tour with the ARVN, his current assignment a MACV post as senior advisor, RVNAF Armor Command, Saigon. Battreall had originally joined the Army as as eighteen-year-old from Omaha, Nebraska, swept up in the romantic patriotism of WWII. He soon had had the distinction of being selected from the ranks for West Point. Vietnam was his first combat assignment and he exulted in it; it was what being a soldier was all about. He felt a close kinship with the Vietnamese he soldiered beside—one he knew that the average GI could never know. He thought it sad that the young Americans asked to die for the Vietnamese saw only the prostitutes, pushers, and dregs of society; it gave them an unbalanced understanding of why they were sacrificing, made outrages like My Lai possible, and fueled the weariness in the ranks.

As for himself, Battreall developed a great and lasting respect for the ARVN after serving with them on a day-to-day basis. He was a man of old-fashioned patriotism and idealism, and thought of his nation's involvement in Vietnam as the most altruistic act a great nation ever made, sacrificing lives and capital to help a struggling nation against communist tyranny, while asking nothing in return. He applauded the invasion of Laos as a vital step to win the peace in South Vietnam. He wrote to his wife, "It is almost childishly obvious that if one wishes to get an enemy off one's back one must strike that enemy where he is. We did not widen the war, the enemy did years ago. We were stupid not to challenge him at the time. If we had done so the war would long since have been over. And all the strident screams in the world won't change these basic facts."

When the 1st Armor crossed the border, Colonel Battreall was at his post in Saigon. It didn't take long to recognize that the reports filtering back had lost their coherency, so he, his sergeant major, and his ARVN counterpart caught a plane to Hue, then a helo to FSB Kilo. There they found that Colonel Luat had left two M577 command vehicles, an ARVN sergeant major, and a half-dozen enlisted men in a rear CP. The APCs were parked back to back beside the I Corps command bunker and Battreall's group spent their days monitoring the radios in them, and occasionally ducking in them for cover when the NVA harassed the command bases with rockets and artillery. As an advisor, Battreall could give no orders to the ARVN and, because of politics, he wasn't allowed to see first hand what was going on in Laos. The frustrations could be tremendous at times.

All in all, Colonel Battreall was guarded about the status of the 1st Armor Brigade at Aloui. His concerns, however, had nothing to do with the caliber of the South Vietnamese soldiers. He considered the troops to be first rate and their commanders superb. Colonel Luat impressed him as a brave commander who led from the front. His counterpart at Armor Command, Col. Phan Hoa Hiep, was also an able officer.

No, Battreall thought, the problem lay not with the combatants but with the plan—with the no-advisors-in-Laos policy. He had begged General Berry for permission to at least overfly the armor's area of operations to get a handle on the terrain and physical disposition of the troops; Berry had no choice but to deny the request and Battreall was one step further removed from the reality of the radio messages from Laos. The armor brigade was attached to the airborne division who were, according to MACV and XXIV Corps, to provide them with logistical support. That is how the Americans defined "attached." Not so with the Vietnamese, Battreall knew, who did not consider an attached unit as a logistical dependent. The airborne made no attempts to support their armor brigade.

Another major problem arose in the airborne's assignment to "secure Route 9" for the armor. To an American officer, such an order meant physically patrolling the road to prevent ambushes and having engineer elements upgrade the surface for traffic. That is what the planners at XXIV Corps had intended; but to the Vietnamese securing a road simply meant being able to bring it under fire. Battreall noted that, on the map, the airborne's LZ Alpha and LZ Bravo sat astride the highway giving the 105mm howitzers there overlapping fire along the entire route. In their minds, the airborne sincerely believed they had accomplished their mission—but the NVA were virtually free to attack the road at will because the paratroopers were not aggressively patrolling it. In addition, the dirt road from Bravo to Aloui was so treacherous that only tracked vehicles could make it; no engineer work was started and no supply trucks got through. Aloui was totally dependent on U.S. Army aviation.

Such problems were bound to occur when U.S. and ARVN forces worked together, but the peculiarities imposed on the Laotian campaign fueled the difficulties, as Battreall noted, "Although titular Senior Advisor, I Corps, the XXIV Corps CG in normal times concerned himself exclusively with his own U.S. units, leaving the advisory function to a brigadier general, Jackson at this particular time. When XXIV Corps Headquarters began planning Lam Son 719, therefore, they did not know their counterparts in I Corps. They wrote a perfectly good plan using standard U.S. military terminology, not realizing the Vietnamese would often nod politely even when they disagreed and that, even when they did agree, they sometimes understood terms differently than the American authors intended. The disconnect between XXIV Corps and reality at the point of contact could not have gone undetected and uncorrected had advisors been at the point of contact."

Some of the difficulties, though, rested squarely on the shoulders of the ARVN. The 1st Armor's initial assignment had been to secure Aloui; this they did with little trouble, and there they sat. General Dong, inexperienced in the ways of war, did not know what else to do with the brigade and Colonel Luat did not pursue any other mission (as Battreall noted, "Initiative by a subordinate, unhappily, never became part of the ARVN character and many, many opportunities were lost.") The 1st Armor Brigade had been able to execute a virtually bloodless attack to Aloui but now they sat on a patch of barren high ground. The terrain around them seriously hampered tank movement, the highway was impassable even to a jeep, and the helicopter resupply was coming under more AA fire every day. Before leaving Saigon, Battreall had seen a MACV intelligence estimate which said no NVA tanks were in southern Laos and none could get there without being detected by the electronic sensors and destroyed by the USAF; he doubted this and was worried, because the brigade had fewer than fifty light M41 tanks at Aloui. He trusted Colonel Luat and his troopers to fight bravely if the NVA brought pressure to bear but, as things stood, he thought a major battle would result in needless chaos and casualties.

Chaotic was the word Okamura chose to describe the developments with the 1st Armor Brigade. Things went badly the third day at Aloui when a bulldozer hit a mine. He was photographing the burnt-out hulk of a Soviet tank when there was another thunderous blast; another dozer had run over a mine and two ARVN were killed. As the brigade returned to the Aloui perimeter, the NVA began mortaring them in broad daylight.

Things were getting dark, Okamura thought.

For five days they tried to sweep onward, but each time an APC would go up in a mine explosion. Okamura was walking down the bamboo tunnel of Route 9 when the lead APC of the latest patrol crossed a stream and exploded. Three bareheaded soldiers stumbled stiffly out of the smoke and collapsed in shock as other ARVN ran forward to help. The driver was pinned under the upturned track and grimaced as blood poured from his mouth. Comrades tried to pull him out, but he died. The NVA began probing the perimeter that first week. Each night Okamura could hear the AKs and RPGs raising a racket somewhere on the perimeter. The ARVN would scatter the brush with return volleys from their tanks and tracks. Mortars hit the camp every night.

One morning Okamura joined a group of ARVN who noisily picked over some dead NVA outside the perimeter. They had walked into the claymores and machine guns the night before, and fifteen dead and one wounded man lay there. The ARVN stripped them of souvenirs, but became more thoughtful and quiet when they saw the NVA had only poor uniforms, no helmets, no food, and some had tattoos which read, "Born in the North, die in the South." An officer muttered to Okamura, "Look at us. Boots, jackets, rifles, food—everything supplied by America." Okamura thought the man had an inferiority complex; all the ARVN seemed robbed of their independent spirit, and he felt it gave the Communists an important edge. The wounded North Vietnamese died, but not before saying his unit had been in the North only five days before. The reinforcements were moving in and Okamura imagined that the NVA had let the ARVN proceed so easily into Laos in order to encircle and destroy them. The troops seemed to sense that too, and morale waned as they sat impotent atop Aloui, under daily shelling.

The ground war in Laos may have gotten off to a slow start, but the air war was a hectic, bloody one from the first day to the last. A pilot summed it up when he told a reporter, "I don't write home much. What am I supposed to say? That I took fire eight times today, and that if I had stayed on those LZs five seconds longer each time, I'd have been dead?"

It was the worst concentration of fire U.S. aircrews experienced in the Vietnam War, frail Hueys going through WWII-style flak barrages. The casualties were high in men and materiel, but the NVA never succeeded in halting U.S. Army Aviation support. Still, for those involved, it was a personal nightmare. CW3 Hawk saw glimpses of it back at the Khe Sanh control tower, the helos coming back with holes torn in them, crewmen dead or wounded, an occasional Chinook dropping off cargo nets of dead ARVN. He saw one of the obsolete UH1C gunships try to take off, so overloaded with ammunition that a skid caught in the perimeter wire—and it abruptly flipped upside down and went up in the flames of old mines and exploding rockets. Another helo hovered with a rope for the crew.

What amazed Hawk the most was the density of air traffic. It was a hornet's nest. Every square yard seemed to be occupied with helicopters and milling crewmen, and the skies were always buzzing; lift-platoons on the move, gunships darting with them, lone ships dropping in to refuel or crash-land. C130 transport planes came in all day, and it was a real challenge to avoid mid-air collisions between the large planes and the helos, whose flight patterns took them right below the cargo planes. Once, Lieutenant Smith of the 48th Blue Stars, having hydraulic problems and heading back for Khe Sanh, contacted the ATC tower to make a landing and was slotted to come in seventh. "You don't understand," Smith called, "this is an emergency." The air traffic controller answered that there were six emergencies ahead of him.

On the northern flank, the ARVN were in position and the 158th Aviation Battalion busied itself with resupply and medevac. On the southern flank, the 1st Infantry Division was still installing firebases along the escarpment and the 223rd CAB had to perform not only the resupply and rescue missions, but numerous CAs under heavy fire. The 223rd had been quickly slapped together and it lacked the cohesion of the Screaming Eagle units; the battalion experienced its share of problems. Lieutenant Smith thought the biggest one was simple battle exhaustion. He had come primed with gung-ho patriotism, but soon was just wrung out. The whole company seemed affected by the routine—flying combat all day, doing night maintenance on the birds, then being up before the sun for another day over Laos. When they lifted from Dong Ha, he could see the big red communist flag across the DMZ and, when they refueled at Khe Sanh, one man always stayed in the cockpit so he could lift off if more mortar rounds came in. The thought that kept grinding in the back of Smith's mind was that it was all for nothing, that it was just a big show of Vietnamization being played out at the expense of American pilots.

Lieutenant Smith had another job which served further to demoralize him. He was company scheduling officer and, at night, some of the pilots came to him, crying over wives and children, begging not to be slotted for Laos again. Smith hated making them go, and he began to hate Kirklighter and Klose for taking them there. He pictured them flying high and dry in their C&C.

The enlisted men were taking it the worst, he thought. They seemed confused about Vietnam to begin with, horrified by their experiences, demoralized with the thought that they were dying for nothing. One night Smith's crew chief came crying to him, saying he had to get off heroin, and he sweated out two nights cold turkey in Smith's tent. Smith was a straight arrow, had never seen anyone light up around him, and was shocked that his chief was a head—the man had always been dependable during the missions into Laos. He told Smith that most of the doorgunners got stoned at night to relieve the pressure. But no one, he said, smoked during combat. What kept them going, Smith figured, was simple comradeship. If Laos and Kirklighter were bad, then the aircrews pulled together that much more. If a man went down, every action was taken to rescue the crew. It didn't matter if you hated the guy's guts, he reckoned, if he crashed, you went through whatever the NVA threw at you to save him. That was the mutual respect they had for each other and if it had been any less, Smith would have refused to fly. He thought of the men in the 48th Blue Stars as heroes, simply that, and he respected hell out of his company commander. Major Bunting always flew the lead ship, "so we automatically wanted to follow."

Sp5 Dennis Lundstrom was also in the 223rd CAB, a twenty-one-year-old South Dakotan flying-crew chief on UHIC of the 173rd Crossbow Guns. He was glad his pilot knew his job expertly, because Lieutenant Colonel Kirklighter made him nervous. Sometimes he could hear on the radio, as Kirklighter ordered them to do something which seemed needlessly dangerous:

"No fucking way," someone would mumble.

"Knock that off," Kirklighter would say hotly.

"Heyyy," someone would cut in, "fuck you," and they'd burst out laughing.

Lundstrom wondered if the colonel baited them along like that to allow them to let off some steam. He couldn't figure Kirklighter out. Sometimes he seemed very brave, but then again it was more as if he were oblivious. Few of the men took the time to analyze it; they just muttered how they wanted to frag his ass. He seemed, to Lundstrom, an absolutely intolerant man who refused to listen to anyone, and who seemed more concerned about the mission than their lives.

Laos changed the war Lundstrom had known. It made him feel like a new guy again. He'd enlisted right out of high school when he'd gotten his draft notice, so he wouldn't have to slog it out as a grunt. He'd gone through high school drinking, driving, and chasing girls, and it had bothered him not a bit when they'd sent him to Nam. He wasn't even very nervous when, after being a supply clerk for two months, an antagonistic first sergeant assigned him as a door-gunner. Then he was shot down, his two pilots badly wounded; he killed four NVA; he saw a dead grunt's brain slide out during a medevac mission, and he was sick for days and wanted to quit. His buddies said you would get used to it. For some sick reason, he thought, you did. In fact, he began to like the action. He made crew chief and, when his tour ended in December 1970, he extended for more combat duty.

But Laos reduced all of the bravado to simply trying to survive day by day. He was shot down once in Laotian territory. Sometimes in the morning, as they cranked up on the Dong Ha pad, a buddy would mutter to Lundstrom, "Hey, I don't think I'm coming back."

"Bullshit, don't even talk that way."

Laos weighed heavily on all of their minds.

During the third week, when they were making a CA to LZ Delta One, a friend who was standby talked Lundstrom into giving him his place on one of the Charlie-model gunships because the friend's good buddy was crew chief on it. When the company came back, two ships were missing, and Lundstrom got the story; the slick his buddy's gunnie had been escorting had hit its skids down into their rotors, and both birds had shattered in mid-air. Eight Americans had died, along with six ARVN passengers. Lundstrom's pilot never volunteered them for resupply missions, but a buddy from Colorado had a pilot who did. When they came back from one his friend had been shot through the face by a 12.7mm—KIA.

Even some of the young pilots turned to drugs and Lundstrom trusted none of them—except for a captain who occasionally smoked smack and was loose and cool in the air. Once a kid WO was assigned to fly his UH1C on perimeter security around Dong Ha and his first comment was, "You got a bucket in here? I'm really getting sick on this smack."

"I ain't got no bucket," Lundstrom shot back, "You better not get sick in my helicopter."

The pilot flew crazily, the skids smacking the surface of the river, and Lundstrom gripped his M-60, terrified, muttering, "Bullshit, bullshit, bullshit." When they landed, he reported the WO to his platoon leader and had the satisfaction of seeing the idiot grounded for the duration of Laos.

Capt. Rich Johnson, operations officer of the 173rd, could understand why morale was so poor during the op. His company commander was shot down at LZ Blue and, in Johnson's mind, it ruined him; he flew only select missions after that. The men began calling him Prettyboy, and Johnson became de facto commander of the 173rd. If the intensity of the air war could affect a professional soldier like that, Johnson recognized what it could do to a draftee door-gunner. It seemed to them worst in the afternoon, when they were preparing to go back into Laos after refueling from the morning trip. Over the radios, they could hear what was happening to those still flying, punctuated by the occasional sight of a Chinook coming over with a slingloaded wreck. Some guys would put on a facade of toughness as they got ready to go back. Others would vomit their lunch of cold C rations before climbing in. Captain Johnson made it a point not to eat lunch because he would be gripped with dry heaves right before he took off; it wasn't until he cranked the engine that he could replace his anxiety with flying skill.

He knew that many of the men took it out on Kirklighter and Klose (claymores blew apart Kirklighter's private latrine and HQ hootch— while unoccupied). They were hated men in the battalion, but were not the monsters the troops thought them to be. As Johnson saw it, they had been assigned a mission and, to carry it out, they had to put some people in precarious situations. And men died. Johnson himself had some shouting matches with Klose at Dong Ha on tactics—but unlike most of the men, he remembered that Kirklighter and Klose were sharing the danger every day over Laos. Big, red haired, and hard drinking, Kirklighter impressed Johnson as one of the toughest and bravest commanders he knew.

And for those qualities, his men—who thought the war over and it was time to go home—hated him.

Despite difficulties, army aviation got the job done in Laos. General Berry was the commander of air operations (with the call sign Big Ben) and his can-do attitude and personal courage influenced the course of the campaign. As Colonel Battreall remembered, "Sid Berry was absolutely superb. He could easily have run the U.S. Army Aviation support of Lam Son 719 from a secure bunker at the Khe Sanh airfield, but he never missed a day commanding it 'eyeball' from his own chopper over the scene of action in Laos. He always made Lieutenant General Lam's afternoon briefings and offered clear and incisive comments on the status of the fighting. I recall vividly one afternoon after he'd been shot at in his helicopter and nearly hit by the 76mm main gun of a PT76 tank. 'Damn it,' he said, 'That's not in my contract!' The point was, of course, that with the exception of Humphrey Bogart in *Sahara* nobody ever tried to use a tank cannon for antiaircraft. We all believed that the Soviets had succeeded in doing what our own ordnance said was impossible: designing a proximity fuse that would withstand the severe setback of a high-velocity tank gun."

There were 90,000 U.S. helicopter sorties into Laos. For four days the South Vietnamese invasion force had a relatively easy time. They cut branches of the Ho Chi Minh Trail, uncovered abandoned bunkers and supply caches, but found only a few North Vietnamese. On 12 February, the first intense firefights broke out around Aloui. On that day the battle for the Ho Chi Minh Trail was joined. President Thieu was unsettled by the casualties (he personally visited ARVN infantrymen on the Co Roc that day) and instructed his commanders to proceed with extreme caution. (Unknown to both Nixon and Abrams, he planned all along to call off the operation if three thousand ARVN were killed.) If Lam Son 719 ever had the momentum to be a daring strike, bad weather was not the only thing which slowed it down.

Each day the tempo and number of firefights between the ARVN and NVA increased. The press gave the impression that the NVA had suckered the ARVN into Laos and were now slamming the door behind them and moving in to annihilate effortlessly. Such a scenario was an exaggeration; the Communists, presumably, had been lying low for the first four days, not to lure the ARVN deeper into Laos but to wait for reinforcements to be shifted from North and South Vietnam. The NVA did not want their foe in Laos for any reason; it put their backs to the wall.

And for that reason, the Communists fought ferociously.

CHAPTER EIGHT:
Defeat

T he U.S./ARVN plan underestimated two important aspects: the speed at which North Vietnam could reinforce its units in Laos and the fierceness of their counterattack. When the allies had invaded the communist sanctuaries in Cambodia, the NVA generally chose to melt away and allowed their basecamps to be seized. But Laos was their last sanctuary and they fought like men defending their homeland. It was conventional war along the Ho Chi Minh Trail in Laos which challenged army aviation with the densest wall of antiaircraft fire of the long war, and the ARVN with the bloodiest sustained ground combat since the Tet Offensive of 1968. No one had anticipated the amount of artillery and armor the NVA would muster.

U.S. Army Intelligence estimated that the NVA had deployed forty thousand to sixty thousand troops to meet the invasion augmented with two hundred Soviet-built tanks; taking the conservative estimate, the NVA outnumbered ARVN two to one. A captured NVA sergeant said they'd been preparing for the invasion since October 1970. The ARVN plan of leapfrogging firebases to Tchepone required speed to succeed; suspected security leaks had given the Communists warning and time to mobilize a defense, and unexpectedly bad weather had hampered any quick assault. Critics of the firebase plan said it isolated the ARVN in tiny pockets deep in enemy territory and allowed the NVA, who knew the land and had the multistranded Ho Chi Minh Trail for mobility, to isolate them and attack one by one.

No contingency plans had been prepared by the U.S. or ARVN.

In mid-February, the hammer fell on the ARVN in Laos as six of their firebases came under increasing pressure: Aloui on Route 9; Hills 30, 31 and Rangers North and South on the northern flank; and LZ Hotel Two on the southern flank. In the face of this threat, the XXIV Corps Deputy Senior Advisor, to ARVN I Corps, Brig. Gen. Charles A. Jackson, was kept busy; co-located with General Lam's CP, his team was responsible for the final coordination of the U.S. helicopter, artillery, and tactical air support to the ARVN. There were many problems involving U.S. firepower, not the least of which was an intelligence report stating that the NVA in Laos knew in advance where the B52s were going to bomb (speculation was that Soviet trawlers off Guam, from where the B52s were launched, were intercepting strike-mission information and had broken the code). In addition, the Communists woefully outnumbered the defenders of the bases, and U.S. firepower alone could not decide the contest between ground troops—especially when the other side knew the terrain, was well deployed and motivated, had been preparing for months, and was willing to sacrifice thousands of troops like cannon fodder.

Things turned particularly hot for the 39th Ranger Battalion at Ranger North. Lieutenant Colonel Peachy's 158th Aviation Battalion flew around the clock to keep them resupplied and to get out the casualties. The conditions were horrendous and Lieutenant Updyke of C Company was involved in a resupply mission which described them all. A lone ARVN stood in the dust of Ranger North, directing Updyke's bird in. He put it down in the swirling dust, the nose to the guide's belly. The door-gunners kicked out the supplies, he pulled up at a turn—and three seconds later an artillery round made a direct hit in the LZ. The ARVN disintegrated in the flash, Updyke's ship rocked from the concussion, and the next ship, piloted by a warrant officer named Doan, was pelted with shrapnel. Back at Khe Sanh, Updyke and others ran to check on Doan. He was okay, but laughed that the only thing left of the ARVN was a hunk of meat the size of a ham. The plexiglass of his Huey was riddled with shrapnel, and flecked with bits of flesh, bone, and hair. Guys were nervously laughing, picking off pieces of meat and pretending to flip them on each other. Updyke knew you needed such a morbid sense of humor to steel yourself against the daily horrors, but he felt his buddies wouldn't have acted that way if it'd been an American who'd been killed.

WO Smith of A Company was going in on another resupply mission to Ranger North when he dropped to a hover over a group of troops on the perimeter. His crew chief prepared to kick out the gear, then suddenly screamed, "Pull up! They're gooks!" The NVA were hugging the perimeter, actually crawling through the wire and firing at helicopters while lying on their backs, in an attempt to avoid artillery and airstrikes. That kind of danger accompanied the aircrews all the time. Updyke, for one, had a wife and three children at home, a Distinguished Flying Cross from Ripcord, and only three months left in a war he thought was useless because the politicians were abandoning it. He could feel the acid burn his gut the entire time he was over Laos and he wished to God a caution-light would come on so he could turn around. It was a shared wish. Once a helo from the 1st Aviation Brigade flew with them into Laos and the pilot radioed, "I'm heading back, I've got a caution-light."

"Roger," the flight leader answered, "What's the problem?"

"The APU warning light is on." The Alternate Power Unit was a small compartment in the fuselage which could be used to jumpstart other helos.

"You dumb shit, that just means your little APU door is open."

The timid pilot stayed with the flight, and Updyke took some pride in the fact that that was the only time he saw any shirking. For all the fear and danger, the men clung to their personal and unit loyalties and did the job. Colonel Davis monitored one telling radio conversation: a USAF Phantom pilot bombed the NVA AA positions in preparation for the slicks, then watched them sail through the blizzards of flak and bullets, and commented admiringly, "Those helicopter guys must have steel balls." Because of the numerous shoot-downs, many of the pilots augmented their standard .38 Smith & Wesson revolvers by carrying M-16 rifles and bandoliers of ammunition in the cockpits.

February 18 marked the beginning of the last act for Ranger North. That morning, the crew of DMZ Dust Off—a Huey medevac from the 237th Medical Detachment, 61st Medical Battalion, 44th Medical Brigade—was waiting on the Khe Sanh pad. An emergency medevac call came in and the crew dropped their C ration breakfast and climbed aboard, two pilots up front; the crew chief; Sp5s Costello, Fujii, and Simpco, in the back. En route to Laos, the aircraft commander came over the intercom, explaining the mission: the 39th Rangers had heavy casualties, the LZ was extremely hot, and two Cobras would escort them in. The Cobras joined the Huey over Laos. Three klicks from Ranger North, they began taking heavy ground fire. The medevac AC decided it was too hot and turned the ship around for Khe Sanh. The Cobras, low on ammo and fuel, turned back, too.

Then the AC changed his mind, banked back towards Ranger North. Sp5 Fujii saw the Cobras disappearing to the east.

The Huey came in low, green tracers from AK-47s and 12.7mms burning lines all around them. Fujii tensed; looking down he could see NVA in the brush at the base of Ranger North and mortar rounds exploding on the denuded, bunkered hill. They landed on the LZ, screaming at the ARVN litter teams to hurry with the wounded and the AC instantly pulled pitch to get out. A mortar round exploded on the LZ as they lifted off and they came crashing back down into the dust. The AC was slumped in his seat, mortally wounded; the pilot, gravely injured from shrapnel, was temporarily paralyzed below the waist. The wounded ARVN were trying to climb off. Fujii and Simpco had shrapnel in their backs; Costello was the only one unscathed. Yanking their radio helmets off, they jumped out amid the continuing mortar barrage.

Fujii and Simpco crawled off looking for cover and a hundred yards down from the LZ found the opening to a bunker. They tumbled inside. Two ARVN were already in it and Costello rushed in moments later. They bandaged each other's wounds, crouching in the bunker while mortar shells kept walking across the hill.

A rescue Huey landed near their disabled medevac.

Somehow, in all the fire, the wounded pilots were carried aboard. Then Costello dashed from the bunker, followed by Simpco, then Fujii. Costello and Simpco flung themselves aboard, but Fujii had just cleared the bunker entrance when an explosion bowled him over. In a daze, he stumbled to his feet and waved at the pilot to get out, the LZ was too hot. He paused long enough to see the Huey miraculously glide off the LZ amid a torrent of fire, then hustled back into the bunker.

There was a PRC25 there and he radioed for all aviators to stay clear of Ranger North. The AA fire was simply impenetrable.

That night, the mortaring stopped for a while and, under cover of darkness, Fujii left the bunker with an ARVN sergeant and walked to the LZ. Fujii opened the fuel release valve on his crippled Huey, draining the JP4 fuel, then they salvaged whatever usable gear they could find. It was the end of the first day of what for Sp5 Dennis Fujii, a soft-spoken, twenty-one-year-old half-Irish, half-Japanese Hawaiian, would be a five-day ordeal.

The reason for the ferocious NVA counterattack was obvious: the allied invasion was hitting them where it hurt. The Ho Chi Minh Trail was being disrupted and supply caches uncovered. While the ARVN on the northern flank found themselves increasingly besieged in their firebases, it was the U.S. Air Cavalry which continued to reap the most finds. The Air Cav was under the control of General Lam, and personally commanded by Lieutenant Colonel Molinelli of the 2/17 Air Cav, 101st Airborne Division. Molinelli had three units to augment his squadron: B/7/1 Air Cav, C/7/17 Air Cav, and the Hoc Bao Company, ARVN 1st Infantry Division. The Hoc Baos ("Black Panthers") were all experienced volunteers, the elite reaction force of the division (arguably the best of the entire South Vietnamese army); they were used to secure downed aircraft since U.S. aero rifle platoons were barred from Laos.

The air cav maintained perhaps the best morale among the aviation units fighting in Laos; the Cobra pilots were selected from the top of the class in flight school, and the Loach crews were strictly volunteers. Over Laos, they worked what was called a Heavy Pink Team or Hunter-Killer Team, consisting of two Loaches, two Cobras, and a C&C Huey. The Loaches flew low and slow at treetop level, trying to draw enemy fire; if shot at, the door-gunner/observer instantly released a red smoke grenade and opened fire with his M-60 as the pilot pulled up. The Cobras, which flew at a high altitude behind the scouts, would then dive in to neutralize the area around the smoke with rockets, automatic grenades, and minigun fire.

The Loaches flew as bait and the Cobras went through walls of AA fire; it was a highly dangerous job. Most of the air-cav crews were young, nineteen- and twenty-year-olds, with hot-rod cars at home, and they went at their work with a sense of cool skill, cocksure daredeviltry, and raw guts. The men of the air cav liked to set themselves apart, wearing starched jungle fatigues and black stetsons with crossed-sabre insignia pinned to the front. When new guys arrived, they were greeted in the roughhouse way of the air cav; while the new ones grinned weakly and shied like ponies in one corner of the unit bar, the vets swaggered in their stetsons and sprayed beer, singing, "You're going home in a body bag, do dah, you'll get shot between the thighs, oh do da day. . . ."

To Capt. John F. Mercadante, of the Bravo Dutchmasters, it was like the bomber pilots in England during WWII: hell during the day;

beer and games of pool in the O Club at night. Before Laos his troop had operated in the Mekong Delta where they rarely suffered casualties and what fire they did receive only heightened their sense of bravado. But Mercadante found from day one that men were dying. No one in the Dutchmasters refused to fly or appeared outwardly frightened, but the swaggering and wild parties disappeared, to be replaced by small groups that spoke in hushed tones. Mercadante, the son of immigrants, kept up his morale because he was proud to be cav, loved the guys he was with, and believed in the war. More than that, all of the heavy fire they took over Laos simply reaffirmed his belief that they were hitting the Communists where it hurt.

The fire was, indeed, incredibly bad. WO Borders and another Dutchmasters Cobra crew were covering a medevac one day, the NVA so close to the ARVN firebase perimeter that the helos couldn't fire for fear of also strafing the South Vietnamese. So the two Cobras nonchalantly did a couple of nonfiring runs down low to draw fire away from the medevac going in. It worked, but Borders was surprised when they all were written up for Air Medals. It was just another day, he thought. You just got numb and kept going.

The cav commander, Lieutenant Colonel Molinelli, was on his second tour and held two Silver Stars, eight Distinguished Flying Crosses, and two Purple Hearts. He was a flamboyant, handsome man whose personal bravery was almost legendary. He often flew lead ship into Laos and, without notifying the command channels, had occasionally gotten on the ground with the ARVN to get a better handle on what was going on. Many of his men considered him the best combat leader they'd ever seen. There were others, however, who resented his the-mission-comes-first attitude; to them Molinelli's own valor was not an excuse to send his men into places made virtually suicidal by heavy antiaircraft fire.

Such occasional disputes did not affect the general performance of the air cav over Laos. In fact on February 18, the same day that the NVA launched their drive against Ranger North, the air cav was knocking another dent in the communist network. At noon, scout and gunship teams reconning west along Route 9 spotted, marked with smoke, and strafed an NVA unit, blowing up one truck and damaging a truck and a tank. In the same area, they discovered three six-inch-wide fuel pipelines and attacked; one pipe was severed and drained fuel on the jungle floor while the other two went up in flames. The NVA poured fire at the diving attackers and a Cobra from A/2/17 caught fire and crashed; the two pilots were wounded but immediately rescued by another helo.

To the south of this action, teams from the Dutchmasters made more finds. A Loach, piloted by a cocky and bold lieutenant named Bruce Cannon, followed vehicle tracks to a solid wall of jungle. He put a burst of minigun fire through the vegetation—and a fuel truck exploded in a ball of fire. Cannon had discovered an NVA truck-park under the triple-canopy jungle. Cannon quickly radioed for tac air but USAF rules-of-engagement prevented them from bombing so close to the main road so he maintained his low-level maneuvering as his door-gunner sprayed with his M-60 and hurled fragmentation grenades. The trucks did not explode so the gunner began putting bursts into the fuel tanks, getting gas on the ground, then tossing white phosphorus grenades. WO Borders came in to provide fire support and could see only the Loach darting below with Cannon shouting excitedly on the radio, then another explosion and a column of black smoke rolling up from the roof of jungle. The Cobras rolled in to finish the job and took some fire, but finally tallied up the destruction of ten fuel trucks, two large fuel blivets, two supply caches, a hootch, and several telephone poles and communication lines which Cannon had spotted down amid the trees.

The day's low overcast deteriorated by late evening, preventing some of the cav teams from returning to Khe Sanh or Quang Tri. Those aircrews were forced to shut down at Lang Vei where elements of the Blues, Delta 2/17, 101st DISCOM, and ARVN Hoc Bao maintained a forward staging area/refuel/rearm point. At dusk, the NVA struck back with mortars, RPGs, and AK-47 fire against the perimeter. Mortar fragments tore a ten-thousand-gallon fuel bladder and JP4 aviation fuel soaked the ground around the airstrip. An RPG sent one parked Huey up in a ball of fire so, while the men on the perimeter returned fire, the pilots ran from their bunkers and revved up their birds before the NVA could destroy any more. Cobras circled Lang Vei, but could not fire on the NVA attack because the U.S. perimeter was not visible in the dark. A quick-thinking young sergeant in the Dutchmaster Blues shouted for his lieutenant and together they dashed almost a hundred yards outside the perimeter; there they ignited a five-gallon can of JP4 which burned fiercely, marking the perimeter. The Cobras dove in on the NVA. Artillery from U.S. firebases pounded in. The NVA attack broke up.

In the morning, Lieutenant Colonel Rosenblum (CO, 101st DIS-

COM) helicoptered to Lang Vei to supervise the replacing of some equipment burnt up in the night probe. He was informed that a young Sp4 in the 426th S&S Battalion, manning the refuel/rearm point, had performed bravely; when the fuel bladder was punctured by mortar shrapnel, the Sp4 had jumped into the berm under fire and had waded through ankle-deep fuel, successfully patching the holes.

"Did you know," Rosenblum asked the man, "that if there'd been a spark, you'd have gone up?"

"Yes, sir," the short, curly-haired kid answered, "but, hell, those pilots needed that fuel."

Rosenblum wrote him up for a Bronze Star for Valor.

Meanwhile the air cav helicopters were sputtering to life at Lang Vei and heading back into Laos. That afternoon they set another pipeline ablaze, gunned down four NVA, and directed airstrikes on NVA tanks and trucks moving down a jungle trail. Coming back at twenty-seven hundred feet a Cobra from the Dutchmasters was hit by AA fire in the main rotor blade. The ship vibrated fiercely, the strained, wobbly pitch echoing for miles, but the pilot made a successful landing at Khe Sanh. The hole in the blade was big enough to put your head through—and the pilot did just that, grinning for the civilian photographers there.

While the U.S. air cavalry wreaked havoc on the NVA, the NVA in turn, tightened the noose on the ARVN.

The initial NVA attack against Ranger North petered out and, on the morning of 19 February they reverted to mortaring the base. Lieutenant Colonel Peachy took the Ghostriders and Phoenix Birds in to resupply the base, and maintained his C&C orbit at about six thousand feet—so high, Lieutenant Updyke laughed, "that his bird looked like a gnat's ass." Peachy ordered two slicks from the Ghostriders to go on in, and WO Smith watched anxiously as two of his buddies headed down. They hadn't even gotten their supplies out before an NVA mortar team raised havoc on the LZ and they had to back off. The pilots were on the radio, clamoring for ARVN artillery or gunships to knock out the mortar, but Peachy ordered two more slicks to give it a try. The pilots reluctantly obliged him, but barely got out alive as mortar shells burst all around them.

Peachy told two more ships to go in.

A kid WO nicknamed Sandy said it for all of them, "Why don't you go!"

"Who was that!"

Sandy identified himself by his Ghostrider call sign.

Lieutenant Colonel Peachy prudently cancelled the mission until air and arty could knock out the NVA mortars. Sandy was given a letter of reprimand, and everyone kept flying.

That night the North Vietnamese launched another full frontal assault against Ranger North.

Sp5 Fujii had set himself up with a PRC25 radio at the battalion commander's commo bunker. It was on the high ground, offering a panoramic view of the whole hill, and Fujii maintained contact with a USAF FAC pilot throughout the day; Fujii calling in the coordinates where he saw muzzle flashes and smoke, the FAC firing WP into the areas then banking off as jets roared in to strafe and bomb. Fujii was wounded, tired, and scared, but he kept his cool and the NVA paid grievously for the firepower he was able to direct in.

He was becoming a hero to the aviators in the area.

At dusk, the NVA mortaring increased from harassment to bombardment. The slopes suddenly came alive with North Vietnamese infantry men charging uphill into the ARVN bunkers and slit trenches. Fujii frantically called Cobras in to catch NVA in the open. Phantoms shrieked low, dropping bombs and napalm canisters. The whole hill was electrified with fire. The ARVN battalion commander was inside the bunker, calmly directing the defense. But other officers were panicking, removing rank insignia and destroying ID cards: better to be captured as a puppet soldier, than a warmongering officer.

Fujii had no intention of surrendering. He climbed back atop the sandbags outside the bunker. NVA were running towards the command bunker. He grabbed an M-16, sighted quickly on a charging figure, fired once, then again, and again as they kept coming.

Within ten furious minutes, ARVN Rangers throwing grenades managed to retake the fallen bunkers and close the gap. The shooting continued throughout the night, aircraft overhead in relays dropping flares and strafing around the perimeter. Fujii sat with his PRC25 and M-16 all night. We're all going to die on this little hill. His fear must have been in his voice because the Air Force pilot orbiting above spoke reassuringly: take it easy, buddy everything's going to be all right. They were simple words but Fujii clung to them. It felt so good to hear another American, to know they were out there trying to help.

In the morning, February 20, the 39th Rangers still held Ranger North. The ARVN around the commo bunker moved as if in a daze, pulling weapons and ammunition from the bodies of ARVN and NVA alike. They formed a tight perimeter around the bunker, Fujii and the battalion commander in the middle. The sun was already blazing.

The NVA began to pound the hill with mortars.

At Khe Sanh WO Fred Hayden was sipping tea in the heavily sand-bagged bunker of the 4/77 AFA TOC, when the call came to mount up. He sprinted across the airstrip and scrambled into the front seat of his Cobra; his co-pilot joined him and in two minutes they were airborne. A series of letters were relayed over the radio. Hayden decoded them on his Whiz Wheel, then banked to the northwest as a second Cobra sailed in alongside. In twenty minutes, they were over Ranger North. Hayden pulled the Cobra up to three thousand feet to get his bearings, watching as other gunships pumped rockets into the disorder below, seeming to hit friendlies and enemies alike. Supply and medevac helicopters circled high, waiting for a chance to get through the ground fire. Hayden pushed his Cobra into a wind-screaming dive and punched off four rockets. He kept strafing until he had expended all his ordnance and was forced to depart for the Khe Sanh to refuel and rearm.

On the ground, the NVA had broken through the perimeter and it was hand-to-hand in some places. Ranger North was going under. Fujii radioed that they could no longer hold out. He was told to hold his ground; rescue birds were coming in as soon as possible.

Meanwhile, the ten helicopters of the Phoenix Birds headed for the base laden with supplies. They had the additional mission of rescuing Fujii and any wounded ARVN they could get aboard before the base was completely overrun. To make Fujii readily identifiable, he was instructed to take off his shirt. Some ARVN saw him and did likewise. The NVA fire was too fierce to penetrate so Maj. Jim Lloyd and Nelson flew through the withering fire and made a quick landing atop the firebase. They kicked out the ammunition resupply and waited for Fujii a few excruciating seconds, blades pumping, fire pouring in.

Fujii had seen the Cobras blaze in, a Huey landing behind them. It was all open ground to the LZ. He ran for it, turning to fire on the run at NVA rushing the commo bunker, AK47 fire kicking up the dirt around him, ARVN running with him falling in the fire. He threw himself inside the cabin, screaming "go, go, go." They lifted off, the door gunners leaning out, blazing madly, the ship vibrating from hits.

The rescue bird was on fire.

Lloyd and Nelson managed to nurse the Huey four kilometers to Ranger South. They crashed on the LZ, but everyone managed to scramble clear before the ship exploded. Lieutenant Updyke could see thick smoke rising from Ranger South; there was no radio contact from the crash, and he debated with himself if he should risk going in. Before he could decide, he felt guilty and relieved to see his friend, WO Doan, peel off from the circling pack of gunships and head in towards the flaming wreck. Doan took several hits but came out of the LZ with Major Lloyd and the door gunners. Nelson and Fujii were still on the ground, and another slick barrelled in. Nelson jumped aboard, but Fujii hollered that he'd stay to help the ARVN on the firebase. Fujii was already a hero to the aviators, but Nelson's rescue also provided a piece of pilot folklore: he was a quiet man who loved spit and polish and as they sped out of the hot LZ, taking hits, Nelson reportedly merely grimaced and pointed to a scratch across the toe of his boot.

Major Lloyd, Captain Nelson, WO Doan, and the three other Huey pilots involved in the aborted rescue won Silver Stars, while the six crew chiefs and door gunners won Distinguished Flying Crosses. They were the first medals awarded to U.S. troops for the Laotian operation. Captain Nelson reportedly only had three weeks to enjoy his Silver Star; pilots of his company remember hearing that Nelson's bird took fire at three thousand feet and turned into a mid-air fireball.

The evening of February 20 and the morning of February 21 were a nightmare. Hundreds of dead NVA could be seen from the air around Ranger North, but many more had broken through the perimeter and were capturing the base. The 39th Rangers, outnumbered, out of ammunition, and exhausted, retreated down one side of the hill. They left about one hundred thirty dead and sixty wounded, and came out with about two hundred men, half of whom were walking wounded. Dozens of private firefights broke out as the survivors ran through the night, intermingling with NVA in the jungle, trying to reach Ranger South. The NVA began mortaring the base and Sp5 Fujii once again set up a radio vigil, calling in suppressive fire. Hueys from the 158th Aviation Battalion began coming in for the wounded at daybreak. Fujii jumped aboard the first bird. The survivors of the 39th Rangers mobbed the helicopters in a panicked frenzy to get medevacked. The AC of the lead ship began shouting frantically, "Get off, get off, get off!" and Fujii did. He started yanking ARVN out of the cabin, the door gunners kicked at them, and the ship finally got airborne with several men clinging to the skids. Fujii watched them fall to their deaths. Colonel Davis instructed Lieutenant Colonel Peachy to cancel the medevacs and make supply drops from a hover until the ARVN commanders could get their troops under control.

The battalion commander at Ranger South sent NCOs to reorganize the LZ and weed out the real wounded from the fakers. It was dark by then; it was another night of mortar and artillery fire before the helicopters returned in the morning. Tac air, air cav gunships, aerial field artillery, ground artillery, and smoke screens were hammered around Ranger South, supressing most of the NVA fire long enough for medevacs to land. This time the ARVN did not lose control, and the wounded Fujii, after five days on the ground in Laos, was finally able to board a Huey. Flying out of Ranger South, Fujii couldn't relax; he was convinced he'd be shot down again, he couldn't believe he was actually getting out alive. The reporters photographed Fujii being awarded the Purple Heart and twenty-six days after being rescued, he was pinned with the Distinguished Service Cross. He was the only televised hero of the Laotian operation.

At Aloui, Okamura thought the position of the 1st Armor was fast deteriorating. An ARVN officer told him there was nothing to prevent the NVA from moving behind them to sow Route 9 with mines, and commented, "We came in in only two days, but it will take us a week at least to get out." Every day 122mm rockets pounded the firebase. Tank patrols that advanced more than two hundred meters ran into blistering NVA fire. Antiaircraft fire hampered the medevac and resupply choppers. The ARVN soldiers seemed to be holding up under the pressure, but they were homesick and tired of sitting and being pummelled. It was time to get out, Okamura thought; a reporter always had that option. He gathered his gear and waited at the Aloui helo pad, just in time for another rocket raid. The shells walked through the area and a fuel blivet burst into flames. As American helicopters appeared, the ARVN atop their tanks and APCs on the perimeter laid down suppressive fire. The second helo landed, and Okamura joined the rush for it. Two paratroopers with slight wounds fell on him as they jumped aboard, and three ARVN officers also climbed in. One tried to draw his pistol to keep other ARVN off, as the helicopter lifted away.

Ranger North was the first domino to fall in the NVA counterattack; the Communists had sustained severe casualties for the victory, but they did not pause. They continued to hammer at Aloui, Ranger South, Hill 30, Hill 31, and LZ Hotel Two. On 23 February, the 223rd CAB went in to assist the ARVN Hotel Two, where the NVA were hugging the perimeter and keeping the defenders underground with mortars. The firebase was on the verge of being overrun, so Lieutenant Colonel Kirklighter and Major Klose circled above with the mission of evacuating the base's 155mm artillery pieces lest they fall into enemy hands.

Marine helicopters, CH53 Sea Stallions of HMH-463, arrived on station to lift the artillery out by slingloads. One of them was being piloted by Lt. Col. Charles Pitman and Maj. Mike Wasco; Wasco was the squadron op officer, but Pitman was the CO of Headquarters and Maintenance Squadron 16 at Marble Mountain. He was in the helo because he was in the process of checking out in the CH53 prior to taking command of HMH-463. Pitman and Wasco, on the radio with the C&C, said the mission didn't look good, but they would give it a try. They and their wingman sailed through the fire and stopped at a hover over the artillery parapets.

North Vietnamese fire drove them away.

The pair of Sea Stallions made another try, some ARVN emerging from a bunker to attach the 155mm pieces, but mortars began impacting atop the dirt knob. As Kirklighter and Klose watched from a thousand feet, a lucky round hit the engine of Pitman's chopper. The helicopter settled atop the artillery tube, blades still spinning, looking, Klose thought, like a chicken hatching an egg. The second Sea Stallion banked in. Ground fire cracked from the trees as the pilot brought his ship to a hover and the door-gunners threw a rope ladder out the rear cargo hatch. Men appeared from the wreck, grabbed the dangling ladder, then held tight as the pilot headed east with them hanging far below.

The radio crackled from the downed Sea Stallion: Pitman and Wasco were still pinned down, and a 12.7mm round had shattered the tibia in Pitman's right leg.

Klose piloted the C&C Huey in and started to set down near the crash just as two mortar rounds exploded in front of them. He pulled pitch and they shot out of the LZ. Most of the enemy fire appeared to be coming from a valley west of Hotel Two, so they sailed in again from due north, veering east at the last moment and heading for a small ridgeline on the firebase which would shield them from some of the fire. They flew in, the ridge to their right, and Kirklighter, in the right-hand seat, took over the controls. He set down the right skid, the other dangling in open air, and the slick hovered bumpily on the crest of the hill. Klose nervously repeated, "Steady, keep it steady!" into his mike as he watched the controls, ready to take over in an emergency, too filled with adrenaline to notice the volume of fire directed at their Huey. Bullets punched holes through the ship and the plexiglass windshield exploded in their faces. The noise around them was overwhelming.

Klose saw Wasco momentarily appear near the Sea Stallion, then reappear helping the leg-shot Pitman towards them. One of the doorgunners jumped out to help them aboard and the sudden shift in weight almost sent the blades smacking into the top of the ridgeline. Wasco and several ARVN tried to load Pitman into the Huey but, in the frantic rush, one of the ARVN stepped on the bandage hastily tied to Pitman's leg. It kept tugging him back out. Pitman finally managed to get the man's attention. He stepped clear, they threw Pitman in again, and he ended up hanging out the door on the other side, peering down at the mountain. Someone jumped on his back and Kirklighter quickly pulled them out of the cone of fire just as two mortar rounds exploded behind them.

They flew straight for Khe Sanh where Pitman and Wasco were transferred to one of the CH53s for the flight to the Quang Tri hospital. (Months later, Major Klose was stationed in Washington, D.C., when a man in civilian clothes walked in with a cane. The next thing he knew, the man was hugging him. It was Lieutenant Colonel Pitman. That night, Klose was invited over for dinner, a block party, for which the whole neighborhood turned out; it was something Klose long remembered.)

The evening of the 23rd, Lieutenant Colonel Peachy was directing a resupply mission for the paratroopers at Hill 31 when he spotted movement outside the perimeter. He sent Cobras in on the position—and by the time the screaming on the radio stopped, the paratrooper patrol had sustained twelve ARVN KIA and thirty one ARVN WIA from the gunships. Lieutenant Updyke was at Khe Sanh when he saw Peachy land and get out of his helicopter with his chin hanging. Updyke didn't particularly like the colonel, but he knew that the man was sincerely regretful.

The evacuation of Hotel Two was completed the following afternoon. Lieutenant Smith of the 48th Blue Stars was in the air when word came that twenty-three ARVN were left in the perimeter. They were about to be overrun. He and two other pilots got on the horn and said they'd give it a try. The three slicks broke from the formation and headed towards the coordinates, as two Cobras and two UHIC gunships swooped in to provide cover. They came in, Smith flying the last slick. AK-47 fire popped furiously below them. Rounds slammed through his ship. He abruptly noticed there were North Vietnamese infantrymen, crawling through the wire, ten yards from the ARVN perimeter bunkers.

A firefight was raging below.

The Hueys set down in the landing zone, mortar shells impacting all around them, and they quickly pulled out, a piece of shrapnel smacking into the tailboom of Smith's slick.

They went in again. The mortars drove them away again.

Milling above Hotel Two, Smith spotted the flash of a mortar round leaving its tube on a hillside five hundred yards away. He alerted the gunships, then watched one of the Cobras dodge a wall of bursting flak to pump rockets into the trees. The mortar crew disintegrated in the explosions. Another mortar promptly resumed the shelling. The two UH1Cs had to depart station to refuel and rearm so, while the two Cobras fired up the jungle, the three Hueys went in for another try. The first two made it through the curtain of mortar shrapnel. Smith came in last. The last few ARVN, running like hell, piled aboard, and he pulled up through the mortar bursts. It was a haunting sight for him to look back and see only abandoned, smoking bunkers and the Cobras banking away.

The North Vietnamese overran the rubble. Airstrikes were called in on them and the helicopter and artillery pieces left behind.

Lieutenant Colonel Molinelli's 2/17 Air Cav had several encounters with NVA in Soviet-made tanks. A scout ship spotted their first tank when he noticed what looked like a hootch moving. On closer inspection, the pilot saw a barrel protruding from the thatch and realized that the hut was built on an A-frame over the tank hull as camouflage. In another engagement, the 2/17 overflew fourteen tanks and rolled in on them firing. The tanks responded with their main guns and 12.7mm flexibles, but the Cobras punched holes in three of them with HEAT rockets, blowing up the crews, and immobilized the other eleven. The USAF came in at night, perfunctorily strafed the column, and reported fourteen kills. But in the morning, the cav found only the three burnt wrecks. The NVA had recovered the rest.

On another occasion, Lt. Col. Joseph Ganahl, commander of U.S. artillery on the border, was in his C&C bird when NVA tanks attacked an ARVN position. His S3 got on the radio to say an airborne forward air controller would direct the battalion's fire on the enemy armor, and that the corps commander was monitoring the frequency. Extremely nervous about all of the brass listening in, the FAC reported it was a good shot, but to drop two hundred meters on the gun target line and go right a hundred. The battery commander answered that his next round was on the way; there was a pause, then the FAC cried, "Holy Christ!" Ganahl thought his men must have dropped a short round into the ARVN, but the FAC caught his breath and said just the opposite was true. The artillery round had exploded between two NVA tanks, bowling them both over. They claimed two tank kills with one shell.

Things were falling apart for the 3rd Airborne Battalion on Hill 31. Their patrols around the base met fierce resistance; NVA artillery, rockets, and mortars pummelled the hill every day, and sappers had been killed in the perimeter wire. General Lam sent the 6th Airborne Battalion into a valley southeast of Hill 31 to destroy the NVA gun positions there. An Arc Light was put on the LZ, but intense NVA fire still forced the helicopters away. They dropped the battalion at alternate LZs, but they were under artillery fire and the battalion retreated in the direction of Hill 31, losing twenty-eight KIA, fifty WIA, and twenty-three MIA in a single afternoon. The 6th Airborne Battalion was helicoptered out, having accomplished nothing.

The death knell for Hill 31 came on 25 February.

At eleven in the morning, 130mm artillery began hitting the base. Hours later a company from the 3rd Airborne Battalion on patrol about a kilometer east of the basecamp spotted an NVA tank and infantry column moving in the direction of Hill 31. They estimated over twenty tanks and two thousand infantrymen. There were only four hundred ARVN atop Hill 31. The company commander quickly moved his men back to the base and the battalion operations officer, a Major Hong, radioed the artillery batteries at Aloui and Hill 30. They began firing on the advancing column, felling numerous NVA foot soldiers, but the tanks rolled through unscathed. Major Hong requested airstrikes, but the ARVN aerial observer, in his circling OV10 plane, was convinced that they must be ARVN tanks, and it took much haggling and an hour before tac air arrived.

The ARVN paratroopers fired madly at the oncoming mass of North Vietnamese, moving in the perimeter wire to the south, as a flight of U.S. Marine A4 Skyhawk jets roared in, led by Col. A. C. Pommerenk and Lt. Col. Jerry T. Hagen. They could see five PT76 tanks—one atop a knoll, dueling point blank with the ARVN artillery on Hill 31, four others rolling down a trail behind the knoll. As the four moved around the hill, two to the left, two to the right, Colonel Pommerenk rolled in. His bombs exploded just in front of two of the PT76s, halting them. Lieutenant Colonel Hagen dove in next, the stalled tanks firing at him with their cannons as he released cigar-shaped napalm canisters. The two tanks were consumed in the fiery billows, the crews burning to death inside. The other pair split up, one tank disappearing into the woods. Hagen blew up the one that remained in the open.

The NVA began traversing to make another attack up the northern slope. They still had about fifteen tanks left.

Moments before the attack began, a heavy gun team from C Troop 7/17 Air Cav, consisting of three Cobras, two Loaches, and a command and control Huey, had overflown Hill 31. Lt. David Ferrell and WO David Lancaster were flying one of the Cobras, and all they could see were the tops of bunkers and a burnt-out Huey in the middle of the perimeter. No one was in sight. West of the hill, the scout ships discovered a group of hootches atop a small hill and the gunnies made their runs low and straight, punching off rockets. The hill rocked with fireballs as a fuel cache went up. The team was heading back to Khe Sanh to refuel and rearm, when word came over the radio that Hill 31 was being overrun. Lancaster commented to Ferrell that the NVA had probably hidden in the brush as they flew over, preparing for their assault.

It was Lieutenant Ferrell's first day in Laos.

Ferrell was from St. Albans, West Virginia, twenty-four years old and married for the last two. He came from a poor family, but had worked his way through college, joined ROTC, and excelled in flight school. His brother, a career sergeant in the USAF, had flown C130 gunship missions over the Ho Chi Minh Trail in 1970, and Ferrell was proud to follow him to Vietnam in February 1971. He joined C Troop at their new tents at Khe Sanh, but there was no time to give him a flight check. The troop commander assigned him to fly with WO Lancaster to learn the ropes. An excellent pilot, Lancaster was young, tall, well educated, and friendly, and Ferrell hit it off well with him.

As soon as the rocket pods were refilled with 2.75-inch flechette rockets and the JP4 fuel nozzle unscrewed, Ferrell and Lancaster climbed back into their Cobra and slammed the canopy shut. In minutes the three Cobras and single Huey were close enough to Hill 31 to see the battle. They could make out the lumbering shapes of several NVA tanks going up the barren slope of the firebase, infantrymen running behind them in a frontal assault. Tracers poured from the ARVN bunker line. Shells exploded and smoke hung over the scene. The airborne FAC came on the radio and directed the gun team to take a high orbit southeast of Hill 31 to clear the way for a pair of USAF Phantoms coming in.

The jets streaked low, one behind the other, flashing north to south over the battlefield, releasing bombs. They pulled up and circled low; then Ferrell watched the lead Phantom dive in again. It dropped napalm amid the North Vietnamese on the hillside, then pulled up from its low dive just as a 12.7mm machine gun cut loose from the treeline at the base of the hill, Ferrell watched astonished as the stream of green tracers nailed the Phantom. The jet seemed to hang in the sky a millisecond; then smoke began pouring out and, a second later, the two pilots ejected, their parachutes opening high up. The Phantom burst into flames, began tumbling through the sky, and exploded in a fireball against the side of a mountain.

The two pilots floated down on the opposite side of Hill 31 from the gun position. They were lost from sight in the jungle.

The C Troop command helicopter immediately radioed that they were going in to get the pilots, ignoring calls to wait for the gunships. The three Cobras, Ferrell and Lancaster in the second ship, peeled off and dropped to fifty feet off the deck racing after the C&C. They darted through a lush green valley, about five hundred feet across, and Ferrell abruptly noticed dozens of NVA infantrymen moving in the elephant grass on the slopes. Most of them opened up with their AK-47s, some high enough in the hills to fire down on the Cobras, and it was like being in a popcorn pan as all three pilots reported taking hits. It was Ferrell's first time under fire, and he could hear a dozen rounds stitch through the tailboom—but training took over and he felt detached from the danger, too intent on getting the pilots to really worry.

The lead Cobra disappeared over a hill ahead of them but, when Ferrell and Lancaster crested it, no one was in sight. They took a guess and Lancaster banked to the left. Unable to raise anyone on the radio and seeing no other helicopters, Lancaster turned the ship around and they zigzagged over the treetops to see if their partners had been shot down. In moments they overflew the C&C Huey which had crashed in a field surrounded by trees. The Huey had only been on the ground a minute or two and the crew waved frantically as the Cobra flew past. Other helos arrived and the third Cobra of the team landed beside the Huey. A doorgunner and a captain were wounded in the C&C, so the Cobra copilot, a new warrant officer named David Nelson, volunteered to stay on the ground while the captain took his place in the two-seater gunship.

Other slicks arrived to evacuate the rest so, because they were low on fuel and their radios did not work, Ferrell and Lancaster departed for Khe Sanh. Once on the ground, they counted thirteen bullet holes in their fuselage and noted their radio cables had been severed. They also found out that two of the Cobra pilots had been wounded, and the injured doorgunner had died while being medevacked.

The search for the two Phantom pilots continued.

The F4 had gone down at around four in the afternoon, and the U.S. FAC and OV10 observer who'd been directing in the firepower had instantly left station to coordinate the search-and-rescue. Such was the policy of the USAF. Accustomed to bombing stationary targets deep in enemy territory, it was an excellent morale booster that, if a plane went down, the airstrike was cancelled and full attention was given to extracting the crew. In cases of close air support, this was done without regard to the troops who had requested the tac air. The policy had previously caused few problems because AA fire in South Vietnam rarely bagged a jet. But the fact that hundreds of NVA with tank support were now free to charge up Hill 31 did not prevent USAF doctrine from taking over. The ARVN 3rd Airborne Battalion was abandoned for two downed American pilots.

Back at the ARVN command bunkers in South Vietnam, Lieutenant General Dong and his U.S. advisors monitored the radio conversations. Col. Nguyen Van Tho (CO, 3d Airborne Brigade) and Lieutenant Colonel Phat (CO, 3d Airborne Battalion) kept a running dialogue from their bunkers in the middle of the shooting on Hill 31. To support the besieged garrison, General Dong instructed Colonel Luat to dispatch elements of his armor brigade. Tanks and APCs from the 11th and 17th Cavalry Regiments departed Aloui and began pushing north, driving cross-country through forested hills. At around five in the afternoon, they were ambushed, a dozen ARVN wounded, two of their M41 tanks and one APC blown up.

What happened next is a mystery.

The official version is that a conflict in orders from two headquarters, far removed from the battlefield and each other, forced the armor to halt in place. Lam ordered them on to Hill 31, while Dong, thinking the base was being overrun, ordered them to stop south of it and wait for instructions. The upshot was that the average nonaggressive ARVN officers reacted to this confusion by remaining where they were. Colonel Battreall, monitoring the armor radios, could envision the stress and frustration in General Dong's CP when in the midst of the chaos over Hill 31, a question was posed of what to do about the ambushed armor. A weak commander with no understanding of armor capabilities, he probably just shrugged.

Colonel Harrison, forced, as were all of the advisors, to get his information secondhand, thought that General Dong's incompetence caused the stalling of the armor relief column, whereas it had been merely a contributing factor to the cavalry commander's own timid spirits. He heard that, after the three vehicles had been knocked out in the ambush, the cav commander had radioed Dong for infantry support to clear the hills, then had sat idling in place, waiting. Dong sent neither reinforcement nor confirmation of his order that Hill 31—with NVA tanks in the wire—must be immediately rescued. The tanks, supposedly, just sat waiting, idling, until they ran out of fuel and more had to be helicoptered to them. "The armor's supposed to be able to charge through," Harrison thought disgustedly, "but they just sat there."

Whether because of the weakness of Dong, the cowardice of the cav commander, or both, the 11th and 17th Cav halted its rescue rush to Hill 31. The 3d Airborne Battalion was truly alone in their fight against a well-coordinated tank and infantry assault, the USAF having forsaken them for their own comrades, the ARVN armor having halted in place to wait and see. The only aircraft above Hill 31 was a helicopter with several airborne advisors aboard. It dipped down to fire an M-60 ineffectually at the surging attack.

At the time that the Phantom went down and air support ceased to exist for the defenders of Hill 31, Lieutenant General Sutherland arrived by helicopter to Lieutenant General Dong's command post. With him was General Weyand (DEPCOMUSMACV); he had arrived at XXIV Corps HQ at Quang Tri that afternoon for one of his frequent visits to the Laotian operation. After lunch Weyand and Sutherland first visited

Lieutenant General Lam and then Brigadier General Phu, who updated them on the current tactical situation. Lam mentioned that Hill 31 was experiencing a tank/infantry attack but, generally had no complaints (commented General Vien of the RVNAF JGS, ". . . another characteristic about General Lam . . . should be avoided by leaders at every level. He would not report bad news or was very slow to do so.")

At the Airborne CP, their last visit, Dong, overwhelmed by the events crashing down around him, poured out a catalogue of complaints to Weyand and Sutherland. He accused General Lam and I Corps of failing to support him, and Colonel Luat and his 1st Armor of not responding to his orders. He also attacked the U.S. air support that his paratroopers were receiving. One of the air force officers present said that the air support was more than adequate. Col. Arthur Pence, senior advisor to the Airborne Division, spoke up then, saying Dong was correct; yes, officially the USAF FACs were on station for the ARVN, but there were a host of problems involving them—not the least of which was that they were looking for two pilots while a battalion was in the process of being overrun.

To Sutherland, Pence was a constant complainer. To the other advisors, he was a competent officer who saw it as his duty to support the ARVN to the hilt. And by doing so, he got himself in hot water. General Sutherland's job was to provide all of the necessary support to the South Vietnamese in Laos and Pence had said, in effect, that he was not doing his job. Pence was a West Point man, on his second Vietnam tour, one not known for his tact; instead of discussing the issue privately, he had embarrassed the U.S. commanding general in front of his counterparts.

There is evidence that the complaints of Dong and Pence were justified. That same day, Colonel Harrison had typed a long letter to XXIV Corps from his command bunker, (25 February 1971) echoing in detail similar complaints:

As the Senior Advisor to the 1st Infantry Division (ARVN), I have experienced considerable difficulty in obtaining adequate FAC/ALO Support for the division for Operation Lam Son 719. . . .

I asked for an ALO to go forward with the CP to Khe Sanh, an ALO normally with the division main CP at Hue to move to the Main CP at Dong Ha. This amounted to one additional ALO requirement.

LTC Vallejo, Air Force advisor to I Corps, told me there was no requirement for an ALO at the Forward CP because all the air support was already planned for operations in Laos and there would be nothing for him to do. He finally agreed to let one go to Khe Sanh. After several days of my repeated requests for the Division ALO to move to Dong Ha, I was told that Colonel Howell in MR 1 would not allow the division ALO to move to the Division Main CP at Dong Ha.

Maj Mahoney, ALO to the division forward CP, moved with the CP to Khe Sanh. He was able to use his communications to get some information of the strikes being made in Laos and transmit requests to the Hammer FAC working the Laos area. The concept of the ARVN officer in the TOC calling a Vietnamese riding with the FAC to obtain information on strikes flown, BDA, and transmit immediate requests just does not work well enough for an operation with the tempo and intensity of Lam Son 719. Having an ALO available at the forward CP is a major assist. Notwithstanding, we are still unable to capitalize on the great potential of tactical air support and achieve the maximum responsiveness the US Air Force is capable of and anxious to provide. . . .

When an air move is underway and enemy fire threatens the success of the move, tactical air support is needed immediately. The Army Air Mission Commander (AMC) must control his lift helicopters and direct the fire of his gunships. The ARVN ground force commander flying in the command control (C&C) helicopter must direct the fire of his artillery and infantry troops and have the friendly forces mark their positions. There is an urgent need for an ALO to be on board the C&C to talk with the FAC to request immediate air as the ALO concurrently coordinates with the ground commander and the AMC. In a dire emergency when a Hammer FAC is not available, the ALO could direct the airstrike himself. On the evening of 23 Feb, I requested the ALO at the forward CP to get another Air Force officer forward so he could be in the C&C helicopter when major air moves were being made. I anticipated no trouble in having another Air Force officer available since in the past 16 days we have had four different officers serve as the ALO at Khe Sanh and the Air Force Officers that remained at Hue have extremely little to do. Unfortunately, I was informed that LTC Vallejo and Col Howell disapproved the use of an ALO in a C&C helicopter in Laos. I simply cannot understand the inertia and lack of "can do" attitude on the part of some middle management Air Force officers when I am certain the Commander, Seventh Air Force, sincerely desires that ARVN troops in Laos receive the most responsive and best possible US Air Force Support.

Colonel Harrison received no static for his complaints about USAF support, merely a formal typed reply from Brigadier General Jackson that, "The contents of your February letter concerning FAC/ALO support is appreciated and has been made known to the appropriate individuals. Every effort is being made to correct and improve the responsiveness of Tac Air support. . . ." Colonel Pence, whose comments were more urgent and made in public, received a different fate. The incident destroyed Sutherland's confidence in Pence's ability to advise effectively; when they helicoptered back to Quang Tri, Sutherland commented to Weyand how lackluster Dong was in comparison to Lam and Phu. He thought the inexperienced and politically-prompted Dong was simply losing his nerve over Laos and was being "supported, abetted, and indeed egged on" by Pence.

At Quang Tri, Weyand caught his plane to report back to General Abrams in Saigon, and Sutherland had to figure out what to do with Colonel Pence who, in reality, had not failed in his professional duties but in his tact. Sutherland ordered his XXIV Corps staff immediately to investigate Pence's charges about U.S. air support, detailing three of them:

1. that there was only one FAC over the ARVN 1st Airborne Division AO when he had been promised two such aircraft
2. that the one FAC Pence said he had was inexperienced with the airborne AO and could not even locate Hill 31
3. that there was only one air cav pink team available to the airborne

Sutherland did not include the story of the Phantom shoot-down. His staff answered that all of Colonel Pence's allegations were false and that, in addition, there had been a rainstorm over Hill 31 which had grounded all air support, making the complaints moot and a probable cover-up of the airborne's failings. Sutherland was furious that neither Dong nor Pence had mentioned this fact (the answer being, of course, that weather conditions had not been a problem when the battle started or the Phantom that had been shot down would not have been over Hill 31 to begin with).

After meeting with his staff, Sutherland radioed his XXIV Corps advisor to I Corps, General Jackson, and detailed his difficulties with Pence. He also noted that the advisor had been a burr under his saddle from the beginning: "Each time that I visited the Airborne Division, Colonel Pence tried to convince me that the Airborne Division should have two FAC's dedicated to the Airborne Division and that they and their aircraft should be based at the Khe Sanh airfield. The Khe Sanh airfield was normally closed by fog until about 1100 hours. It was not prudent for us to station FAC aircraft at Khe Sanh since they had to be able to get airborne at any hour of the day or night. They could only do this from the Quang Tri airfield. Lieutenant General Dong, abetted by Colonel Pence, refused to accept the realities of the situation."

Sutherland asked Jackson to confer with Lam on whether he should relieve Colonel Pence of his duties. Jackson's answer was no surprise.

The slopes of Hill 31 were a killing ground as the third NVA attack took advantage of the disappearance of the jets to charge from three sides—tanks from the northeast, infantry from the northwest and south.

Overhead Lieutenant Colonel Molinelli and Charlie Troop 2/17 Air Cav homed in, diverted by General Lam from an extended recon to the north. The scene below was confusion on the grand scale. The USAF and numerous helos were darting above the trees, looking for the two pilots, while some eighteen hundred meters away, the ARVN armor sat impotent, seemingly frozen in place because they perceived themselves to be outgunned. Molinelli sent his Cobras in on the NVA running up Hill 31, but their antipersonnel rockets ricocheted harmlessly off the tank armor.

On the ground, the ARVN paratroopers fired furiously from their bunkers, killing many of the charging North Vietnamese in their tracks. The tanks tore through the wire and the ARVN fired LAW rockets from twenty yards; they scored numerous hits but did no damage with the small rockets because they had not been properly trained in the vulnerable spots of a tank. The firebase artillery had been mostly disabled by previous shellings, but two 105mm howitzers were wheeled around in their parapets. They fired point-blank, destroying two tanks. The rest of the armor made it to the top of Hill 31, foot soldiers pouring in with them.

The NVA swarmed into bunkers and trenches. Combat was hand to hand.

From above, the American aircrews could only look on helplessly. WO Smith of the Ghostriders, who had been heading with his company to evacuate the survivors, watched the Phantoms lay napalm; the chaos on the radio when the jet went down had resulted in his company's being put in a circling pattern two miles south of Hill 31. From his perch, Smith could see tracers, puffs of explosions, an occasional darting figure—then three Soviet-made tanks crashed into view and began doing pedal-turns atop the ARVN bunkers to cave them in. Someone on the radio told Smith to head back for Khe Sanh.

Their rescue mission was cancelled.

A squall-line and heavy clouds rolled over Hill 31, and Lieutenant Colonel Molinelli saw the last of the NVA tanks rolling uphill into the clouds and out of sight, even as his Cobras fired at them from the valley. Finally the weather forced the USAF out of the area, and Molinelli also departed to refuel.

At fifteen minutes after five, Colonel Tho ordered the firebase evacuated. His executive officer and twelve soldiers immediately managed to escape down the southern slope of Hill 31, followed by Lieutenant Colonel Phat and twenty more ARVN, and then by Major Hong with another twenty men. Colonel Tho remained in his command bunker to go out with the last of his paratroopers.

Moments later, all communication with Hill 31 was lost.

The North Vietnamese charged victoriously across the fog-shrouded firebase and there were some last, isolated bursts of fire. Exhausted ARVN paratroopers raised their hands in surrender. The NVA surrounded the command bunkers and Colonel Tho and some of his staff emerged to be greeted by AK-47 barrels. By seven that night, the NVA were securing Hill 31, while the groups of ARVN survivors who had run away in the chaos hid out the night in the jungled valley.

Ironically the two air force pilots were not located by the search and rescue efforts that had been diverted away from Hill 31. Lieutenant Ferrell had the opportunity later to speak with some USAF officers who said the pilots had wandered for three days in the jungle before finally being picked up.

In the morning, 26 February, General Jackson walked over to the command bunker of the ARVN 1st Infantry Division to tell Colonel Harrison that he was now temporary senior advisor to the airborne, replacing Pence. He was still responsible as SA to the 1st Division but, since they were doing well and Phu was a competent commander, Harrison felt secure in leaving to catch a jeep for the two-kilometer ride to General Dong's command post. Harrison was not all impressed by his new counterpart; Dong seemed like a politician, a friend of the president, a palace-guard officer who'd probably been made a general to insure his loyalty to the government should another coup occur. He was not well versed on tactics and made little attempt to monitor the day-to-day status of his units.

Meanwhile, that morning, Lieutenant Colonel Molinelli led a recon flight over Hill 31 to determine exactly who still held the position. He could see several tanks, some artillery pieces, and a few people walking around the base; they went down for a closer look and were greeted with heavy NVA fire. In response, General Dong ordered the survivors of the 3d Airborne Battalion, augmented by the now-moving ARVN armor, to counterattack. Two hundred meters from the firebase, they were halted by intense NVA fire and eventually fell back with an additional twenty-seven dead and forty-one wounded.

The ARVN tankers were up front during the engagement, losing four of five M41s to RPGs, but blowing up a number of NVA tanks on Hill 31. Back at his CP, Colonel Battreall and the other advisors were elated at the 17th Cav's reports on the brigade net as they reported twenty-two tank kills. And in this, the 1st Armor Brigade found itself once again embroiled in controversy. General Sutherland completely dismissed the report as a fabrication by Luat; the fact that the NVA tanks had scored not a single kill in such a supposedly fierce battle added fuel to his fire. The truth, most likely, was somewhere in between—the ARVN tankers, in fact, doing their duty and engaging the NVA tanks on Hill 31, but, in the heat of battle, unable to distinguish between live tanks and those knocked out the day before, they probably thus claimed an exaggerated number of kills.

General Lam also did some exaggerating of his own, using the reports to claim that parts of Hill 31 were back in ARVN hands. Perhaps that is what some of his field commanders were claiming, but U.S. aerial recon showed no ARVN on the hill. The NVA also left it, as they had no reason to maintain an open position once they had knocked the South Vietnamese off.

On 27 February, the Bravo Dutchmasters were in the air again over Laos, the pink teams doing low-level scouting in the AO of the ARVN 1st Infantry Division. Lt. Ronald Babcock was flying one of the Loaches and his door-gunner/observer was the scout platoon sergeant. A man in his forties, the sergeant was not required to fly, but he volunteered to show the young draftees that old lifers could be as tough as they were.

Skimming low over the trees, their Loach was nailed by NVA fire. Babcock radioed that they were going down. The C&C Huey, piloted by Capt. "Mother" Waters, commander of the troop's lift platoon, chased after the descending ship. (Waters claimed his nickname came from some virile exploit, but his troops loved him and called him that because he watched after them like a mother hen.) As Waters zipped down in his Huey, the Loach crashed on a dirt road, and Babcock and the platoon sergeant, jumping out, ran like hell across a grassy clearing. North Vietnamese in the treeline cut them down with their AK-47s. Waters brought his bird to a ten foot hover over them and called on the radio that, from their appearance, he had no doubt they were dead. The C&C crew chief, Sergeant Seaman, dueled the NVA in the treeline with his M60—until a burst from a 12.7mm tore through the Huey. Seaman's ankle was shattered, a ten-inch hole was blown through the floor, the fuel tanks ruptured, and aviation fuel sloshed in the helicopter. Captain Waters managed to pull out and get them back to Khe Sanh.

Another helo went into the crash site but was also driven away by intense fire. Lieutenant Babcock and the platoon sergeant were declared missing in action, and the aircrews simply kept flying.

Relations between the U.S. and ARVN were not superb, as General Berry noted in his journal: "0630, 22 Feb 71. General Lam, the ARVN Corps Commander, is the decision-maker for the operation in Laos. General Sutherland commands the US supporting operations and has little real influence on what General Lam does in the Laotian operations, at least on Lam's tactical decisions. . . .

"0515, 26 Feb 71, Quang Tri. General Sutherland has great pressures on him. This Laotian operation must succeed. Sutherland is the senior US field commander working with the senior Vietnamese field commander, LTG Lam. Sutherland had a large role in planning the operation. Now it's Lam who commands the ground forces in Laos while Sutherland commands the supporting US forces. Command of ground forces in Laos is the decisive element. Therefore, Sutherland lacks control of the decisive element in the campaign. Yet, from the US point of view, Sutherland is the responsible field commander. There is no unity of command in this very difficult operation. That's a major weakness and vulnerability. . . .

"0600, 27 Feb 71, Quang Tri. There is a vast potential for bitterness, recrimination, and misunderstanding between the South Vietnamese and the Americans involved in this operation. If the operation were a great success, everyone would be happy and swapping congratulations. But as the operation bogs down and losses mount, Americans tend to blame the Vietnamese for having been too cautious and conservative in their ground maneuver plan and too unaggressive in their tactics. Vietnamese will tend to blame Americans for having failed to provide the air support, helicopter support, logistical support promised at the beginning of the operations."

Ranger North was overrun on 20 February. LZ Hotel Two was evacuated and abandoned on 24 February. Ranger South was evacuated and abandoned, and Hill 31 was overrun on 25 February. The evacuation of the 2d Airborne Battalion from Hill 30 began in earnest on March 2 when the 158th Aviation Battalion flew through murderous fire in a resupply-medevac mission. In the midst of a shelling, ARVN mobbed the Hueys. One of those who deserted on a helicopter was the ARVN battalion commander of Hill 30. The evacuation was called off while airstrikes came in, and the helicopters were diverted to the armor. Chinooks came in to Hill 30 with resupply and artillery-extraction missions, but were driven away by the intense AA fire. The evacuation was finally completed three days later despite fire from the NVA tanks.

The only base among the six hit in the NVA counterattack which did not fall was Aloui, held by Colonel Luat's 1st Armor Brigade. With the airborne and ranger units pulling out on the northern flank, the pressure on the brigade was intense. Those in the most danger were the men of the 17th Cavalry (reinforced with two companies from the 8th Airborne Battalion and survivors of the 3d Airborne Battalion); when Hill 31 fell, they found themselves cut off. They were alone in the hills and, without orders to attack or withdraw, they simply sat and were pummelled.

The situation only served to aggravate General Sutherland's impatience with the 1st Armor. He considered the armor typical of the "elite" ARVN units, more concerned about polished boots, comfortable barracks, and a sparkling motor pool, than about taking to the field to fight the war. He was tired of complaints that Laos was not tank country (aerial photos of what appeared to be ditches were often thirty-foot ravines), and would respond acidly that the NVA tankers seemed able to get around. The answer may have been that they knew where the good trails were. The ARVN complained that their M41 tanks only had 76mm guns, while the NVA T54s had 100mms.

In all quarters, the friction grew.

Sutherland blamed most of the difficulties on Colonel Luat whom he tried without success to convince Lam to replace, and who he, personally, felt was "a martinet, incompetent, and a coward." He thought that the failure of the armor to come to Hill 31's rescue was not the result of a conflict of orders, but of Luat being shocked into inaction by the report of NVA tanks. He thought that the friction between Generals Lam and Dong was heightened by Luat playing one against the other. Following the collapse of Hill 31, Sutherland received a radio call from General Jackson at I Corps; he said that Luat had arrived on a resupply helicopter, uncalled and unexpected, and that Lam had furiously ordered him to get back to his unit in the field.

Colonels Battreall and Hiep saw Luat that day—tired, but cheerful and confident—and understood that Lam had called him for an update of his brigade's situation. Battreall heard nothing about Lam being angry, and was convinced that Jackson's report to Sutherland about Luat skulking out of combat was based on a personal grudge towards Battreall. Jackson and Battreall had long been at odds, and Battreall thought the general's personal dislike for him was prejudicing his reports on the ARVN armor, Battreall advised. Whatever the cause, Luat's brief visit to the I Corps command bunker was the only time he was not with his brigade in Laos. In the midst of all of the attacks on the armor, Battreall thought bitterly, why did no one ask why the 17th Cavalry continued to hold its position after the airborne had withdrawn? If they were cowards, why didn't they bolt the five kilometers south to Aloui?

The 17th Cav's position was indeed grave. Isolated in the hills, the NVA had been able to bombard them and maneuver infantrymen close enough to fill the air above them with lead, keeping the helicopters away. At noon on 27 February, the North Vietnamese tried to overrun the position with a wave of tank and infantry. Jets and gunships came to their aid and, when the smoke cleared, the ARVN were still holding their ground. The skirmishing continued until the night of 1 March, when the NVA launched another major attack.

For the second time, the 17th Cav held.

Colonel Harrison urged General Dong to do something, either reinforce the 17th Cav or order their withdrawal to Aloui. Dong just shrugged, bewildered under the pressure of command. On 3 March, the NVA attacked again and Colonel Battreall listened anxiously to the radio reports. The ARVN were taking fire from three sides and had tank shells exploding to their rear. They had suffered a hundred more dead and wounded; ten more APCs were destroyed and two attempts to resupply them and evacuate casualties by helicopter had been driven away by the hornet's nest of fire. Dong was unresponsive to the situation, Lam was at a XXIV Corps briefing, and Battreall did not know to whom to turn. He feared the 17th Cav would be completely overwhelmed, so he and his counterpart, Colonel Hiep, took matters into their own hands. They collared Lieutenant Colonel Vallejo, USAF advisor to I Corps, and, after five minutes on the radio, he had six B52 bombers diverted to the 17th Cav. The Arc Light came in like close air support, the hills disappearing in explosions several hundred yards from the surrounded ARVN, and the NVA attack was halted in its tracks. Battreall and Hiep radioed them to break contact and the armor-airborne task force withdrew to a better position to allow helicopters to come in for their wounded. Then they continued a rearguard action to rejoin the brigade at Aloui.

At Colonel Hiep's suggestion, Colonel Battreall and his sergeant major joined him on a helicopter for Da Nang. Hiep thought it advisable to be out of the area when General Lam returned, lest he be angered that a mere colonel had stepped in like that. They spent the night in Hiep's private home, then signed out a jeep in the morning to return to FSB Kilo. With the sergeant major driving, Battreall joined a U.S. ammunition convoy on Route 9 and arrived, caked in red dust, hoping Lam had better things to worry about by then. Colonel Hiep, meanwhile, reported to President Thieu in Saigon. His observations and recommendations were that General Dong of the airborne and General Khang of the marines were failing to perform, and that, unless the 1st Armor Brigade were given some viable mission, they should be withdrawn from Aloui before the NVA could make Route 9 completely impassable. Hiep then went to XXIV Corps to organize fifty men from each ARVN armor regiment to go back with him as replacements to Luat's mauled brigade.

PART THREE:
Americans at War

CHAPTER NINE:
The Rockpile

As the ARVN fought in Laos, the U.S. ground forces continued their simultaneous effort to keep Route 9 open and the new firebases secure. To do so, General Hill and the 1st Brigade, 5th Mechanized Infantry Division, were initially concerned with the Rockpile, that incongruous jutting of jungle-covered granite north of Vandegrift. North Vietnamese rocket teams with infantry support had taken advantage of the high perches just west of the Rockpile to bring Vandegrift and Route 9 under almost daily shelling. Casualties had been inflicted on the American units in the area, and it fell initially to Lieutenant Colonel Meyer's 1st Battalion, 77th Armor, to scout the Rockpile area and flush the enemy teams.

In the same time frame as the 8 February crossing into Laos, a patrol under 1/77 control found two recently abandoned NVA basecamps in the hills three kilometers west of the actual Rockpile. They held many anti-tank mines, and 60mm mortar and RPG rounds. The next day, Meyer helicoptered to join the unit on foot as they continued patrolling, pushing north of the 3/5 Cav pioneer road in the hills, and west of the Rockpile. The captain in charge appeared nervous to have a battalion commander on the ground with him, and his fears for the colonel's safety were soon justified: at noon, NVA opened up from a bunker with AK-47 automatic rifles. The GIs returned the fire, located the bunker, and the forward observer called in artillery support. None came. Meyer grabbed the radio and spoke to the battery commander, "We needed that arty five minutes ago." Still none came. Finally Meyer radioed for a combat-engineer vehicle with a 165mm demolition gun to be dispatched. It clanked up through the thick brush and blasted shells into the NVA bunker.

The patrol moved up, found two dead North Vietnamese, and the captain joked to Meyer that he was welcome along any time. Things were off to an easy start.

To press the NVA, Meyer ordered one of his tank companies to sweep the high ground around the Rockpile. In support, the battalion scout platoon and a detachment from the 1/61 Mech Infantry were attached to the tankers. As they rolled north from the Vandegrift perimeter, Sp4 Spurgeon of the battalion snipers jumped on one of Lieutenant Revelak's scout tracks, hoping to see some action. The patrol halted below one of the smaller hills, and the tanks proceeded to deploy in the heavy underbrush to lob shells uphill.

Lieutenant Revelak said something about a reconnaissance team up the hill being stuck in an NVA bunker complex. He made a head count of the men and said they were going uphill "light" (without rucksacks). Spurgeon noticed uneasily that a disproportionate number of the men had dark-green fatigues and new jungle boots. He noticed a Puerto Rican sergeant beside him, a tall guy with a beard, looking nervous. Spurgeon asked if he really thought there were any NVA up there.

"There're definitely some dinks on that hill. Lots of 'em." Spurgeon was feeling gung-ho. "Good."

But that didn't mean he was crazy. Everyone else was wearing helmets, but he'd turned one down in favor of the bravado of his bush hat. The sergeant's comment got to him and he grinned, "I'll take that steel pot now." A grunt on an APC laughed and tossed him one. The tanks ceased firing and the patrol pushed out. A Kit Carson Scout took the point, the Puerto Rican sergeant following him, the rest of the scouts and 1/61 grunts in trace behind them. The hill was steep and lush with heavy green foliage, but a one-foot-wide trail wove up through the tangle and the grunts snaked up single file. The jungle canopy enveloped them from above. They splashed across a stream, only two feet deep but fifty yards wide, and hauled themselves back into the wall of brush on the other side, continuing uphill. It was a clear day and not a shot was fired. Spurgeon had been through a year of patrols without a single serious contact and he disgustedly thought this was going to be another useless walk in the sun. He bummed a Salem off one of the grunts and continued trudging along.

They stopped amid the brush, forming a hasty perimeter as the Kit Carson and sergeant pushed on. Spurgeon waited with the grunts, the 1/61 lieutenant standing with an o.d. sweat towel around his neck and a helmet over his bush hat. Spurgeon, fed up with the humping, sarcastically asked, "What now?" to the lieutenant and his RTO.

A single shot broke the silence from the point.

Then a long burst of automatic fire followed.

The patrol crouched in place amid the high shrubbery, not sure what was going on or what to do. Then Spurgeon saw something tumbling end over end through the air and the lieutenant was shouting "Chicom!" The grenade exploded thirty feet from Spurgeon, and he looked up terrified to see seven more arching down towards them. The NVA were lobbing them from the high ground. GIs began heaving grenades uphill and Spurgeon watched the stunning sight of a half-dozen U.S. grenades sailing up, spoons popping off in flight, while a dozen NVA stick grenades sailed downhill. They bounced and fizzed and sprayed shrapnel over the patrol. Everyone was firing back from the prone. A North Vietnamese mortar added to the cacophony. Spurgeon, pumped with adrenaline, got up clutching his M-14 rifle, screaming for them to charge. No one moved. No one was giving orders, and he finally jumped back down, afraid he'd accidentally be shot from behind if he actually ran forward.

"Medic! We need a medic!" men were screaming, hidden in the brush.

Spurgeon dropped down in the bushes beside three black GIs who were spraying their M-16s and throwing grenades into a patch of burning elephant grass. Spurgeon fired blindly into the smoking brush and lobbed his last two grenades. To his right, he could see men trying to outflank the NVA. They were halted by the heavy fire. He was kneeling and firing when another grenade bounced in. He grabbed his ears, it boomed, and his right knee suddenly stung. He yanked up his trouser-leg to see a tear in the cloth and a scrape on his skin; a piece of shrapnel had kicked him without drawing any blood. He rolled away towards Lieutenant Revelak who was down flat on the slope, fire raking near him.

Someone was moaning, "I'm hit, I'm hit," and Spurgeon crabwalked towards the sound. A medic was balled up in the grass. He patted over his field jacket, looking for the wound. He finally found a tiny shrapnel hole which barely bled, and it dawned on him that the man wasn't dying, but was just scared. He wrapped the medic's arm around his shoulder and they rolled downhill.

The shooting continued without letup, and soon the patrol was out of grenades and short of ammunition. Men began shouting, "We're leaving, let's get outta here!" and the patrol retreated down the trail. Two or three GIs at the end tried to drag the body of the sergeant with them—the first shots of the ambush had killed him. Spurgeon grabbed his shirt, the others his feet and arms, and they laboriously scurried down the path, sliding on their butts. The NVA opened up with a renewed fury, volleys of AK slashing the leaves and limbs above them. The dead man's shirt ripped off of him as they tugged. Spurgeon grabbed his wrist. His helmet bounced off. A GI ahead of him tumbled, a ricochet swelling his eye. Spurgeon stopped, enraged, and fired his rifle uphill. Someone down the trail yelled to pop smoke to mark them for supporting fire so Spurgeon tugged a yellow smoke grenade off of the M-16 bandolier tied to the dead sergeant's waist.

The AKs kept hurrying them along, sounding like popcorn in a pan.

They reached the stream and made a pell-mell dash across it, running and falling. Lieutenant Revelak tried to hoist the dead sergeant on his back, but the body was too heavy and they tumbled into the water. The AK fire increased, roaring above their heads into the far bank. Spurgeon began crawling, his head and back above the water, his rifle submerged, his mind paralyzed with the thought of a bullet smashing through his forehead. He threw himself behind a small rock in the middle of the creek. Several grunts splashed back across to get the body which had been dropped, and Spurgeon felt like a coward. "Let them do it," he thought, "this kid ain't getting shot." Tears of fear stung his eyes. The NVA fire was too heavy. The men ran back, leaving the dead sergeant.

Spurgeon bolted for the bank, grabbing handfuls of elephant grass to haul himself up. He stopped at the edge of the water, sitting in the mud, turning to fire. Water sprayed from the bolt at each shot. They finally straggled back to the tank site and a helicopter landed. The crew chief hopped out to take a photograph as Spurgeon and another GI helped the medic aboard. Another chopper came in; about seven men had been wounded.

The grunts took a breather on the tanks, wearily smoking and talking. Spurgeon was exhausted. It had been his first real firefight and he'd not seen a single NVA. He felt they'd been beaten because they'd underrated the power of the NVA on that hill. A U.S. Navy Phantom roared in dropping bombs and the grunts cheered inside. The second pass splashed napalm, then rockets, then it made a strafing run. The pilot radioed he was taking ground fire, then reported "dusting a dink" with a rocket.

Firepower was brought to bear against the hill all that night.

In the morning, Lieutenant Colonel Meyer arrived. He reviewed the firefight. The captain in charge had been back with the tanks instead of up with the patrol. He had not aggressively responded to the NVA ambush, but had allowed them to get the upper hand; he had ordered a withdrawal not based on what he saw personally but on the excited reports of a young radioman. And the body of an American soldier had been left behind in the chaotic retreat under fire. Meyer relieved the captain on the spot; the man resigned, saying, "Yes, sir," and disappeared. Meyer directed more fire against the bunkers atop the hill, then took out a foot patrol to retrieve the body. Although they recovered the dead sergeant without any contact, it was obvious that the NVA had more than just a few rocket teams in the Rockpile hills. Reinforcements were needed to clear the high ground.

The reinforcements sent by General Hill were Lieutenant Colonel Coast's 4th Battalion, 3d Infantry, Americal Division, which was airlifted from Khe Sanh to Vandegrift on 10 February. That first day, Alpha Company 4/3 manned some old marine dugouts on the perimeter, and immediately came under 122mm rocket fire. When the shelling stopped, the grunts stood on the bunker line to cheer on a pair of Cobra gunships which pumped rockets into a neighboring ridgeline.

The men spent the night in the flimsy bunkers listening, detached, as an occasional one-two-two exploded somewhere else on Vandegrift. The whole battalion was going to CA into the Rockpile area the next morning; and Pvt Russ Morse knew they'd be stepping into the shit. He was tense, but he wasn't collapsing, and that was because they had a good platoon. Lieutenant Dewing had his shit together, Morse thought; they called him Mad Dog out of respect for the lieutenant's willingness to share the risks. And the guys themselves, Morse reckoned, were just dynamite. They did their best, and it irked him that the war protesters and draft dodgers seemed to be getting the hero's treatment back home. It was something they rarely talked about in the field. Most of them didn't want to be in Nam. But Morse thought it was the only honorable choice, even if it was a lousy choice. You just did your job.

Sitting in a bunker that night, Lieutenant Dewing was having similar thoughts. He was deeply moved by the performance of his grunts, only two of whom were not draftees. They were mostly just kids, nineteen-year-old working-class kids like his friend Morse, who smoked dope and flashed the peace sign, and couldn't give a shit about the army or Vietnam—and who would risk their lives in a moment for another GI. Underneath the veneer of being rough-and-tough killers, he thought, they were caring, dependable men. All you had to do was treat them with dignity; they would refuse orders from a screaming second lieutenant, but go on the hairiest patrol for someone who led them personally. As for Dewing, he was there by choice. He'd grown up a high-school athlete in the Alaskan outback country, and had dropped out of college to join the army in a moment of apathy after his girlfriend had broken up with him. In retrospect, he'd never regretted the move. A stint with an engineer unit in Vietnam had earned him a recommendation to OCS; he'd arrived for his second tour as a lieutenant in October 1970. He'd come in to the Tan Son Nhut airbase aboard a commercial jet filled with captains and lieutenants, many of whom jumped at the chance when the reception clerks asked who wanted to go to the support commands. After a year in the rear and primed with the gung-ho attitude of OCS, Dewing had been adamant about going to the infantry. He'd volunteered for everything he got in Vietnam and, at the age of twenty-three, Lieutenant Dewing felt content leading the First Platoon in combat.

The sun broke through the overcast on the morning of 11 February as the grunts of 4/3 made last-minute preparations on the Vandegrift helicopter pad. Slicks and guns from the 14th CAB took the lead elements into a hilltop LZ west of the Rockpile. C Company went first; it was a hot LZ; a Huey and an OH58 Kiowa Scout were shot down, and a firefight around the crash site killed two Americans. One dead NVA and an AK-47 were found in the brush. The helicopters were destroyed in place, the crews extracted.

While the initial CA was being conducted, Captain Spinning's Alpha Company waited at the helipad. Helicopters came back from the Charlie Company insertion, riddled with bullet holes, and the men began boarding. They knew this was it—a hot LZ and birds down—and some of the men got shakey. Pvt. Morse could feel the hesitation well up in him and he asked Lieutenant Dewing if he could stay at Vandegrift since he was slotted for an R&R the next day. Dewing said no, they needed all the men they could have; and Morse agreed to postpone his leave until after the op. As he hustled towards the birds, he noticed two GIs, one black and one white, refusing to board the helicopters; the black GI muttered, "I'm not going out there to get killed." It was the last Morse ever saw of those two.

They climbed into the cabins, hunkered under their gear, and sat for a long time as the blades churned and the cabins vibrated around them; the engines shut down and still they waited. Finally, word came to go, the blades picked up to a dervish pitch, and Alpha Company watched Vandegrift skim away underneath them and the hills of the Rockpile rise to the north. Morse sat beside Denny in the second slick, M-16s across their laps, legs hanging out the doors; they touched down in the LZ with a few AKs sputtering from the treeline, and Morse bolted out, jumping behind a fallen tree with a Charlie Company grunt. The NVA fire dried up and the rest of Alpha CA'd in without difficulty.

After a brief huddle, they moved out in file down a thin mountain trail. Morse took the point, grinning back at Buddy-Fucker over the dead North Vietnamese sprawled inside the LZ, then stopped at the edge of the perimeter. Dewing gave him general directions and Morse led the patrol, moving slowly down a well-used path. He came to a lesser-used fork, followed that to the top of the ridgeline, then descended the other slope; it was shaky footing straight down. After three exhausting hours of humping, they took a short break, then more patrolling along the slope until dusk when they set up their night defensive position on the trail. The fog and cold rolled in around the mountaintops. Colder than a nun's butt, Dewing thought; the men had no blankets or extra shirts so they lay shivering miserably on the cold ground.

The sun was breaking on the horizon and Morse had just opened a C ration breakfast when three M-16 shots popped from the edge of the perimeter. He grabbed his M-14 and ran over to see the Staff Sergeant and Buddy-Fucker lowering their rifles. They said they'd gone to take a leak and had spotted a dink on the trail. He'd run away before they'd gotten a bead on him.

Things calmed down and Alpha moved out again down the path, First Platoon up front, Morse again on point. He hated the trail for it followed the narrow crest of the ridgeline, the slopes falling away like cliffs on either side making their movement predictable and thus ambushable. He wanted to hack through the brush on the side. Three hours of patrolling yielded nothing and the company halted, strung out along the trail to take five. The company leaders stood talking and, as was routine, Captain Spinning assigned Lieutenant Walker's Second Platoon to take over the point.

Morse sat in the brush, his fatigues soaked with sweat, watching Second Platoon file past, Lieutenant Walker on point and two GIs named English and Moran walking slack. The lone NVA they'd spotted weighed on his mind. It was too quiet out there. Some premonition clicked in his head and he was tempted to fake it—to shout, "Dinks!" and start shooting, halting the move. He let the thought pass, knowing that would simply pinpoint their exact location to the North Vietnamese—as if they didn't already know.

Morse walked over to Denny, sat down, lit up a cigarette—and the whole world suddenly went up. A Chinese claymore slambanged under the canopy of trees, spraying chunks of metal down the path, AK-47s drilled from the brush and, in a millisecond, Lieutenant Walker was blasted with shrapnel and hurled against a tree stump, English and Moran were blown away, Morse and Denny were throwing themselves into the bushes, Chip was down with shrapnel, and five other GIs were screaming in pain. It was all chaos and noise. Behind him Morse could hear Lieutenant Dewing shout, "On line, move out!" and someone started pouring down fire with a pig. He glanced at Denny and they rolled to their knees, firing in the direction of the NVA. Morse emptied two magazines, jammed in a third, rose from his crouch to move towards the casualties, and a sudden stinging explosion rippled through his back and side. He spun, and two more rounds punched through his stomach. He collapsed and the pain exploded through him. He couldn't move his legs.

A stray M-16 burst from behind had hit him; a medic from Second Platoon scrambled over to patch him up.

Dewing jogged forward to the point of contact and saw Lieutenant Walker dropped at the foot of the stump. He was peppered with shrapnel along the right side of his body and was bleeding badly—it looked as if his helmet had saved his life. Dewing hesitated a moment, but Walker shouted, "Go on!" and Dewing ran past. In a few minutes, it was all over—the NVA emptying a few AK mags then disappearing back into the jungle, no one seeing a single one of them. Dewing got on the radio to call in artillery on the slope that the NVA were probably moving down. The company FO, Lieutenant Cunningham, ran up and took over, directing a roar of air and arty into the jungled valley below them. The company formed a hasty perimeter while the medics worked on GIs moaning in the grass. There were two dead and eight wounded. Medevacs circled but the trees and brush were too dense for them to land, so they had to use a jungle penetrator. One at a time, the dead and wounded were strapped in the basket and winched up to the hovering helicopter by a cable.

Morse was the last out, two guys dragging him, as he heard AKs open up on the hovering bird. It remained in place and Morse loved those pilots. As he was winched up, he could see muzzle flashes below him and heard the zing of an AK round go past him, but he was too drowsy on the medic's morphine to realize he was in danger.

12 February had been a bad day for the grunts, but Alpha Company humped the rest of the afternoon on patrol. After another freezing night, they returned to sweeping the ridgeline, getting further and further away from the battalion command post set up in the original landing zone. Instead of patrolling single file, they put out five point men—one on the crest, two more on each slope—with the rest of the company following in a skirmish line behind again.

It was obvious that the ridges they were patrolling had long been the site of war. Lost in the undergrowth, they found many U.S. gas masks (poison gas was not used in Vietnam so, when infantrymen were issued protective masks, they routinely dropped them in the brush on the next patrol to lighten the load they were humping). They also found that an occasional tree had been sawed down by North Vietnamese soldiers for their bunkers. The stumps would have been like white dots looking skyward as a signal to U.S. reconnaissance planes, so the NVA had rubbed dirt on them for camouflage. Dewing was impressed by such attention to detail; the enemy they were hunting were professionals and all of the grunts had a lot of respect for them. While they saw evidence of bunkers being built, they saw no bunkers.

The terrain was rough going, with sharp inclines and steep hills, and the thick brush and trees slowed progress. Tall clumps of elephant grass had to be pushed through, and Dewing was amazed when the metal blades of a few machetes actually snapped in half as exhausted grunts clubbed at the grass with them. Like all tough humps, it turned into a plodding monotony of aching muscles, sweat-drenched fatigues, and mumbled curses at the lifers, the oppressive packs on their backs, the hills, the sun. Heavy fog shrouded the mountains, disrupting regular resupply to the company, and water became critical. There was little to drink, none to waste on washing or brushing teeth, and the grunts began looking around, as they patrolled, for bamboo stalks which had water inside.

On 14 February, Captain Spinning decided it was becoming too exhausting and passed the word to drop the rucks and travel light. One platoon halted to guard the equipment until helicopters could get in for them, and the other two platoons continued on, the men putting their C ration cans in pockets, and carrying nothing but weapons, ammunition, and half-empty canteens. They were moving up another hill on the ridgeline when Dewing got a call from the Loach scouting ahead of them, "You got some traffic ahead of you. Dink in a bunker." The company came upon a small clearing where they could make out the NVA dugout in the brush, an elaborate construction that looked as if it would withstand artillery. The Loach orbited it, the door-gunner throwing smoke and frag grenades. It banked off and Dewing shouted, "Chieu hoi, chieu hoi!" Surrender! There was no response from the bunker, so he cautiously jogged forward. Seeing a figure move inside, he dropped down, threw in a grenade, and scurried back. Sergeant First Class Rojas, of another platoon, crawled forward and tossed in two more frags. The sergeant waited a bit, then climbed into the bunker and dragged out the body of the North Vietnamese soldier killed by the blast. The grunts curiously gathered around. Someone pulled out his wallet, and they passed around several black-and-white photographs of the dead soldier with his wife and children. That brought the whole war down to a personal level for Dewing; this guy was a draftee like us, he thought, just a rice farmer from Hanoi fighting for his country. It was the first time he'd thought of his enemy as a human being, and he was amazed at the man's courage. Whereas the Americans would send several men to do a job, the Communists had just sent one. And he died fighting, all alone, one man against a whole company.

15 February. The bunker of the dead NVA sat atop a little hill, and the 4/3 jump command post moved into it. Early the next morning, a battalion element reported contact with about two dozen NVA. Three GIs were wounded and the enemy slipped away in the jungle. Two hours later, the GIs ambushed an NVA patrol and reported killing fifteen enemy soldiers. By noon Alpha Company was leaving the battalion area for another hump, but Captain Spinning was concerned about the sightings of the NVA groups. He told Lieutenant Sheridan to take his Third Platoon back down the trail in the direction they'd come and check for any NVA who might be trailing them.

They moved down the path, and were in the valley between the command post and a small hill, when the sudden roar of another Chinese-claymore ambush thunderclapped. AK-47s hit the platoon in the draw from the hill. Lieutenant Sheridan went down with dust and bamboo splinters blown into his eyes. Two grunts behind the point, Benjamin Burgos-Torres and David Comber, were killed instantly by the claymore. The point man, Pfc Julian Marquez, charged towards the NVA ambushers, only to be shot dead in the brushy slope of the hill.

The platoon fell back.

Dewing's First Platoon was still at the CP when the ambush was sprung and, before the lieutenant could say a word, the grunts were up and rushing downhill towards the fire. It was an instantaneous reaction, the company falling on line, firing into the jungle, unable to see any of the NVA. A platoon of NVA were firing from the hill and it was impossible to move forward without heavy casualties. The overcast was too low to bring in the gunships, so Captain Spinning shouted to fall back. The company began pulling back, dragging their wounded with them, but leaving the three dead men who were right under the enemy guns. The NVA fired on the retreat and Pfc Barnhart flopped forward, shot in the foot. The round had hit the sole of his foot, ripped through to the ankle, and he lay clutching his leg in intense pain. Dewing jumped down beside him and could see the copper-jacketed AK-47 bullet protruding from the canvas of Barnhart's jungle boot. He plucked out the bullet, put it in Barnhart's hand, and curled his fist around it, telling him to keep it for a souvenir. Then the medics helped him limp back, with the rest of the grunts, jogging between the trees.

At the command post, medevacs came in for their six wounded. The company spent the night there, everyone nervous about the next morning when they would have to go back to get the bodies of Burgos-Torres, Comber, and Marquez. Dewing was hurt that a young fighter like Marquez had to die like that, but he really felt sorry for Comber. Comber was new to the company and scuttlebutt was that he'd had a rear job until he'd pissed off a sergeant major.

It was still chilly and brisk in the morning and the fog hadn't burned away, when the helicopters came in with a resupply of water and the company's rucksacks. Dewing took a detail down to the only suitable LZ in the jungled area, a crater on the other side of their hill position. The choppers came in at a slow hover, door-gunners kicking out the rucks and

"Donkey Dick" water blivets; and then the North Vietnamese opened up with a mortar. The first round fell short and exploded in the valley as they scrambled for cover. The next one whistled over their heads and burst in the opposite valley, and Dewing shouted to get back before the NVA bracketed them.

The grunts scrambled hand-over-hand uphill, dragging the gear.

Dewing ran to the crest of the ridgeline before realizing one of his men was still back in the open area, hunkered down in the crater, afraid to move. He shouted to come on but the kid hesitated another moment, then scurried over the rim of the shell hole, dragging his ruck. The NVA had the range by then. Another shell exploded as the kid popped up, and he flopped back into the crater. Dewing and Sp5 Larry Gann, a super medic, scrambled down the hill. They tore off the GI's shirt. He had only seven minute shrapnel holes on the left side of his chest but he was dying. Gann worked quickly and efficiently, getting a plastic trachea tube down his throat so he could breathe, and starting an IV in his arm. A medevac was requested.

They put the wounded man in the helicopter but he died en route.

In the afternoon, Alpha Company mounted up again and moved slowly towards the three bodies in the jungled draw. They were again met by a torrent of fire. They shot back futilely into the bushes and fell back before they suffered any casualties. This day, though, the grunts had some revenge for their frustration and fear. They were moving back along the ridgeline when NVA were spotted in the valley below them, pulling away from the hill mass. Lieutenant Cunningham quickly got on the radio and called for TOT—Time On Target, several batteries of artillery firing simultaneously into the same kill zone. The air rushed with the freight-train sound of incoming artillery, and the valley floor literally erupted around the dozens of NVA swarming through the trees. The grunts crouched on the hilltop and cheered inside as the FO watched through his binoculars and kept up a running commentary on the massacre. He said he could see groups of NVA trying to run away, a blinding flash, then shredded foliage and pieces of bodies strewn about. To the grunts it was sweet, sweet revenge.

The fighting did not end that night. As the grunts settled in their foxholes for another black night of fog and chill, the NVA sent probing teams creeping through the brush. The company's 4.2-inch mortar team did an expert job dropping shells on the edge of the perimeter, driving the enemy away. By that night, someone in supply had helicoptered more than fifty Arctic Mountain sleeping bags to Alpha. Dewing, with four hours to sleep, climbed in, feeling snug, just thankful for the warmth. He was sleeping when the whole world seemed to come ripping apart and he bolted awake, terrified. Airstrikes were pummelling the valleys on either side of the ridge. No one in higher headquarters had taken the trouble to alert Alpha Company.

On 17 February, the company was again met by a hail of fire when it tried to get to the three bodies, but pulled back unscathed. The grunts began calling the NVA-held knoll Track-meet Hill for all of the times they'd run up and run back. It was grinding the men down—some worse than others. Captain Spinning was using the captured NVA bunker as his CP, and Dewing was inside with him when a grunt stumbled in, crying and shaking. He had cracked up from the stress. A medic grabbed him, Dewing and the others reassuring the sobbing man, "It's all right . . . don't worry about it." He was slated for a medevac. There was a lot of peer pressure among the grunts for each to hold up his end and the man was afraid he'd be laughed at. He wasn't. Sometimes Americans can be such vindictive bastards, Dewing thought. But it made him proud that the grunts had shown only compassion for a fellow soldier who simply couldn't take it anymore.

Another soldier in Alpha Company also quit for less tangible reasons, and with less drama. He had performed well during the unsuccessful attacks to get the bodies and was in for a Bronze Star. The day after he earned the medal, he told his platoon leader that there was no way he was going up again. The story spread like wildfire among the grunts, and Captain Spinning told him he would be court-martialled. He left the shooting war aboard a helicopter, bound for trial, and it amazed Dewing how a subtle, unspoken shift in a man's mood could make him a hero one day and a coward the next.

On the evening of 17 February, Captain Spinning, Lieutenant Cunningham, and Lieutenant Dewing sat down once again to discuss the next attempt to get the bodies. They were frustrated, but there was never a question of abandoning the mission; it left a bad taste in their mouths to leave dead Americans to the Communists, and the officers felt it would be disastrous for morale if anything but a maximum effort was made to recover soldiers, dead or alive. The only thing they hadn't tried was coming in from two angles, so that if the NVA ambushed one column, the other could still move in. They agreed that this time nothing would stop them.

They moved out the next day at noon. Captain Spinning walked point in one column. Out of sight on the other slope of the ridgeline, the First Platoon advanced. Staff Sergeant Kegerreis walked point with Dewing walking slack behind him. The rest of the platoon followed single file, a good distance between them so they wouldn't be bunched up if the NVA let loose with another claymore. They walked to the side of the trail, where the NVA had previously hacked away the underbrush, making it relatively easy going. Keg, on point, was wearing a helmet and flak jacket, and set a cautious, deliberate pace. Dewing followed, a thirty-round magazine in his M-16, twenty-four more mags wrapped around him in bandoliers and an empty claymore bag, and three grenades in each pocket.

It was cold and overcast, the dampened forest a gloomy gray.

Staff Sergeant Kegerreis led them to the bodies without a shot being fired, then spotted an NVA bunker in the brush. Keg moved for it, Dewing behind him. Then as Dewing watched, everything happened too quickly for fear to surface; a bareheaded North Vietnamese popped waist-high from the bunker, his AK-47 pointed at them. The silence was shattered by the metallic burst. Something thudded into Dewing's hip, and Keg spun back, tumbling over him head over heels at the impact of the AK rounds. Dewing dropped down, frantically grabbed a grenade from his pocket, yanked the pin out. The NVA dropped back down to reload and Dewing lobbed the frag into the bunker. There was a muffled boom from within and he waited a second. The North Vietnamese soldier did not reappear. He crawled quickly to Keg, who was lying in the brush, wide awake although the AK had raked him from the waist up. The meat was blown off his right forearm. Dewing tugged off the sergeant's flak jacket and wrapped two compress bandages around the bare bone to stop the bleeding. He talked to Keg, to keep him out of shock, until a medic ran up from the platoon column to take over. The rest of the grunts fanned out around them. There was no shooting. The NVA were gone.

Jesus, Dewing thought, this is eerie.

The silence was the cue to the NVA that their man in the bunker was dead, and they opened up with mortars. The grunts hugged earth. Dewing could still walk and felt no pain, but he noticed a bulge of flesh sticking through a small hole in his trousers. He ripped at the cloth and could see a small bullet hole in his hip; there was an AK-47 round in him.

The bodies of Burgos-Torres, Comber, and Marquez were lying where they'd fallen; the cold nights had prevented them from decomposing. The grunts, used to the VC down south who booby-trapped anything and everything, used grappling hooks and ropes to tug at the bodies, but they were clean. An occasional mortar shell whistled in, hurrying the grunts along as they rolled the dead men onto litters fashioned of ponchos and hardwood branches, and started dragging them back up the hill. The mortar rounds hit the treetops, sending fragments spraying down like rain. Dewing was walking back with the rear of the platoon when he noticed other GIs moving slowly past them, towards the bunker they had blown.

At the hilltop, he saw the battalion operations officer and asked, "Who are the guys in the clean fatigues?" The major said a battalion from the 101st Airborne was moving in and their whole battalion was pulling out.

The ridge was a scene of windy confusion as helicopters came and went, the Americal conducting medevacs and extractions in the midst of the Screaming Eagles combat assault. Dewing climbed aboard a Huey with Keg and two men from the 101st who had shrapnel wounds. He noticed they had clean fatigues and black jungle boots; after eight days in the Rockpile, his grunts looked like bums. He sat cross-legged on the metal floor, his rifle and rucksack gone, and Keg lay flat on his back beside him, still conscious. The helicopter lifted off and Dewing asked the door-gunner if it was okay to smoke. He lit up and Keg rolled over and smacked his lips. The lieutenant placed the cigarette between his lips and the sergeant took a long drag.

They landed at the 18th Surgical in Quang Tri at around four in the afternoon. When they came in, a medic asked, "What's wrong with you."

"Well, I think I've been shot," Dewing replied.

Since he was still on his feet, hardly bleeding, and in little pain, Dewing was ushered to a bench while Keg was immediately wheeled into surgery. Dewing watched, very impressed with the professionalism of the doctors, nurses, and medics.

There was a CBS-TV News camera crew there and they interviewed Dewing. He felt automatically hostile towards the press. It seemed that every time they came to a firebase, they scrounged around for the biggest malcontent to put on television. He felt the reporters had stained the bravery of his grunts with their constant harping on drugs, fraggings, and refusals. He was angered that My Lai had been made synonymous with all activities of the Americal Division. He saw no atrocities, only tragedies. Once, before Laos, his man Morse had been on point when they were patrolling triple-canopy jungle at dusk. Morse, hearing Vietnamese voices coming down the trail, had waved the platoon down and opened fire. He'd thrown a couple of frags, and moved forward with some grunts, firing from the hip. When they'd parted the brush they'd found two dead little boys, a dead papa-san, and the mama-san, hit in the chest, side, and legs wailing over the bodies. A medic had patched her up, given her morphine, but they'd heard she'd died on the medevac. There had been no weapons, packs, or VC documents on the bodies. It had happened in a free-fire zone, but that hadn't made Morse feel any better. The whole platoon had felt gutted, an attitude rarely reflected in press reporters.

Dewing resented the newsmen and gave them a hawkish line.

The reporter asked why they'd kept going back for the bodies.

"I don't believe in leaving anything American behind."

The interview was aired on the network news before Dewing's parents had even received notification from the army of his WIA status.

The medics eventually got around to Dewing, giving him a tetanus shot and X rays. A doctor returned with the X rays and said he'd been hit by a ricochet AK-47 round. The bullet had hit the ground first, lost its copper jacket, then the lead slug had bounced into his hip. He was lucky; had the round been going full force, it would have shattered his pelvis. He was carted into an operating room and the anesthesiologist strolled in—just back from a Hawaiian R&R and decked out in a beach hat and a brightly colored tourist shirt. He gave Dewing a spinal, joking that it was working when you could scratch between your legs and not feel anything. Then the doctor operated and removed the bullet. There was little pain involved and, after the quick surgery, Dewing said he was starving. They told him to wait for midnight chow, but the last time he looked at his watch before falling into exhausted sleep it was half past eleven.

The next day, he saw Keg for the last time, in bed with two tubes in his nose and an IV going. Then he was air evacked to the 67th Semimobile Evacuation Hospital in Qui Nhon. He arrived there stinking like a grunt would after three weeks in the bush without anything but drinking water, so the nurses finally taped his wound with fourteen layers of plastic and ordered him to the showers. He spent forty-five minutes under the hot nozzle. It was unbelievable. Later he sent a postcard to his grunts, addressing it to Captain "Take-the-hill" Spinning. Alpha Company had gone into the Rockpile with one hundred and twenty-two men; they came out with eighty-eight. The battalion as a whole was credited with one hundred and twenty-two NVA kills.

It was Lieutenant Colonel Sutton's 3d Battalion, 187th Infantry, 101st Airborne Division that combat assaulted into the Rockpile to replace the battered 4/3. The welcome for the Screaming Eagles was an ugly one. Echo Recon went in first, CAing to the bottom of the 4/3 CP hill which was in the process of being evacuated. Charlie Company followed them in, landing atop the hill in the middle of the Americal pullout and a mortar raid, and in half an hour they had two dead and a dozen wounded. The grunts called it Purple Heart Hill. The battalion operations officer, Major Scharnberg, helicoptered in only to be seriously wounded by mortar shrapnel.

The battalion executive officer Major Euell White, monitoring the chaos by radio, heard that dead Americans were found in the LZ from the pellmell pullout of 4/3. Artillery was directed against the area and Bravo Company went in next to CA atop a knoll west of Purple Heart Hill. Artillery pasted the jungle, the helicopters circled, arty lifted, and they sailed in.

The LZ was cold.

The next day, 19 February, an Arc Light was directed just northwest of the Rockpile and things began to quiet down in the area. For the battalion's Delta Company, the move to the Rockpile AO was mostly more of the same. They were airmobiled to relieve C Company atop Purple Heart Hill. The sheer hilltop was too small, so the CP set up atop it while the rifle platoons filed onto the fingers on patrol. The routine was set again and there were only a few times when the enemy was close, when the grunts had some excitement and could grasp at some reason for their being there. One night the North Vietnamese dropped mortars on them and Sergeant Silvers, a little red-haired guy who was sharp with the mortars, lobbed a few rounds at suspected locations. The NVA fire stopped for a while, but then more rounds whistled in and it was clear that, somewhere in the jungle, an NVA mortar crew was watching, firing, moving. One day on patrol, Delta overran an NVA basecamp moments after the enemy had hastily retreated. They found abandoned gear, food still cooking.

So, mostly, Delta Company and the others in the battalion did their work diligently, but with few results. There were bad moments such as when Captain Edward's senior RTO rotated home and Daugherty was selected to leave Second Platoon to replace him. He did not want the job; he liked the men in his platoon and had come to trust and respect Lieutenant

Stephen. He suspected the captain's abilities and felt that the job was a burden. It made each day in Vietnam go by a little more slowly. For Daugherty that was the whole point; he could see no sense in Lam Son 719. It was just another no-win operation that had to be survived before he could go home.

The enemy was the sun, the terrain, the hundred-pound rucks and the lifers who thought up the patrols. It was immersion foot, jungle rot, snakes, and scorpions. It was Lieutenant Colonel Sutton himself who broke the monotony one day when he helicoptered to the Delta CP to, as Daugherty cynically noted, "check on the morale of the troops and all those wonderful things lieutenant colonels do." As far as he was concerned, visiting lifers were a waste of time; they didn't seem concerned about clean rifles, fields of fire, or registration of artillery—only shaves and haircuts. The hassles from officers and career NCOs to clean up were a pain. The last time the colonel had dropped in, Daugherty had been in the process of growing an oversized Frank Zappa mustache and goatee. The captain bugged everyone to shave, but Daugherty'd been in one of his difficult moods so, when he'd seen the colonel get off the bird, he'd loaded his face with shaving cream and was holding a mirror in front of himself. The colonel had walked by, said hello, moved on, after which Daugherty had wiped his face clean. The captain had been pissed, but the young grunt had figured he'd owed it to himself.

The colonel had been with Delta only a short time when two NVA mortars opened up. Lieutenant Colonel Sutton immediately departed aboard his C&C, while rounds exploded on both sides of the narrow ridge the company occupied. Lieutenant Stephen could see smoke rising from the jungle. It was too close to hit with air or arty so he told two M-60 gunners and three M-16 riflemen to open fire. They poured two thousand rounds onto the spot where the NVA tubes were located and the mortaring abruptly stopped.

They debated whether to dig in or pull out until Lieutenant Colonel Sutton flew back in. He said aerial recon had spotted several North Vietnamese coming up the ridge towards them. While the officers talked, Daugherty sat with a medic from Texas shooting the breeze.

He thought he heard a pop.

He turned to the medic, "Didja hear that?"

"What?"

"Incoming!"

They scrambled for cover as the air filled with a succession of pops and explosions. The NVA finally got their range, so the men grabbed their gear and tried to outrun the shelling. They sprinted down the ridge, Lieutenant Stephen's platoon in the lead. A hundred yards downhill they hit the valley and discovered an NVA trail in the jungle. It was well used, had commo wire, and was foreboding enough for Stephen to leave three men to guard it for the rest of the company. A hundred yards up the opposite slope, they set up a hasty NDP as the rest of the company jogged up, having successfully outrun the mortars. Stephen watched amused as overweight Captain Edwards straggled in and passed out in a sweaty pile.

In the morning, they went out to retrieve their claymore mines. They were gone. The NVA had crept up, cut the wires, and taken them.

From that hillock, Delta Company continued their patrolling. Captain Edwards kept Lieutenant Stephen on point every day. He thought it was because the CO was angry with him for the antics of some of the grunts in his platoon. Sometimes, at night, they would shout, "Heyyyy, Captain!"

"What is it?" would come Edwards' nervous reply.

"Fuck you, fuck you!" the grunts would bellow, mimicking the sound of jungle lizards.

Stephen thought it was funny secretly, but told the captain he couldn't stumble around the NDP in the middle of the night looking for whoever was shouting. Edwards was not amused. So it was Stephen's platoon again on point when they stumbled into an NVA bunker complex in the valley east of Purple Heart Hill. The point man turned the corner of a jungle trail and walked right into several North Vietnamese. He opened fire, putting them to flight. The platoon quickly secured the abandoned complex—and there was shooting off and on, for the rest of the day. Some NVA strolled in at sling arms, and ran away astonished with M-16 rounds zipping past them. Three bunkers were full of dud U.S. bombs of all sizes, and in another Stephen found a crude map with the bunker complex detailed and arrows pointing to D Company's hill. He quickly radioed Lt. Mike Daltan, leading the platoon behind him, and had no sooner gotten off the horn when several NVA walked into Daltan's people.

Back at the company command post, Sp4 Daugherty got a report from Stephen's platoon, of six blood trails, two heavy and probably fatal. Edwards, all excited, told Daugherty to take point and the two of them moved alone into the brush as automatic-rifle fire popped at the base of the ridge. Daugherty walked slowly and quietly through the jungle, thinking, "This is crazy! The gooks're scattering, our guys are firing up anything that moves, and we're just strolling down into this." He came to a small clearing in the jungle, levelled by artillery, and stopped short—he wasn't about to walk across an open area during a firefight. Captain Edwards came up from behind and walked right into the clearing. Daugherty was about to call him back to cover when Edwards spun around and jumped back. He tried to hide his massive body behind a slender tree.

The captain said he'd seen a man dash through the trees on the other side of the clearing, but they held their fire, unsure whether the figure was American or Vietnamese. Daugherty thought Edwards suddenly looked very hesitant. He told Daugherty to radio the trail platoon and have the last man in their file make a noise. They didn't hear anything, confirming that the CO had spotted an NVA. But the platoon RTO said all the North Vietnamese had bugged out. Edwards, nonetheless, seemed unwilling to keep moving, Daugherty was getting disgusted with the whole thing, and he finally snapped, "If it was a gook, he's gone now."

He started back down the hill and the captain trailed behind.

By the time they hooked up with Stephen's platoon the grunts were cleaning out the bunkers. There were almost forty of them, sundecks on top of some, an underground cooking shack, and makeshift showers at a nearby stream. Daugherty was impressed with the NVA bunkers; from ground level, they were hidden amid the brush and almost impossible to see even when you knew where they were. Men began destroying the bunkers and captured gear while others followed the blood trails. A couple led to the stream and a few grunts waded in, but could find nothing. Nonetheless, Daugherty thought that the guys looked happy, content that, after weeks of humping and sweating, they had made a solid contact, come through unscathed, and had done a little good. The grunts just seemed disappointed that they had no tangible evidence of their success in the form of a North Vietnamese body to count, kick, and take pictures of.

It had been a long war for Major White, the battalion executive officer. When he'd been commissioned in '62, after ten years as a sergeant, the advisors were being sent to Vietnam in growing numbers and the career men would joke that they all would be going to Vietnam soon. White believed in the war and the Domino Theory, but to him the tragic mistake was made when the president landed the troops and Americanized the war; the Asian mind, he thought, would always beat the impatient American.

He'd gone over in '65 as an advisor to a Vietnamese Special Forces battalion in Project Delta and lasted three months before he was seriously wounded. He'd come back again as an advisor by Christmas of '67. The ARVN battalion he'd been assigned had held a party in his honor when he'd arrived. In a large tent, an ARVN officer had proposed a toast to White and the United States for coming to help the Victnamese people in their struggle for freedom against communism; he'd said that America would never let them down. When he'd finished they had called for White to give a speech, the expectation seeming to be that he would reciprocate the assurances. But, he had only felt comfortable saying what he'd felt to be true, that the Americans had come with the best of intentions and that he hoped they would stick it out—but that the U.S. government was very responsive to public opinion which, in turn, was being shaped by adverse media coverage. He had told the ARVN officers that the patience of the American people would probably run thin and the government would be forced to forsake South Vietnam.

By the time he arrived for his third tour in '71, Nixon was finally doing what White thought should have been done all along—turning off the Americanization of the war and building up the ARVN through what was now labelled Vietnamization. But, as he perceived it, the spirit was not that of success but of bucking up Saigon long enough for the U.S. to retreat with some face. It was such an incredibly different war they were fighting this time. Now the mission was to minimize casualties rather than destroy the enemy. There were some exceptions to the rule—Operation Lam Son 719 being the most dramatic example—but the battalion was mostly restricted to defensive action and local patrolling. It chafed professional soldiers to speak of anything less than aggressiveness and total victory, especially in a unit with the proud reputation of the Screaming Eagles, but battalion headquarters often got subtle messages from brigade about not taking any chances.

They were hanging it up, White mused, cutting loose and leaving Vietnam to the Communists. No one seemed to have any illusions that the ARVN had reached the point of being able to go it alone. And with that sense of defeatism, the battalion was a changed entity. White attended a battalion commanders' conference during which the brigade commander gave them a little speech about having to instill in the individual trooper an understanding of the purpose of the conflict so as to raise morale. White interjected that that would be hard to accomplish because, the way they were disposed now, the purpose wasn't even clear to him anymore. The colonels gave him irritated stares; they were good men, he thought, but he had hit a raw nerve within all of them. No one wanted to admit that there was no purpose in what they were doing. They were preparing to leave, and the Communists were going to conquer in their wake.

Despite the doubts, Major White was a professional soldier. To give less than his all, even to a losing cause, would have been a disgrace to the uniform he proudly wore and a disservice to the commanders and men of the battalion. So the war continued for him. This time around, he spent much of his efforts with two new headaches brought on by the winding down of the war: the increased number of malingerers and malcontents ghosting in the rear, and the drug problem. Heroin was epidemic in the battalion, as easy to buy as cigarettes. White was always suspicious of Salem smokers because the mentholated cigarettes were the easiest to load. He saw only one man with track marks; smoking and snorting were the norm, for heroin was easy to hide in vials and, unlike marijuana, it was odorless when smoked. The joke among the draftees was that you could take a toke with one hand and salute a lifer with the other. It was a quagmire in which he and a couple of old hardnosed sergeants did their best to catch GIs for possession and have them court-martialled. Many of those apprehended turned informant on other users and pushers in order to get easier sentences. White suspected collusion between the dopers and some of the young GIs in the criminal investigation division office; too often, records of a man's crime were lost before the trial. The major and the sergeants heard through the grapevine that there were frag threats against them. No one ever actually tried.

The drug problems in the rear spilled over into the problem of shirkers in the field. For every one-hundred-thirty-man rifle company, about ten of the men would be playing an angle to stay at the 3/187 Rear at Camp Evans. It was a constant struggle for White to round up the dope addicts, black militants, demoralized kids, and slackers and helicopter them back out to the field. The shirkers quickly found they had a confederate in the battalion surgeon. He was a young draftee, antimilitary and antiwar, who saw his job not as that of keeping up the field strength but of getting kids out of combat. White suspected that some of the slackers may have threatened him for his cooperation. A favorite trick was to complain about ear problems, whereupon the doctor captain would send the soldier on an air-conditioned vacation as an outpatient at the Phu Bai hospital for audiometer tests. He would then write the soldier a light-duty slip and try to have his commander keep him permanently out of the field. Major White asked the division surgeon to have a talk with the doctor about discriminating more between real patients and loafers, but it did not help.

The company commanders did not appreciate White's efforts; they would rather have a smaller unit they could depend on, than one beefed up with heads and nonhackers, and as soon as the shirkers started complaining, the captains usually allowed them to depart on the next resupply helicopter to pursue whatever excuse they had dreamed up this time. A small percentage of the men in the 3/187 simply did not do their jobs, but most of the problems did not extend to the grunts hunting and being hunted around the Rockpile. Considering the constant problems in the rear, White thought it no small testament that those young grunts actually in the bush, although demoralized, were loyal to each other and to good leadership, and did as much as anyone could expect of infantrymen.

Sp4 Jack Kucera was a twenty-one-year-old in Weapons Platoon of Bravo Company 3/187 Infantry. He was from Milwaukee, Wisconsin, and had grown up with little concern about the war until his third year in college. He'd been majoring in biology, not sure what he'd wanted to do with his life. When he'd sat down to think about it, he'd concluded he was only in school to dodge the draft. That had seemed an ignoble reason, so he had dropped out, allowing himself to be drafted, and had been proud when assigned to the 101st Airborne—his father had served with them in WWII. It was Kucera's service with the Screaming Eagles that shaped his new opinion on the war. During the first week of the operation, his eleven-man platoon was not resupplied. They threw their C rations into a community pile, each man getting two spoonfuls. Then they went four more days without food, until they got dizzy just standing up with their packs on. But they had all hung together during that miniature ordeal, and that kind of comradeship made Kucera think they must be doing some good in Vietnam. And if it weren't for the "candyass" protestors back home tying the hands of the government, he reckoned, the war would have been won long ago.

Bravo Company CA'd into the Rockpile area atop a hill west of Firebase Scotch. Scotch was just north of Purple Heart Hill, along the same ridgeline, and the Echo Recon platoon held the foxholes ringing it. The valley between Bravo and Echo was literally crawling with North Vietnamese; the grunts could sit in their foxholes and watch NVA on the move through the jungle. Each time, they pumped 81mm mortar fire at them and called in airstrikes—once cheering the breathtaking sight of an Arc Light bombing on an adjacent valley. At night the NVA in the valley mortared Echo Recon and sent probes against the Bravo hill. The North Vietnamese never fired, but just crept up to observe, and the GIs responded to every noise in the black jungle with a dozen grenades. Once Kucera was trying to get to sleep when he heard movement ten yards outside the perimeter; he grabbed a frag, the pin stuck, and the noise crept away down the hill. Every morning, a helicopter would drop off an emergency resupply of grenades.

On their fourth night in the Rockpile, 21 February, the NVA hit just before dawn. Scotch was blanketed with fog, Kucera watched across the valley on perimeter guard, when suddenly all hell broke loose. Green and red tracers intermingled in the mist as NVA sappers overran the hill, and Echo Recon fought to retake the position. When it was over, there were seven dead North Vietnamese amongst the Echo foxholes and several blood trails leading away in the elephant grass. The medevacs came in at first light and, true to the bravado spirit of reconnaissance units, the three men who'd been wounded hobbled unaided to the helicopter. While the Bravo mortar team stayed in position, the rifle platoons airmobiled to Scotch to sweep the perimeter for bodies and survivors. A diary found on one of the dead enemy soldiers indicated his sapper team planned to hit the Bravo hill next.

The rifle platoons, plus a Screaming Eagle sniper team, helicoptered back to the hill and every man was awake on the perimeter line that night. The snipers, using Starlite scopes, opened fire with single shots at around midnight. The North Vietnamese fell back. In the morning, the Americans swept the slopes and found blood trails. It was funny, Kucera thought, that the press always talked about inflated body counts, but in a situation like this, where NVA had obviously been killed but no bodies were recovered, 101st Airborne Division policy dictated they could claim no kills.

Soon afterwards, helicopter scouts over the valley reported a massive bunker complex and Bravo Company mounted up to go on patrol. Their two Kit Carson Scouts refused to go. Kucera decided that they were basically tough troopers but were spooked at the sight of all those NVA down in the valley; they knew full well what their former compatriots would do to them if captured. When a helicopter landed to drop off food and ammunition and pick up their extra gear, the two Vietnamese tried to jump aboard. The grunts managed to drag them off, but then they simply sat down and refused to move. The GIs then took their M-16s away and said they would leave them behind, so the Kit Carsons finally relented.

They spent three days patrolling the valley before being lifted to Khe Sanh for a rest. On the first day, they found flashlights and bloody bandages, remnants of a few nights before when Bravo had seen lights in the valley and had called in arty. Coming up another small hill, they suprised a few NVA and opened fire, but the NVA escaped into the jungle. On the second day, they happened upon an NVA high-speed trail, a fabulous construction with logs built like steps down the mountainside. They NDP'd right on it, setting up M-60s at either end. Kucera used his E-tool to scrape away a flat spot on the side of the slope so he could sleep without rolling down. Before being airlifted out, they did find the complex. They hauled many NVA packs and 122mm rockets out of the thirty abandoned bunkers. Battalion wanted the 122s extracted so the grunts had to hack an LZ in the jungle and hump the rockets to it; Kucera watched, glad he wasn't one of those fingered to be a pack mule, as the grunts cursed and humped towards the LZ with hundred-pound rucksacks on their backs, and communist rockets in their hands.

In early March, additional units were dispatched to augment the 4/3 and 3/187 scouring the hills around the Rockpile. The 2d Battalion, 1st Infantry, 196th Infantry Brigade, Americal Division operated primarily down south out of Hawk Hill on Route 1, but had been on the eastern DMZ since soon after the operation had commenced. It had been mostly quiet along the North Vietnamese front and, when ARVN units moved in to take their place, the battalion was opconned to the 11th LIB HQ at Dong Ha. The battalion commander was on R&R at the time so the exec, Maj. Hugh Peppers, set up his command post in a small hootch on the base.

The 2/1 was just getting organized for the move into the mountains when Major Peppers called the commander of C Company, Capt. Gerald Downey, into the CP hootch. He described the objectives, then said one company was to be immediately detached to 4/3 for what would probably be the most dangerous segment of the battalion's mission. Captain Downey's company had not performed as well as expected on the DMZ, and he wanted to redeem himself. He also thought that the exec was an outstanding officer who had probably set this whole scenario up to give him the chance; as soon as Downey volunteered his company, Peppers accepted. The grunts in Charlie Company were less than enthused and responded with sullen stares at Downey when he passed the word.

They were helicoptered to Vandegrift, landing precariously among the many choppers crowded on the small landing zone. They were quickly ushered off the LZ into a small depressed patch of raw earth. They were to be CA'd out that day. Downey watched his grunts flake out in the field with the foot soldiers' eternal problem of bored waiting. It was a clear blue day and the sun was savage above them, the heat sticking like paint to their bodies. It was all dust and noise around them, helos coming and going, truck convoys refueling nearby, giant M48 tanks clanking about the perimeter. The grunts sat, fatigued and bored, shed of helmets, idly smoking and talking.

Sometimes Captain Downey could only stare helplessly at the infantrymen of his company. His background certainly hadn't prepared him for the demoralized attitudes and absurdities unique to Vietnam that faced him as a combat commander. He was himself a patriotic small-town kid from California, who'd enlisted a year out of high school in '65, going from private to lieutenant in OCS, and commanding a platoon in the 101st his first tour. Now he commanded a factionalized, dispirited company of draftees and lifers, whites and blacks, heads and juicers, each clan usually grumbling against the other. He knew that, in the rear, a sizeable portion of his men turned on and a few were soldiering while supporting heroin habits. He saw no fraggings, drug use, or open disobedience in the field; the men did their jobs, but most of it was just going through the motions.

Downey could think of few times in American history when it might have been harder to be a company commander. He saw the young captains caught in the middle of the announcement of phased withdrawals, pressed from above by the lieutenant colonels and majors, who saw their career-enhancing war fading away and who were anxious to squeeze whatever combat they could out of it before they all went home, and from below by the troops, who were convinced the war was a farce that was soon to be ended, and that any more deaths were useless and wasted. Captain Downey soon discovered his young lieutenants sided with the disaffected grunts. His three rifle-platoon leaders were all competent and shared a common sense of identity, he thought. "They hated the war, misunderstood their role in it, disliked the Army and career officers, and had important plans for their futures as soon as they were shed of their uniforms. In each case they had been draftees before being commissioned."

In the field, his lieutenants often employed evasive tactics designed to look as if they were carrying out the mission while actually cutting down on the platoon's chances of bumping into the enemy.

All of which left captains like Downey, still trying to fight a war, constantly compromising between gung-ho battalion commanders and fed-up, reluctant draftee grunts. It was an extremely unpopular position. "In truth," he said, "I failed at least as often as I succeeded. On the good days everything went fine, you accomplished the mission, killed the enemy, and lost no men. On the worst of days the battalion CO screamed at you all the time, the troops were sullen and angry, the enemy kicked your behind or deftly managed to avoid your best laid ambushes, and your lieutenants were unresponsive to your orders without being insubordinate."

Downey did not feel loved by his men; he felt tolerated and reluctantly obeyed.

The doubts and hypocrisy of the situation were not only wearing down the troops, but had muddied Downey's thoughts also. He had graduated from OCS with the intention of being a professional soldier, but since then had soured on that career choice. He felt his patriotism drain at the reception his uniform received back home, was angered at the way politicians seemed willing to let American youth die for votes, was frustrated with the no-win attrition tactics of two successive presidents. And, even at the ground level in Vietnam, he'd seen enough politicking to turn him off.

For example, last Christmas Eve his company had set up in a fog-covered field in Antenna Valley, when the battalion operations officer had radioed that the Christmas Truce was in effect. This dictated that his company was to hold its position and avoid contact with the enemy. The Communists, knowing the rules the Americans imposed on themselves, had taken advantage of it. A platoon of NVA, moving to a better position, had filed right past one of Downey's platoons, the last North Vietnamese in line turning to wave mockingly at the grunts. An hour later, a perimeter claymore had exploded and Downey, unwilling to send his men into a foggy night with NVA spotted in the area just to make a possible body count, had decided to wait until morning to check it out. But the operations officer had radioed from the rear, "Check it out. We may need proof that it was a defensive action in case we get charged with violating the truce." Downey's protests had been met by the battalion commander coming on the air to reinforce the order, and a squad finally moved out into the fog, trudging past Downey with hot stares. They bumped into a party of NVA, carrying away one of the North Vietnamese. As the sergeant threw a grenade it short-fused, nearly blowing his hand off at the wrist. The medic, who raced through the no-man's-land to treat the casualty, radioed that the sergeant would lose his hand if a medevac didn't get in immediately. But the local medevac commander had grounded his birds because of the fog, and could not be reached via radio because the pilots were all at their Christmas party. It'd taken a U.S. Marine helicopter crew, defying the weather, foggy mountains, and orders not to fly, to come in and pick up the wounded soldier.

Downey had been disillusioned by such games in combat, by an army which fraudulently awarded medals to officers, by having to push kids through a war he thought they were losing. He found it harder and harder to maintain a disciplined command, when in the back of his mind he'd lost the faith. "What my men did," he said, "was halfheartedly run their missions and fail to search diligently for the enemy. My feelings about the war and its inevitable end were changing by then and I must admit that I tolerated a great deal of mediocrity in the name of caution."

Charlie Company had not been waiting long at Vandegrift when other elements of 2/1 began choppering in, and Downey watched amazed that so many helos could maneuver in such a small LZ. The op officer and two other company commanders joined him on the berm beside the LZ. Before long, a reporter and his Vietnamese cameraman appeared, asking permission to talk with the troops, and Downey pointed to the waiting infantrymen. The reporter came back a bit later and collared the operations officer while his cameraman filmed the interview.

"Major, is there any truth in the rumor that American troops are going to be introduced to the ground combat in Laos?"

"I don't know anything about that."

"Well, what are you going to do with all these troops and helicopters?"

The major shrugged, "I really can't say."

"Is is true that you are going to the rescue of the South Vietnamese who are being slaughtered by the NVA?"

Exasperated, the major locked eyes with the reporter and said, "I don't know." The man irritably motioned his cameraman to stop filming and stomped off. As soon as he was out of earshot, the officers broke into laughter, one of the captains joking, "I can see it in tomorrow's headlines—Major in command knows nothing!"

An officer from 4/3 walked over, asking for Downey, and said, "Your lift birds should be coming in about an hour. Tune into the air channel and monitor it. I'll be back with some maps in a few minutes."

They were still standing on the berm when the terrible sound of metal ripping metal screeched above the landing zone. A Cobra and a Huey had collided in midair over Vandegrift. Downey snapped up to see a torn rotor blade slowly whirling towards them and everyone ducked to the ground, except the major, who had his back to the scene. Another officer grabbed his collar and jerked him down as the broken blade flew directly over their heads, over the huddled soldiers on the low ground, over a fuel truck driving up from the fuel depot, and crashed loudly against the turret of an M48 tank.

Officers were counting heads. No one on the ground had been hurt.

Downey kept waiting, but no choppers called on the radio. It was getting dark. He had no idea where he was going, and he was worried that nightfall would cancel the CA before he had his whole company on the ground. He had just decided that, if the birds were not there in five minutes, he would not allow the lift to start, when a sergeant from 4/3 ran up, panting, and handed him a fistful of maps "Here's your maps. Your LZ is marked on the first map. The colonel says to tell you he's sorry he couldn't get this thing in better order, but you'd better get going right away."

"Fine, but where are my birds?"

The sergeant pointed to a staggered trail of ten slicks making the approach to the LZ. "Those are yours. They've been trying to talk to you for five minutes!"

"I haven't heard anything on the air channel."

The sergeant squinted, confused, then blurted, "Air channel? Hell, those ships are on the arty channel! The air channel's been compromised."

Down in the shallow area, Downey could see his forward observer standing beside the tank, frantically waving the men toward the landing helicopters. Downey told his RTO to turn to the arty channel and started towards his men, just in time to hear a pilot shout over the radio, "Why the hell have you people been on the wrong channel!" In five minutes, Charlie Company was in the air and Downey sat on the metal floor of one of the birds, trying to orient his maps, the radio tucked against his shoulder, Lieutenant Colonel Coast counselling him, "Move off your LZ about five hundred meters and go into a night perimeter. I'll call you tonight and give you tomorrow's objectives and mission. I'll do my best to get out and visit you in the next day or two."

The LZ was a level spot in the Rockpile foothills; it was a cold landing, but they lost another bird when the pilot, having hovered nervously at eight feet over the top of the elephant grass as the infantrymen leaped out, veered away too sharply and smacked blades into a tree. The rattled crew was evacuated and the grunts stripped off the two M-60s for their use. The company began hacking through the thick brush towards their hill and a FAC plane circled overhead, getting on the radio with Downey. He said he had a couple of very bored jet pilots running low on fuel, and asked if they could expend their ordnance on the ridgeline. Downey said to have at it, and the GIs paused to watch the jets shriek in, pumping rockets at nothing. There were a couple of small secondary explosions but Downey was not impressed, figuring it was probably just grenades or C4 abandoned or lost by other units passing through the area.

By seven that night, they were digging in along the slope of the ridgeline. The next few days, they made several patrols but, much to Downey's surprise, no enemy were found; it was not the dangerous mission he had envisioned. The biggest noise was a spectacular airstrike to destroy the crashed slick. On the fourth day, Lieutenant Colonel Coast helicoptered in with the water resupply and told the company to move closer to Route 9 the next day. They were to continue their daily patrolling in the high ground, and be prepared to move to the highway as a reaction force if needed. From the other slope of the mountain, they had a better view of the road and surrounding terrain. It was mountainous, highly vegetated, easily capable, Downey noted, of hiding entire NVA divisions. Signs of the fighting were all around; burnt-out trucks on Route 9, blown-up enemy bunkers, chunks of equipment and bodies. They found a jungle boot with a rotting foot in it, and a splatter of brain plastered to a bunker support.

But that's all they found.

Perhaps the tough fighting with 4/3 and 3/187 had forced the NVA in the area to retire; perhaps they were simply hiding in the jungle and biding their time; and maybe it was a little of both.

After about three weeks in the hospital, the doctor caught Lieutenant Dewing playing football in the surf and rightly decided he'd recuperated enough to rejoin his unit. At that time, he'd been going through physical therapy at the 6th Convalescent Center at Cam Ranh Bay and he only needed his lieutenant's bars and an ID card to start catching rides up north. At Chu Lai, he hitchhiked a flight out to the 4/3 Rear at LZ Bronco and spent the day swapping lies and war stories with a young GI who'd been a super troop in his platoon but was now in the rear as company clerk because he knew how to type. It was there that Dewing learned that he and Keg had been given impact awards of the Silver Star for John Wayneing the NVA bunker.

At Bronco he got a new rucksack, picked up a half-dozen machetes for the platoon, and caught a USAF flight to Da Nang. He hitched a ride on the back of an ARVN's moped to the nearby U.S. Marine compound and spent the night drinking beer with an old friend who was an engineer lieutenant there. He spent half the next day sweating in the Da Nang airport until he heard that a C130 was leaving for Khe Sanh with a load of 81mm mortar ammunition. The plane having set down on the Khe Sanh airstrip, the air force crew hurriedly shoved the pallets of ammo out and the loadmaster shouted, "Get the hell outta here!" Dewing jumped from the still moving aircraft. On the side of the strip, he accidentally ran into the battalion exec, who had a small CP set up adjacent to the airfield. They had hardly exchanged greetings when NVA shelling began and they hustled for a bunker.

Dewing managed to catch a resupply bird to his platoon that afternoon and found them in the flatlands below the Rockpile. A new staff sergeant was there. The grunts told Dewing of their latest travails: they had been in the mountains, fog had kept away resupply for six days, and they had had to rummage down old trails looking for C rat cans they'd discarded to lighten the load on previous humps. Shortly after getting back, Lieutenant Colonel Coast called him up to the battalion field CP to welcome him back. They sat on the perimeter berm and shot the bull. Coast was a very personable commander and Dewing felt proud when the colonel confirmed that he was to be decorated, saying, "There's a lot of colonels that are flying around at six thousand feet that are getting Silver Stars but, lieutenant, you can be proud of yours. You've earned it."

The infantry operations around the Rockpile had, by early March, severely tempered NVA activity in the area. Yet nothing ever went easily in the debacle-prone Americal Division. Once Dewing was listening to a radio at the 4/3 CP hill, when another unit on an adjacent ridge took fire.

He listened to the platoon leader call for artillery and get none; then he saw a Cobra gunship bravely come screaming down from a high altitude, roaring fire, and inadvertently strafe the American position because the smoke grenades they'd pitched at the enemy had blown back over them. Dewing saw the little puffs erupt on the hill at the same time the man on the radio screamed and the line went dead; a moment later, a new man came on the radio saying his lieutenant was hit. In the same period, a 101st Airborne night patrol wandered into the Americal AO and hit a mechanical ambush. The Americal troopers automatically directed fire towards them, and the ambushed Screaming Eagles, thinking they were being hit by NVA in the dark, returned the fire. Both platoon leaders called for artillery support and it took an artillery officer in the Fire Direction Center to realize that the calls for supporting arms were within a few hundred yards of each other. He radioed for both elements to stop firing and the mistaken ambush abruptly ended.

Lieutenant Dewing sat in the elephant grass at daylight, watching the medevacs go in and out.

CHAPTER TEN: Patrol Action in the Hills

To effect some type of blocking operation against the NVA withdrawing from the Rockpile area, General Hill directed Lieutenant Colonel Meyer to step up the patrolling of his 1/77 Armor at the base of the hills. The 1/77 AO encompassed the Rockpile and the stretch of Route 9 from there to Vandegrift; the tank and infantry patrols of the battalion task force made sporadic contact as the Americal and 101st mopped up. Most of the men in the armor battalion had never been in combat before, not counting mines and rockets, but they generally performed well.

The battalion had a set pattern in their AO. To cover the highway, teams of tanks and APCs were posted at intervals, camped on the side of the road. If a supply convoy were ambushed, the nearest team moved towards the firefight. Such tactics resulted in several skirmishes and the destruction of two or three RPG teams. In addition, day and night foot patrols were conducted to keep the main body of NVA at least out of 82mm mortar range of the highway. Each unit commander additionally was taxed to establish twenty-four-hour observation posts on the high ground, using starlite scopes, field radars, and other electronic devices to monitor NVA movement in the hills and to call in fire support accordingly. Fighting was only sporadic for the 1/77, but its area was infiltrated with NVA who maintained constant surveillance of all the units in the area. If a platoon consistently slacked off, didn't wear flak jackets, or man the fifties, they invited attack.

Ironically, the single most insecure place in the 1/77 AO was its base-camp at Vandegrift. Set in a lush valley surrounded by low ridges, it was subjected to almost daily 122mm rocket raids, but the more telling danger came from the North Vietnamese sapper teams that lurked in the area. At least twice they penetrated the perimeter to blow up equipment and raise general hell, and there were numerous other shooting incidents. The perimeter consisted of only some culvert-and-sandbag bunkers and a single roll of concertina wire; what was worse was that the soldiers manning it were generally unenthusiastic rear-echelon support troops from various XXIV Corps and USARV units. One of the sapper raids occurred before dawn on 1 March; the battalion command sergeant major, Roy Nelson, was in the CP bunker when a gigantic roar lit the sky and shots cracked from the perimeter. No one was willing to move for fear nervous sentries might shoot them. In the morning, Sergeant Major Nelson joined Lieutenant Colonel Meyer to inspect the damage and determine where the NVA had infiltrated. Dug-in fuel bladders containing forty-five thousand gallons of JP4 and ten thousand gallons of diesel had been blown up; burnt enemy equipment indicated that one of the NVA had gone up in his own explosion. Meyer and Nelson talked to the perimeter guards; they were young draftees, lackadaisical, not particularly interested in what was going on. Although they weren't flagrant about it, it was obvious to Nelson that they were pot heads. One of the men said he had seen two NVA creep through the wire and dart past his bunker. Nelson asked why he hadn't done anything and could only shake his head when the GI said he hadn't wanted to give his position away. The sergeant major was taken aback; the soldier hadn't even taken the time to alert anyone. He might have been too stoned.

Such problems with inexperience, and lack of motivation and discipline, also intruded, upon occasion, on the field performance of the battalion. Sp4 Spurgeon accompanied one five-man patrol on a ridgeline overlooking Vandegrift. It was a miserable day. The grunts wearily trudged through the mist and cold, using cigarettes to burn away the leeches that dropped on them from the wet leaves. The sergeant leading the patrol was a shake'n'bake who must not have wanted trouble with the men because, when they stopped for the night, he posted no guards and simply sat down to start a big fire and talk the night away. Eventually Meyer overflew the patrol in his C&C, saw the fire, and ordered the whole patrol extracted that night.

Lieutenant Colonel Meyer was a staunch disciplinarian who came down hard on the problems he saw. Once, he and Sergeant Major Nelson drove up to inspect a lone tank outpost outside Vandegrift, and found no one out on the ground to watch for the marauding RPG teams. Meyer shouted for the tank commander, held a Field Grade Article 15 and busted the man from staff sergeant to sergeant. On another field inspection, Meyer was riding a tank to one of his line companies and monitoring the radio. First he heard the GI at a company outpost radio the captain to warn him that the battalion commander was coming, then the captain radio all of his tank crews to get into their helmets and flak jackets. Meyer's standing order was always to wear the body armor in case of ambush or booby-traps, but as it was a hot day, the young captain was letting his grunts flake out. Meyer didn't need a subordinate who, by feeling sorry for the men, would get them killed; as soon as he reached the CP tank, he told the captain, a West Pointer, that he was relieved of command.

On the whole, though, the 1/77 Armor performed the job at hand. A hard line commander, not well liked by his men, Meyer was, nonetheless, a good leader. He often accompanied his troops on their armor and foot patrols, enduring the dangers and field conditions of his grunts. Sergeant Major Nelson, who had been wounded four times on a previous tour with long-range reconnaissance patrols of the 9th Division, thought Meyer a fine officer and that the men, lifers and draftees alike, performed professionally in the field. The drug and race problems which had exploded at Quang Tri were shoved beneath the surface; they were not completely gone, Meyer knew, but, given a viable mission for the first time, the young draftees were doing their jobs. And, Nelson noted, for all their bitching, most of the grunts did not balk at their new hardships. After weeks of finagling with XXIV Corps, Nelson managed to get a shower and laundry sent up to Vandegrift, only to discover that he had to order the grunts to use it. They had a reputation to uphold and they prided themselves in their raunchy, dusty appearance as a sign that they were not REMFs or FNGs.

Sometimes reporters would come to Vandegrift and Meyer would explain what 1/77 Armor was doing. Most did not seem interested, Meyer remembered. "I had reporters seek out other units than mine because my troops were just doing their duty without any of the race and dope problems that made stateside headlines. They went looking for problems elsewhere."

Working simultaneously to hunt for the NVA in the hills around Khe Sanh, Vandegrift, and the Rockpile, was P Company, 75th Infantry (Rangers), 5th Division. A small, elite unit, Papa Ranger worked in six-man teams and conducted seven-day operations. They had to carry enough food, water, and ammunition to last the week because, once inserted into the jungle, their only contact with other Americans was by radio. Their mission was to patrol for the NVA rocket teams and to lay ambush on NVA trails. Their success depended on stealth; therefore, they received no resupply in the bush because a hovering helicopter would pinpoint their location to the enemy. And because they did not have the security of a thirty-man platoon, the six-man teams had to be resourceful and daring if they were to win. Every man was a volunteer and if someone wanted to transfer out, he could do so anytime.

One of the men who embodied the spirit of professionalism in Papa Ranger was Sp4 Harry E. Walters, Jr., an eighteen-year-old from Lebanon, Pennsylvania. His father had made a career in the army because of hard financial times and as soon as the young Walters had turned seventeen he too wanted to sign up. He'd dropped out of high school and gone in three days after his birthday, his father having agreed to sign the enlistment papers only if he took the teletype-repairman option so he would have a trade when discharged. Walters had said sure, had volunteered for the infantry within a week, and then had reenlisted to get to Vietnam. His father had been slotted for a second tour there, but his son's volunteering had automatically disqualified his father for another year in the war. When he'd hit the 5th Mech in December, 1970, he had immediately volunteered for the brigade ranger company. As for the war, Walters had been soured by the cities where it seemed most of the Vietnamese were just out to rip off the GI; but in the bush, where he could see little village children with hardly any clothes and ribs sticking out from hunger, it had made him feel America must be in Vietnam to help. Walters was young, athletic, motivated, and exactly what the rangers wanted.

Walters was in a team which had been dropped into the Khe Sanh mountains on the first day of the operation to guard the advance force. They had seen no NVA, but now, with the increase of activity around the Rockpile, they were going back. Walters and his five partners boarded a Huey; a Cobra and a Kiowa Scout flew escort and, as they lifted from the Quang Tri strip, other rangers threw the thumbs-up sign. The first night, they heard an NVA mortar being fired and, taking a guess at the location, the team leader called in artillery. In the morning, they came upon some fresh tracks on a thin jungle path and the leader decided to follow them. They filed silently down the NVA trail, especially alert, for the enemy couldn't be far ahead. Walters ruck was kicking his butt as they labored up the ridgeline, and he slipped, the barrel of his rifle jamming into the mud. They stopped for a quick breather atop the crest and he tried to scrape the muck away with a stick; the point man joked that if they did catch the dinks, ". . . just say, here's mud in your eye." They kept moving through the thick brush on the spine of the ridge.

A burst of AK-47 fire suddenly startled Walters back into reality.

The three rangers ahead of him disappeared from sight in the bushes, and he immediately hit the prone, levelled his M-16, and fired at the chattering sound of the AK. He didn't know exactly what was going on and it amazed him that his mind was really a million miles away as his trained reflexes had him calmly firing and changing magazines. He wasn't thinking about what he was doing, the situation not yet registering in his mind, the sound of his own rifle strangely seeming far away.

It was Walters's first firefight.

The first sound that clicked in his mind was that of the team leader scrambling back from the point, yelling to throw grenades and fall back. They ran back thirty yards before realizing there were only four of them there—the point man and RTO were missing. Two of the rangers fired blindly through the foliage at the NVA, while Walters and the team leader waded back through the heavy vegetation to find their people. They began calling their names but no one answered. Walters spotted the RTO's ruck and radio sticking from the bush on the side of the hill, and shouted to the team leader that no one answered him. "I think he's dead!" He scrambled down the hill and grabbed the pack, but no one was in it. The team leader followed him down and crouched in the bush calling for air support on the radio. They kept shouting names and, finally, a nervous reply came. It was from the point man. Walters ran towards the sound and found the man lying in the grass, splattered with blood. A graze wound over his eyebrow poured blood, and a dozen AK rounds had stitched across his waist—all of them, miraculously, hitting an ammunition bandolier and doing no more than scaring hell out of the soldier. Walters began helping the point man up the hill, when he heard the RTO yelling from the top. Walters was wildly relieved (he had gone through basic training with the man) and answered with, "Get your ass down here and help me!" It turned out the RTO and the point man had not answered because they had heard each other in the brush and each had thought the other was an NVA.

They were struggling up with the wounded man, when more AK fire splattered nearby. The assistant team leader ran through the brush towards the NVA, and fired a LAW right into them. It must have been an NVA mortar team they'd bumped into, because the rocket explosion set off a chain reaction that made them think the whole top of the hill was going up in smoke. Helicopters were overhead and a pilot directed the team to a bomb crater a couple of hundred yards down the trail. While a Cobra shot in low to lay down cover fire, a slick lowered a jungle penetrator and they hung tight as the bird lifted them up and out. An airstrike followed their departure.

Other rangers met the helicopter when it dropped them off at Quang Tri—they always monitored the radio reports of their comrades—and they made sure to visit the wounded man in the hospital. Said Walters, "We never abandoned anyone in the field. Dead or alive, if six went out, six came back. Always. The leadership in P Company was superb, the morale, camaraderie, courage, and dedication of our people were unequalled. As far as drug abuse, fraggings, racial friction, and combat refusals, they were nonexistent in Papa Company. As far as I'm concerned, my association with the men of P Company Rangers was one of the best experiences of my life."

Two men from Papa Rangers were killed on a mission near the Rockpile. They were in a different team from Walters, but they were friends and he didn't want to talk about it. Sp4 Spurgeon, however, was there. He'd been tagging along with a 3/5 Cav platoon when, one night, a helicopter came in, lights off. It deposited five rangers, in camouflage paint and bush hats, and Spurgeon was surprised to see that a buddy of his, a short guy with glasses and the nickname Recon Smitty, was one of them. Smitty had wanted to join the armor snipers, but Spurgeon had talked him out of it because he was still new; so Smitty had turned around and volunteered for the rangers. He was very excited about his new unit and told Spurgeon it was his first mission.

The next morning, the rangers moved out into the jungle and, almost immediately, there was a burst of automatic weapons fire and shouts on the radio. By the time the cav platoon got there, the shooting was over. Only two rangers were still on their feet. They said they'd walked right into an

NVA unit; the lead North Vietnamese had dived for cover as they had, but the second NVA had stepped forward with an RPD machine gun and shot down the three men at the end of the patrol before they could get down. Two Americans were KIA, one WIA, and the enemy had vanished.

Spurgeon helped carry out one of the dead men. It was Recon Smitty.

Back at the 1/77 bunkers at Vandegrift, Spurgeon regaled the snipers with an exciting version of what happened. When he got to the part about Smitty getting shot in the face, one of the men, a Mexican-American named Felix, suddenly snarled to cut the bullshit. Spurgeon took offense. He shot back, "You know and always have known how I've operated and how I talk, Felix! I'm not glad Recon's dead. Just because I'm not crying now, doesn't mean I wasn't crying up in those hills when you or anyone else wasn't there to see me! He was closer to me than anyone else because I met him first; he was my security first. I talked him out of the snipers for the very same reason we're talking about him now. I carried his goddamned body and loaded him onto the bird, for God's sake!"

Felix looked down and muttered that there was more to it. He was just so goddamned sick of Spurgeon's fanatic zeal.

"Felix, you and I and everyone else who's a sniper ought to be prepared for things like this. We're volunteers, goddammit, we're fucking killers. That's our fucking job! Recon volunteered for the Rangers, he's dead, tomorrow one of us will be dead. We volunteered! If you can't take it, Felix, transfer to the mess section or be a truck driver. For God's sake, go back to being a supply clerk. Wilds went back to driving a tank with his old outfit, Bravo Company. We're still friends. No one's going to laugh at you. We're sure as hell not laughing at Wilds."

Felix was crying, but he stared at Spurgeon with hate.

He grabbed Spurgeon's collar, twisted it in his hand, pulled him towards him. Spurgeon grabbed Felix's collar, and they stared into each other's eyes. Spurgeon let go first. Felix walked away. Spurgeon stood there, suddenly aware of his furiously pounding heart.

At the same time that the Rockpile was being fought over, the 3d Squadron, 5th Cavalry, under Lt. Col. Robert B. Osborn, was enduring its own struggles—mostly against the terrain and the weather.

The 3/5 Cav had been tasked to construct the pioneer road from the Rockpile to north of Khe Sanh, as an alternate route to the main logistical base in case Route 9 was blocked. Working in tandem with the brigade's A Company, 7th Engineers, construction began on 30 January. C Troop patrolled the eastern starting point. At what was to be the western anchor of the pioneer road, Captain Stewart's A Troop had previously secured a patch of rolling hills surrounded by thick jungle. Although Alpha was isolated, the NVA did not hit them. (Their most serious problem occurred when they began running perilously low on C rations and ammunition. Stewart reported this to Osborn, who helicoptered ahead with ten cases of C rations. That was not nearly enough, so First Sergeant Bradley took four APCs with trailer hitches to Khe Sanh. Through persuasion or thievery, the gruff old sergeant returned with three hundred cases of C rats and crates of ammunition.) On 8 February, the engineers, with B Troop providing escort, linked up with A Troop. Lieutenant Colonel Osborn set up the squadron command post in the clearing Alpha had secured; the command vehicles went into wide trenches, the cooks put up a mess tent, and the engineers bulldozed a berm around the camp. Since the CO's nickname was the Wizard of Oz, the basecamp was christened Emerald City and the pioneer road became the Yellow Brick Road.

The official name was the Red Devil Drive, and using it was a shaky venture; one lane and muddy, it was carved right into the sides and tops of mountains, virtually straight up and down at some points. The entire area was forested ridgelines, and the 3/5 Cav took to the hills to conduct patrols to keep the NVA away from the road. The North Vietnamese did not make a show of force against the pioneer road, but they were out there. The first night after the rendezvous, Alpha Troop split into platoon laagers and Captain Stewart was on the radio with his lieutenants, making sure they set up strong NDPs. Squadron and brigade policy dictated that positions were to be constructed at dusk to avoid observation by the enemy; Stewart thought that was bullshit and ordered his men to set up while it was still light. That gave them time and light to set up well and to hell with the NVA seeing them, he thought, because, if the RPG screens, trips, and claymores are well situated, he can't get through. That night the NVA hit the NPD of Lieutenant Boyd's First Platoon; no GIs were hit, and in the morning, they found two or three dead North Vietnamese outside the wire.

Sometimes at night, the cav men could see 122mm rockets flashing from their tubes, and would fire their Sheridan tanks at them and call in artillery. Other times they could look through their nightscopes and, seeing NVA pilfering their old positions, would direct in more arty. The NVA usually stayed shadowy. Sgt. Louis Forrisi was with a platoon of the

3/5 patrolling a valley between Emerald City and the Rockpile nick-named the Punchbowl. He wrote in his diary: "Our first day in the Punch Bowl was to search for another of these phantom NVA artillery spotters that higher-ups say are calling rounds into Khe Sanh. So someone gets the idea he's in a group of trees in the middle of the place. . . . Khe Sanh is miles away up in the hills and here we are far below it on a valley floor. But we are ordered to assault this treeline. The lieutenant plays the game by lining up the platoon and letting go with everything we have for about five minutes. After this show, we dismount and walk through what is now a burned out bunch of trees and all that's there is two dead snakes. Every night we move to one of the three positions the engineers prepared for us while they were cutting the road at the beginning of the operation. The ground surveillance team is with us constantly now. And then radar picks up movement every night, but at long ranges. So we lob a few mortar shells in that area and find nothing there in the morning. Every day we'd patrol a different area of the Punch Bowl, checking out the woods or under the culverts the engineers put under the road to prevent washouts. The night went by quietly. It was like the war didn't exist."

But the war was always waiting and watching, and men died. One of them was Sp4 Steve Warner; he was killed in action on 14 February 1971, days before he was to rotate home. Two weeks earlier, on the first night of the op, Hq&Hq Troop had stopped at the foot of the Rockpile, the APCs running to recharge their batteries and the night defensive position hastily set up so they could move quickly. Sgt. Charles W. McKenzie, Jr., a twenty-two-year-old draftee from Salem, Ohio, who worked on the TOC track, was more than nervous that night. He could remember as a kid hearing his father and the other WWII veterans sitting on the back porch telling stories, so he'd tried to soldier well in Vietnam, avoiding the drugs and discontent—but he had only two weeks to go in-country and the Rockpile had a bad reputation. Sp4 Warner introduced himself that night—he was a small, bespectacled man with the Information Service Office, USARV. He sat down with McKenzie and a couple of other GIs to ask them questions and shoot the breeze. An Ernie Pyle type, McKenzie thought, an experienced guy with a personable manner that put you right at ease. Warner opened his pack, stuffed with pistachio nuts, Slim Jims, Kool Aid, and such and they sat talking, eating, and drinking Cokes. McKenzie felt his anxiety drain away.

Two weeks later, McKenzie was sitting in the TOC APC with a couple of radiomen as Lieutenant Colonel Osborn bullshitted about a previous tour where his helicopter had been hit and had had to autogyrate down. McKenzie was just waiting for transport back to Dong Ha to process home. Word came over the TOC radio: Alpha Engineers and 3/5 Cav escort hit in an RPG ambush while laying a culvert over a mountain stream. Two Americans killed, three wounded. An APC pulled into camp and it hit McKenzie like a weight when someone dropped Warner's fantastic pack into the dirt and said that the army photographer was dead. All McKenzie could think was: man what a stinking waste. He was glad Warner's body was not in sight. Osborn picked up the broken camera, splattered with blood; he threw it to a GI standing there and told him to clean it up so Warner's next-of-kin wouldn't have to see it like that, then told an officer to make sure an Army Commendation Medal Citation was written up. Then the colonel sat back down and, to McKenzie's disgust, nonchalantly continued with his war story. A bit later, a major landed in the C&C bird and ushered Sergeant McKenzie aboard. McKenzie slumped in the seat with his gear; this was his last day in the Vietnam bush.

The firefight on the night of 28 February was the worst one Sgt. Larry White ever experienced. He'd enlisted in the army a naive seventeen-year-old from Kentucky and had ended up in Germany. Then he'd reenlisted—he was so gung-ho to get to Vietnam. Now he was a nineteen-year-old buck sergeant commanding a Sheridan tank in Alpha Troop 3/5 Cav. The eight weeks he'd been in Nam, so far, had changed him. Whatever sense of glory he'd been looking for was not easily found, but what was obvious was that most of the guys didn't give a shit about blowing grass in the field, the war, or the lifers. Before long the frustration and bitterness had eaten into White also. He was introduced to marijuana, and his new philosophy could be explained in the squadron's favorite piece of helmet graffiti, STAY HIGH AND KEEP LOW.

Sergeant White was in Lieutenant Johnson's platoon but, since Lieutenant Kincer's Third Platoon was undermanned and alone, he was dispatched to them. He hooked up with them at around three in the afternoon and joined their circle of vehicles, three Sheridans and six APCs, on a small elephant grass-covered hillock. At dusk they posted guards and sacked out around the vehicles. Lieutenant Kincer walked around to each vehicle every ninety minutes to check on things.

It was just another night.

White was sleeping in the grass beside his tank—when an explosion jolted him to his feet. He awoke to instant bedlam: men screaming, tripflares shrieking up, fifties and sixties sweeping the wire around them like some sustained Mad Minute. The North Vietnamese were assaulting their little perimeter. White scrambled barefoot to the top of his Sheridan, screaming at the driver to get out of the commander hatch, and jumped behind the fifty. He could see shadows darting in the tall elephant grass and he joined the roar, pounding out rounds. His loader jumped into the turret to slam shells into the breach, as White fired the main 152mm gun with his TC override control. The driver crouched on the back deck, firing an M-79 grenade launcher. White shouted at the gunner to stay topside and the GI knelt behind the turret, breaking open crates of .50-caliber ammunition.

Jesus, it's a nightmare, White thought, firing wildly at shadows and muzzle flashes. Rocket grenades whooshed by, exploding inside the perimeter. Another RPG screamed in from the right and burst through the turret ring. The explosion sent shrapnel burning into White's legs and feet; and the main gun, radio, and electronics on the tank instantly shut off. He glanced down inside the turret. The loader was slumped over, an arm blown off, his head caved in, brains splattered on the metal around him. Another shriek, and another RPG smacked into the Sheridan, this one from the left. The gunner screamed; White saw him jump off the back deck, tumbling as he landed, and then noticed the man's foot lying on the deck, pulsing blood. The driver, a little new guy, dropped his M-79 and bolted, diving headfirst into a mortar pit for the duration. White heard someone running towards his tank and turned to see Lieutenant Kincer coming to help—he suddenly disappeared in an exploding RPG round. When White opened his eyes, Kincer was down with an arm and leg in tatters. A medic jumped on his tank. White was bleeding but in no pain and he shouted, "Go to the lieutenant!"

He didn't know Kincer was dead. He kept shooting.

Forty yards to his right front, the darting shadows suddenly came into focus and he could see three North Vietnamese rising up from the elephant grass. They wore green fatigues and sandals, one was toting an RPG launcher and the other two had extra rounds and satchel charges. A second later, two more NVA popped up on the left and White didn't even have time to think as he pulled a long sweeping burst across them with his fifty. He saw the bodies fall back, the bullets punching them like baseball bats. A sixth NVA emerged from the grass, drawing back to throw a satchel charge, and White blew him away in turn.

For thirty minutes the little hill was a cacophony of weapons, shouts, and flares, until gunships streaked in, strafing the edge of the perimeter. The NVA attack faded away and White noticed the empty ammo boxes and expended brass and links piled around him. He'd fired ten thousand rounds. When the sun came up, the medic bound his superficial shrapnel wounds. Several North Vietnamese lay dead in the brush and wire. White was bitter over his gunner and loader, and when he saw the driver, he exploded.

"You no good sonuvabitch," White screamed, "Get out of my sight or I'll blow your fucking head off!"

"I'm sorry," he said quietly, "I was scared."

"So was I. Keep your fucking distance from me."

A Loach landed in the battered perimeter and Brigadier General Hill and Lieutenant Colonel Osborn stepped out. They walked about, talking to the grunts, saying that the numerous blood trails indicated they'd defeated a numerically superior enemy force, "Outstanding job, men." The whole nine yards, White thought, the lifers are just eating this shit up. He was standing there, filthy, sweaty, his feet bandaged, and Hill stopped to talk with him for a few minutes. "Good job, trooper, we'll see a citation written up, and don't worry about your tank, we'll have it fixed in no time." White simply said, "Yes sir." But he was raging inside: Well, what about my people? Loader's dead, gunner's crippled, they were damn good friends, you gonna fix them? We're expendable, he surmised, like a can of C rations you use once then throw away. It was a shocking new thought to him: Nobody gives a shit about you lifers being out here. His only concern was that their presence might draw fire.

The next day, an M88 dragged White's gutted Sheridan back to Emerald City. He had just dismounted when a sergeant major was shouting in his face to shave, clean up, put on his jungle boots.

"Well, I'll tell you what, sergeant major. We've been out for weeks. Ain't got no soap, ain't got no reason to shave. Gear's fucking blown away by RPGs. Main gun's down, radio and electronics is down. My crew's fucking wasted. And you want to start telling me about shaving?"

The sergeant major patted him on the shoulder, "Young sergeant, don't you worry. I will get you some gear." He got on the radio, a helicopter came in with parts, and the sergeant major hustled the mechanics over. It took three days to piece the tank back together, and White was sent right back to the field, since his wounds weren't serious enough for a medevac.

The skirmishing around the Yellow Brick Road continued at a sporadic pace, and eventually the brigade's Papa Rangers were inserted into the mountains. Sp4 Walters's six-man team was helicoptered to a small knoll carpeted with elephant grass where they set up an observation post and put booby-traps out around them. These consisted of frag grenades, the fuses screwed out and replaced with smoke grenade fuses which went off instantaneously, rigged with trip wires. Their first day went by quietly, and Walters sometimes found himself forgetting where he was, taken in by the sweeping beauty of the mountains.

In the morning, two rangers went out to retrieve the grenades.

Walters was getting his gear ready when a grenade suddenly boomed and AK-47s opened up. The four of them jogged downhill, tree to tree, and found the other two men at the prone, one wounded, firing into the bushes straight ahead. They shouted that they had four dinks. Walters crouched behind a tree, shooting at the muzzle flashes, until they noticed that the NVA fire had stopped. They cautiously walked down at a crouch, still firing. Two North Vietnamese were sprawled dead in the bushes. They set up a hasty perimeter, found a blood trail, but pursued it with no results. The team moved back to their hilltop with their wounded man, who had shrapnel in his leg and back. He'd been hit, it turned out, by their own booby-trap—when he'd seen the four NVA walking towards him, he'd started to run back, but his foot had snagged the trip wire.

A helicopter came in, taking the wounded man and dropping off two boxes of ammunition and a ranger lieutenant. The teams were usually extracted after contact, since the NVA then knew the location of the six men, but the lieutenant said that the area was hot, and higher-ups wanted the contact pursued. They were getting organized for the patrol when one of the rangers spotted three NVA five hundred yards away in the valley below their hill, walking unaware in an open area. The team's M-60 man shouldered his machine gun, took slow aim, and squeezed the trigger. Walters watched the tracers burn into the group, saw two of the NVA collapse and the third sprint for a treeline. The rangers laughed and patted the gunner on the back, calling him a damn good shot, while the lieutenant brought artillery to bear on the grove into which the NVA had disappeared.

The team spent a second night on the hill.

In the morning, they were scheduled to be picked up, and three guys were picking up their M-16s to make a quick walk around the slope to secure the LZ for helicopters; then they all abruptly heard swishing on the hillside. Instantly they dropped side by side in the tall elephant grass, weapons on full auto and trained at the approaching sound. Walters canted his head to get a better view through the thick grass and saw a bare head bob into view ten yards away; he was walking up the hill right to them. It was the NVA point man.

He could see the man's eyes.

The team leader cut loose and, just that fast, Walters was pumping rounds, the North Vietnamese point man in his sights slamming to the ground.

The NVA patrol fled without firing a shot.

The rangers quickly fanned out, finding two bodies and a blood trail. One of the NVA had a Chinese or North Vietnamese pocket manual, complete with photographs of U.S. vehicles, crosses marking the spots most vulnerable to rocket-propelled grenades. At the same time, a platoon from the 3/5 Cav appeared at the base of the hill, and a foot patrol beat the bush to the top. They got geared to follow the blood trail. The cav point man looked gung-ho; the cav lieutenant must have trusted him because he insisted his man walk point. They pushed off down the hill, the grunt on point, followed by his lieutenant, the ranger team leader, Walters, and the rest of the rangers and grunts.

They filed through the high grass, then came to some thick brush a hundred yards out. They started pushing through, uncomfortably crouched over. Walters was coming through the bramble when a sudden grenade blast pulsed his adrenaline; then M-16s and AK-47s dueled in sharp bursts. He scrambled forward. The point man was down with shrapnel. Walters joined the shooting, but the firefight dried up in a minute. The point man said he'd come upon two NVA carrying a wounded man, but one had spun and tossed a grenade. They searched the brush, finding a dead North Vietnamese and a blood trail. They were getting ready to pursue, when an explosion echoed from the hill; the cav lieutenant got a radio call from his vehicles that some NVA had snuck in and cut loose with an RPG. They moved quickly back to the grassy knoll, where medevac and ranger extraction helicopters came in.

The results of those three days were two GIs wounded, against seven North Vietnamese killed and two wounded. These American soldiers were still winning their part of the war.

But not all of the men were rangers; the troop commanders in the 3/5 Cav had their share of difficulties in leading the reluctant draftees. Captain Stewart of Alpha Troop was a case in point. Sergeant White, for one, respected Stewart's leadership, but there were a minority of GIs in the troop who were generally surly and unresponsive to orders. The grunts of the 3/5 rarely made contact but, when there was a firefight, it always seemed to happen to Alpha. The men had developed a salty, don't-tread-on-me attitude so, when their captain was relieved of command, Stewart inherited an already rebellious situation. Some of the grunts did not adapt well to Stewart's all-army attitude.

And the drug problem didn't help.

The GI who had tried to balk, the first day of the operation, fell apart in short order. He began suffering through heroin withdrawal, and had to be kept under guard on the platoon leader's track because he seemed crazy enough to go for a grenade. A helicopter finally ferried him away to the drug amnesty program. He was released in a week and ghosted in the rear, despite Stewart's repeated attempts to have him returned to the field. The GI finally came back—for one day, before he helicoptered back to Dong Ha on a complaint he filed with the inspector general. Stewart could not court-martial the man for drug use because he had voluntarily surrendered to the amnesty program. Stewart did, however, catch a second addict going through withdrawal and filed charges against him.

About two weeks into the operation, the troop got their first batch of mail. First Sergeant Bradley sorted it out and found a package addressed to a mechanic on the maintenance track who was a suspected drug pusher. Stewart and Bradley called the young GI to their APC, gave him the package, and mockingly requested him to open it right away. Inside were some cans of food—and a test-tube-size vial of white powder.

"Hey," the mechanic blurted, "I don't know what that is, sir!"

Stewart said they could either send it in for chemical analysis to see if it was heroin, or destroy it and forget it. The GI opted for the latter, and Stewart walked over to a small bonfire where men were drying out clothes and poured the powder in. The GI visibly cringed as he watched his heroin go up in smoke.

A night or two later, Stewart was asleep when an explosion woke him. No shooting followed, so he shrugged back to sleep, thinking a sentry had fired an M-79 at the shadows on the perimeter. In the morning, he saw the shrapnel gouges from a grenade in the side of his APC and realized that he'd been fragged. He didn't know whether it was a warning or a serious attempt on his life, nor could he prove who was responsible. He was convinced, though, that the smack freaks had done it for disrupting their heroin supply. He assembled the troop, stared at the GIs on the maintenance track, and snarled, "You guys better get me next time because I'm going to kill you myself if you don't. It won't do you any good, anyway, because the first sergeant's going to look after me."

First Sergeant Bradley stepped forward to say damn right.

Captain Stewart rotated home, unscathed, in March. Scuttlebutt said that someone later tossed a frag at Bradley; it only served to make the gruff sergeant angry, and he also went home in one piece.

Those certainly were not the only fraggings. The 3/5 Cav had a bad reputation for such activities. Every time units rotated to the rear, there were threats and scare frags; searches through tents and bunkers would turn up grenades hidden in milk cartons. One night the sniper squad was put on the roofs of the 3/5 Cav Rear in Dong Ha to deter marauders. It was this atmosphere which helped one bland private first class to attempt to kill Capt. Wayne R. Young, the commander of Bravo Troop. Near the end of the operation, Captain Young rotated into Third Platoon, the poorest in the troop. True or not, the rumor got around that they had been scheduled for a rest break in Emerald City or Khe Sanh, but that Young had volunteered them to stay in the bush.

Three heroin addicts bitched the night away in their APC, about how Young had cancelled several resupply missions so they could keep pushing for the dinks, how he'd volunteered them for more shit, how they should frag a lifer like him. One of them, the bland pfc, took the talk to heart. He was—and it was the word that came first to his mind—irritated. A tough firefight they'd been through, the cold weather, rain, mud, the lack of hot food and baths—it was made all the worse by the perceived callousness of the captain. Conditions had simply reached an unacceptable point for the young soldier. He did not consider trying to talk with Young, for he didn't think the captain would listen; and the fragging talk of his buddies acted as a catalyst in him. The pfc was going with the flow when he took three claymores that night, wired them under what he thought was Young's APC, then unhesitatingly set them off. The floor of the APC blew open. In the ensuing scramble, it was discovered that Young was in a different track; the platoon mortar track had been destroyed, and four GIs sleeping nearby had been wounded. The unspooled detonation wire led directly to the APC of the three junkies. They were put aboard a helicopter for court-martials, the private charged with attempted murder, the other two with conspiracy to commit murder for urging him on.

The would-be fragger ended up in Long Binh stockade, and was interviewed by the reporter Linden, who wrote: "The magnitude of what he attempted still escapes him. At one point before his trial he looked up and asked naively, 'Look, wouldn't it save everybody a lot of trouble if I took a Section Ten {discharge in lieu of a court-martial} and went home?' Later, after he was convicted of attempted murder and sentenced to ten years at hard labor, he was asked how he would have felt had the claymore mines he had rigged actually killed his CO. {He} said, 'I'd have been tickled pink.' {He} is a passive man, easily impressed by the impulses of his peers. He seems to have no strong convictions on any matter, not even his own fate. Murder is generally associated with ruthless people driven by desperation or greed, and not with lackluster men . . . who cannot comprehend that what they attempt is murder. Murder was not in his heart, it was in the air, and what he attempted is more aptly described by the Army term for killing: to neutralize. Bland, affable {he} is a typical fragger."

There were even more. After Sp4 Spurgeon extended his tour he was sent to Charlie Troop 3/5 Cav on the Dong Ha bunker line. He noticed that the draftees in Charlie hated their lifer first sergeant for pushing them too hard on trivial police calls and shining boots when they were in from the bush. One night Spurgeon was sitting atop his Sheridan when someone broke in on the radio. The sound of an exploding claymore blasted through the speaker; then a GI came on the horn laughing, "Did ya hear that? Ha, ha guess who that was? Ha, that's right, baby!" The first sergeant was medevacked with a limb blown off, and the next morning the captain held a troop formation and called the fragger—whoever he was—a cowardly swine.

As Linden put it, murder was in the air. For example, White knew of a sergeant and his new crew who had pulled a short stint of perimeter security at the Khe Sanh airfield. The sergeant was sitting on his tank one afternoon, writing a letter, when an ARVN ran from the other side of the vehicle, a case of U.S. C rations under each arm. He fired a warning shot from his M-16 but did not halt the fleeing ARVN. He put his second round in the thief's back.

The ARVN died instantly.

There was an investigation of sorts. When the sergeant was asked if he'd really done it, he grinned, "No way, Top."

"I don't give a fuck what you tell the MPs, troop," the first sergeant growled, "but don't lie to me. Did you shoot that gook?"

"Yes, sir, I did."

But nothing really came of the investigation.

It was like hide and seek. Weeks went by when platoons in the Punchbowl and along the Yellow Brick Road would never see a single NVA; then out of nowhere ten or fifteen minutes of terror, called contact, would erupt. And even then, they usually never saw their foe. One morning late in the campaign, Sergeant White was in the lead Sheridan, an M88 towing a disabled APC was behind him, and another Sheridan brought up the rear. They were heading east on the Yellow Brick Road towards Emerald City, escorting the downed track out of the Punchbowl. Without warning, a North Vietnamese sprung from the elephant grass thirty yards ahead and, before White could swing the fifty around, let go with an RPG and dropped back down. The round missed his tank by feet and exploded against the driver's hatch of the M88.

The two Sheridans opened up with their fifties and 152mm main guns, aiming at sounds in the thick grass. AK-47s and RPGs cracked back at them. The wounded M88 and attached APC rolled back; then over the embankment. Two mechanics climbed out and ran up to the Sheridans. It was an eternity of perhaps five minutes before help arrived, a platoon from Alpha Troop crashing in at full throttle. They raked the roadside with fire, and the NVA faded off. The new captain, Stewart's replacement, was with them and it was White's first look at him. The look did not inspire confidence; the captain was prematurely bald—his helmet had been lost in the brush—he had horn-rimmed glasses and looked sweaty and shaken. He looked like an FNG. They made a quick dismounted patrol off the road and found a blood trail. Then a party of GIs climbed down to the M88 to recover the dead driver and salvage gear from it. White unhooked the .50-cal while a couple of grunts lifted the driver out. He was a gory mess, arm and face charred, splattered with blood, his scalp opened in an ugly slice that exposed the skull.

The next morning, White had his tank in a trench on the Emerald City berm line. He was relaxing, sipping a beer, when the new captain came up and snapped, "You stand up and salute when you talk to me—and get rid of that beer."

White followed orders, hating the games.

Lieutenant Boyd took over as troop exec, and later complained that he had had to run Alpha because the new captain would constantly commute to the rear and take extra R&R leaves.

And so it went for the men of the 3/5 Cav in their skirmishing around the Yellow Brick Road. It was the scene of some successes by the U.S. ground troops committed to the operation; also of some disasters. Lieutenant Christian, West Point '69 and executive officer of Bravo Troop, had the sorry experience of eavesdropping on one of the debacles. Early one day in February, he picked up the troop's payroll at Khe Sanh and helicoptered a ride to the First Platoon under Lt. Steve Overstreet. They held the middle position of the Bravo line in the Punchbowl. Night was falling by the time he finished handing out the MPC notes, and Christian had the choice of paying the troops and staying overnight with either Second or Third Platoon. He had commanded Second when he'd first arrived in Vietnam, many of his men were still there, and the new platoon leader, Lt. Bob Allen, was competent. Christian felt safe with them. On the other hand, Third Platoon had a bad reputation for heroin and incompetence (for example, one GI in the platoon, mishandling a case of C4 explosives, had totalled an APC, killing three GIs and wounding four in the process). Their platoon leader had been injured on the first day of the operation when his APC threw a track, rolled on its side, and the fin on a loose mortar round split open his calf. A lieutenant took command. He too had a bad reputation, having been relieved of command earlier and shuffled away to another job. Since Bravo Troop was short of officers, Lieutenant Colonel Osborn had elected to give him another crack at commanding a platoon.

Lieutenant Christian decided to play it safe and hitched a ride to Allen's platoon. After paying the troops, he sacked out on a litter beside a track in the Second Platoon laager. It was around four in the morning, when Allen shook him awake and said to follow him to his command track, so they could monitor the action—all hell had broken loose on the little grassy knoll held by Third Platoon.

They sat in the APC, listening to the chaos on the radio.

North Vietnamese were in the perimeter wire, two Sheridans and two APCs were ablaze, and Lieutenant Overstreet, whose platoon held an adjacent position, was trying to scream sense into the Third Platoon lieutenant over the radio. Overstreet had his 81mm mortar crew pump HE and illumination shells around the embattled platoon, and radioed the troop commander for permission to crank up and haul into the firefight. The NVA would probably be waiting in ambush for such a move, so permission was denied. On the hill, confusion abounded. The lieutenant refused to leave his APC, so the platoon sergeant took command. The sergeant was hit, an RPG round penetrating the turret of his Sheridan, the explosion blowing off the gunner's head and the sergeant's leg. But the sergeant remained calm, tied his belt as a tourniquet around his stump, and stayed on the radios, trying to direct return fire and bring in artillery around the hill. The squad leaders scrambled from hole to hole around the perimeter, trying to get the terrified troopers up to return fire.

On their own accord, the NVA faded back into the night.

In the morning, Lieutenant Christian took an M88 recovery vehicle to Third Platoon to help get their downed vehicles back to Emerald City. He caught up with the platoon along a jungle trail, halted because a Sheridan in the lead had thrown a track and the crew was repairing it. Christian asked among the soldiers what the hell had happened; it turned out just to have been a continuum of foul-ups. Squadron policy was never to stay in one spot longer than two days, but the lieutenant had been lazy, had complained to the captain, and had received permission to stay another day. Even though this meant the NVA probably had his platoon under observation, Jones neglected to register his 81mm mortar around the perimeter. And for some reason, the lieutenant did not trust claymore mines and, despite the advice of the platoon sergeant, did not employ them. The results of this were one GI killed, seven wounded, two tanks and two tracks burned out by rocket-propelled grenades, and the demoralization of the platoon. A heavy blood trail had been found in the elephant grass, and the frustrated officers in squadron headquarters decided no one could have lost that much blood and lived. They reported one NVA confirmed killed.

Christian was so upset that he jumped off the M88 and stomped along the halted column looking for the Third Platoon lieutenant. No one knew where he was. Christian finally found him sitting on a rock in the middle of a jungle stream, dangling his feet in the water. He looked so distraught that Christian turned around and left without saying a word other than to tell a trooper to take his M-16 and cover the lieutenant in case the NVA reappeared. The good news was that the man was relieved of command a second time and sent to a rear job in Dong Ha. The bad news was that the courageous platoon sergeant, who lost his leg during the firefight, died in a hospital ward in Japan.

Sometimes, though, the grunts had their vengeance.

Working off of the Yellow Brick Road on the second day of April, Lieutenant Allen's platoon had its revenge for the casualties Bravo Troop had suffered. At around four in the morning, a GI with a Starlite scope on the perimeter spotted an NVA patrol north of them on a hillside trail. There were about twenty of them, walking single file, noisily griping their way through the brush, seemingly convinced that the night belonged to them. Allen radioed his troopers to hold their fire until the NVA saw them, or until they were close enough to ambush. A grassy field of some five hundred yards separated the platoon's position from the NVA column; and when they walked into an open spot, the night erupted. The 152mm main gun on a Sheridan tank fired a flechette round which sent ten thousand razor-darts scything through the North Vietnamese; in the same instant, the 81mm-mortar crew began dropping illumination shells and the troops opened up with their fifties and sixties, raking the now starkly lit hillside. In the morning, the grunts picked among the corpses, finding enough severed arms and legs and mangled torsos to claim a body count of nineteen. Sergeant White was monitoring the radios at Emerald City when the report came in. A North Vietnamese unit had been massacred; not a single American had even been wounded. It was the best feeling White had ever had in the field. It was just so damn good to win sometimes.

Working in coordination with the 1/77 Armor and 3/5 Cav in keeping the NVA off balance was the 1st Battalion, 61st Mechanized Infantry (Lt. Col. Arnold Stallman). They worked the furthest east during the op, mostly in the grassy hill country around the Cam Lo Bridge, Dong Ha, and the eastern DMZ. Stallman's 1/61 TOC was a concrete bunker at a muddy knob of a firebase called Charlie Two, situated between Dong Ha and the DMZ. A sister firebase called Alpha Four (known as Con Thien in the days of the Marines) was a bump in the rolling hills to the north. The battalion did not work as a single command; A Company was sent to Vandegrift and C Company to the Rockpile, opcon to 1/77 Armor, while B Company was the reserve at C2 patrolling the Z and the muddy roads that connected the firebases. On occasion the companies rotated assignments.

The grunts of the 1/61 Mech were as reluctant and fed up as any soldiers of the time. Their most recent source of bitterness had come from a foot patrol during which a sergeant in Alpha Company had gotten lost leading a night ambush patrol. They'd walked into an old Marine minefield outside A4; four GIs had been blown apart, one seriously wounded, and only the sergeant had come through the night physically unscathed. That had been around Christmas time and the mood of the battalion could be read in a slogan written on a track at Alpha Four: SANTA IS DEAD.

Nevertheless, the battalion continued to perform its mission.

One of those who served was Pfc Michael J. DeAngelis, an assistant machine-gunner in Bravo Company. Age twenty-two, from a middle-class family in Hartford, Connecticut, he had taken his draft notice with a mixture of pride and relief. His father had fought in WWII; and DeAngelis had gone to Vietnam in October 1970 with a belief he never lost: that it was America's role to help people who wanted to be free. He also had gone with a piece of advice stuck in his mind. A buddy of his had been a Marine grunt and, when DeAngelis had been on leave prior to departing for Nam himself, the ex-infantryman had given him three codes to survive by: No one likes a new guy so keep your mouth shut and do what you're told. Don't let your mouth write a check your ass can't cash. And, the key one, pick out the best grunt in the outfit and follow his example. "If you survive the first three months," his buddy had told him, "only bad luck will kill you."

When DeAngelis rotated into Bravo Company, he stuck with Sgt. "Wolf" Garet, his nickname from the fact that after eight Dear Johns in Nam, he still had seven girlfriends left. The young sergeant was a brave, dependable man with plenty of bush sense. What Tarzan was to the jungle, DeAngelis thought. And he reckoned that, if Garet was the best, most of the grunts were at least giving it their all. The problems arose mostly in the rear. The three line companies rotated for standdown at the 1/61 Rear in Quang Tri every two weeks, or whenever the combat situation allowed. They would come in at night, shower, shave, get clean uniforms, and soak up the mess hall beer and steaks. The next day was spent cleaning weapons, repairing APCs, and being inspected; then mounting out back to the field at four the next morning. If the standdowns were a time to relax, they were also two days of heated friction. The most prevalent was between the grunts and the rear-echelon lifers. The REMFs seemed afraid of them, DeAngelis thought, as if they knew that pissing off a grunt could result in a vengeance grenade. But they hit them with a harsh regimentation of uniform inspections, police details, shaves, saluting, haircuts, and all the rest. DeAngelis thought the process was to make them hate the rear so much they'd want to get back into the bush, and he resented the ploy as chicken-shit.

Even Bravo Company fell upon itself in the rear. DeAngelis was lucky in that he stayed away from the dope and was easy-going enough to get along with almost everybody. He could stand back and watch. He saw four factions in Bravo, two of them were mean as snakes. The Chicanos and American Indians were a friendly bunch, but the blacks stuck together and had a militant core who cruised around purposely looking for trouble. They were the most violent. There were rednecks, rough factory kids and farmboys, who listened to C&W, got blind drunk, and loved to harass "them niggers." And there were the heads, who usually just wanted to avoid all of the fights and indulge in marijuana. The camaraderie was strange, DeAngelis thought; those who were close were brothers, and the rest hated each others' guts. One USO show in the EM Club turned into a race riot among the 1/61 REMFs. He was convinced that if the hatreds had been allowed to boil long enough in the rear, some of the grunts would have killed each other.

But all of the troubles ended the moment they drove past the Quang Tri wire. The common denominator, he surmised, was hating Charlie and taking care of each other. Even the most militant of the blacks packed away their prejudices, took some solace in falling into tight-lipped silence around the whites, and soldiered with the best of them. There were no drugs in the field. One of the company pot heads was on DeAngelis's track. His nickname was Pockets because he kept everything he owned in them, and he was an original Haight-Ashbury hippie who'd been caught up in the draft. He hated the war but, in the bush, he was a man you could count on.

DeAngelis even considered the leadership in Bravo to be good. The captain was known as Jungle Pimp, after his initials, and he worked with a good mixture of careful planning, caution, and assertiveness. The platoon sergeants also used good judgement. None of the leaders needlessly risked their lives, and even the battalion chaplain went on patrol with them. They were all heroes, DeAngelis thought, but they cursed the war and bitched and the word hero was something they would never have chosen for themselves.

Bravo Company and the rest of the battalion adhered to standard mech-infantry procedures. Each day became a repetition of the one before. The company was assigned ten grid squares on the map to search for a week, and they split up into the four corners of the AO. The tracks established platoon laagers, guards were left behind, and the grunts fanned out on dismounted patrols, usually sweeping out less than a mile before returning. When they travelled mounted, the deltas followed in each others' tread marks to avoid mines. If they took fire, the entire column immediately wheeled about, laid down return fire, and charged, chasing off the NVA.

On most days, nothing happened.

Nights were the hairiest, and construction of the NDPs followed a careful routine. They moved just prior to dusk so the NVA couldn't fix their positions and mortar them at night; the GIs quickly broke into preassigned groups to unload the APCs and set up. The tracks formed a circle in the elephant grass, platoon and mortar tracks in the center, RPG screens in front of each vehicle with engineer stakes; rocket grenades would explode against the fence allowing only shrapnel to spray through. In front of that, each track crew wired several claymores, some of them booby-trapped with grenades to deter NVA sappers, who were adept at crawling in and turning the mines around to face U.S. positions. Around the whole setup a spool of concertina wire was staked down and, thirty yards out from that, trip flares were stuck in the ground with wooden stakes, taut wire zigzagging from flare to flare.

Between each track, the grunts dug two foxholes, claymore firing clackers unwound to the holes, one man awake at all times between each APC. They brought the M-60s into the muddy holes with three thousand rounds per gun. Before dark the gunners would study the terrain, then stick branches into the dirt in front of their holes to indicate terrain features, so even in the pitch black they could fire without sight simply by touching the barrel against the stick that indicated the area at which they wanted to fire. Even if the infantrymen were filthy head to toe, the weapons and ammo were cleaned and oiled and laid across C rat cardboard to keep them out of the dirt. They usually didn't have Starlite scopes, so when the wind rushed through the elephant grass they would sit, nervous and tense, the grass above their helmets, unable to see even their hands, the noises playing with their minds. To keep the NVA similarly off-balance at night, Bravo deployed MAs and ambush teams.

On most nights, nothing happened.

Even so it was numbing and exhausting, DeAngelis thought; the men always seemed to be sleepwalking. Yet, for an untested, middle-class kid like him there was some good to be salvaged from the experience. It was his first real test, and in his mind, he had passed.

DeAngelis never considered himself a very lucky person; as far as he was concerned, he used up all of his luck in the war—for instance, the time he was in the showers at C2, but it was the mess hall that took the rockets; or the time the AK-47 round, meant for his back, was deflected by a little tab of metal inches away from him, while he was firing the M-60 on his track. He thought his transfer saved his life. DeAngelis, who had junior-college training in mechanics, was sent to D Company, the battalion service outfit, located at Quang Tri. He spent his time at OJT, learning to maintain the tracks in the motor pool, and to hate lifers. They were pigs, he thought, never satisfied with anything, always hassling someone. "Lifers are like flies," was the draftees' joke, "they eat shit and bother people."

The mechanics were often dispatched to Charlie Two, where the overriding problem was the living conditions. The firebase itself was simply a bare earthen mound, covered with bunkers, surrounded by wire and mines. Bunker life was austere; ramps had to be built in them because the bottoms were swamped from the monsoon and had become home for rats and snakes. They pulled guard duty atop the bunkers to avoid the rats, but even when they lay wrapped up in a poncho they could feel the things scurry over them. Some GIs were bitten and, when a rat crawled into a man's sleeping bag, they declared war. They put C ration crackers on a berm; then, using a red-lensed flashlight to spot the approaching rodents, they nailed them with M-16s. By morning they had thirty-five rats stacked up.

The next biggest problem was the North Vietnamese Army. Almost every day, fifteen or twenty 122mm rockets thudded into C2, sending almost everyone leaping for bunkers. DeAngelis could look from his underground shelter at some of the bravest men he'd seen; the firebase artillerymen who manned their guns during rocket raids to return fire.

On occasion there would be a need for the men to go to the field to tow in destroyed APCs or to walk the morning minesweep patrol between C2 and A4. The problem was not how to scrounge up a volunteer, but which one to pick, since almost every man would step forward—a sign of dedication which DeAngelis thought the lifers were not impressed by. The most lonely feeling he ever had was walking point on the muddy road in the cool, misty morning, with nothing but wet fields of elephant grass and three APCs following several hundred yards behind. Field duty was all a matter of chance. Once DeAngelis's track went to Vandegrift to tow a downed APC back to Charlie Two. He was waiting to cross the Cam Lo Bridge on his way back, when some APCs roared up from the opposite direction, headed towards Vandegrift. They stopped, asked if DeAngelis had just come from the west, and shook their heads in amazement when he said yes. They said that it must have been the tracks right behind him that had been RPG'd; then they continued their dash to the trouble spot.

On 24 February, word came down that the Delta Company mechanics were going to convoy to Vandegrift to handle the damaged vehicles there. They were sitting in their cots in a bunker that night when a young staff sergeant nicknamed J.D., one of the few lifers DeAngelis liked, collected a bunch of C ration apricots and ate them. That was a bit of bravado on his part because a battalion superstition was that apricots led to ambushes and rockets and injuries; but DeAngelis's warning, "Why tempt fate?" was met by J.D.'s cynical response, "That's a crock of shit." In the morning, they were packed up to leave for Vandegrift with Bravo Company when Charlie Company rotated back, weary and filthy and towing several APCs. J.D. left DeAngelis and three other mechanics to handle the new wrecks, then departed with the Bravo tracks.

Three days later, these four took an APC down Route 9 and made it to Vandegrift without a shot being fired. As they pulled inside the wire, DeAngelis shouted to the sentry, "Is this the right road to Hanoi?" The GI laughed. Sappers had been shot in the wire, the night before, and he could see one of the North Vietnamese corpses lying stiffly against an earthen berm. His legs had been blown off. A few GIs were gathered around, laughing as they switched legs around on the dead man so he looked pigeon-toed. Vandegrift was a noisy, dusty place with traffic roaring in and out, but it struck DeAngelis that most of the GIs seemed to be just milling around, trying to look busy.

They shut down in the motor pool and asked for J.D. Instead they got a bad story. The soldiers there said that, a couple of mornings back, they'd been sitting around boiling some sunrise coffee, while J.D. had stood shirtless on the lowered cargo ramp of an APC, shaving out of an upturned helmet. A couple of 122mm rockets had dropped in from across the perimeter. The GIs had scrambled inside the track, but J.D. had stayed put, laughing at their timidness. Then another rocket had exploded near the motor pool and J.D. suddenly had fallen to his knees, doubled up. He'd grabbed a flak jacket and had pressed it against his stomach to hold in his intestines. The men had quickly hauled him all the way inside the track, and he had been medevacked as soon as the shelling had stopped. After the operation was over, DeAngelis returned home briefly on an emergency leave and on his way back to Vietnam, visited J.D. in a Washington state VA hospital. He looked bad, had a cane and a colostomy bag, but was in good spirits. They joked about the apricot jinx, and J.D. said to tell a staff-sergeant friend of his that he still wanted the ten dollars he'd won in a card game the night before he was wounded. DeAngelis didn't have the heart to tell him that the sergeant had been blown away in another rocket attack.

Tragically, the worst shelling the 1/61 Mech Infantry took came after the operation was over and they had rotated to Charlie Two for a breather. They were lining up for chow at dusk when the rockets started whistling in and the men scrambled for cover. Men crammed inside the nearest bunker, one which doubled as a beer hall—then a single 122mm rocket made a direct hit on the sandbagged roof and, in one screaming flash, twenty-nine GIs were dead.

It even made the papers.

CHAPTER ELEVEN: Convoy Duty on Route 9

The primary goal of the American ground operation was to maintain Route 9 as a viable supply line to the ARVN invasion force in Laos. In this mission, they were successful. The needed materiel got to the front and Lt. Gen. William J. McCaffrey (Deputy Commander, USARV) could rightfully record with pride, "The support of the operation was one of the major logistical feats of the war. The equivalent of more than four divisions received supplies that travelled, for the most part, over a single road and into a single airhead."

The task facing General Sweeney and the Da Nang Support Command was monumental. Most of the materiel was moved by truck and the final tabulation of traffic monitored on Route 9 during the operation came to 1,163 U.S. convoys (20,995 vehicles) and 621 ARVN convoys (22,858 vehicles). A thousand vehicles a day hit Route 9.

But there were many difficulties that surfaced, and the problem-solving began in earnest on 7 February. That morning General Sweeney telephoned Colonel Richard Morton, commander of the 8th Transportation Group at Qui Nhon, informing him that at 1400 hours an L23 would arrive at his base. Morton was West Point '49 and winner of the Silver Star and three Purple Hearts as a lieutenant in Korea. He was disgruntled, having pressing problems in his own area to contend with, and had no idea what could be so important in MR1. He took his sergeant major and a major with him. It was a brisk evening at Quang Tri when they checked with Colonel Konopnicki at HQ, 26th General Support Group, SUPCOM. In the morning, Sweeney arrived by air and the three commanders got down to the business at hand.

"It was from Konopnicki that I discovered the real reason for my presence," Morton said, "it was that the highway for Lam Son was in shambles and getting worse. Our highers in USARV and MACV had been obsessed about leaks concerning the operation and had limited their planning to only the highest staff officers at both headquarters. Accordingly, no one who really worked on the plan had spotted that the weak point was the paucity of surface transportation assigned to the gigantic task."

For the next two days, Sweeney, Konopnicki, and Morton heli-hopped throughout the AO in Sweeney's helicopter—from Camp Eagle, Vandegrift, Khe Sanh, to Lang Vei—talking with commanders and enlisted men. A firmer picture of the problems plaguing the supply line began to emerge. Route 9 from Dong Ha to Vandegrift was a two-lane, all-weather, paved surface where convoys could average twenty-five mph. A few sections had been washed out in the monsoon and had yet to be repaired, but the major problem lay in the thick elephant grass which flanked the difficult leg of the highway. NVA ambush teams could infiltrate through the heavy foliage and open fire on convoys from only a few yards away. Colonel Morton tried to get an engineer Rome-plow company to level the underbrush, and to have combat units assigned sectors along the road to prevent ambushes. He was unsuccessful on both counts, receiving no explanation why engineers were not dispatched, and being told by infantry commanders that the battalion operations pushing the NVA into the countryside were a more viable answer than falling back on the highway itself.

From Vandegrift, the highway turned into a one-lane dirt road which twisted to the Laotian border, and only allowed convoys to crawl along at eight mph. The physical adversities on this leg of Route 9 were many. The road was hemmed in by underbrush and was subject to ambush, particularly at the makeshift bridges. At some points, the roadside fell into hundred-foot ravines and was without guard rails; many trucks and cargo trailers plummeted off the side. The dirt was composed of red laterite clay which quickly pulverised into a fine dust, two feet deep in places, which rose into great clouds and made driving a very real hazard. They called it the "Khe Sanh Red" and it worked its way incessantly into noses, hair, eyes, mouths, food, drink, engines, and weapons.

Perhaps the most frustrating aspect of travelling the dirt path of Route 9 was caused by the ARVN convoys. Because the road was one way, convoys had to be coordinated carefully and when the South Vietnamese were given the choice of when they wanted to run their supply trucks, they chose most of the daylight hours, leaving the nights and the NVA to the Americans. "Conference after conference failed to get ARVN to yield one second of their times," Morton said. "I was most unhappy about how little our own highers knew about this situation and what little pressure they put on ARVN to change."

At that early point, the only U.S. transportation units making the run were the six truck companies of Lieutenant Colonel Alvin Ellis's 39th Transportation Battalion. Morton was most impressed by Ellis's performance: "He was a first-class commander who got the job done under woefully inadequate conditions. Al frequently led the convoys in person from Vandegrift to Khe Sanh and return." The supplies were pushed through, but the battalion has suffered accordingly. Morale among the truckers was low; the 666th Truck Company had a driver refusal, and the company first sergeant was later fragged. Trucks were burned out. The clouds of red dust had done most of it. In interviewing battalion drivers, Morton thought that they hated the dust more than the enemy; it was their only topic of conversation to him. At Quang Tri, SUPCOM sent the 2d and 63d Maintenance Battalions out to work on the problem and, Morton remembered, "Within two weeks of my arrival you could not put another vehicle into their compound. My deadline rate which averaged five percent in Qui Nhon soared to 35 percent in Quang Tri. The curses of the drivers who lost their vehicles to laterite and had to be taken to the maintenance battalion echoed far and wide. Lam Son needed fresh truck assets and needed them yesterday or even last month."

Thievery between units for parts and vehicles became rampant.

On 10 February, Maj. Gen. Walter Woolwine (Deputy Commander for Material, USARV) arrived at Quang Tri and plans for recovery were shaped up. General Sweeney was to return to Da Nang to supervise the convoy movement along Route 1 from there to Quang Tri. Although Colonel Morton was technically senior to Colonel Konopnicki, the latter had been on the scene longer, was more familiar with the problems at hand, and was to be the local logistical commander with his 26th GSG HQ in Quang Tri. In conference, Woolwine, Sweeney, Konopnicki, and Morton agreed on a six-point plan to revamp the flow of supplies to the ARVN:

1. despite the strain it would put on the logistics in MR2, the HQ, 8th Transportation Group would move to Quang Tri to work in tandem with HQ, 26th GSG
2. also bearing in mind the problems it would cause in MR2, two additional truck companies would be shifted north
3. another battalion headquarters would be moved to work with the 39th
4. ten armored gun trucks would be dispatched to escort convoys
5. seventy-five five-ton tractors were needed to compensate for the maintenance shortfalls
6. fifty fifteen-ton semi-trailers would be moved in to replace losses

By 20 February, the situation along Route 9 began to improve. On or about that date, Colonel Morton's headquarters arrived via C130. Also brought to the scene were fresh drivers, new equipment, and gun trucks. The second battalion to join the 39th was the 57th Transportation Battalion of SUPCOM, commanded by a black lieutenant colonel named Frank Francois. The two battalion commanders were well respected by the logistical commanders: Francois working hard to get the supplies from Da Nang to Vandegrift; Ellis working equally hard to continue the chain to Khe Sanh. The convoys went well protected by MP vehicles, some APCs, and most importantly, the gun trucks. They were an example of battlefield improvisation which had developed because simply mounting a machine gun, as per army regulations, did not protect a thin-skinned truck. The solution was to reinforce a five-ton truck with steel planking (some had APC hulls fitted atop the bed); then put three or four soldiers in the cargo bed, arming them with whatever could be scrounged together—.50-calibers, grenade launchers, numerous M-60s, even an occasional minigun. All of the gun-truckers were volunteers. If a convoy was ambushed, it was the gun truck which hauled into the fire, engaged the enemy, and extracted the truck drivers. The sight of gun trucks in a convoy probably deterred many North Vietnamese ambushers along Route 9.

Nevertheless, problems abounded. The truck convoys began meeting the requirements, but could not always unload at their destinations. The problem was with forklifts; as Morton recounted: "Forklifts require a skilled operator, spare parts, good mechanics, etc. If you are missing any one of these ingredients, you are doomed to failure. The entire chain of command endeavored to solve the forklift problem by rushing more and more forklifts to Quang Tri, Vandegrift, and Khe Sanh. Khe Sanh was a case in point. The number of operational forklifts there in mid-February was eleven. We must have hauled in twenty or more over the next two weeks. But, on March 1 or so, the number of operational forklifts was still eleven. As a result, many of my trailers were arriving at the airhead and there they sat for days or even weeks. A loaded trailer just sitting is a tremendous waste; we began taking fifteen-ton semi-trailers from everywhere in Vietnam and even Okinawa."

This problem occurred at Quang Tri also, where trailers full of ammo sat crammed and waiting at the Ammunition Supply Point. One night in February, an NVA sapper team successfully infiltrated the base perimeter and sent several tons of ordnance sky high.

Through it all, the truckers kept hauling the supplies, enduring bad driving conditions every inch of the way, and occasional bouts with rockets, snipers, and ambushes. The official assessment of the casualties of the Da Nang Support Command and 504th MP Battalion along Route 9 was 11 killed, 55 wounded, 14 fatal traffic accidents, and 68 nonfatal accidents.

Once a week, Lieutenant Malmstrom and one of the checkpoint MPs would race their jeep down Route 9, making it within sight of Vandegrift in under twenty minutes. They would be out to look for any stalled trucks, and would time it so they could see Happy Hour, the rocketing of Vandegrift which happened almost every night at around five to seven. Malmstrom had not taken any incoming at Khe Sanh and felt sorry for Major Butler and Lieutenant Doyle, especially Doyle, who'd picked Vandegrift precisely because he'd already seen enough action. Whenever he could, Malmstrom hitched rides on convoys between Khe Sanh and Vandegrift, to keep his map updated on where the road had been widened or where bad turns were, so he could better brief convoy commanders. He also went to advise the officers on any problems that might develop, but usually everything went smoothly and he just sat and sweated out the ride.

Along the route, Malmstrom would usually see a few abandoned trucks, a five-thousand-gallon fuel tanker crashed at the side of the road and burnt out, and the gutted shell of an APC, its rear ramp blown off and junk scattered around it. Communications were poor, so he didn't know if the vehicles had been blown away three days or three years before. Either way, when they drove past, he had the tendency to tighten up on his flak jacket, finger his M-16, and look down the column of trucks to see if everything was okay.

Malmstrom was lucky; none of the convoys he was on drew fire.

As far as he was concerned, the worst enemy was the terrain and the elements. At night fog covered the road, cutting visibility down to zero, and the drivers had to concentrate every inch of the way. When it rained, the mud road literally turned to red ice. On a hot day, Route 9 was a blizzard of red dust, sun glare magnifying the problems of maneuvering the twisting, narrow road. There was no good time to drive. Some trucks missed turns and Malmstrom organized the wrecker crews to drag vehicles up and to medevac truck drivers with concussions, broken bones, and bad cuts. Once, at the checkpoint, a GI was doing maintenance under his truck when another truck bumped his. Malmstrom hefted him into a jeep and they sped to the Khe Sanh medical bunker, where he was immediately taken out by helicopter. Malmstrom didn't think the GI would make it; his head was literally crushed like an egg.

What impressed Lieutenant Malmstrom the most about duty on Route 9 was the good morale and hard work of the soldiers involved. It was just the opposite of what he was accustomed to at Cam Ranh Bay. It was an odd truism of Vietnam 1971 that the farther away from combat, the worse morale became. Cam Ranh Bay was one of the safest places in the country and Malmstrom couldn't imagine spirits going any lower. Drugs were the biggest problem. When the battalion chaplain sent out an anonymous questionnaire, 25 percent of the men said they smoked heroin daily and an additional 20 percent smoked marijuana and opium. The leadership was no help; he saw two lieutenants smoke grass, heard rumors of a captain on smack, and knew most of the older NCOs carried around bottles. Malmstrom thought most of the transportation corps officers were divided into two groups; easy-going managerial types who cared more about efficiency than about troops, and hard-core ex-infantrymen. Out on convoy, the draftees were without much supervision and grew resentful of authority; there were a few scare fraggings on battalion commanders. A lieutenant Malmstrom knew had an M-16 jammed into his stomach by an enlisted man enraged at his attention to discipline. Racial friction was another quagmire. Two sergeants in Malmstrom's company hated blacks and refused to promote them. The blacks grumbled openly, and the battalion commander ordered Malmstrom to promote several qualified blacks over qualified whites. The next night, one of the sergeants appeared at the company orderly room, drunk and complaining. There were unending scuffles between the races which erupted one night in the EM Club; the blacks slowly moved to the back, the whites gathered up front; then a person or persons unknown chucked a WP grenade through the front door. Malmstrom drove to the emergency room to find a doctor pouring water onto a friend's stomach which was burning with white phosphorus.

Disgusted with the war and the army, some of the young officers at Cam Ranh Bay even refused their end-of-tour medals.

Malmstrom saw no such problems at Khe Sanh. He didn't have time to look for dope among the troopers, he thought cynically that the men hadn't set up their dope supply line yet nevertheless, it never disrupted the work at hand. In the convoy staging area, the truckers were always ready to help; if someone needed maintenance. Everyone cooperated to get the job done. When ARVN hung around, asking questions about vehicle repair, the GIs showed them what to do. When it came to the convoys, they drove in all conditions around the clock, fighting sun glare and veils of dust in the day, and fog banks at night. Sometimes the GIs only got a few hours of sleep under their trucks before Malmstrom roused them at three in the morning; they would climb unhesitatingly back into their trucks and head out to get more supplies. He thought they did a great job and, as far as Malmstrom was concerned, the logistics of the operation would have fallen apart if not for the daily endurance of the GI and ARVN truckers, who braved treacherous roads and bad weather day after day to get the goods in. Maj. George H. Chase would have been the first to agree with such an appraisal of morale. He was a New Yorker who had served as a young officer in Korea and was recalled from reserve status in 1967; in Vietnam he was made the information officer of the Da Nang Support Command. With eleven combat correspondents, Chase hopped between the various SUPCOM units at Da Nang, Quang Tri, Dong Ha, Vandegrift, and Khe Sanh, taking photographs and doing stories. There were numerous outfits spread out along the Quang Tri front, from POL fueling pits, ammo supply points, helo slingloading pads, mechanic workshops, convoy units to the main area at Khe Sanh, designated FSA-II under Maj. Charles Lutz.

The men had a job to do, Chase was proud to report, and they were performing superbly. He knew things weren't perfect: he heard one story of a truck going off the road and ARVN pilfering it at gunpoint. He knew that mama-sans were selling dope in plastic baggies, and he had to relieve some men for drug use. But those were not the stories that Major Chase did; his view was that the civilian press was covering the troublemakers, that it was the military's job to report on the majority of dedicated soldiers who did their jobs without recognition. He and his crew wrote the good news stories to show SUPCOM's professionalism—for instance, the time when General Sweeney and his sergeant major helicoptered, starched and polished, into the dust bowl of Khe Sanh to chat with Major Lutz, make an inspection tour, and pin a Bronze Star on a young, mustached, grease-splattered staff sergeant for his hard work as a maintenance man (the sergeant's comment: "I was damn sure surprised. I was just doing my job like everyone else up here."). Chase hitched rides on several Route 9 convoys and a truck driver was quoted, "We have put on beaucoup miles, but no one seems to mind. There's a reason behind it all. We understand that and it makes a lot of difference."

Chase was greatly impressed by the hard work of all involved, and his major disappointment came in trying to get the civilian press corps to take an interest. The reporters he saw ran the spectrum from big television names, to small town newspapermen, to freelancers trying to make a career, to a few old-fashioned muckrakers. He had limited success with them. Once he had ABC-TV News lined up to do a story on the convoy runs, but they cancelled at the last minute; the morale of the GIs seemed to dip for a moment after that, Chase thought, as if they figured no one really cared. Chase knew enough about journalism to understand the problem. Reporters had to follow the dictates of their editors who knew that, by 1971, a headline like GIs GET SUPPLIES THROUGH ON ROUTE 9 didn't sell papers, but GIs FRAG OFFICER did. Many of the reporters seemed to have preconceived notions on the "evil" of American involvement in Vietnam, and their minds were made up as to what type of stories they would pursue. Sometimes Chase became so frustrated he confronted reporters and told them that what they were doing was a disservice to the nation.

Every man had his own version of what was really happening.

Another convoy was forming up at Da Nang for the run to Khe Sanh, and the men waited, exhibiting a variety of emotions—some calm, others excited, a few almost shaking with nervous fear. It was blistering hot and most of the truckers waited in the shade of their vehicles as forklift crews filled the truck beds. Some of the GIs lit up to mellow out for the ride. Sp4 James Brock of the 23d MP Company, Americal Division, was not alarmed by the dope smoking; he was there to provide convoy security, not to chase pot heads. It didn't matter anyway, he thought; a few of the MPs also used grass, most drank, but it never interfered with their job in the field. Besides, if they were to be measured by their outward appearance, he surmised they would not have measured up; the smell of dew was in the air and almost everyone, including Brock and the MPs, had long hair, mustaches, and peace medallions, while the truck drivers had flak jackets emblazoned with logos like "FTA" or "Is this trip really necessary."

But the men got the job done, Brock reckoned, and that's what counted.

They finally pushed out with about forty supply-laden trucks, plus three MP jeeps, two V100 MP gun vehicles, and overhead helo escort. The MPs rotated duty on Route 9. For Brock, a twenty-year-old Arkansas country boy who believed in the war, it was his third trip to Khe Sanh. The other two trips had been harassed by snipers; no big deal, he thought, just part of the job. Brock rode front seat in one of the jeeps as radioman, the driver beside him and an M-60 gunner in the back seat. Things changed on Route 9. The weather grew cool and misty. The terrain became more primitive. The threat of enemy action became more serious; dotting the road were units from the 5th Mech, a few tanks and APCs deployed to the side with RPG screens around them, some of the grunts sleeping in the shade while others kept a monotonous lookout. If a convoy was hit hard, they were the reaction force.

Brock was a short-timer, so he slumped in the seat as they bounced along, talking about going home. The gunner knew he was Regular Army and joked back, "Well, you're a lifer, you'll be back next year anyway."

"No way, man!"

The NVA ambushed them after the convoy passed Vandegrift. Bursts of AK-47 rattled from somewhere in the roadside brush, snapping Brock out of his doldrums with a painful whack to his leg. The MPs and one gun truck poured suppressive fire into the bushes, and Brock burned off a magazine from his M-16 in the cacophony. In seconds they zipped past the ambush point, losing no one. At first Brock thought his leg had been blown off, it hurt so bad, throbbing from the hip down. An AK round had passed just below his kneecap, punching a hole in one side and leaving a cut on the other that barely bled. He tore open his trouser leg and wrapped a bandage around the wound.

When they pulled into Khe Sanh, they hauled for the med bunker and Brock limped inside. A medic simply rewrapped the wound and, since it was not serious, Brock elected to return to Da Nang via the unloaded convoy rather than call for a medevac. At the Da Nang hospital, he was stitched up, put on light duty for two weeks; then he spent a few more days in the field before rotating home. Before he left, he was pinned with the Purple Heart and an Army Commendation Medal for Valor. The decoration was for "commanding" the MP jeep during the ambush and "refusing" evacuation for his wound. Brock figured the Army was looking to hand out medals for anything.

It was a hot day at Quang Tri as a twenty-truck convoy, with gun trucks between every fifth vehicle or so, was being loaded with food, water, and ammunition. Someone was asking for volunteers to ride shotgun and Sgt. John Michalak, a twenty-one-year-old Chicago kid, decided that he'd go. At the time, he was a USAF technician temporarily assigned to the TOC at Quang Tri; he was tired of working at his desk in the stifling, windowless bunker and wanted to get out and see what was happening in this big operation they'd been called up for. An Air Force buddy also volunteered and they rode in the seventh truck, a gun truck, sharing the back with four GIs. When the convoy rolled out, the men did not diligently man their guns but slumped in the truck bed to light up. Ah, sweet reefer, Michalak thought, as the soldiers shared their joints; it had been hard to score grass at Quang Tri after their USAF team had moved up, and the only ones who seemed to have any smack were the black GIs, who were not easily approachable. The four soldiers spoke bitterly as they drove along, bitching about the convoys, about just wanting to go home, about the damned weather which either turned the road into a muddy trail or, as on this day, covered them with sweat and caked them with red road dust. Michalak felt sorry for them: Man, they got it rough, always in the field, getting shot at and pushed around by the lifers. Route 9 turned into dirt as they sat talking. The lead of the column disappeared around a bend in the road—and the blast of an RPG suddenly sounded. Michalak popped up to look over the armor plating just as a second RPG exploded against a tree and he caught a spray of wood chips across the front of his flak jacket. He shit his pants and jumped back down as AK-47s cracked from hidden spots in the roadside tangle. The convoy kept moving, gun trucks raking the brush, Michalak getting keyed-up and manning the fifty. He pounded out seventy-five rounds. As they rounded the bend, they could see the result of the first RPG, a truck shoved to the side and burning. The crew scrambled aboard another truck and the shooting petered out as they quickly outdistanced the wreckage, and continued for Khe Sanh.

By '71 the U.S. Marine Corps was practically out of Vietnam. Its small contribution to the Route 9 convoys was C Company, 11th Motor Transport Battalion, III Marine Amphibious Force, detailed to work under the 26th GSG. On 14 February, with the revamping of the assets along the road, another small detachment of marines was committed to the Quang Tri front. This was the Communications Platoon, Headquarters Company, 11th MTB. At least one of the marines, Cpl. Carson C. Bartels, was glad of the prospect to see some action. Bartels, a radioman and jeep driver in the platoon, was a square-jawed, bespectacled twenty-one-year-old from Cedar Falls, Iowa. He'd joined the marines in '68, right out of high school, too young and naive to really care about the issues of the war, but he had been raised with a sense of duty to the nation. He'd also wanted to prove himself. The Marine Corps had seemed like the place to satisfy both urges. He'd already done thirteen months in Vietnam, 1969–70, a hard tour with the 7th Marines south of Da Nang.

After five months of spit-and-shine stateside duty, he had volunteered for a second tour in Vietnam.

For Bartels, his new post with the 11th MTB was nothing but listlessness and hassles. He lived comfortably in a Da Nang basecamp and ran routine convoys on Route 1, an area so secure by then that lone vehicles could leave the perimeter without the security of a convoy and not worry about enemy ambushes. It was a boring routine and Bartels was practically the only man in his platoon with any combat experience. The rear was no luxury to him, with its oppressive heat, smell of diesel and burning dung everywhere, sullen stares between black and white Marines, and a dullness so pervasive that some Marines smoked pot every off-duty day. So, when the word came that they were heading north, Bartels was filled with enthusiasm. No one knew the details, but the prospect of being involved in a major operation in the midst of the withdrawals gave the morale of the marines a boost.

They loaded the commo gear always carried on convoys aboard a command jeep, four trucks, four semi-trailers, and a wrecker. Only a small group was going; a captain, a lieutenant, a gunnery sergeant, and fewer than a dozen enlisted men. They departed Da Nang going north on Route 1, Bartels driving the command jeep with the captain beside him. They tied a bright-orange, waterproof tarp on the roof of the jeep, so a Sea Knight flying above them could keep the convoy easily in sight. The helicopter was in radio contact with Bartels and flew ahead of them, skirting from one side of the road to the other, looking for possible enemy ambushes. There was no shooting. Just a Sunday drive, Bartels thought, par for the course. Route 1 was a modern, two-lane, blacktop highway and mopeds, Citroens, and buses with people clinging all over them zoomed by the Marine column. Villages and cultivated rice paddies flanked the route. The highway skirted the east coast of Vietnam and, off to their right, the marines could sometimes make out the inviting blue shimmer of the South China Sea.

Ten miles out of Da Nang, the villes became fewer and the foilage thicker. A few more miles up Route 1, they neared the Hai Van Pass where the road cut through a jungled mountain. The road began to wind uphill, dropping off sharply to one side, and a few junked vehicles sat rusting in the brush over the edge. Infantrymen from the 1st Marine Division were in bunkered and barbed-wired checkpoints every few hundred yards, situated so that they could make visual contact with the ones on either side. Coming downhill from the pass, the convoy hit the flat hedgerow and paddy country around Camp Eagle. North of Eagle, the highway went straight through Hue City, the old imperial capital of Vietnam. Bartels was amazed; it was a beautiful city with concrete buildings, sidewalks, telephone poles, and even a huge white church in a grove of trees. Crossing the Perfume River on an old French span bridge they passed the Hue Citadel with its eighteenth-century walls and towers.

The country continued to change; fewer civilians, more jungle, and the sight of misty mountains ahead. Bartels had never been so far north and the whole area felt different, like a war was still going on.

Quang Tri City looked like a big shantytown of shacks and markets, beggars, trinket sellers, prostitutes, and pushers. Dong Ha had become a logistical center; it was dusty and noisy, helicopters coming and going from several LZs, crisscrossed with roads, motor pools, aid stations, bunkers, and hootches.

The convoy started rolling on Route 9 and, within a few miles the elephant grass, scrub brush, and rolling hills began rising into jungled mountains. After a few more miles, the road curved south in the direction of Vandegrift. Bartels stared in fascination at the Rockpile; it was like taking a trip back in time, he thought, to places the marines had made famous in the years past. The Vandegrift Combat Base was another eerie sight to Bartels. It had been completely overgrown when the army reopened it after two years of abandonment, but the recent clearing and digging had exposed the old trails and bunkers. Rotted sandbags and abandoned gear was littered in the elephant grass. It was like pulling into a ghost town.

Everything was muddy. Trucks and APCs were parked at random, a few helicopters squatted in makeshift LZs; there were sandbagged culvert bunkers, commo wire stretched atop the mud, some concertina wire thrown up around the stacks of supplies. One of the first things Bartels noticed, as they pulled into Vandegrift, was several tanks ringing the perimeter; they were hidden in the tall grass with sandbags piled around them. Behind them the perimeter was encircled by a single coil of concertina wire and foxholes were dug in along it.

Mountains surrounded Vandegrift, deep green with jungle.

The small marine contingent spent the rest of the day running supplies to Khe Sanh and Lang Vei. At Khe Sanh, Bartels could also see where the old Marine positions had been. They all knew what their fellow Marines had gone through during that famous battle and, at least for Bartels, there was a strong feeling of tradition and pride in those mountains.

Before dark, the platoon returned to Vandegrift. They pulled their trucks side by side in a neat row along the main trail in their little area, and put their personal gear in a small van. They slept in ponchos on the ground.

The protection around them consisted only of some flimsy wire and some unimpressive looking GIs sitting in foxholes. The second lieutenant in charge of the perimeter on their side of the compound appeared to be nineteen or twenty, and seemed to have no idea what was going on nor any real control over his troops. The soldiers themselves looked sloppy. When the sun went down the men in the foxholes kept on talking and smoking. Bartels remembered the field discipline of the marine grunts on his first tour and was amazed at what he was seeing; he could only think the soldiers were poorly trained and inexperienced draftees. The Marines decided they would have to perform their own security. The captain made sure that they all knew where everyone was, in case anything happened during the night, and set up sleeping times so that two men were always on guard.

Bartels had finally fallen asleep when a sudden crash startled him awake. Everyone was yelling. He shook his head, thinking for a second that he was dreaming. An Army truck, barrelling down the road, had rammed into their row of trucks, and now the driver was backing up and smashing into the trucks again. Bartels saw his captain jump up and run to the truck. He grabbed the soldier from behind the wheel, and shook him by the collar, screaming in his face. The GI was high as a kite. In a minute or two, an Army major emerged from a nearby tent and took the stoned soldier away.

In the morning, they moved out from Vandegrift towards Khe Sanh. The country was beautiful. It reminded Bartels of Colorado, with high green mountains stretching as far as you could see. It was misty and cool and sometimes you couldn't see the tops for the fog. The only intrusion into the wilderness was Route 9 and Bartels thought it was a joke to call this narrow dirt path, usually too slim for two trucks to pass easily, a highway. The brush and trees grew right up from the sides of the road, giving the drivers an uneasy, hemmed-in feeling.

A sign had been posted along Route 9, with the Vietnamese translation beneath the English:

KHE GIO TO CALU

FRIENDLY PATROLS

both sides of road

DO NOT RECON BY

FIRE!!

Khe Gio was a large bridge near the Rockpile, and Ca Lu was another name for Vandegrift. Bartels saw only one patrol while driving on Route 9, a line of infantrymen sweeping in the Rockpile flatland. As far as he was concerned, no one was in control between Dong Ha and Lang Vei. Three or four times he heard the muffled pops in the hills along the road, and could see a splash of mud or water. Snipers. The drivers would try to push their trucks faster through the mud. Men on the cab-mounted fifties would join the tank in shooting back, and they would try to outrun the fire. They always made it in one piece.

On that second day, word came that one of the platoon drivers had become so exhausted, he'd fallen asleep at the wheel and run off a steep embankment. The marine was medevacked. The deuce-and-a-half truck had not been destroyed, so the lieutenant and Bartels took the jeep and another marine took the wrecker to go retrieve it. They went first to Dong Ha to pick up an M88 recovery vehicle with seven GIs aboard. Heading west again, they found the crash site just outside Khe Sanh. Bartels found it ironic to be out in the middle of nowhere, with no infantry support, to recover one crashed Marine truck, while along the way they had seen at least six Army trucks, abandoned with only smashed radiators and broken axles. Bartels was not surprised: it seemed to him that the Marines always took better care of their equipment and were able to use what the Army would have replaced.

Bartel's worries were justified. As the retriever winched the truck up, an NVA cut loose with an AK-47, sending Bartels and the rest jumping over the edge of the road. The GI on the retriever fired back on his fifty, evidently cowing the sniper, as they got out with no further problems.

That night the platoon again secured inside the wire at Vandegrift. Around midnight, Bartels was jerked awake by mortar rounds exploding around the base. There were no bunkers for the Marines, so they could just flatten in the grass and mud. Everyone kept low for the minute or two the rounds plopped randomly about; then a lucky shell exploded on the small LZ up from the main camp road. A JP4 fuel bladder went up in a roaring burst of fire and the whole area lit up like daylight.

The next morning, 16 February, the platoon drove to Dong Ha to pick up more supplies. There they were informed that the supply problem for which they had been called up was taken care of and they could return to Da Nang. The Marines were back by lunchtime. Corporal Bartels was glad he'd been able to spend at least those three days and two nights in Operation Lam Son 719.

Others were not coping as well. For Sp4 Carney of the 39th Transportation Battalion, the mud, the cold rain, the rockets and mortars, the shot-up convoys on Route 9 were adding up to destroy him. It just kept up day after day with no break; he couldn't have imagined anything this bad. The worst carnage he saw was when a convoy returned to Vandegrift one morning, after having been hit in a night ambush. Carney had watched the convoy form up hours earlier inside the perimeter at Vandegrift; he'd been feeling strange, depressed and suicidal, and had gone over and said, "Hey, I'll go with you as shotgun." But the battalion sergeant major, an older black man whom the men considered a cool head among the lifers, pulled him to the side. He could see what a wretched state Carney was in; the drugs, violence, the absurdity and waste were falling on him, beating him. On his last run, a sniper had put two rounds in the side of Carney's truck and he hadn't calmed down from that yet. So the sergeant major told him to forget it, to get some rest; and Carney watched the convoy roll out. When it came back, a wrecker was towing the remains of a gun truck which had taken a direct hit. A couple of bodies were laid out in the wreckage. Blood and pieces of flesh were splattered on the metal. Carney felt himself getting sick, felt his bitterness at the lifers grow as he watched them bringing out their cameras.

The good morale that Carney had seen when they first moved out had quickly evaporated. They'd been enthused at the rumor of invading North Vietnam, but were turned off when they saw it was to be an ARVN operation in Laos. They saw it as another useless political battle, and the support troops, who'd rarely even heard a sniper down south, were shocked by the ambushing and horrid driving conditions into which they were thrust. It was all confusion, Carney thought, like some deranged, violent carnival. They were running around like headless chickens. That's how he saw it. Ideas of rebelling against the lifers floated in his head.

As the battalion mail clerk, Carney had another duty which further depressed him: he had to collect the personal effects of the KIAs and ghostwrite the letters to the next of kin for the colonel to sign. During the day, he worked in the command hootch, handling the battalion mail. At night he pulled perimeter foxhole guard. About three times a week he picked up his M-16 and rode shotgun on the convoys. Once a week he would catch a ride to take the mail to Camp Eagle and Da Nang. He was required to be back at Vandegrift by night and thought catching a helicopter back from Da Nang would be quicker and safer; the battalion commander personally cancelled that idea by telling him, "You're in a transportation unit. You'll go in a truck. Everyone in this unit is going to take the same chances." Fucking colonel, Carney fumed, he's just trying to play the macho trucker, with no practical concern about the safety of his men.

The convoys were bad. He would hitch up with them at Vandegrift, the gun trucks running front and rear of the column. The GIs painted big, elaborate slogans on their gun trucks: DAUGHTER OF DARKNESS, KING KONG, CANNED HEAT, EVE OF DESTRUCTION. A few of the men loved to get out on Route 9 and tear up the countryside with their weapons; some thought they had a job to do, some got stoned as much as they could, and Carney went because he was ordered to. He tried to make most of his convoys with a young mustached buddy named Don. Don was a heroin addict. And if it wasn't the convoys, then just being at Vandegrift was bad. The rockets usually hit at dusk, like clockwork, when the trucks were pulling into the maintenance area and the men were lining up for chow. There was the cold gray silence, the sudden shrieks, the scramble for foxholes, then six or seven explosions; then the silence again until the U.S. artillery batteries at Vandegrift boomed out counterfire.

The nights on the perimeter were a mind-boggling terror to Carney. He was too fragile for war, his nerves constantly on edge. He would sit in his muddy foxhole, holding his uncleaned M-16, and stare out into the black. "All that's out there," he told himself a hundred times, "is some stinking wire—and thousands of Communists. Oh God, they can kill us all any time they want to." He talked to some sentries on the perimeter who said that an NVA sapper, wired down with explosives, had tried to creep through the wire. They'd shot him and the man had exploded. One night it all came too terrifyingly close, when Carney was in the command hootch and the rockets began thudding in. He ran for a culvert bunker, the last rocket exploded; then came the rattle of automatic weapons fire and screams of, "Sappers in the wire!" Carney peered from his bunker and could see the lieutenant colonel standing atop a truck, shouting for his men to organize around him. This dude, he thought, is insane. Satchel charges exploded in one area of the camp. Carney bolted from his bunker, then saw the grass stir beside him. He didn't know if it was a sapper, the wind, or another GI, but he whirled towards it firing his M-16 on automatic. The filthy weapon jammed and Carney freaked out, making a mad scramble for another bunker. Two soldiers were hunkered inside, staring hotly down their rifle sights into the blackness around them. On the perimeter, truck drivers and clerk-typists fired wildly at shadows while the NVA sappers slid away.

Carney succumbed to the situation and sought his escape through drugs. He was smoking joints for breakfast and drinking obestol to wire himself up for the day. Obestol was like cough syrup, but was really narcotic speed. The speed made it easier to do his work, but prevented him from sleeping when he had a few moments off. Some of the truckers told him that heroin would bring you down, so he began mixing skag and methanol cigarettes. The pot, speed, heroin, and booze were ruining Carney. He did not give a fuck. He got trashed every day, sitting around the motor pool with his buddies, keeping an eye out for the lifers. Shit, he thought, everybody's doing it. They used to laugh about the battalion commander whom no one ever saw asleep. "That lifer is so afraid of getting fragged," they joked, "he's jacked up on speed twenty-four hours a day."

The dope was easy to get, even along the Quang Tri front during the operation. There were few civilians in the area, but along the road, at

Dong Ha and Quang Tri, they began to appear: beggars, kids with boxes of trinkets, and the cowboys, Vietnamese teenagers on Hondas, selling dope—sandbags filled with marijuana, vials of heroin, opium, and dew joints machine-rolled and packed in cigarette cartons.

Carney was horrified by it all; he didn't want to die and he didn't want to kill anyone. "You get so fucked up you don't care," he said, "You force yourself into another world." And he was in another world, one which shattered his senses and brought him a deep rage at his government, the lifers, even his own father, whom he blamed for his being in this hellhole. The old man never even used to talk to him; then, nonchalantly, he had threatened to bar Carney from his home if he were to go to Canada. "You don't want me in your house!" Carney had screamed at his father on the day he'd gotten home, "Don't worry, I'm leaving!" They didn't speak again for four years.

The worst convoy Carney ever was in didn't even make contact. There had been shooting along Route 9 during the night, and in the morning there was hesitation about opening the road immediately. The sergeant major wanted him to stay in the compound, but Carney argued that he had to get to Da Nang. They had sent word that they had the DEROS orders for several men in the battalion. Carney knew that one extra day on Route 9 could get them blown away and he wanted to get those orders as soon as possible. The minesweep teams hit the road and Carney sat back to wait, sipping Black Label and smoking joints. Word finally came that the road was clear and his truck headed east. Carney was riding shotgun, Don was driving, and two AWOLs, who wanted to score on the prostitutes and get some dope in Da Nang, sat in the back. All four soldiers were stoned. They were making the windy curves near the Rockpile when they turned another corner, and came upon a truck right ahead of them. It was just sitting there in the cold morning air—on fire, two dead GIs hanging out the doors. Don hit the brake and there was a moment of stunned silence. Carney had a camera on his lap. Without thinking, he raised it and took a photo through the windshield. Then the realization hit. They shouted to each other, "Let's get the fuck outta here!" and Don hauled to the side of the road. They jumped out with their M-16s. The road was hemmed in by a tall wall of elephant grass; they couldn't see a thing. If the truck had hit a mine, they were safe, but if it had been hit by an enemy RPG team, they were in trouble—four guys out in the woods without a radio. They fired blindly into the elephant grass and Carney heaved his four grenades. When the rattle and echo died away, there was only more silence. Two Cobras that had been circling dove in and threw a couple of minigun bursts into the field where they'd been shooting. A moment later, some trucks and a wrecker rumbled up from the direction of Vandegrift, shoved the burning truck out of the way, and they continued on for Da Nang.

From his end of the supply line in a sandbagged tent at Khe Sanh, recently promoted Colonel Rosenblum thought that the truckers were heroes. He watched them come in day and night from perilous road runs, crawl under their trucks to sleep while the supplies were being unloaded; then climb back into their cabs to hit Route 9 again, that being the only sleep they got. They were doing a super job.

Rosenblum worked in tandem with General Smith (ADC for Support, 101st Airborne), getting the trucked-in material to the field via choppers. He also ran the refuel/rearm points. Rosenblum, who had less than two months of logistical experience after an infantry career in Korea and Vietnam, felt that, if ARVN failed, DISCOM would be blamed for not providing sufficient support. So he worked himself and his troops hard, and his four battalions performed well.* The 426th Supply & Service (Lt. Col. Ken Jacobs) handled transportation for DISCOM, manned the refuel/rearm stations, and rigged helicopters with external loads. The 5th Transportation (Lt. Col. William Beasley) performed the maintenance, supply, and repair of the division helicopters, while the 801st Maintenance (Lt. Col. Richard Nidever) maintained all divisional equipment. The 326th Medical (Lt. Col. Robert Day, M.D.) ran the division medevac service.

The biggest task of Rosenblum's list was keeping the refuel/rearm points running at Dong Ha, Mai Loc, Vandegrift, Khe Sanh, and Lang Vei. The delay in building the airfield and the two weeks of convoy problems had kept the 300,000-gallon fuel reserve at Khe Sanh from being up

---

*There was, uncharacteristically, a fragging incident in DISCOM during the operation, in a supply company at Camp Eagle. Someone blew the captain's hootch apart with a claymore mine. The captain miraculously escaped with only shrapnel in his arm. No one was brought to justice for the attempted murder although three angry soldiers, who had been transferred to the rear for being troublesome in their infantry units, were suspect.

to par, and it was only reached because of a great effort by DISCOM and the 26th GSG with tanker trucks and slingloaded bladders. The choppers worked out of the points all day long, and the tankers came in throughout the night to replenish the fuel supply. It consisted of long hard days for all involved, punctuated by rocket raids; and Rosenblum had an added burden: not only was he responsible for supporting U.S./ARVN units committed to Laos, but at the same time DISCOM had to maintain its services in the entire 101st Airborne AO. His twenty-five-hundred-man force was spread thin. Fortunately, when he asked General Berry for reinforcements, the general had a hundred men straight from the replacement centers given two or three days of training, then had them immediately dispatched to the refuel/rearm points.

Additional supplies reached Khe Sanh via the U.S. Air Force airlift. Shutting down C130 operations in much of South Vietnam and shifting these capabilities to MR1, the 7th USAF brought in an average of five hundred tons per day. The army forklift crews at the airfield (augmented by the U.S. Marines of C Company, 1st Shore Party Battalion, III MAF) unloaded the material from the C130s, which landed about every fifteen minutes on peak days. A record of one thousand tons was recorded one day and, throughout the campaign, 2,734 sorties were flown to bring in 28,333 tons of cargo. Enemy fire was not a problem to the C130s; during the '68 siege, shellings prevented the large planes from ever fully stopping, but in '71, a half-dozen of these craft could be seen waiting along the strip at nearly any given time. There were difficulties, however. The secondary assault runway was opened to C130 traffic on 15 February, but the main strip was not finished until 1 March. Then, eight days later, a C130 lost its landing gear and tore up seventeen hundred feet of runway. It was not repaired until 21 March, and logistical support suffered accordingly.

Despite the occasional snafus, the logistical lifeline usually flowed unabated. Konopnicki and Rosenblum were a good team, and they joked amongst themselves, "This is either a logistical nightmare, or the greatest logistical effort that the U.S. Army has made in years." They knew the answer to that question. Major Klose of the 223d CAB saw Rosenblum and the 101st DISCOM in action at Khe Sanh; the helicopter pilots had a saying: "Go haul two for Rosie," which meant that whenever you had free time, to bring two slingloaded blivets of fuel to Colonel Rosenblum. The aviators loved him. He kept them flying.

CHAPTER 12: The First Regiment of Dragoons

For the men of A Troop, 1st Squadron, 1st Cavalry, the month of February 1971 had been hit and miss. When they patrolled Route 9 to secure engineer teams, nothing happened, but when they pulled perimeter security for the artillery, they got shelled. The worst came towards the end of the month when they moved into the bush south of Lang Vei. "It was Bad, Bad, Bad," Sergeant Keefer wrote home. They were to spend five weeks in the area. The troop commander, Captain Pierson, split the unit up, each platoon assigned a different position from which to conduct patrols. First Platoon was dispatched to a grassy knoll called Hill 400, a miserable place, freezing, muddy, and watersoaked when the rain clouds rolled over; a parched and brittle oven when the sun came out. There was no water to spare on washing and before long, the grunts were unshaven and grubby, their fatigues and skin worn to the colors of the earth.

The top of Hill 400 was ground to dust when the Sheridans and APCs moved in, and it became a garbage pile of poncho shelters, dead grass, discarded C rats, and more GI battle junk. The elephant grass was above their heads at the edge of the perimeter; the dozen tanks and tracks of the platoon were parked in a circle amongst the tangle, weapons trained downhill. Hill 400 was only a bump among the rolling hills that made up the whole area around Lang Vei, the hills rising and dipping, branching off in fingers, the mountains of Laos rising to the west and forming the horizon. The tops of most valleys were thick with clutching brambles where nothing could be seen.

Hill 400 was worst when it was dark. "Night time rolling around again," Keefer wrote home. "We got where we hated to see it come. Because with it we knew the sappers with RPG's and satchel charges would come. And the nights got so cold and lonely." When the sun went down behind the Laotian mountains, the fog rolled in so only the crests could be seen, like islands in a moor. Sergeant Keefer assigned four men to be awake at all times, one at each compass point; and they sat atop their tracks in helmets and flak jackets, the fifties' butterfly handles before them, staring into the settled gray mist. The fear of sappers kept the men awake during the first part of their two-hour watches, but then exhaustion set in. You patrol all day, catch RPGs both night and day, the mind clouds, and before long you are so tired you don't give a damn. When Keefer checked the perimeter at night, he was frightened when he found men asleep at their posts. After finding three guards out of four asleep one night, he assembled the platoon and told them he wasn't going to have any more of that. The next night, Keefer was pulling guard when his buddy, Sgt. Robert Greene, was suddenly shaking him awake, muttering, "What kind of example are you setting?" It was two in the morning, and Keefer was shocked; the last thing he remembered was sitting there, staring over the gun shield at the night sky, concentrating on staying awake. Finally, every night, Keefer had the platoon pull a Mad Minute, firing all the weapons and chucking hand frags around outside their circle, as much to deter NVA sappers as to wake guards up. There was no doubt in his mind that on some nights the entire platoon was asleep atop that hill.

During the day, Keefer got his platoon missions from Captain Pierson via the radio from his position in the hills, and the platoon would mount out. Their patrols were aimed at rooting out the NVA harassing Route 9. They rarely found anything. Sometimes they would bust jungle, the vehicles actually rising up in the face of the brush before crashing down and ploughing through. Making dismounted foot patrols through the mashed areas, they found numerous bunkers and tunnels underneath the crushed foliage, and would harass each hole with a couple of M-16 bursts and hand frags. There was no way, with their limited resources, to get at the bunker networks.

On rare occasions, the platoon added a few North Vietnamese soldiers to the operation's body count.

Weather and resupply were among the many problems plaguing Sergeant Keefer's platoon on Hill 400. It rained a lot, a cold northern rain that combined with the cool night air to shock him. He couldn't believe that in Nam he could actually see steam on his breath. The platoon was ill-prepared for the weather; they had few jackets and blankets to begin with, and were forced to wear the same soaking wet fatigues day after day. On some nights, Keefer watched with pity as young GIs curled up miserably against the cold, teeth chattering, crying from the numbing pain. When the rains came, the engineer trails clogged with mud, helicopter support was hampered, and its priority was for the ARVN in Laos. The platoon did without C rations and water, ran short of trip flares, M-79 rounds, tank rounds, mortar rounds, and track blocks. When it rained, they held their plastic canteens under leaves to catch the runoff. When they found NVA rice, they kept it for themselves.

The recruiting posters called it the New Action Army. Keefer jeered; they can't even keep their combat troops supplied. They just don't give a fuck, he thought. What sustained Keefer were his friends; some deep sense of patriotism, which he never lost; and the feeling that he was good. Back home he was just another aimless dropout punk, who had been a constant problem for his widowed mother. In Nam he was a sergeant of infantry who knew enough about the bush to keep his people alive. It was the first positive thing he'd done in his life, and he was proud. In the jungle, he felt like a man.

He turned down his R&R to stay with the platoon.

One day, as usual, the platoon was low on water and C rations, and Keefer got so fed up he took matters into his own hands. He and his friend, a black kid, Pfc Larry Robinson, decided to drive cross-country to Route 9, try to scrounge some supplies off the convoys on the road, then hustle back before Captain Pierson radioed in and discovered they were gone. Keefer, Robinson, and two other GIs left Hill 400 in the mortar track, Keefer driving because his regular delta, Pfc Ester Wolf, was on R&R. Not knowing if the replacement was experienced, Keefer bumped him from the drivers hatch. It didn't matter. Six hundred yards out, as they were busting jungle down a steep hill, they threw a track and the APC ground to a halt. They jumped off; the bush around them was almost suffocating, reaching maybe thirty feet up, even arching down onto the crippled vehicle.

Night was falling and there was no time for help to come before morning. They prepared for a bad night, and counted up their resources: 500 rounds of M-16 ammo, twenty hand frags, and one smoke grenade. They had eighteen hundred rounds for the fifty but, with the APC stuck going downhill, the barrel was aimed at the ground. They also had the 81mm mortar mounted inside the crew hatch of the APC, but it too was now pointed at an odd angle and the overhead foliage prevented its use. It was a stomach-churning night, the four of them sitting silently in the pitch black in the thick jungle, just waiting for the NVA to creep up and slaughter them.

The night passed without incident.

In the morning, the squadron commander, Lt. Col. Sheldon Burnett, flew to Alpha Troop's command post in his C&C Loach. Typical, Keefer thought, we need a dozer to cut us a path out of this tangle and they send us a colonel. The CO departed shortly and a bit later Captain Pierson arrived at the downed track. An engineer dozer began ploughing a zigzag path up the steep slope. Pierson chewed Keefer out for taking such a chance against orders; then a bigger source of irritation, Burnett's visit, welled up and he muttered, "You ain't going to believe this. The colonel told us that you all needed haircuts and baths so bad that he's going to send his own personal barber out to the field when he gets back to battalion headquarters."

Keefer, Robinson, and the other two GIs who'd sweated out the night looked at each other, mumbling, "Great, just what we need to hear."

North Vietnamese artillery was erupting near the platoon, and the tracks vibrated from the rumble. Keefer jumped into an APC and slammed the cargo hatch shut. Only the platoon medic, a tall and thin soldier called Doc Slim, was inside. Keefer flipped on the red lights and was shocked to see Slim sitting like a statue, drained and crying. Slim never held back in the bush, but the shellings were eating at him, and he pleaded with Keefer, "I just can't take it any more. . . . You gotta send me in."

"Nobody could call anybody a better friend," Keefer said, "but I can't send you in. We wouldn't have a medic if I sent you back."

"Look, you've seen more wounded than I have. You can do everything that I can. You can take care of things."

"Yeah, you're right, I can take care of the guys. But that's your job. I hate being platoon sergeant, but I was the best man for the job. I'm going to have to make sure that as many of these guys get home as I can. If I send you back, Slim, and we get in some heavy contact and somebody gets wounded, I can't leave my command track to go help 'em out. They're all counting on you for that. They're your friends. If I sent you back and we hit some heavy shit, and lost some guys that were close to you, could you take that home with you? You'd always wonder if it could have been different if you would've been there, if you could have helped out."

Doc Slim mustered a small grin, "Yeah, you're right. . . . I don't know what I'm thinking of. Thanks, Keef, I appreciate you telling me that."

"You'd have told me the same thing. And this talk did me as much good as it did you, 'cause I've been feeling the same way you have."

On the afternoon of 4 March, a platoon from Alpha Troop was hit by RPG and AK-47 fire; a Sheridan and APC were reported destroyed, eight GIs wounded. There were no reported enemy casualties. You sit in a position long enough, Keefer knew, and the NVA will map you out and kill you with sappers and ambushes. The only way to prevent this was to disrupt them before they started; he decided to take a night ambush patrol down Hill 400 at dusk to see if the North Vietnamese were moving on them.

Five men volunteered to go with him and they pushed out into the dark night at half past eight, filing wordlessly through the elephant grass of Hill 400. They began crawling slowly through the tangled bramble at the base of the hill, taking an hour and a half to move eight hundred yards, then settling into their ambush position on one of the engineer trails in the jungle.

After an endless wait, they saw lights moving through the brush. Flashlights: Keefer counted five of them. A North Vietnamese patrol was moving on the path, brashly carrying flashlights in the pitch black jungle, confident that no Americans would actually be out this late. Keefer estimated that there were fifteen NVA walking towards them. He got on the radio to Captain Pierson who turned him over to Sgt. Neil Whipple. Whipple handled the troop's 81mm mortar section, and he was good. The night was still, black, and hushed when the thunks of mortar rounds leaving their tubes echoed softly in the calm. Then the rounds arched down from the sky and erupted in a thunderclap of shrapnel. Several flashlights spun wildly in the air. Got 'em! Keefer was elated. Blew away at least five or six of them!

He moved cautiously down the trail towards the impact area to check it out, but an unseen NVA threw a grenade at him. It exploded nearby and he scrambled back to the patrol, pulling them back to Hill 400. Back on the radio, he had Sergeant Whipple put a heavy concentration of 81mm fire on the trail. When the mortar fire lifted, Keefer wanted to scout for bodies and further NVA movement. Robinson, Wolf, and two other grunts volunteered to go with him. They were wading through the elephant grass on the hillside when Keefer got nervous. The farther they went into the black, the more convinced he became that the NVA would be waiting in ambush this time. He only had four men with him. Two hundred yards out, he turned the patrol around, leaving the body count and possible ambushing to the imagination.

At first light, Keefer had the platoon mount up to sweep the ambush site, leaving only a couple of tracks atop Hill 400. It was still cool and foggy in the valley, the sun gray behind clouds. They halted where the jungle grew thick, and fanned out on line. Keefer prepared a squad-sized patrol to move into the brush with the help of Sgt. Randall Hughes, an older family man from Tennessee. Hughes was both a new guy and a lifer, but Keefer thought he was one of the best men in the platoon. When Hughes had first arrived, they'd already been on the Laos border and he'd told Keefer, "Look, it's your platoon and you're running it. You know what the hell's going on. Just ignore the fact that I got an extra stripe. You keep me posted on what's going on, and show me what I'm going to need to know to take care of these men."

The vehicles were still getting organized, when the patrol moved out, Keefer on point, Hughes walking slack. Keefer was impressed; most lifer sergeants he knew wouldn't even accompany the patrol, let alone walk slack. They had only gone a short distance down slope, when Hughes tugged at the back of Keefer's shirt. "Wait a minute, Sergeant Keefer, let me take point." The patrol paused amid the brush and Hughes put a hand on Keefer's shoulder, pulling him back a bit. "You took out the patrol last night. Let me take point, it's only fair." They were side by side, Hughes walking forward; then Keefer saw the flash of movement out of the corner of his eye. To their left, the crack of explosions and the smoke of backblast was followed in the next second by two RPGs exploding at their feet. Keefer was propelled backwards, the concussion slamming into him like a baseball bat on the bridge of his nose, a burst of lights before his eyes. He could feel himself falling backwards, dazed, then, crashing down hard into the bushes. He landed on his back, the wind knocked out of him. Then he realized everything was quiet and, gasping for breath, screamed out for the patrol to fire. He snapped back from the concussion, could see nothing but bushes and hanging vines around him; then he realized Staff Sergeant Hughes was lying beside him, still in the grass, blood running from his ears, nose, and from a wound in the side of his head. He looked dead and Keefer felt sick. He screamed for the medic.

Robinson was the first to scramble down beside him. Keefer lay quietly, still coming out of shock, suddenly aware of the hot shrapnel in his face, chest, and arm. The left side of his body had been peppered. More men moved forward along with Doc Rose, a red-haired kid who'd come in as a replacement when Doc Slim had rotated home. They helped Keefer and Hughes stumble back; Robinson came out last, covering their retreat.

Cranking up to return to Hill 400, Ollie told Keefer that Doc Rose had tried to hide when the shooting had started and had only gotten moving when Ollie'd prodded him with his M-16. Sorry bastard, Keefer thought; the new medic had been a slacker since he'd arrived, a smartass with a chip on his shoulder.

Pulling to the top of Hill 400, they found that another Alpha platoon had moved in; they'd captured two North Vietnamese and had moved to the hilltop to call in a helicopter for them. The two NVA sat in some lawn chairs, untied, both of them barefoot and wearing fatigues, glancing around uncomfortably. Keefer was surprised to find a third injured GI on the hill. His nickname was Yo-Yo and he'd been run over by an APC. Typical, Keefer thought; his nickname told it all. He was a California hippie who couldn't figure out the first thing about the infantry. When the RPG ambush had been sprung, a driver had backed up his APC to find a better vantage point to give support fire, running over Yo-Yo's legs in the process.

He lay on a stretcher, shot up with morphine, but still in pain. Keefer sat beside him and Yo-Yo asked how the old staff sergeant was doing. Keefer said it looked bad, that Robinson had told him Hughes was bleeding from multiple head wounds and might lose an eye.

Hughes was led over and sat down. Yo-Yo looked over and said, "Oh, man, I'm sorry to hear you're going to lose your eyesight."

Keefer looked at him sharply—you never tell a man he's hit badly, it might send him into shock. "For two cents," he snapped, "I'd knock your teeth out."

Hughes was levelheaded; he ignored them.

Keefer and Hughes shrugged off Doc Rose, so he squatted beside them filling out their WIA tags. The other platoon's medic worked on them, taking off their tattered shirts and tying bandages around their wounds as they stood behind an APC, grunts snapping photographs. Hughes calmly smoked a cigarette as he was being bandaged; Keefer ducked back into his track to retrieve a prized possession that he wasn't going to let out of his sight—the photo album from his first tour, wrapped in plastic. The NVA prisoners sat a few feet away. Cold wind swept the hill. The mountains were shrouded by fog.

Keefer drank from a canteen as he waited for the medevac, and cursed himself for getting wounded. It was stupid; the NVA knew the U.S. troops always ran body-count patrols after contacts, and he shouldn't have been so confident when he walked into the brush. They hadn't even gotten the tanks and tracks organized to give effective fire support before he took the patrol out. He figured that NVA, wounded in the mortar ambush and unable to limp away, had probably caught them with the RPGs. A single Huey finally flew into Hill 400. Robinson and another grunt rushed forward under the slapping blades with Yo-Yo's stretcher, and slid him into the cabin. Then Robinson darted around the nose of the chopper to help Keefer and Hughes aboard. Finally they were up and gone.

The phantom war continued. The same night that Alpha hit the NVA with mortars from Hill 400, North Vietnamese sappers hit Bravo Troop with RPGs and satchel charges. Bravo reported two dead, thirteen wounded, a Sheridan and an APC destroyed—but no NVA bodies found. Seventeen hours later, at 2000 hours on 5 March, an Alpha ambush team led by a black lieutenant had fifteen NVA walk into the kill zone of their MAs. The jungle resounded with blasts and screams, and the tally was eight North Vietnamese killed, four weapons captured.

The grunts of the 1st Battalion, 11th Infantry had been sharing the travails of the 1/1 Cav along the Laotian border and Route 9, working in tandem with the armor to keep infiltrating teams of NVA sappers and artillery forward observers away from the highway supply line. The only way effectively to accomplish this mission was to get in the jungle with the enemy, to hump, sweat, and search (and often to succumb to frustration because most patrols produced nothing).

The battalion's Alpha Company, under Captain Bodenhorn, shared this jungle experience; their exception, though, was that they had been placed opcon to the 1/1 Cav. It was from Lieutenant Colonel Burnett that Bodenhorn took his orders and received his resupply. Alpha Company first made solid contact at the beginning of March. The first was when the second squad of Second Platoon, patrolling off a trail they'd located, surprised two North Vietnamese soldiers. They killed them both. The next day, a claymore ambush reaped a bloody harvest—seven dead NVA from an artillery observation party. Bodenhorn ordered the mangled corpses searched and the GIs found maps which showed both U.S. artillery firebases on the border and the NVA mountain artillery positions in Laos. They were packed aboard a chopper for Lieutenant Colonel Burnett.

The next few days of patrols went anxiously, but quietly. On 7 March, the Second Platoon and Captain Bodenhorn's command group patrolled all night, then moved out for another NDP and began digging in at around two in the afternoon. Bodenhorn sat in the grass and checked his platoons on the map: he and Second were about four klicks north of Route 9; First, about two klicks west of them; Third, a scant klick from Laos; and Weapons was dug in along the highway. Around him the GIs had dropped their helmets and rucks and were sweating in the hot afternoon, digging foxholes and hacking at the thick underbrush with machetes to clear fields of fire.

That afternoon Lieutenant McConnell and Third Platoon were NDP'd atop a small hill. The platoon RTO, Sp4 Mike Castro, was a Mexican-American from Arizona who had had to leave his pregnant wife when the draft notice had come. He just wanted to do his time and go home, but somehow Castro couldn't extinguish an ember of pride from serving with Alpha Company; he never touched drugs, and was impressed by the leadership of Bodenhorn and McConnell and the camaraderie of the platoon.

Lieutenant McConnell heard noises in the valley below their hill, and told Castro to call in artillery fire. After it lifted, they moved out to search the area, and found abandoned NVA spider holes deep in the brush. They followed the line of dugouts up another small hill, until the footpath branched. A sergeant took a squad down that fork while the rest continued on, McConnell and Castro right behind the point and slack men. The chilling crack of AK-47s erupted from the direction of the sergeant's squad, answered by M-16s.

Then they too were caught in the ambush.

A volley of AKs tore into them. The slack man was hit, and McConnell was flung back into Castro's arms, a bullet through his neck. They tumbled into an NVA dugout, the radio harness painfully wrenching Castro's back. The North Vietnamese began moving around their flanks, and Castro alternated between his PRC25 radio and M-16 rifle. He emptied twenty magazines into the underbrush. Support fire was denied because the NVA were too close; he screamed for a medevac. They began pulling back before the NVA could box them off, crawling away one at a time, shooting continuously. Castro and three grunts grabbed McConnell and, as the fire kept slashing around them, they ran, crawled, fired back, kept dragging the wounded lieutenant. Their frantic tugs and the thorny bramble tore McConnell's clothes off. Cobras finally roared in behind them, covering their retreat, and a medevac beat overhead.

At the company command post, Bodenhorn was still watching his men dig in when his senior RTO got off the radio and said Third Platoon was in heavy contact.

Captain Bodenhorn relayed the information to Lieutenant Colonel Burnett, and requested an immediate helicopter so he could be dropped off at the platoon CP and work his way down to his men in the ambush. Burnett replied that he would be en route in ten minutes. Bodenhorn checked his M-16, and his .45 side arm; he hung more grenades on his web gear, and slung a LAW rocket over his shoulder. Figuring the colonel would arrive in a Huey slick which would accommodate several people, Bodenhorn picked three others to go with him: his senior RTO, the company forward observer, and an infantryman with an M-79 for security. They waited at their makeshift jungle LZ, and the C&C came in for a landing. It was a Kiowa Scout from the 5th Mech which seated four people max and already had three people in it, WO Randolf J. Ard in the left pilot seat, Burnett beside him, and the squadron sergeant major in the back seat. Bodenhorn walked to the front of the helicopter, hunched under the blades, and held up his green memo pad for Ard to see. On it he had written frequencies, call signs, and coordinates of the Third Platoon CP and a guess at where the contact was.

The sergeant major hopped out to allow two passengers in the back seat, and Bodenhorn climbed in behind Burnett, lugging a radio with the company and squadron frequencies. His forward observer, Lt. Jerry Castillo, boarded the seat behind Ard, also carrying a radio but one with the freqs for the fire support channels. As they lifted off, Bodenhorn noticed that, while Burnett and Ard were plugged into helmet radios, there were no headsets for him and Castillo.

They could not communicate with the pilot or the colonel.

The Third Platoon ambush should have been a short, four-kilometer hop to the northwest, and Bodenhorn peered through the Plexiglas window, expecting to see smoke or movement. But there was nothing, and the helicopter seemed to be sailing due west. He could not hear what Burnett or Ard were saying over the radio, had no idea why they were going off course, and before long it was obvious that they'd headed west too long.

They had crossed the Laotian border.

The Kiowa Scout suddenly dropped from two hundred to seventy-five feet, slowing down over the green hills, and Bodenhorn looked out the window over Ard's shoulder to see yellow smoke rising from the ground. He quickly keyed the radio to Third Platoon and asked if they had popped smoke.

The man on the radio said they had no smoke out.

Bodenhorn lunged from his seat, frantically grabbed Ard's shoulder, and shook him, screaming over the turbines that his platoon had not popped smoke—just as the staccato sound of an RPD machine gun and AK-47s cut loose. Bodenhorn glanced out the side door to see a group of North Vietnamese below. They were clear as day, firing from a brushy hill. Rounds came from two sides, tearing through the tailboom and engine. They were going down fast, Bodenhorn losing his balance. They smashed into the brush in a metal-crunching screech, coming down hard on the right side of the bird and tumbling.

Bodenhorn was the first to wake up, slouched in his seat. The helicopter was nestled upright in some thick grass and brush, the foliage high enough to conceal the crash site. Everything had stopped moving; nothing was on fire. He moved slowly—felt pain. His right eye was bruised shut, his left eye gashed and bleeding badly, impairing his vision, his face was cut and his shoulder dislocated. His M-16 was gone. God, he thought, what a screw up. For who knows what reason, they had flown past the platoon ambush, crossed into Laos, and the NVA had suckered them down with a false smoke marking. The correct procedure for marking a ground position with smoke grenades called for the commander in the air to order his ground element to pop smoke, whereupon he would identify the color he saw, get a confirmation and only then come in to land. This was designed precisely to prevent the enemy from listening to the U.S. radio frequencies and luring helicopters with captured smoke grenades. Either Ard or Burnett had violated procedure and now, as a result, they were crashed and cut off. Bodenhorn could understand such a mistake from a young pilot like Ard—he'd heard he'd only been in-country a few weeks—but not from a supposedly experienced cavalry lieutenant colonel.

Bodenhorn struggled out the door, then slowly pushed through the brush to the pilot's door. He pulled Ard from his seat, but both of his legs were pinned under the crushed instrument panel, and he lay awkwardly on the ground, his feet pinched up inside the open door. The young pilot was injured, but still coherent, relatively calm, and when Bodenhorn handed him his mayday radio, he got on it. Bodenhorn then waded back to the colonel's side. Burnett was in a bad way, the force of the crash having collapsed the panel, door, seat, and having crushed metal around him. He was encapsulated and it would take metal-cutting tools and several hours to get him out.

Lieutenant Castillo had been hurled in the crash and lay pinned under the wreck, badly bruised, ribs cracked, an arm broken and a shoulder wrenched. Bodenhorn pressed his one good shoulder to the tailboom, and shoved with his legs, allowing Castillo to roll his legs out from under. He checked on Castillo, who was hurt but hanging tough, then went back to Ard and took the .45 from his holster. He thrashed around in the brush for their M-16s, and finally tossed Castillo's brand-new rifle to him. Then he found his own in the grass, both handgrips knocked off and the pistolgrip broken. He was very nervous about whether it would work or not.

They'd been on the ground for fifteen minutes. Burnett was stuck in the crash, Ard was lying half on the ground and whispering into his radio, Bodenhorn and Castillo were leaning against the bird on Burnett's side, trying to raise anyone on the squadron, battalion, and company radio nets. The NVA who had shot them down from the adjacent hill must be looking for them, Bodenhorn realized, and it was becoming painfully clear that, if they had to run, there was no way to take Burnett or Ard with them. He was thinking it over, when they heard the voices of at least six Vietnamese coming downhill, breaking brush towards them. As they got closer, the machine gun atop the hill and a couple of NVA with AKs reconned by fire, not spraying, but walking lines ahead of them in the brush. It was erratic, but Bodenhorn froze, heart pounding as bullets cracked past fifteen feet away.

Five yards away, there were more voices. He heard two Vietnamese talking back and forth, walking towards them, pushing through the brush with their rifles. He and Castillo grabbed their M-16s, rolled over in the tall grass, and aimed at the sounds. Footsteps crunched twigs; then an AK barrel parted the grass beside the front of the helicopter and two NVA appeared. They peered at the wreckage, freeze-framed for a moment in Bodenhorn's rifle sights: khaki fatigues, khaki pith helmets, AK-47s.

Lieutenant Castillo fired. His rifle jammed.

Captain Bodenhorn opened up with his broken M-16, dropping both North Vietnamese soldiers from nine feet.

With the rifle burst, the NVA moved quickly. More voices and thrashing came down the hill. The volleys of AK fire slashed closer; Bodenhorn thought they were trying to get them to open fire again and give away their positions. He held his fire. It didn't matter. The first Chicom stick grenade sailed from the brush, bounced off of the helo, and dropped in Castillo's lap as he leaned weakly against the wreck. He managed to flip it away with his good arm just before it exploded. Another frag was lobbed over the helo and boomed in the brush. The third Chicom bounced off of the helicopter, hit Bodenhorn's leg, and rolled six feet from him. He painfully curled into a tight ball to shield himself, and the explosion sent a two-inch chunk of shrapnel ripping into his inner thigh. Bodenhorn threw two grenades into the brush from where the stick grenades had come.

The NVA stopped lobbing grenades.

Overhead a single UH1C gunship appeared, overflew them, then took a heavy barrage from the hillock. The Huey flew on, Bodenhorn figuring that they must have been short of ammunition, or that the NVA fire was too intense, but convinced that the pilot had seen them. Realizing that the NVA machine gun could prevent a ground team from being inserted to rescue them, Bodenhorn armed his LAW rocket. He held it over his head, took a guess at the NVA position, and squeezed the firing button. The 66mm shell flashed from the tube, exploding in the brush over a hundred yards away. The machine gun fell silent. Bodenhorn figured that only by a fluke could he have actually hit the target, but he hoped the NVA might have been fooled into thinking that other troops were in the area so they would break down their weapon and retreat to a safer location.

He searched the sky for rescue helicopters. It was a clear, cloudless afternoon. No one was in sight.

They'd been on the ground for forty minutes, the sun was setting, no support was apparent. More NVA could be heard coming down the hill, then splitting to break bush on both sides of the crash site. Boden-

horn could hear them to the front, to the right, to the left. In a few minutes they would be surrounded, then captured or killed. This was it, he
thought, they had to escape and evade. Only he and Castillo could walk,
and only then by supporting one another. Burnett and Ard were hope-
lessly pinned in the wreck. Bodenhorn felt a sudden sense of ease when
he made the decision to abandon them. He rationalized that it was logical, trying to maintain his self-control. He limped over to Sheldon
Burnett and pulled the radio code book from his pocket; he still could
see no major wounds, but the colonel was fading in and out of con-
sciousness, and there was nothing to say to him. Bodenhorn kneeled beside Ard and told him they were taking off for the south and he was
sorry, but there was no way to free him from the wreck. Randy Ard
nodded, saying nothing.

Bodenhorn glanced guiltily at the two dead North Vietnamese
sprawled in the grass a few feet away. He realized that by killing them he
had probably signed the death warrant for the two men he was leaving
behind.

Captain Bodenhorn and Lieutenant Castillo departed fifty minutes after the crash. They crawled through the brushy tangle, an excruciating
struggle in their condition, Bodenhorn practically blind, his one good eye
slowly closing. As they were leaving, they heard voices converge on the
crash site and then the banging of metal, as if the NVA were rapping the
helicopter with their rifles. They were eighty yards away when another
UH1C gunship came in on a single gun run, firing flechette rockets. They
seemed to explode right on the downed bird. As it got darker, they
watched another aircraft come in, an F4 rolling in for a one-bomb airstrike. The Phantom screamed into a low pass, slicing over the crash site
and hill, a two-hundred-fifty-pound bomb exploding in its wake.

Bodenhorn and Castillo hobbled through streambeds and down thin
trails in the Laotian jungle, moving generally south, figuring they
would have to hide out during the night, and hoping they could find
Route 9 in the morning. They splashed down one stream, Bodenhorn
smearing blood from his face on the leaves and boughs; then they re-
traced their steps and continued down another creek. Forty-five minutes
after retreating, on a dirt trail, they heard people coming down it towards them. Bodenhorn and Castillo wearily looked at each other, too
exhausted to run, no place to hide. They got down in the grass, Castillo
clutching his .45, Bodenhorn raising his battered M-16. A Vietnamese

came down the trail, point man of the patrol, wearing a GI steel pot and carrying an M-16.

Bodenhorn recognized the ARVN airborne patch on his sleeve. The South Vietnamese escorted them for an hour down the trail to Route 9, then lifted them into a truck. They were driven to LZ Bravo, about six kilometers inside Laos astride the highway, the Laotian home of the 11th Airborne Battalion. It consisted mostly of sandbagged mortar pits. The ARVN medics worked on them and that night, Bodenhorn was put on the radio to the battalion's advisor in Vietnam. He gave his initial report and the advisor said a medevac would come in the next morning.

At seven A.M., 8 March, as a Huey landed at the post's makeshift LZ, the ARVN carried Bodenhorn and Castillo from the medical bunker on stretchers. The helicopter took them to B Medical Company, 75th Support Battalion, 5th Division on the Khe Sanh strip, then to the 18th Surg at Quang Tri. Bodenhorn saw Lieutenant McConnell there, a bandage around his neck, only able to wave due to the damage done to his throat. From there Bodenhorn followed the standard evacuation chain to Da Nang, then to Camp Zama, in Japan, the William Beaumont Hospital in El Paso, Texas, and finally to outpatient rehabilitation at Letterman Army Hospital in San Francisco. Later some of his grunts visited him in the hospital. They said that, when news of the crash reached the CP and Second Platoon, the platoon leader didn't have a chance to give an order before the men were slinging on their gear, expecting to be CA'd into the crash site. It was the only gratifying note for the most wretched day of Phil Bodenhorn's life.

Lieutenant Colonel Burnett and Warrant Officer Ard were declared missing in action. Command of the 1/1 Cav passed to Lt. Col. Gene L. Breeding, who had been a classmate of Burnett at West Point. Three days after the action, the story was released to reporters at Khe Sanh. The army spokesman accurately described the NVA ambush, but mistakenly told the press that Burnett had had radio contact with the soldiers on the ground and that he and Ard had been seriously wounded and appeared dead to the two officers who had escaped. The names of the survivors were not released, so the press could not follow up on the story.

The presumed death of a squadron commander was met with dispassion by General Sutherland, who was informed of it by General Hill the next day. He said, "For a reason which I don't recall the decision was not made to employ the Air Cavalry and the Hoc Bao to attempt to retrieve either Lieutenant Colonel Burnett alive or his body.* . . . Burnett had no mission nor units in Laos. He had no reason or authority to take his helicopter over the Laotian border."

Most of the grunts in Burnett's squadron were not sorry to see him go. Sergeant Keefer offered a profane eulogy, "The colonel finally got what he was looking for. I think he was looking for the glory of dying in combat. I hate to say that, but to me he got just what the fuck he deserved."

A couple of days after being wounded, Keefer had his wounds cleaned and was on his way back to his platoon aboard a resupply Chinook. A new lieutenant and staff sergeant were also choppered to Hill 400 to take over First Platoon; "Got a new first lieutenant today," Keefer jotted in his diary. "Don't look like he'll be too good." Perhaps the officer didn't like Keefer's hippie appearance or didn't want to take advice from an unschooled kid, but he cut it with Keefer when he told him, "You've been running things your way. Now I'm here and I'm going to run them my way. Now I'm going to show you the right way to run things."

This guy was another lifer, Keefer thought, disgusted, another Regular Army—Regular Asshole. He was bothered most that the lieutenant seemed to be playing a kind of popularity contest with the platoon. Night patrols were scary, but they kept the NVA off balance, and Keefer had run several and wanted them to continue. The new platoon leader called them off, much to the chagrin of Keefer, who thought that this would give the edge to the North Vietnamese; he was also upset that the slackers seemed to step right up and embrace the new lieutenant, making him feel good but eroding the field discipline of the platoon.

The lieutenant lasted a week.

They were sitting atop Hill 400, some of the men lighting C4 to keep warm, dry out clothes, and heat up some C rats and coffee. At dusk Keefer felt the old nervousness creep in; the NVA liked to hit at twilight, firing a couple of RPGs when there was still enough light to see by and knowing they could escape because by the time the Americans got organized and cranked up their tracks to pursue it would be dark. To chase

---

*That day they were successfully rescuing, under heavy fire, seven downed crewmen of the 174th AHC from the vicinity of LZ Sophia Two. That was a major ARVN success story, the tough Hoc Bao killing sixty NVA and rescuing all of the Americans.

into the jungle at night was to invite ambush and chaos. Keefer shouted at the GIs on his side of the perimeter to put out the fires, lest the NVA use them to sight in on. A few moments passed and he could see the new lieutenant and maybe ten men warming themselves around a fire built beside the command track in the middle of the laager.

Keefer wearily mumbled to Robinson beside him, "C'mon, Larry, I guess we better go over and educate this guy on some of the finer points here."

They ambled across the hill. "Sir, you better have your men put out them fires over there. It's just about time the enemy's going to be hitting us soon. They'll use them fires to zero in on us."

The lieutenant bristled at this challenge to his authority. He locked eyes with Keefer. "I don't need you minding my business. Mind your own business. I know what I'm doing. You and Robinson go on back over to your side of the laager."

The GIs around the fire laughed. Idiots, Keefer thought.

"All right," he said, "but I suggest you put them fires out."

Sp4 Ron Smith, sitting in the back of the command track with Doc Rose, was amused to see his buddy Keefer piss off the lieutenant again. He was relaxed, listening to a Carpenters tape on his cassette player—then an RPG cracked from a neighboring hillock. Smith stared, shocked at the projectile lobbing towards them. Keefer and Robinson were screaming to get down, but the lieutenant stood bewildered. Smith saw the RPG hit. It seemed to explode right on the lieutenant's leg, and he spun around like a top, then collapsed with a shuddering scream. Doc Rose poked his head out the door to look, then started backing up but Smith booted him out with a kick to the ass. Rose fell out and went flat as more RPGs shrieked up the hill. Men on the perimeter were putting down bursts from their fifties, while Keefer and Robinson ran back and dragged the lieutenant to cover in the back of an APC. Ain't been here long enough, Keefer thought as they helped the sobbing man, to know that hit the dirt means hit the dirt.

Doc Rose went to work on him in the track and, in the glow of the red lights, they grimaced at the devastating effect of the explosion. It looked as if the lieutenant would lose his legs and penis. Rose shot him up with morphine and the screams slowly subsided; then the medic looked up from the bloody bandages and muttered, "Man, he ain't going to make it through the night."

They radioed Captain Pierson for a night medevac and the answer came back shortly: none was available. It had been rainy all day, the clouds were low, and no helicopter could get up in that weather. The lieutenant's shit is in the wind, Keefer thought, but I can't tell him. He and Robinson ducked outside the track to hash it over. The squadron command post at Lang Vei had an aid station, but muddy roads and several kilometers of no-man's-land were between them and it. Keefer was tempted to let the lieutenant bleed to death in the track, rather than risk his men by trying to evacuate him cross-country, but he knew he couldn't. They couldn't watch a man die in front of them without at least doing something, wise-ass idiot or not.

Keefer was alone in the APC with the lieutenant for a moment, when he mumbled through his pain and morphine stupor. He said that he should have listened, but he hadn't wanted to send out patrols because he hadn't wanted to get anyone killed.

"Well, it's too late for that shit now," Keefer answered, "We're just going to have to see what we can do for you."

Deep down Keefer was bitter that some of the GIs had been willing to ignore his experience in keeping them alive, and had sided with the lieutenant because he didn't press them as much.

Finally they cranked up to go, a single track making the run. Keefer took the fifty hatch, Wolf drove, and Ollie and Robinson, Keefer's best friends, volunteered to ride shotgun. The four of them were an inseparable team. Doc Rose went too. "Like it or not," Keefer snarled at him, climbing in the back to keep the lieutenant alive as they made their mad dash to Lang Vei. They left the perimeter, lights out in the pitch black, crashing through brush until they found an engineer trail. They churned to one muddy hill and the track refused to climb it, the treads merely spinning mud, digging in deeper. Keefer tensed behind the fifty, his entire body crackling in preparation for the RPG that he knew was going to slam into them at any second. Wolf jammed it into reverse and they lurched out of the mud. He drove a few yards to one side and hauled up the road again from a different angle. The treads finally found passage, and they drove up and over the long, gradual hill.

They continued along the narrow, muddy trail, splashed across a stream, then hit Route 9, the bumpy highway a luxury in comparison to the jungle run. They weren't going to make it, Keefer sweated, this was suicide. Every hundred yards or so, an RPG burned out of the brush in their direction, all of them going wide because the track was moving fast, lights out, and the NVA had only the engine noise to aim at in the darkness. Somehow they made it to Lang Vei. At the command post, they were told to stay overnight rather than risk another run through unfriendly jungle. Keefer, Robinson, Wolf, and Ollie talked it over; they had Doc Rose and the mortar track and if the platoon were to be hit again during the night they would need both. The four decided that their place was with the platoon. They left Lang Vei at around midnight, roaring back the way they had come, ducking another volley of blindly fired RPGs. Keefer had counselled the gunners to fire only if NVA sprang out of the bushes right on them with satchel charges, so muzzle flashes wouldn't give away their exact position. Ollie and Robinson kept their cool, the engine sound wasn't enough of a target for the NVA, and they made it back to Hill 400 unscathed.

It had been an impossible feat as far as Keefer was concerned. He felt that the four of them deserved Bronze Stars at least, for saving the lieutenant's life. They won no medals; they never even heard if the platoon leader made it home okay.

PART FOUR:
A Renewed Effort

CHAPTER THIRTEEN:
Victory

By 28 February, it was obvious that the airborne and ranger drive on the northern flank had been ground to a halt. On that date, General Lam flew to Saigon to confer with President Thieu on an alternate plan. The president had previously sent I Corps a directive to have the Vietnamese Marine Division replace the 1st Airborne Division and press on. Such a switch would have been extremely difficult under the combat conditions in Laos, and it was obvious that Thieu's orders were politically motivated; he wanted to spare his "elite" paratroopers further bloodshed.

General Lam presented an alternate plan. Instead of replacing the Airborne, let them remain in place to screen the northern frontier, while the ARVN 1st Infantry Division took on the weight of the drive to Tchepone. General Phu and his troops were making a good showing of themselves and, at that time, they had eight firebases along the escarpment on the southern flank. The last, LZ Brown, was over halfway to Tchepone. Lam called for three more landing zones to be established along the escarpment (LZ Lolo, LZ Liz, and LZ Sophia Two), followed by a fourth (LZ Hope) to be placed near Tchepone and the area searched from there. Thieu agreed.

One of the problems that had been made apparent in the first phase of the campaign was the lack of coordination between the U.S. and ARVN. General Lam was at FSB Kilo, while General Sutherland was at Quang

Tri, while most of the I Corps HQ staff officers were at Dong Ha, while the unit commanders were in command posts spread across the Khe Sanh plateau. On-the-spot decisions during the battle were hard to come by. For example, the reserve forces at Khe Sanh were never once committed, not even when firebases were overrun and the defenders outnumbered. On 1 March, the U.S. Joint Coordinating Group was established at FSB Kilo; controlled by the commander of the 108th Artillery Group, XXIV Corps, it was colocated with Lam's field headquarters, and included representatives of XXIV Corps, 7th Air Force, and the 101st Airborne. Its purpose was to provide the second phase of the campaign with quick and responsive U.S. aviation and fire support.

Once again the crucial factor was this support. As General Berry wrote in his after-action report, "Probably no one unit in the history of air mobile operations was presented a more demanding and challenging task than that assigned to the 223d Combat Aviation Battalion to conduct the assaults 3 to 6 March. Four landing zones were selected along the escarpment which had to be sequentially assaulted to successfully execute the 1st ARVN Corps Commander's plan. Indeed, because of the NVA success at Ranger North and South and at Objectives 30 and 31, the fate of the entire operation was to be determined during this critical four day period."

On 2 March, the Dutchmasters of the 7/1 Air Cav were assigned to conduct photo reconnaissance along the escarpment to Tchepone to determine the best landing zone locations. Captain Mercadante flew only irregularly because of his duties with the troop rear, so he volunteered, flying front seat in one of two Cobras. They came into Tchepone at 8,500 feet and immediately began taking 37mm and 57mm fire; flak bursts appeared around the Cobras and Mercadante couldn't help but think, what is this, a rerun of *Twelve O'Clock High?* He began taking photographs from the cockpit as they pulled up to 11,500 feet, the flak following them the whole way. They radioed for USAF tac air, and a pair of Phantoms came on station. Mercadante asked the FAC what altitude the guns topped out at and was told 12,500 feet for the 37mm, and 16,500 for the 57mm. Incredible, Mercadante thought, it was virtually impossible to get above those guns without oxygen. There was no safe airspace over Laos.

The next morning, the ARVN 1st Infantry Division prepared for LZ Lolo. It was a hill mass atop the escarpment. The ARVN 3/1 was to be inserted, with the 223d CAB controlling the CA using additional helicopters from the 14th and 158th Aviation Battalions. This was to be followed by an airlift of a reinforced artillery battalion. Lieutenant Colonel Kirklighter took his helicopters from Dong Ha, rendezvoused at Khe Sanh with Major Klose, and made plans; then once more they crossed the river into Laos. The ARVN infantrymen, waiting in lines at LZ Delta, peeled off, a squad to a Huey, while guns and command ships circled. Up high again, the staggered trail of choppers beat westward. Down below, it looked like virgin forest. The land was calm. But the sky was filled with noise and motion, metal birds cutting forward, wind slapping the blades, turbine engines screaming, chatter on the headsets.

Major Klose took the C&C ship down over Lolo, while Kirklighter and the ARVN battalion commander on board decided on two LZs atop the ridge. Smoke grenades billowed yellow and the guns went in to prep, Cobras shark-nosing down at a hundred-and-seventy mph, miniguns flashing at two thousand rounds per minute. Trails of expended brass fell from the sky. There was no return fire from the jungle canopy. With the Cobras maintaining a scouting orbit, the first slicks lit atop the bombed hill and the ARVN disembarked. The first few Hueys went in and out, one at a time, without difficulty. Kirklighter sent in two ships at a time to more quickly beef up the ground elements.

The first pair of Hueys settled down. All hell broke loose.

And that set the stage for the day; despite the heavy tac air prep, the NVA hit LZ Lolo with the fiercest concentration of fire seen in the operation. Seven of the first ten slicks into the hot LZ took hits. Almost immediately four Hueys were down. Kirklighter maintained his C&C circle, controlling the guns, directing in more flights. The slicks kept coming, dropping ARVN, returning to Vietnam to refuel and pick up more troops.

It was semi-controlled chaos.

"Roger, Black Cat, go on in there, go on in there and land as close to the smoke on the high ground, where the smoke is crossing, where the Lima Zulu is."

"Taking fire! Taking fire!"

Pandemonium on the radio: "Yes, I seen the red tracers. We got it in the tailboom, I believe."

"Roger, we have guns on the way."

"Okay, let's hurry 'em up."

"And chalk six is taking fire."

"Roger, where from?"

"I don't know. It's just down, ah, straight below us. Just a minute, we'll get you coordinates."

". . . . there at the two o'clock position, down on the river."

"Okay, divert south of the river."

"Okay, where we took fire is approximately four-six-three-eight."

Into the LZ, they flew fire streaking up at them, door-gunners going in hot crew chiefs screaming to move, ARVN jumping out. Up, they circled back to Lang Vei or Khe Sanh to refuel, then to get more troops, then to go back through the fire, radio headsets buzzing with a constant stream of commentary. The NVA gun crews fired furiously. Another flight of Hueys came in with ARVN, Cobras rolling in to suppress fire. Doorgunners on the trail ship popped smoke out on the LZ for the next flight. Kirklighter was on the horn, "Do you have it now? Black Cat, do you have that smoke?"

"Yes, I sure do. . . . Hold off, I'm coming down to the mark."

Slicks came in, taking fire before they were even close to Lolo.

"Aw shit, I was going to tell you, you're not supposed to fire unless you can see the fire."

"Hell no, I didn't even get a round off."

"What was that pop-pop?"

"Hell!" came the door-gunner's high-pitched exasperated reply, "that was somebody shooting at us!"

So much fire tracked the flights that ships went down before they could even disembark the ARVN passengers. One crashed in the Laotian wilderness, and another chopper broke pattern to cover him while rescue ships came in. A commander shouted to keep the insertion going.

". . . that's affirmative, sir."

"Roger, get him back in business. If he's over that downed bird, get him back with his flight and proceed with your SOP for the recovery. Over."

"Roger, sir. Boats-six, Red Dragon Zero-nine. . . ."

"Hi, this is Boats-six. Roger, you got a recovery aircraft on my bird now. I'm coming on out of the LZ."

"Roger, your flight with you?"

"Negative, I let them go ahead. I got chalk two in charge of the flight now."

"Roger, roger, we have recovery in process."

". . . You've got recovery, now stay with the mission! Over."

"Roger, sir."

The last helicopter of the Black Cats came out of Lolo and popped more smoke; the next flight descended, taking fire, losing two Hueys, two-nine and two-six, still short of the hilltop.

"Two-nine's on fire, two-nine's on fire, going down."

"Did you see the fire?"

"Fire from three o'clock, from that ridgeline that they just passed over."

Pandemonium on the radio, a calm voice came on, "Okay, hold it, hold it down,"—then a ball of fire below them brought more shouts.

"Six, we got a fire."

"It just exploded."

"We got two ships down. One just crashed and burned."

More fire: the flight left two-nine and two-six, making the final descent approach to Lolo, Kirklighter watching from his C&C, trying to counsel them in, "They got twenty-three millimeter all the way down this flight path. You've got to remain south of the river, grab some altitude coming in here, start your descending approach into the LZ."

They descended to the unsettling sight of Hueys still in the LZ, unloading troops, which meant that they might have to overfly the LZ—and possibly have a helo, lifting off at that moment, crash into their underside.

"Tell these guys to unass this thing!"

"Get out of the LZ, you got aircraft on short final."

Coming back from the LZ, choppers passed the two crashed ships.

"Jesus Christ, that thing went up."

"Can we go back and see if them guys are okay?"

Long bursts of M-60 reached down to protect the crews.

A Huey went down through the fire to the crash site, the crew of two-six jumping aboard, except for the missing copilot. An excited voice called from the LZ, "Roger, one-seven has gone in and picked up two-six and a full crew off that ship! We're coming out of the LZ at this time. . . . My ship's running a little rough. We took a lot of fire. Don't know if I had any hits or not. I believe I've got it under control now."

The next flight on the long approach to Lolo took fire, took hits.

"Okay, what's your status? Do you have the LZ in sight?"

"Negative. I broke off the LZ on long final and I'm heading back inbound to Kilo Sierra at this time. I got a gunner hit in the head, some of the troops hit, and the aircraft's hit pretty hard, and I was losing fuel, but it stopped losing the fuel now, so I'm just heading back to Kilo Sierra."

"Okay, who have you designated as your. . . ."

Brigadier General Berry and Lieutenant Colonel Kirklighter, maintaining separate C&C orbits around LZ Lolo, stayed on the radio with each other. The NVA were good; they had allowed troops to be inserted before they threw their ring of steel around the landing zone. Once troops were on the ground, a CA had to be continued at all costs because the alternative—trying to extract the troops under heavy fire—meant chaos and additional casualties with no gain. The enemy understood this. All Berry and Kirklighter could do was radio for all available aircraft to divert to Lolo. Artillery pummelled the jungle at their directions. Cobras made screaming dive runs, pumping rockets and minigun fire into NVA positions. Jets flashed in, tumbling bombs and napalm into the triple-canopy ridgelines around Lolo. Tracers continued to float up from the forest, black and white puffs of flak rounds continued to explode. The sky over Lolo filled with smoke and circling machinery.

The 48th Blue Stars came in with cabins full of ARVN, flying behind the eight Hueys of another company. Five miles from Lolo, a flock of Cobras picked them up to escort them, every fifth slick shadowed by a gunship. Lieutenant Smith gave the thumbs up to his gunship pilot. With two miles to go, he heard an explosion and looked back to see only an ashy spot in the sky a hundred feet away where the Cobra had been. A radar-controlled flak gun had erased the ship and two pilots, and more pandemonium broke out on the radio.

"It was a midair collision!"

"It wasn't a midair collision!"

"Roger, get the hell outta there!"

"That looked like radar."

"Sure is, bigger'n shit."

"Sonuvabitch exploded."

"Did you see that. Goddamn."

"Let's cut the talk."

Coming in, Smith could see USAF jets making low gun runs around Lolo, heard them on the guard freq saying they couldn't neutralize all the NVA emplacements. The LZ was hot, the scene terrifying. The hill was pounded to dust, trees four feet in diameter broken like toothpicks. Parts of downed helicopters were strewn in the upturned earth, dead ARVN lay where they had fallen among the shattered trees. The South Vietnamese on his bird clambered out; then Smith was pushing the cyclic back and they were hauling up and out, taking fire, circling around to make the run back to Vietnam.

Sp5 Bill Wilder of the 174th Helicopter Company had already made several gun runs to Lolo, refueling and rearming at Khe Sanh between each trip. He was crew chief on a UH1C gunship. They were going in again, flying cover for his company's two lift platoons, when he saw flak burst all around one of the slicks. It trailed smoke in its descent. Wilder got on the intercom to his pilots, leading them towards the wreck. Their wingman peeled off to cover. Fire cracked around them and Wilder sprayed bursts back into the foliage. They were rushing forward at treetop level, popping over the trees—and spotted an NVA 12.7mm gun. The crew must have been moving, because they were in plain view in a field of elephant grass. They were wearing T-shirts and khaki trousers, Wilder noted, one NVA in the gunner's seat, the two loaders wearing sunglasses. Having fired at a different helo, the crew began swivelling around for the UH1C but the gunship sailed by ten yards away. Wilder, braced in the door, fired his M-60 in a long burst and the three North Vietnamese bounced into the grass.

Losing sight of the downed bird, they bounced to five hundred feet, spotted it again, and directed in the rescue slick. They were hit as they circled giving cover with their minigun and sixties, but the ship was still flyable. Another burst hit the rotors and the Huey began vibrating. Another burst, and they lost hydraulics. The pilot made a controlled crash on a thin dirt trail. It ran north-south and Wilder figured that it must be a branch of the Ho Chi Minh Trail. Their wing ship also took hits and crash landed on the path. The door-gunners laid some precautionary bursts into the treeline, but there was no return fire and everyone was okay. They began destroying their gear so the enemy would not get it, Wilder disconnecting the three radios and the voice scrambler, putting them out of commission with his .45. Then he pulled a pin which dropped the minigun into the dirt. Two lift ships flew in under fire, after dropping ARVN on Lolo, and the downed crews hefted the miniguns and climbed aboard.

Over Lolo another ten-ship company went in; then the flight leader was on the radio, "Okay, so we lost one aircraft in the LZ. We did get the crew out, is that correct?"

"Six, this is one-seven. Roger, I've got chalk four's crew with me, but I do not have his copilot. I repeat, I do not have his copilot."

"Does the crew know what happened to the-copilot?"

"That's a negative. We've asked them. They. . . ."

"Okay, was his aircraft burning?"

"Roger, his aircraft was definitely on fire. Very hot. The ammo was popping off."

"Okay."

"And six one-seven, we took a lot of fire and we'll be shutting down at the laager pad to check it out. I think we've sustained some hits."

Two Cobras and two Hueys came on station over the burning ship.

"Okay, did you get two-six himself out?"

"Roger, I have two-six himself."

"And the enlisted crew members?"

"Roger, I have the charlie-echo and the gunner."

"Okay, did they ever see the guy get out of the aircraft, the copilot?"

"That's a negative."

"He probably didn't because that thing went over on its right side and then it exploded."

"Boats six, Boats one-seven. The gunner just said that he got the co-pilot out and the copilot was walking around the LZ."

Another Huey went through the fire and found the copilot, still alive, down the slope from the hilltop LZ. Crew extracted, the air-mission commander said. "Let's all regroup at POL."

To avoid the intense fire, Berry and Kirklighter tried bringing the slicks in one at a time to the escarpment face. They approached through the river valley, then came in to land, one skid against the crest, the other hanging free, the ARVN jumping out the one side and scrambling up the hill. It usually worked, but the NVA fire continued unabated. Twenty helicopters radioed that they were inbound from the east, taking fire; ARVN wounded were on board, two slicks down. A voice on the radio said, "That's a helpless feeling to have to pull off an LZ like that and know that those guys are down there."

There was more firing.

"We got a slick autorotating to the dirt road. We are dropping down to take a look."

Lieutenant Colonel Kirklighter and Major Klose were in their C&C orbit above the battlefield, when 23mm fire began bursting around them at all angles, looking like bright puffs of white cotton. Four exploded in line behind the tailboom, then the fifth burst outside Klose's left-side door. The ship jerked in space, shrapnel tearing through in screams, and blood suddenly splattered the Plexiglas windshield in front of them. The crew chief, a young spec five, was down with a wounded hand. There were holes in the floor and ceiling of the Huey. Kirklighter radioed for the battalion exec, Major Davis, to continue the assault as Klose turned the ship around. They settled down beside the medical bunker at Khe Sanh and the crew chief was taken inside. Klose then flew to the nearby refuel/rearm pits and set down, leaving the engine running and the blades pumping. A nozzle was screwed in and the JP-4 turned on; then they stared in amazement as the fuel began spraying out as if from a garden sprinkler. Dozens of shrapnel holes had punctured the belly of the ship. The fuel was quickly shut off and Klose, jumping back to the controls, lifted away from the fuel blivets. He sat down, shut off, and another helo was readied for them.

Lieutenant Colonel Kirklighter was sweating in his flight suit. Christ, he thought, this a bitch.

In minutes they were airborne again and headed for LZ Lolo.

Over the landing zone, Major Davis was the temporary air mission commander. His normal duties had nothing to do with combat flying, but he was a man of courage and got into Laos any chance he could. By the end of the day, over five hundred ARVN soldiers had been inserted atop Lolo and, despite the murderous fire, had secured the hill. However, the second phase of the insertion, the airlifting of the artillery, had to be cancelled because it would have been impossible for the big Chinooks to hover long enough for the slingloaded pieces to unload without being blown out of the sky. The day had taken a heavy toll in helicopters, the official tally being seven shot down and thirty-five damaged.

On 4 March, the 223d CAB with the 101st and 158th Aviation Battalions cranked up to complete the move to Lolo. The ARVN 4/1 Infantry and the regimental command post were airmobiled to the firebase, enemy fire having lessened considerably from the day before, then the choppers continued west to LZ Liz. ARVN artillery on Lolo pounded the site designated as Liz, five kilometers further along the escarpment: sixty airstrikes and numerous gunship sorties further pummelled the area. The helos came in with the ARVN 2/1 and artillery, through heavy fire, and secured Liz. Heavy smoke blocked vision around the LZ and General Berry, on station in his Huey C&C, later wrote, "What transpired was an alternating stream of assault helicopters and large cargo helicopters in a stream of combat air traffic which would rival that of a large international airport on a foggy day."

Official toll for the day was one Cobra and one Huey downed, twelve helos hit.

The next day, the ARVN hit LZ Sophia Two, about four kilometers west of Liz. The 2d Regiment secured the hill in the face of heavy fire, and artillery and supplies were brought in ("The coordination had become so polished by this time," a 101st ABD report read, "that CH-47s and CH-53s were able to begin resupply of artillery and ammunition almost concurrently with the troop insertion."). Enemy fire was heavy; two Cobras, two UH1Cs, and two Hueys were shot down. Seventeen other choppers were damaged around the three new firebases. Firefights flared as patrols began moving out.

But the door to Tchepone had been opened.

The deserted and bombed village called Tchepone, in reality, had no military value. The NVA supply caches were in the surrounding mountains, not in the town proper, and the supply lines ran to the east and west of it. But the name Tchepone rang with political significance. The South Vietnamese and foreign press had made it an invasion symbol (with no rebuttal from the RVN government) and the military was ordered to go after the propaganda coup. As one ARVN general noted, " . . . the ARVN effort now seemed to be more directed at setting foot in Tchepone than trying to destroy the NVA logistical system which was the real objective of the offensive."

All was not for naught, though. In three days, U.S. Army Aviation had survived the heaviest AA fire of the war and had moved two full ARVN regiments (1st and 2d) thirty-five miles deeper into enemy territory, a major victory in itself. Also, the military objectives were in no way completely abandoned. Time and effort were going to be exerted in Tchepone for propaganda, but the selection of the landing zone was reassuring; LZ Hope was four kilometers northeast of Tchepone—where it belonged militarily, not politically. The ARVN 2d Infantry Regiment was designated the assault force into LZ Hope on 6 March. The aviation support was to come once again from the 223d Combat Aviation Battalion, 1st Aviation Brigade.

On 5 March Colonel Battreall went to the I Corps HQ Bunker for General Lam's daily decision briefing. The subject was Tchepone. The 2/17 Air Cavalry was to escort the troop-carrying helicopters, and their new commander, Lt. Col. Archie Rider, had just returned from a personal reconnaissance of the area. It was Rider's first day in command of the squadron. His helicopter had almost been blown out of the sky, and he was rattled. He frantically tried to convince Lam that the hills around

Tchepone were alive with AA positions. He wanted to postpone the CA, and General Jackson seconded the opinion. Battreall had never been enthused with Lam as a decisive commander, but he was impressed when Lam thought for a moment, then said forcefully, "No! We have B52. We will use them, and then we attack."

That ended all further discussion.

The CA to LZ Hope/Tchepone by the ARVN 2d Regiment was coordinated by the 223d CAB. It was the most complicated air move of the operation, an hour and fifteen minutes required for each helo pickup, flight, insertion, and return. It was seventy-seven kilometers from Khe Sanh to Tchepone. On the morning of 6 March, the helicopters began gathering on the Khe Sanh strip. Three hundred choppers sat in the fierce glare of the sun and the swirling red dust, while their crews waited.

It was a stunning sight, but also a worrisome one; before long, the first 122mm artillery shell impacted in the perimeter wire. The NVA walked their bombardment onto the strip, creating massive confusion as the aircrews rushed for their ships and bolted into the sky. Two men were killed on the ground in the shelling but, amazingly, the three hundred helicopters managed to get airborne above the artillery without losing a single ship.

Meanwhile Lieutenant Colonel Kirklighter, Major Klose, and the ARVN regimental commander were in the C&C bird. They had gone in ahead of the main body to recon LZ Hope. They circled the last firebase along the escarpment, Sophia Two, so as not to alert the NVA of their intentions. The area was pocked with craters from the B52 Arc Lights, and the last landing zone was a clear spot carved out of the jungle with a Daisy Cutter (the detonator extended several feet from the nose of the bomb so that it exploded above ground, felling trees with fifteen thousand pounds of explosive). The ARVN commander confirmed that the LZ was suitable for the insertion and they returned to Lang Vei to refuel. They were headed to Khe Sanh to join their armada when General Berry got on the radio to inform Kirklighter that the airstrip was being shelled, the helicopters were already airborne, and everything was to continue ahead of schedule. If the helicopters had left Khe Sanh in succession, as planned, the first company would have been halfway to Tchepone before the last company had even started its engines. Instead they were burning fuel as they waited in circling patterns. Kirklighter and Klose radioed the pilots to play it by ear, dipping into refueling berms when they could, and it worked itself out.

Phantom jets flew continuous airstrikes around Hope and caused numerous secondary explosions. That firepower, combined with the Arc Lights of the previous night, must have devastated the NVA antiaircraft crews in the area because only a minimal amount of fire was directed at the choppers. Six crewmen were wounded, fourteen helos hit, and only a single Huey was shot down, its crew immediately rescued. In ninety minutes, the ARVN 2d Infantry Regiment was on the ground and securing the area against minimal resistance.

Tchepone had been taken.

The next morning, Berry wrote in his journal, " . . . Yesterday was a good day. We seized our objective. We had very few casualties. . . . What a glorious relief!"

CHAPTER FOURTEEN:
The Great Withdrawal

How long were the ARVN in Tchepone before they started screaming to come out, Lieutenant Smith thought bitterly. A few days, was it? And then began what the aircrews cynically referred to as the great withdrawal, marked, Smith noted, by a graveyard of American helicopters.

The plans for invading Laos had not envisioned an army of occupation; the ARVN were to strike to Tchepone, destroy Base Area 604, then withdraw. MACV and XXIV Corps (not to mention the White House) hoped they could destroy the NVA logistical systems until the onset of the rainy season in May, and then make their withdrawal through BA 611 and the A Shau Valley, wreaking further destruction along the way. The ARVN high command had never wholeheartedly embraced that option; when Tchepone was taken, the South Vietnamese had the choice of reinforcing and continuing the fight, or of pulling out as soon as possible. They opted for the latter. The ferocity of the North Vietnamese counterattacks was the main factor in this decision. Intelligence had failed accurately to gauge the great rate at which the NVA could reinforce southern Laos, and even the successful drive to Tchepone had been met with fierce resistance in an area that was still hot. Lolo, Liz, and Sophia Two were under daily shellings and the patrols in the area made numerous contacts.

This phase of the operation could be summed up by noting, for example, that the 1st Regiment, working off of Lolo, had killed hundreds of NVA, discovered tons of supplies, and cut important communist communication lines to the southwest. At the same time, the line battalions were taking heavy casualties, and the bombardment of Lolo kept away practically all resupply and medevac helicopters.

The combat in those jungles was conventional warfare.

To make a propaganda coup of the Tchepone victory, no planned withdrawal could begin until the rubbled village was occupied. Two battalions of the 2d Regiment swept through the valley from LZ Hope. Ironically they had the easiest task, since the NVA caches and commo lines were not in Tchepone and the area was not heavily defended. Okamura, the reporter, joined up with the search battalions, and was correct in writing that the mission was "partially propaganda, partially fishing."

The 2d Regiment walked up the slopes of Sophia Two on 9 March.

With that completed, General Lam reported to the Presidential Palace in Saigon. He met with President Thieu and General Vien, and detailed the campaign as he saw it. In one sense, victory had already been achieved: for every ARVN casualty, ten had been inflicted on the NVA, and, although an early withdrawal meant numerous caches would go undisturbed, they had already destroyed enough supplies to halt the planned communist offensive. In his opinion it was time to get out. The terrain beyond Tchepone was mountainous and so deeply thicketed that ARVN armor could make no headway without knowing the concealed trails. In addition, the NVA were still well dug in. Lam's troops were outnumbered and bloodied, and there was no large reserve. Thieu and Vien agreed it was time to withdraw.

When General Abrams was informed of the order to retreat, he met with Thieu and Vien. Aggressive as always, he suggested that the ARVN 2d Infantry Division be sent into Laos to continue the offensive. President Thieu let his feelings be known when he said that would be fine if a U.S. infantry division were also sent in. The matter was dropped at that point.

In Laos the ARVN began destroying the tons of material they had uncovered (numerous underground storage areas had been unearthed by the B52 strikes) and pulling back to their firebases to be airmobiled out. The NVA, who had enjoyed numerical superiority throughout the entire campaign, pressed relentlessly at the withdrawal as, with each day, there were even fewer ARVN to face them. Combat around the firebases was horrific, casualties high on both sides. The first unit out was the 2d Regiment from Sophia Two on March 11-12; there was surprisingly little fire to hamper the move.

No other unit was blessed with such a bloodless exit from Laos. For U.S. Army Aviation, the spirit of the withdrawal was, as General Berry noted, to "Get them out as fast as you can." He further noted in his after-action report, "The objectives of LAMSON 719 had been achieved. What remained was the very difficult task of disengaging from the enemy and conducting an orderly withdrawal from Laos. The retrograde operation in land warfare is one of the most difficult to conduct successfully. The difficulty of withdrawing the ARVN forces from Laos was compounded by the terrain, weather, and the aggressive enemy who had been severely embarrassed by the ARVN's ability to penetrate deep into what had been their sanctuary. . . . U.S. aircrews used every trick in the book and invented several new ones to get the job done. Fuel loads were lightened to allow more ARVN troops to get on each helicopter. It looked as if there was no control of the withdrawal during the last days; however, the more troops which crowded on each helicopter meant that less helicopters were subjected to the intense hostile fire in and around every pickup zone. An example of the intensity of the fire around the pickup zones was that 75% of the helicopters used sustained bullet damage during that period."

LZ Lolo, held by the ARVN 1st Infantry Regiment, was the deepest base in enemy territory after the evacuation of Liz and Sophia Two. It had been under attack since the initial insertion. Within a week, the NVA had maneuvered to encircle the bunkered knob, while 120mm rockets and 130mm artillery pounded the firebase round the clock. Sappers raised hell inside the wire. It was virtually a siege. The Cobras of the 4/77 AFA flew constantly to strafe the NVA creeping in the wire, directed by an ARVN who spoke English fluently and whose calmness had earned him a good reputation among the American aircrews. They called him Quebec Whiskey. By 14 March, as the North Vietnamese moved to isolate the withdrawing units, Lolo was cut off. The AA fire was so intense that medical evacuation for the South Vietnamese was impossible, resupply extremely hazardous.

On 15 March, the regimental commander issued an emergency request for small-arms ammunition. It went to the 223d CAB at Dong Ha and Major Klose volunteered to fly as air-mission commander. Five slick crews also volunteered to fly in five slingloads of ammunition. Captain Johnson and one of the best pilots in the 173d Robinhoods, Capt. Henry Pomije, flew the lead ship. They picked up their thousand-pound slingloads at FSB Kilo, then departed for Laos in one-minute intervals.

Klose circled the boulder outcropping on which Lolo sat, directing in air-strikes and gunships. One of the Cobras was hit and fell from the sky in flames. But the two wounded pilots crawled away from it.

The lead Huey came in towards the face of the escarpment—and Klose suddenly saw a stream of green 12.7 tracers stitch across its tailboom. The Huey shuddered and veered away, Johnson and Pomije valiantly refusing to punch the slingload which slowed them down in the ground fire. Pomije radioed Klose that he had taken hits but that no caution or warning lights had come on. He turned the ship back around, hovered over Lolo, and gently put the slingload of ammunition on the ground. Then Johnson and Pomije banked the Huey and hovered over the bunker line, looking for the Cobra pilots. Rounds ripped through the helicopter.

Klose screamed on the radio, "Get the hell outta there!"

They maintained their orbit over Lolo and radioed the location of enemy guns to chalk two, boring in next. It hurtled in high and fast, not slowing down or dropping low with its slingload. Johnson mumbled to Pomije, "What the hell is he doing?"—just as the slingload of ammunition was released from two hundred feet, hit the middle of the perimeter in a cloud of dust, and splintered in all directions. Klose exploded on the radio, chewing out the pilot. When finished, the pilot cut to the company frequency and said nonchalantly, "They won't have to uncase that shit." The other pilots came in and dropped their slingloads softly. All five Hueys were riddled with fire.

Captains Johnson and Pomije went back for the Cobra pilots. They emerged from a bunker, waving a red NVA flag they had found, then jumped aboard the slick which pulled out with sixty-five bullet holes in it. Quebec Whiskey got back on the radio, directing the Cobras on NVA attacking the perimeter. During the night, tac air pummeled the NVA. Quebec Whiskey was either killed or wounded in the battle, because another Vietnamese took over the radios. In the morning, 16 March, the 1st Regiment pulled out, leaving five damaged howitzers, destroying three more in place, and abandoning their dead and whatever couldn't be carried.

The 4th Battalion was left behind to conduct a rearguard defense.

The ARVN 4/1 Infantry was immediately hit by NVA artillery which wiped out the battalion command group, including the commander. As they moved on foot to the northeast, they were under almost constant fire and, at noon on 17 March, the North Vietnamese launched a heavy assault.

The battle raged for two hours; the ARVN radioed that they had killed five hundred NVA, but had lost fifty men themselves. Helicopters of the 223d CAB went in through heavy fire to medevac their many wounded. Sergeant Keith, Intelligence NCO with the 101st Airborne, was flying as an observer on one of the Hueys that was diverted towards Lolo. Cobras zipped in ahead of them, and heavy fire cracked from the escarpment. Keith's slick banked off, but then went back in to get a fix on the gun positions. The tracers began streaming at them—then, suddenly, the Huey lurched in space, the floor exploded. Keith didn't even realize he'd been hit until he looked down. His left leg was literally disintegrated, all white and red, the kneecap gone, and Keith muttered into his radio mike, "Oh damn, I'm hit, I'm hit." His radio cord was severed. The copilot turned to look back in the cabin and almost fainted when he saw Keith—he just shook his head and laughed back, "I've done it now!" The crew chief helped him lay back. He was in shock until the chief straightened out was left of his leg; then the pain shot through him. There was no morphine on the helicopter so all they could do for Keith was tie a bandage around the stump. Blood kept seeping onto the floor. Keith's glasses were speckled with it. When he looked up in the vibrating helicopter, he could see bits of his bone and flesh embedded in the ceiling. The pilot struggled to control the bird as all the warning lights flashed, and Keith knew that if they had to ditch in Laos he'd bleed to death before a medevac got in. He was a professional soldier and didn't want to go through life crippled; he forced himself to mumble, "If you want to die you can die right now . . . no, I don't want to die." Keith patted himself, finding other wounds, and kept smiling at the shaken copilot who glanced back at him. The pilot kept the Huey together and headed for Khe Sanh, radioing for medevacs in case they went down. Gunships peeled off to cover them.

When they shut down on the strip, medics from Bravo Med rushed up.

Keith was badly in pain, coming out of the Huey. He was taken to the underground medical bunker. Medics cut off his clothes, stopped the bleeding, kept talking to him, asking questions. A medevac came in soon and he was ferried to the 18th Surg at Quang Tri. He babbled in his morphine stupor, passed out when they started the IV, and woke up five hours later, coming out of it with terrible nightmares and with his left leg amputated. Later he told a reporter, "The pilots I had flown with came in that evening and said a lot of good things to me. That set me on the road to recovery. From then on I had no problem about my mental attitude."

By nightfall the survivors of ARVN 4/1 were seeking refuge in some bomb craters at a bend in the river at the foot of the escarpment. The North Vietnamese surrounded them in the dark and shouted with loudspeakers for their "brothers from the South" to surrender. The battalion had not been supplied for six days and was short of ammunition. They did not surrender. They radioed for more bullets.

Lieutenant Smith had shut down from a day of flying when an emergency call came to Dong Ha for immediate resupply to the survivors of 4/1. Smith had no idea what ARVN unit that was but, when volunteers were asked for, he and WO Del McClure stepped forward. They flew out in a single slick, with door-gunners, tracing down Route 9 at thirty knots and fifteen feet because of ground fog, taking several hits before they even reached Khe Sanh. They shut down on the airfield, checked the tiny holes in the skin, then had a thousand-pound cargo net of ammunition slingloaded under their Huey. An air force major briefed Smith and McClure in a command bunker, "The ARVN are surrounded. We've got them on the Fox Mike frequency. They're instructed to pop a strobe light when you come on final. You're to go straight into the strobe light. They're on the neck of a river. Punch your load off right at the strobe. Take an immediate right turn. They're completely, 360 degrees, surrounded by the enemy. No lights, no dash lights, no nothing on the helicopter. Take a turn to the right and the river's on the right. When you get shot down, you can head for the river."

When, Smith noted, not if.

They departed Khe Sanh with volunteers from the 173d in a second Huey also towing a slingload of ammo. A line of napalm burned red and yellow below them, pointing to the ARVN position, and a USAF pilot came on the horn to say he had splashed nape on the NVA but was still taking ground fire. Smith contacted the South Vietnamese on the FM freq and told them to turn on their strobe light.

Several strobes popped in the dark. The NVA were on the radio.

Just then NVA fire began cracking past Smith's Huey and they aborted the mission with eighteen hits at one thousand feet. Back at Khe Sanh, the major said that they had to give it another try, so they cranked up again, Smith and McClure still flying lead. Ground fog had rolled in around the Khe Sanh plateau from the east, and they churned slowly through it at thirty feet, following the dirt road of Route 9 with landing lights on. They figured that if the fog had also blanketed the Laotian side of the border they would abort the mission; if not, they would instantly climb high as they hit the clear. In Laos the road forked and Smith followed the trail which seemed to go west. It actually made a gradual southern run through a small valley. The fog got thicker, a few rounds cracked below them, and Smith radioed the second chopper that they must be lost and to turn around for Khe Sanh.

Then, abruptly, they were in thicker fog. It was a void, pitch black and foggy on the valley floor—and McClure was seized with vertigo; he felt the chopper wildly spinning in different directions when actually it was flying straight and level. He shoved the cyclic all the way forward. Smith flipped on the spotlight to see where they were just in time to see a mountainside looming before them. With blades clipping at the treetops, Smith cut off the light, punched the slingload, grabbed the controls, and went to instrument flying. They levelled off, but the sudden shift in weight had jerked the craft and McClure frantically grabbed the controls again, pulling the cyclic all the way back. The black dot on the console attitude indicator showed they were flying almost straight up, Smith screamed, "I've got the controls! You've got vertigo!" as he punched McClure in the face and wrestled back the cyclic. Oh God, his mind screamed, we've bought the farm. Somehow, they levelled off again and made an ascent into the clouds between two peaks. Lieutenant Smith pulled them up to eight thousand feet and finally broke out of the clouds; then he shot a GCA radar approach back to Khe Sanh.

They made it back safely, nerves shot, the ARVN still out of ammunition.

By sunrise on 18 March, the stranded 4/1 had accomplished its mission covering the retreat of the 1st Regiment. By noon, the 223d CAB was almost finished extracting the regimental command post and the 1st, 2d, and 3d Battalions. The reporter Saar was at Kilo and saw the first four slicks, " . . . cross a melancholic expanse of gray sky." The wounded had been evacked first. Saar watched and wrote his notes later, " . . . One man topples out and lies still until rushing colleagues bear him gently to an ambulance. The rest can walk, the stiff-legged stumble of the exhausted wounded, and with their drawn, grimace-set faces, tattered uniforms and filthy dressings, they come painfully toward us like some terrible march of the damned.

"Then, in air-tearing fleets of Hueys, the unwounded survivors arrive. That first step back to the soil of South Vietnam is for each man a moment of pure joy—the dazed grins, the helpless laughter, the jubilation of friends celebrating joint survival, with arms flailing round necks and shoulders. It takes no oracular powers to understand that in the past six weeks these men have seen fighting they never expected to survive. Yet they have come back, and despite their long unwashed griminess and tatterdemalion fatigues, each man has a steel pot and a rifle, and somehow they have the carriage of the tough, dependable soldier."

"They look good," Saar commented to a pilot.

"Yeah, what there are left of them."

Saar spoke with a crewcut U.S. Marine captain, an ARVN advisor, who watched his returning troops with controlled emotions. The politics of the invasion forbade him from accompanying his charges into Laos and his comments betrayed guilt, "I wish we could have gone with them. We trained them, lived with them. It's kind of like cheating."

The 223d CAB immediately took off again to get the last of the regiment, the 4th Battalion, which was cut off four kilometers east of Lolo. They were in an area where the escarpment tapered off to the river flatlands, still in the higher part where thick scrub grew, seeking shelter in the craters produced by their USAF close air support. Of the 420 men of the 4/1 who went into Laos, only eighty-eight were there. All of the officers were dead and sixty-one of the survivors were wounded. Their final position measured only sixty meters in diameter. A sergeant was in command, and his only link to the vital U.S. air power was a single PRC25 radio. The men were exhausted, outnumbered, almost out of ammunition, and surrounded by the NVA.

Another attack would destroy them.

As soon as the main extraction of the regiment was completed, General Berry got into a C&C orbit above 4/1. Lieutenant Colonel Kirklighter and Major Klose joined him, calling in all available helicopters and directing in more airstrikes. The Phantoms tumbled bombs and napalm around the battalion's crater, sixty-eight airstrikes in all, keeping the North Vietnamese at bay. A flight of Cobra gunships, led by Capt. Keith M. Brandt of D Company, 101st Aviation Battalion, came on station in response to Kirklighter's call for assistance. The ARVN on the radio called Brandt, "We're completely surrounded. You expend on my smoke." He hurled his last smoke grenade from the crater and twelve Cobras rolled in right on top of it.

Captain Brandt stayed over the ARVN all afternoon. Three times he expended his ordnance into the NVA, flew back to Khe Sanh to refuel and rearm, and returned to the crater. He stayed in contact with the ARVN sergeant and dodged the NVA fire on low-level flights to pinpoint 4/1's exact location and calculate the best approach route for the rescue birds.

It was almost five in the afternoon before the 173d Robinhoods began trailing from the east, Captain Johnson flying the lead with Lt. John Trapani. Captain Brandt was still circling the area, out of ammunition but aware that the ARVN had no smoke grenades left to mark their position. He volunteered to lead the slicks in and contacted Johnson, "This is Music One-six. Follow me, Robinhood Three, and I'll lead you to the friendlies."

The Cobra and Huey darted in at treetop level but overshot the crater as NVA fire exploded around them. The Cobra shuddered, trailed smoke and fire, but Brandt was still on the radio, "I've lost my hydraulics and my mast is on fire." He brought his gunship into a slow, 360-degree turn towards the ARVN, with the slick still following him.

Brandt lined Johnson up with the crater and shouted in the radio, "There it is! Twelve o'clock, a hundred meters I'm going to try to make the river."

"No sweat, buddy," Johnson answered, "I'm right behind you."

Smoke and flames dragged in the wind behind the Cobra. The rotor rpm slowed as he fell towards the riverbank treeline.

Captain Brandt was on the horn, "I've lost my engine and my transmission is breaking up. Good-bye. Send my love to my family. I'm dead." Then, the Cobra became a ball of fire and crashed into the trees. Captain Johnson brought his Huey to a hundred-foot hover over the burning wreck, and thought he could see an outline of the pilot and copilot lying in the flames. Johnson and Trapani looked at each other, knots forming in their throats.

Major Klose's voice screaming over the radio brought them back to reality, "The troops are at your six! Get'em, get 'em!"

Klose was not being heartless. He had watched Brandt die from his C&C; he could feel the lead weight sink in him and thought, My God, that man was a true hero. He'd given his life for others. Klose wanted to put Brandt in for the Medal of Honor.

But the battle was still being fought.

Johnson landed his Huey and it was chaos. Twenty-four ARVN scrambled aboard, filling the cabin, hanging from the M-60 mounts and skids—one even opened Johnson's door trying to get in with him. They lifted off and Johnson looked back at the survivors in the cabin; their fatigues were shredded, many were without weapons, some had bandages, and one had a hole in his head where once he'd had an eye. They'd just come out of hell. Heading back for Kilo the ship began losing rpm because of the weight, and could not return fire with ARVN on the guns. Johnson did not resent the ARVN; they had fought bravely, and had scrambled aboard now as any man would when a rescue bird came in. But they were going down from the weight.

Johnson ordered his crew chief and door-gunner to throw three ARVN off. They were kicked off of the skids at several hundred feet.

The second Huey in the 173d trail popped up with a dozen ARVN, but was hit on takeoff and crash-landed east of the position. Another slick went in to rescue the crew, and the extraction was temporarily halted as more firepower was laid around the crater.

Two hours later, Lieutenant Smith was flying lead ship for the 48th Blue Stars. Three kilometers from the crater, he could see green tracers burning past him, a couple smacking into his Huey. He radioed ahead to the orbiting C&C, "Do you have the flight in sight?"

Klose gave an affirmative, saying gunship support was coming and to go into the LZ.

Smith insisted he had no contact with the guns.

Klose said they were coming, the LZ was cold, get in there!

The North Vietnamese fire tapered off as they made the final approach to the South Vietnamese position, Smith flying low over the brush. He darted towards where he thought the LZ was, then spotted the ARVN a hundred meters away and quickly hopped over to them. He landed in the one-ship LZ, then stared flabbergasted at the ARVN rushing towards his ship as if someone had fired a starter pistol. The first ones shoved their dead battalion commander aboard, and jumped in. Smith pulled pitch as more ARVN clambered on. The blades bent, the rpm light flashed on, and Smith just managed to get into a transitional lift, give it fifty pounds of torque, and glide away at a shallow departure angle with ten ARVN in the cabin and two hanging from the skids. The crater fell into pandemonium. Smith could hear the pilot of chalk two screaming, "Goddamn!" in the radio, as he sat for a few seconds in a five foot hover, then flew off with ARVN swarming on the skids. The third Huey sat on the ground, overloaded, and couldn't get airborne again until the crew chief and door-gunner punched some of the South Vietnamese out of the cabin.

They were flying back at three thousand feet when the crew chief told Smith that one of their skid riders had just fallen off.

The line of Hueys followed Smith back towards Khe Sanh, the last of the South Vietnamese aboard. More ARVN soldiers lost their grips on the skids in the freezing wind and flew tumbling through the sky.

Smith was a hundred feet from the Khe Sanh strip when the engine stopped, the fuel line finally having ruptured from a hit. He made a controlled crash, then sat shaking in the cockpit. He watched the rest of the company coming back, one slick weighted with too many ARVN. It lost control on landing and bounced to a halt on the runway, its skids sheared off, an ARVN skid rider crushed underneath.

By Captain Johnson's count, of the eighty-eight men in the crater at the beginning of the day, they got thirty-six back to Khe Sanh alive.

Reporters crowded around the strip, photographing the South Vietnamese clinging like insects to the helicopters, interviewing frightened and excited pilots who poured out bitter comments about the panicky ARVN. That's how the ordeal of the 4th Battalion was reported back home, with the inference that the ARVN were cowards. The U.S. command thought otherwise; the ARVN battalion had been fighting hard for six weeks, had successfully defended the pullout of their parent regiment, and was surrounded and out of ammunition when the pickup birds finally came. "I don't know what the press was trying to prove," Lieutenant Colonel Kirklighter said, "I didn't see him hanging from the skids. It does not mean that the unit panicked or acted unmilitarily. It only means that some soldier looked around and, hell, he's the last son of a bitch on the ground and he's not going to be left behind. I'd jump on the skid too. And so would you."

On the afternoon of 19 March, Lieutenant Colonel Peachy's 158th Aviation Battalion controlled a pullout in the airborne sector. Under heavy fire, they managed to evacuate the 2d Airborne Brigade Headquarters, many wounded paratroopers, and some artillery pieces.

Next to come were the 2d and 7th Airborne Battalions, scattered and disorganized on the jungled mountains. WO Smith of the Ghostriders had just flown two resupply missions into Laos, and had shut down his machine on the pad at the 1st Airborne Division CP when word came to mount up again. The whole company, eleven slicks, was going in to get the stranded paratroopers. They began taking heavy fire as soon as they crossed the border and one or two of the Hueys had to turn back with serious hits. They made it to the assigned coordinates, a small clearing on a knoll, and Smith could make out ARVN clustered in the brush, firing from their hastily formed perimeter.

He could see mortar rounds exploding around the LZ, as he sailed through a crossfire of 12.7mm and AK-47 tracers. One round punched through the main rotor blade. First one M-60 stopped firing, then the other, and the crew chief screamed, "They're jammed, let's get outta here!"

"Long as we're here," Smith shrugged, "let's see what we can get."

WO Smith brought the Huey to a ten-foot hover. There was a mad scramble and, within seconds, ten ARVN were hanging from the skids. He pulled up through the fire as the crew chief and door-gunner hauled the men into the cabin. They dropped them at the airborne CP, traded their jammed machine guns for a working pair from a wreck, and prepared to go back again. A captain, the new company commander, came over then and told the copilot to get out; he took the seat to Smith's right. They were almost to the paratroopers again when Peachy came on the horn and cancelled the mission. The ARVN advisors wanted more time to organize the troops via radio.

Smith and the captain were headed back when an emergency call came over the radio. A UH1C was down and they were to extract the crew. They were told to fly on the deck while Cobras led them in. Smith was tempted to pop up to several thousand feet to see for himself, but he obeyed the Cobra pilot leading him. "Go left, go right, okay, flare now!" He brought the Huey to a hover over a jungle clearing, as instructed, and looked through the Plexiglas at his feet. The crashed gunship was nowhere in sight, but he could see figures in the brush fifty feet away—and he realized they were shooting at him. His face suddenly recoiled as if a sledgehammer had hit it and the bullet crashed out the windshield in front of the captain.

Reflexively, Smith grabbed the cyclic between his legs with one hand and reached for his face with the other. There was no blood; then he realized where he'd been hit. The round had come through his door, punched through his lower left side and tumbled out just under his right shoulder blade. His spine had been hit and his legs were paralyzed straight over the foot pedals. There was no real pain; it was numb. As he slumped uncontrollably to the right, gripping the cyclic, the Huey veered from its hover, and he shouted at the captain to take the controls. The captain hesitated a stunned moment, then grabbed the controls and pulled them out of firing range. They banked around for Vietnam. Smith occupied his mind by staring at the control panel. The engine oil pressure suddenly dropped to zero, and the temperature gauge spun up. He shook the captain's shoulder and pointed.

The captain made a controlled crash in the dust of Route 9, still in Laos. They sat vulnerable on the road, the door-gunners sweeping the brush with fire, tracers burning back at them. Smith could hear whistles in the treeline, maybe bugles, and thought, God, I'm going to die. Then he noticed he really wasn't scared. The firing was getting heavy but he was going into shock from his wound, floating into a world of detached bliss. Another Huey, piloted by a buddy nicknamed Muddy Waters, landed right behind them to rake the trees with M-60s, while a medevac bird darted in. The crew chief and door-gunner hauled Smith from his seat and ran to the medevac. They laid him in, then joined the captain running to Muddy's slick. The two Hueys lifted up under fire. The fifth member of the medevac crew, a young medic, worked on Smith as they flew towards Khe Sanh. Harold Smith could feel nothing below his waist.

The airborne advisors stood in a tense cluster at the CP as the Hueys of the Ghostriders came back from Laos. The reporter, Saar, stood nearby as the slicks shut down on the strip cabins empty of ARVN. The pilots joined a huddle.

"I don't know who the hell is running that, but there's NVA right alongside the landing zone and .51 is hitting inside. Six ships hit, one went down, and one aircraft commander hit in the spine so he can't move his legs. What are they trying to prove?"

"We started taking fire from a klick out."

"That's two of my birds got shot up today. They can stick this flying up their ass. What are they trying to prove?"

The height of the debacle, Saar thought, that's what this is. He'd been at the airborne CP for several hours, watching the Hueys coming and going, disgorging over a hundred dead and wounded paratroopers. Almost all of the dead were barefoot and wrapped in ponchos tied with cords, or in U.S. body bags. They were stacked like firewood, weapons and gear piled beside them. " . . . And among the helmets, is one drilled front and rear with odd precision by a Kalashnikov bullet. . . ." he wrote. The underground medical bunker, made of sandbags and carved earth, was a hell of moans and screams under hazy flourescent light. The wounded lay in blood and bandages, just off the choppers, still wearing their muddy uniforms. There were a hundred casualties, so many that they filled the bunker and had to be carried to a troop tent.

The ARVN are losing, Saar thought. He did not think the ARVN were collapsing because they were cowards; in fact, he considered them reasonably well trained, equipped, and led. But, in the final analysis, it is the spirit of the troops on the ground, when all things are equal, that will determine the victors and losers, and the ARVN lacked the fervor and conviction of the North Vietnamese. His attitude must have been obvious to the ARVN; when he was standing with fellow journalist Okamura, some airborne officers asked, "Okay, what would you do if you were the general?" Okamura smiled broadly. "Do you mean a Vietnamese general," he said, adding fierce emphasis on the end, "or a Japanese general?"

Saar returned to the Ghostriders on the strip. Word came to try again and they bitched and cursed, but climbed into their Hueys. It seemed to him that they flew not out of charity for the South Vietnamese but because of personal and unit loyalties. He was still there when the slicks returned, fended off by the intense fire before they could get the ARVN aboard. One of the ships settled on the strip, hit so many times that it reminded Saar of a target drogue. An armored seat in the cockpit was laid back and dripped blood on the metal floor. The pilot, a popular young lifer captain, had had his leg shot apart. A young warrant officer ran up, threw his hat to the ground, and shouted in anguish, "The sons'a bitches just ain't worth it!" The door gunner, a handsome kid, blond hair sweaty against his forehead, stared, haunted, at a hole torn in the metal just above his head. Pilots smiled at him. He wandered aimlessly off the strip, shaking his head. "I can see going out there for GIs," someone grumbled, "but it's not worth it for these guys. What are they trying to prove?" Curious ARVN paratroopers edged closer to have a look at the shot-up Huey. The pilots screamed at them to get the hell out. The advisors jogged over to lead the ARVN away.

That night Saar joined the ARVN doctors for supper in their underground mess; it was a fine affair considering the surroundings, with the surgeons' servants putting liquor, tea, and food on the table. Saar thought the lighting was dramatic, with pools of light and shadow playing against the sandbags. The scene was made even more dramatic when an American advisor noisily cleared his throat from the shadowed bunker entrance. Conversations at the table hushed. The advisor spoke awkwardly,

"About the two refusals by the medevac birds today . . . wanted to say that we are going to find out what happened." The advisor excused himself and Saar noted, "There is laughter and normality, but another dividing line had been drawn between allies."

On 20 March, the 2d and 7th Airborne Battalions broke contact with the NVA and regrouped on a ridgeline. The paratroopers, about six hundred of them, held the eastern portion of the hill mass and the NVA fired on them from the west. Lieutenant Colonel Peachy controlled the extraction with birds from his battalion and the 223d CAB. North Vietnamese mortar fire plastered the LZ, so Peachy directed in airstrikes and gunships. At the same time, he courageously escorted each slick in through the foggy valley. Some ARVN were pulled out, but several choppers were hit and went down. Peachy himself was seriously wounded when his C&C was hit.

The initial extraction was cancelled.

The helicopters settled back at Khe Sanh to refuel, rearm, and reorganize. Lieutenant Smith was standing beside his Huey when a pilot with a 101st patch ran down from the medical bunker, screaming about his copilot, "What the hell you send us in there for! There's no way to get in there, you're just leading us to a death trap!" Other pilots held him; he seemed upset enough to go for a commander.

The weather got better. More USAF strikes hammered around the ARVN paratroopers, a naval smoke barrage was laid to the west of the LZ, and the aircrews cranked up to give it another try. Smith was flying chalk eight; a hundred yards short of the LZ, green tracers burned by his ship. There were hits and the engine conked out. Smith brought it in for a controlled crash in a field of low brush, everyone jumped out unscathed, and, before the rotors even slowed down, a UH1C gunship was darting low to cover them. It was from the 48th Joker Guns and piloted by Smith's buddy, WO Fred Cristman, nineteen, of North Carolina. Cristman flew past, raking the brush with his minigun, while a Huey bore in. Smith and his crew climbed aboard it and they headed back for Khe Sanh.

The rest of the helicopters continued into the hot LZ. Cristman's gunship was hit, crashed into the ARVN perimeter, and was hit on the roof by a mortar round just as the crew jumped out. Cristman, his copilot, and the crew chief were thrown to the ground. Only the door gunner, Sp4 Paul Lagenour, survived the direct hit, with shrapnel wounds in his left arm. The North Vietnamese tried to overrun the LZ but the paratroopers opened fire as they pushed Lagenour to a radio. He directed airstrikes and gunships on the NVA and their attack petered out.

The second extraction attempt was halted.

The ARVN still in the LZ clustered around Lagenour all night as he stayed in the radio. He was a young kid and he sounded scared to Smith, who listened with the other crewman at Dong Ha, but he was holding himself together well under the pressure. Support fire was brought to bear throughout the night.

By the evening of 20 March, only a few remnants of the 1st Infantry Division remained in Laos: the 2d Regiment CP, 2/2, 4/2, 1/3, and an artillery unit. They were located near Delta One, the division's last firebase along the escarpment. A pickup that day by the 223d CAB had gotten the ARVN 3/2 back to Vietnam. Those still in place repelled a night attack and, in the morning, the 14th and 223d CABs came in to get the survivors.

Some infantry and artillery units remained at Delta One to provide support if the NVA launched a final assault during the pullout, while most of the ARVN organized in clear spots around the perimeter. Lieutenant Colonel Kirklighter, having been told he had 550 men to evacuate, figured eighty slick loads would do the job; he and Klose circled high, letting the company commanders run a simple daisy chain. The Hueys went in two or three at a time. There was no NVA fire. Kirklighter figured the NVA were just glad to see them get the hell out.

He finally broke in on the radio, "What's it look like down there?"

A company commander said, "We still got a helluva lot of people down here."

Kirklighter advised the next company flying in, which soon departed with ten more cabins full, and with the report that more ARVN were milling around the area. Ten more Hueys came and went, and their trail ship reported still more troops on the ground. With a hundred slicks already having gone in, Kirklighter and Klose finally brought the C&C down. They were astonished to see some 500 ARVN on the ground; they had been told they were to get 550 and had already taken out 500, but were only halfway through. Slicks kept going in. Kirklighter got on the radio to Colonel Harrison at Kilo and said he would keep pulling the men out, but suggested jokingly that he check their identification because he had no idea who they were. Back at Kilo, General Phu and Colonel Harrison were ecstatic; not only were their last battalions being extracted without difficulty but hundreds of missing soldiers who'd been written off as dead were straggling to the last pickup zone.

Kirklighter and Klose returned to thirty-five hundred feet to supervise. They saw some vehicles several kilometers away, coming east on Route 9. They were running a well-disciplined road march with about fifty meters between each vehicle. Kirklighter ignored them until it dawned on him that no ARVN armor was still supposed to be that far west. The pullout from Delta One was progressing smoothly, so Klose took them down for a look. From a bit closer, they could make out the dark spots on the road as tanks but couldn't tell if they were of U.S. or Soviet make. Kirklighter got on the radio to General Berry at Khe Sanh. He confirmed that there were no ARVN units in that area.

Before long a flight of F100s rolled in to strafe. Kirklighter and Klose departed to watch from a safe distance. The jets roared down from four thousand feet straight at the tanks, dropped their bombs at practically ground level, then pulled up and came around for another pass. They hit the lead and rear tanks, blocking the column, then strafed leisurely—a field day, Kirklighter thought, as he watched the fireworks of snake-eye bombs and twenty mike-mikes. One of the jets made its turn so that Kirklighter found himself looking down the tailpipe and, at the same time, able to see the intended target in a direct line below the plane. The pilot unleashed his ordnance at low level; then he simply flew straight into a gently rolling hill. Kirklighter was shocked. The pilot may have been hit, but there had been nothing erratic in the flight; Kirklighter knew pilots could become locked on a target, mesmerized, and lose touch with everything else. That's what he thought had happened, for the jet had simply followed its dive path into the ground, nose first. The jet exploded and burned in the grass, and Klose felt a particular pang of remorse. The bodies of the two pilots would never be recovered, thus they'd be carried as MIA; though he knew they were just ashes, their parents would never know for sure.

A radio call came from the last company commander over Delta One. They had everyone out of the PZs and were heading for Kilo. Klose turned the C&C around and headed back, as the jets continued strafing and smoke rose from several burning tanks. At Kilo they made a head count: 919 soldiers had been pulled out that afternoon. The ARVN 1st Infantry Division was finally out of Laos.

On the afternoon of 21 March, the choppers went back to pick up Sp4 Lagenour and the ARVN paratroopers still on the ground. They walked east, the wounded door-gunner calling in airstrikes along the way, and grouped at a small hill for the extraction. This is reportedly what happened: The first slick filled with ARVN; Lagenour ran towards the second, but mobbing ARVN shoved him aside and he tumbled into a ravine, out of sight, the helicopters departing without him.

Lagenour was not seen again until eleven days later. He walked east the whole time, travelling by night, sleeping by day, eating leaves and rice, evading NVA units in the area. Twice he was almost captured, and once a U.S. gunship almost killed him. Thirty kilometers and eleven days later, Sp4 Lagenour was found by a U.S. armored patrol west of Khe Sanh. Lieutenant Smith was detailed to investigate the incident, but Lagenour was medically evacuated to the United States before anyone could talk with him. The impression among the aircrews, however erroneous, was that the lifers wanted Lagenour out of the way before he could tell anyone what he'd seen with the ARVN.

As the general withdrawal continued, General Berry and Colonel Ghai, deputy commander of the ARVN 1st Infantry Division, planned a raid into BA 611 in Laos to keep the enemy guessing and off balance. The always tough Hoc Bao Company conducted the successful foray. This completed, Berry bid his friend and comrade, Ghai, goodbye and asked him how he thought the war would finally end.

"It will never end," Colonel Ghai said. "It will go on forever."

CHAPTER FIFTEEN:
Ambush Alley

The ARVN 1st Armor Brigade was also pulling out via Route 9. The North Vietnamese were waiting for them. It was a chaotic and bloody episode, made even more dramatic as American armor and cavalry units rushed to the border to hold the road against repeated ambushes. At the same time, they were trying to evacuate the U.S. artillery in the area before their firebases were overrun. For the American ground troops in the operation, it was perhaps the most sustained action they ever saw.

Captain Downey, observing Route 9 from his hilltop perch, remarked, "It was quite exciting to watch our convoys come charging around that bend with all guns blazing and the NVA rockets coming back at them. Although it became much less a charming scene when you reminded yourself that men were dying down there in some very horrible ways. The color of the tracers, rockets, and explosions was awesomely beautiful. In every case the ambush was overcome or silenced and my arty FO helped by directing howitzer fire against the NVA. The guys from the 5th Mech and the other armored cav outfits were a brave and tough bunch of men. They fought their way up that road every day, sometimes several times a day, and each time they went they knew what to expect. They behaved in a way that would have made the original General Patton proud. If it had been World War Two, someone would have written exciting stories about them. Ernie Pyle'd have loved 'em."

The border firebases were held by the 8/4 and 2/94 Artillery, XXIV

Corps, who had moved into position on 9 February. Until then they'd been living in the mud at Vandegrift and Khe Sanh; for Pfc James Keeney, a radioman with C/2/94, this had been an eye-opening week of war. He was nineteen, from the small farming community of Chillicothe, Missouri, a country boy who'd answered the draft unhesitatingly when his number had come up. He arrived as a new guy in January, during a standdown in Da Nang, and the first thing he saw was a burnt-out personnel carrier. It had hit a mine, two men had been killed, and the artillerymen talked of revenge on the enemy. That's what Keeney had expected of Vietnam. But the rest of the standdown was a confusing experience, a shock to see that things were not as he'd thought they'd be. The blacks and whites shunned each other: there were fistfights. Night guard on the bunker line consisted of pot parties and prostitutes who were allowed inside the wire. About half of the battery turned on with grass, but there were a half-dozen men hooked on heroin and they frightened Keeney; they seemed paranoid and crazy enough to kill you if they thought you'd turn them in.

It wasn't until the road-march to Vandegrift that the battalion changed into what Keeney expected from the army and Vietnam. The drug use dropped dramatically, and the artillerymen tucked away their differences to work as an effective team. The soldiers of 8/4 and 2/94 set up on the border off Route 9 at a place called Lao Bao. It was simply a ragged circle in the jungle, trees knocked down, the ground pitted and uneven, and quickly pulverized to dust by all of the machinery pulling in.

They were still digging in that first day, when the NVA began shelling from Laos. Keeney and a buddy nicknamed Whitey jumped into a little bunker meant for one and scrunched up, Keeney terrified at the roar around them and the dirt clods bouncing into the entrance. Most hunkered in holes, waiting it out in a cold sweat, but a staff sergeant in 2/94 jumped up amid the explosions, gathered some volunteers, and ran to one of the 175mm pieces. They climbed aboard and managed to fire several rounds towards the NVA before a shell exploded directly behind them, hurling the men dead or wounded from the cannon.

The NVA shelling finally stopped. Men warily got up. Medevacs came in. Keeney and Whitey climbed from their bunker to see the staff sergeant standing nearby, amid some other GIs, holding his helmet which had a big shrapnel hole in it. He was drained white and shaking. The sergeant was a big, bald, well-muscled Southerner, and Keeney considered

him a macho, beer-chugging type. He also didn't think much of his dash
to the artillery piece. It was stupid, he thought; instead of keeping his
men under cover and calling for support fire, the lifer got gung-ho and
ran to do it himself. And two of the guys with him got blown away. But
Keeney couldn't drag up much anger at the sergeant. He'd exposed himself to the fire, had taken his chances alongside his men. In a way, he
thought, I guess he's a hero.

Sp4 Pat Hallman, a draftee in B/8/4, had no problems determining
who was a hero and who was not. When the sergeant and volunteers ran
out into the flying steel to return fire, he thought they were the greatest.
They'd gotten up and tried. He stood there shaking inside after the shelling, exhausted from his first moments of combat, and hurting inside from
a terrible thought. He hadn't been able to move when the artillery was
pounding in. In the American rite of passage known as war, his greatest
accomplishment had been to cringe in a hole. At the age of twenty-one,
he felt like a coward.

Sergeant Hatfield struggled with his own doubts that day. By four in
the afternoon, 8/4 had repacked and moved back towards Lang Vei, leaving 2/94 on the border alone, and leaving Hatfield to wonder why they
had even gone forward. They had gotten people killed for no reason that
he could see; the difference of a couple of kilometers made no difference
in their fire missions into Laos, and he wondered why higher had sent
them within range of the NVA guns to begin with. His anger increased
that night as they set up near Lang Vei; some of the GIs told him a friend
of his, a young man also from Washington whose parents he knew, had
been one of those killed in the shelling. Hatfield could have cried. It was
all such a game, Hatfield thought, and that day he could feel himself in
sympathy with the bitterness and frustration of his men. He was a professional soldier, saw Vietnam as a neccessary evil, but so often it all
seemed such a useless waste.

His only consolation was that the draftees in a unit he had considered
garrison, learned to fight day-by-day, and some were even decorated for
genuine valor.

The batteries were booming out rounds from Lao Bao into Laos, and
Pfc Keeney was standing around watching when the captain told him to
hustle down to an engineer truck unloading supplies to get a case each of
soda and beer. He was walking towards the truck when a distant boom
and shriek hit his ears above the sound of their own artillery, and he

threw himself down. Fifty yards ahead of him the truck exploded. A few more shells impacted around the perimeter; then there was silence except for the horrible screaming from the gutted truck. Keeney ran over. Three GIs were sprawled dead around the wreck, mangled by shrapnel. Two other men lay there, one in shock with an eye blown out, the other screaming with his leg split up to his crotch.

They were just fish in a barrel, Keeney thought.

Sights were seared into the memories of those down in the gun pits. When Sp4 Hallman crawled from a hole after bombardment, he could only stare, too scared to do anything, at the wounded gunner before him. The kid leaned against the treads of a 175mm SP, drained white, smoking a cigarette and mumbling to the medic working on him, "I'm going home. . . . I'm going home. . . ." His legs were a bloody mess, his flak jacket practically ripped off of him. They heard later, he died on the medevac. Another man in the battalion put an M-16 to his foot to get out. The worst of it for Hallman was when a buddy, a hard-working religious kid from the South, got blown away. He'd been at his post on the guns and couldn't hear the whistle of incoming over the roar of outgoing. He died instantly. A sergeant came back from R&R with a case of booze; they sat in a bunker that night, not celebrating as they had planned, but drowning their sorrows in alcohol. Hallman felt that a little piece of him had died, and self-hate pounded at him as if he thought he could have done something to save his dead friend. The shellings were cracking him up.

Sgt. Drayton Markle was dispatched with four Dusters and one APC of A/1/44 Artillery, as perimeter security to Lao Bao. It sat like a bulge into Laos. They set up on the southern side of the perimeter, down a small grassy slope so they could hear but not see the 2/94 Artillery. The Co Roc was ahead of them across the border river so they buried their vehicles up to the turrets to protect them. It was just plain shitty, Markle thought, the North Vietnamese dropping in a couple of hundred rounds a day on their little perimeter. You could see the puffs of smoke on the Co Roc, hear the boom and whistle and know you had only seconds to scramble into the nearest bunker or hole.

It was tough, but Markle tried to keep his spirits up by concentrating on the funny things. One hot meal a day was flown in by helicopters in thermite cans, and as soon as a dozen men lined up for chow, the NVA observer would start another shelling. Everyone would run for cover. It would let up in about ten minutes; then heads would start popping up like moles. The first man would get brave and go back to get some chow, another line would form, and the shelling would start all over again. During another bombardment, Markle and a buddy, an Sp4 named Jack Wooten, got gung-ho and ran to their Duster to return fire at the Co Roc. Wooten was pumping rounds amid the incoming when he suddenly asked Markle for his helmet. Markle handed it to him with a puzzled look, because no one put much faith in the GI steel pot to stop anything, and Wooten grinned, "Yeah, I know, but it just feels better." Markle thought the funniest thing he saw happened when a chaplain set up a makeshift altar beside a truck in a bulldozed ditch. About fifteen artillerymen sat on a mound listening to the sermon when the chaplain held up his hands in a blessing—and a boom echoed from the Co Roc. Before Markle could even get to his feet, the chaplain turned and, with his hands still up, bent over, he dove between the truck and the trench wall. REMFs always take everything seriously, Markle thought.

But the bad things were all around and even a trooper like Markle who believed in what they were fighting for couldn't help but be worn down. It pissed him off to see ARVN convoys going by on Route 9 with lumber and steel planking, when the GIs had only sandbags and culverts. There was the time that the barrel on one of the 175mm guns broke in half from metal fatigue, then fired and flew across the perimeter to shatter the skull of a GI sitting on a perimeter bunker, his back to the gun. He never knew what hit him. Another morning Markle woke to see a 175mm SP blown up and a path gouged behind the wreck. The story was that the crew had put in the wrong charge; the breach block had blown off like a cannonball and had caught the gunner in the chest, hurling his body so hard he dug the trench. The two artillerymen beside the gun were caught in the powder blast.

The 8/4 Artillery, camped between Lao Bao and Lang Vei, was the first ordered back from the border. The 2/94 Artillery was the next, but unlike the peaceful withdrawal of their sister battalion, theirs became a trial by fire. On the afternoon of 18 March, Bravo Battery at Lao Bao packed up to move. At the same time, a platoon from the 1/11 Infantry was mortared while holding the road open for them. One GI was killed, six wounded. Whatever could not be loaded on trucks, and whatever vehicles would not start, were abandoned. The NVA shelled Bravo Battery as they hit the road, at a toll of sixteen wounded artillerymen, plus the destruction of much of their equipment and vehicles. Of the materiel left behind, all was blown up by the accurate NVA bombardment except for a broken-down 175mm left in its berm.

At around five in the afternoon, after the departure of B Battery, Alpha Battery prepared to follow. To Pfc Steven Rhodes, of Aberdeen, South Dakota, nothing could have been better. The op had started on an ugly note for Rhodes during the convoy north. A friend had been tossed off of their truck when the driver'd swerved around a shell hold. By the time they had run to the man, a medic was doing mouth-to-mouth; the friend's head was smashed. He'd gasped for air, turned blue, and died on the medevac. At Lao Bao, the shellings had been hitting home, and most of the last few days had been spent underground with some buddies, the earth shaking as if a train was rumbling past, shrapnel pelting off of the sandbags, dust clouds rolling in the bunker entrance. A few nights back, Rhodes had crouched in the bunker with his M-16 at the ready while artillery impacted in a treeline behind him and green AK-47 tracers erupted along the perimeter. Sappers were probing the wire; a quad-fifty, with the cynical slogan PARIS PEACE TALKS on the turret, instantly streamed red tracers in return. He heard the gunner shout, "I got one!" and things quieted back down.

It was getting too close for comfort as far as Rhodes was concerned, and he gladly threw his poncho, cot, and footlocker into a commo truck. His buddy took down a peace flag that they had flown over their bunker, torn with shrapnel holes, and packed that too. In a half hour, the battery was ready to go. They abandoned two trucks, four trailers, and an eight-inch gun that would not start. An artilleryman manned an M-60 atop the FDC track; behind that Rhodes climbed into the commo truck and squeezed among the stacked gear, able only to see rewards due to the side boards. When they hit the road, fire snapped at them and the M-60 gunner raked the brush in return. The commo truck veered to one side and Rhodes saw a helmet lying on the road. He thought someone must have dropped it. With another sharp veer, he saw a jeep on the side, smoke rolling from under the hood: then a body came into view—sprawled on the road, the head blown, nothing remaining but a bloody stump and a pool of blood. They stopped, another truck pulled up behind them, and a sergeant quickly hooked up the wrecked jeep. They took off again, headed for Lang Vei.

Charlie Battery had also been scheduled to leave Lao Bao that afternoon, but the NVA artillery and ground ambushes along Route 9 prevented it. That night Pfc Keeney manned a perimeter bunker with two other artillerymen, unaware that they were cut off and alone. The North Vietnamese knew, though, and a sapper squad moved against the semiabandoned perimeter. The brush moved in the darkness, and Keeney choked to see shadows gliding through the elephant grass. He shouldered his M-16. The sappers crept forward through the high grass; the artillerymen sat silently watching from the bunker, the moonlight catching the details—a dozen sappers, stripped to shorts, smeared with charcoal, and carrying satchel charges. They stepped into an open engineer trail and Keeney fired. A body tumbled in his rifle sights. They sprayed on automatic, a tracer hit one of the satchel charges, and it exploded amid the group. The shooting petered off. In the morning, Keeney took a photograph of the dozen North Vietnamese soldiers spread-eagled on the road. It was the first time he'd killed. He was a hard-muscled, broad-faced, country boy with a country boy's sensibilities. He felt no regret. Them or us, he thought, simple as that.

That evening, 18 March, the gears to withdraw the ARVN 1st Armor Brigade from Aloui were set in motion by General Lam at his nightly I Corps briefing. Until then, the brigade had been pummelled by NVA bombardment and attack. They had held their ground, but little good had come of it, as Colonel Battreall noted in his after-action report: "In the period 4–16 March the Bde received a plethora of instructions from both Div and Corps variously directing it to seize objectives deep in enemy territory, block at ALUI, move 'as far as possible' in one or another direction, not to cross this or that grid line, etc. The result was that the Bde blocked a km or two north and west of ALUI. . . . The principles of the Objective, Mass, and Unity of Command were violated."

Lam directed that the 1st Armor begin its eastward road-march the next morning, and allocated two troops from the 2/17 Air Cav to General Dong for use in covering the withdrawal from ambushes. That evening Colonel Battreall received a radio call from General Sutherland, their only personal contact during the operation. Sutherland was concerned about the numerous disabled vehicles the brigade had at Aloui and offered to dispatch a company of ARVN M578 recovery vehicles with which to tow the downed armor.

"What am I going to do with a company of dragon wagons?" Battreall answered, "the road is not passable."

Sutherland sputtered, obviously hearing this for the first time.

Battreall was shocked at how far removed XXIV Corps was from the realities of the battlefield, but he surmised that it was not the fault of Sutherland or his staff. It was the recurring problem of having no advisors in Laos, and the disjunctions that resulted. This one happened because the U.S. had intended the ARVN Airborne to physically secure Route 9 against the NVA and improve the dirt trail, while the ARVN had interpreted the instructions merely to mean they should bring Route 9 under artillery fire. The highway was in wretched condition west of LZ Bravo, usable only by tanks and tracked vehicles. Not even a jeep could make it to Aloui.

Early the next morning, Colonel Luat and the 1st Armor departed Aloui, bringing out their damaged vehicles, towed by like vehicles. An FAC pilot overflying the abandoned basecamp reported four NVA tanks closing towards it. The two air cav troops which were to have screened ahead of the armor to detect ambushes were diverted by Dong to his airborne units. Thus, the 1st Armor was left to travel the narrow, terrain-restricted road with no flank or scouting security.

The first NVA ambush came before eight in the morning at a stream crossing between Aloui and LZ Alpha. The lead tanks were sloshing through the water when the North Vietnamese cut loose from hidden jungle positions. The lead tank was hit and some of the ARVN panicked, abandoning four vehicles in the stream, some of the attached paratroopers continuing alone down the road in chaos. In three hours of fighting, the ARVN managed to subdue the NVA fire long enough to move two of the abandoned tanks to the side so the rest of the column could continue. The brigade kept moving, leaving one disabled tank in the water and cutting loose seventeen of the disabled vehicles they were towing so that the remaining ones could move and fight when more of the inevitable ambushes occurred.

North Vietnamese units followed the withdrawal and moved into the ambush site with PT76 tanks and infantrymen who clambered aboard the ARVN vehicles. The Dutchmasters of the 7/1 Air Cav, overflying the area, glimpsed a bewildering scene of ARVN and NVA tanks in the same area. They had a moment of shock until they comprehended that there were NVA firing from the ARVN tanks. A Cobra pilot, WO Marvin "Doc" Beck, roared in to unleash a 2.75-inch rocket into the engine deck of one of the PT76s on the road. The tank blew up, blocking the path, and USAF jets arrived to demolish the seventeen abandoned ARVN vehicles. Back at Quang Tri, Beck painted a tank silhouette on the nose of his gunship.

In the morning of 19 March, Pfc Keeney climbed wearily from his bunker only to look shocked at the scene around him: the Lao Bao perimeter looked like a ghost town. Where A and B Batteries had been, there were now only abandonned 175mm and eight-inch guns, stalled trucks, empty bunkers, piles of expended shells, stacks of live ammunition, cartons of C rations, and other odds and ends. Groups of ARVN straggling out of Laos walked through the abandoned perimeter; Keeney thought they looked wild-eyed and hungry, only one or two still carrying rifles. The ARVN ducked into the bunkers to stuff their shirts with C rations and the artillerymen shouted at them to clear out. Someone fired his M-16 over their heads, not too concerned about how close he came, and the ARVN scurried into a bunker. Then they crawled away in the brush; like snakes, Keeney thought, damned cowards.

By noontime the gravity of their situation began to hit them. It was hot and dusty, and down the road they could hear shots and explosions. A helicopter weaved bumpily over the perimeter, shaking from hits, and sailed towards the ground. A hundred yards from the wire, it lurched forward and burst into flames on impact. A patrol of artillerymen quickly moved out to rescue the crew, but there were no survivors. Phantoms pummelled the area around them, a couple screaming low over Lao Bao doing victory rolls. Victory rolls, he thought, my God, what do those pilots see out there? How close are the gooks?

The NVA shelling started again and they scrambled underground. The truth suddenly hit Keeney like a dead weight—they were cut off— and he felt scared, forgotten, glad the jets were on his side. Several hundred artillery rounds exploded on Lao Bao as they crouched in the bunkers, some of the men bitching.

"What the shit's going on?"

"Here we are fighting for a bunch of chicken-shit ARVN, and they leave us!"

By nighttime Keeney was back in his bunker trying to sleep. He'd been able to sustain his flagging spirits during the day because all of his buddies were pulling together in the face of crisis. But that night, alone in his dugout, he could feel his morale sink. Oh God, I'm never going to get home, his mind kept repeating. This is it. Boy, Jim, you've really blown it now. You're trying to be the all-American hero, and now you're going to die in this God-forsaken country. For nothing.

On the morning of 20 March, helicopters dropped off three teams from the Long Range Reconnaissance Patrol (LRRP), 1st Brigade, 5th Mech Division into the AO of the 1/11 Infantry. The five-man teams, wearing bush hats and camouflage fatigues, were inserted at various points along Route 9 to pinpoint the location of the NVA who'd hit the road. At nine o'clock, one of the teams found two mines in the road which they blew in place. Then they were ambushed, and the LRRPs called for artillery support. As soon as the arty lifted, they were promptly hit by 82mm mortars. They called in more firepower, and turned up one dead North Vietnamese and an AK-47 rifle.

The NVA fire kept up.

General Hill alerted the commander of the 3/187 Infantry to prepare his C Company as a reaction force, possibly to CA in. Meanwhile he ordered Lieutenant Colonel Breeding of the 1/1 Cavalry to dispatch immediate reinforcements to the LRRPs. The closest cavalry outfit was two platoons of Bravo Troop, under Capt. Carlos A. Poveda, a thin Puerto Rican. Bravo clipped down Route 9 only to be ambushed themselves. A raking of AK and RPG fire killed one GI, wounded five, and damaged an APC and a Sheridan. Captain Poveda pulled the two platoons back and called in arty and air on the south side of the road where the NVA were dug in. Napalm and five-hundred-pound bombs raised smoke and Bravo swept forward again; they were met by a level of fire undiminished for all the U.S. firepower employed, and another trooper was killed. More air and arty were called in on the NVA. Bravo moved forward a third time and was again forced back in the face of heavy fire.

Captain Poveda was coming in last, covering the retreat, when his APC hit a mine. He and his crew, one of them wounded, were cut off and left behind in the disorganized withdrawal. A Huey went down on the road nearby and its crew joined the pullout. Bravo troop reorganized on Route 9 and two tracks went back to rescue Poveda and his crew. They tore full throttle down Route 9 on a Thunder Run, the fifty and sixty gunners laying down a constant hail of lead into the roadside brush, and the men climbed aboard one of the APCs.

The retreat under fire continued.

Sgt. Jim McCormack, twenty, a draftee from Waterbury, Connecticut, was in one of the LRRP teams which initially did not make contact. He knew it to be a bad area, though; the night before, his five-man team had crouched silently in the jungle as a North Vietnamese unit filed past. This morning was clear and sunny when the choppers deposited them on

Route 9 and, in short order, they walked into an abandoned NVA bunker complex. Another chopper dropped off demolition charges to blow the bunkers.

They were doing this when someone on the radio told McCormack to get his team to haul ass back to the highway.

They heard heavy firing as they moved back, and proceeded with caution, not wanting to be mistaken for the enemy. They emerged from the brush into chaos—a 175mm SP was abandoned on the road, Sheridans and APCs were hauling east in clouds of red dust, fire cracking in both directions. Grunts on the tracks shouted to come on, and the LRRPs ran like hell to get behind some armor. One young Lurp hustled towards a truck dragging a water trailer just as an RPG blew the trailer away: he collapsed in shock. McCormack and the others threw him into the truck bed, then climbed to the deck of an APC. The NVA raked them with fire and they returned it, McCormack firing his M-16, amazed to see North Vietnamese in broad daylight ducking from bush to bush.

They acted as if they owned the place.

Bravo Troop kept hauling east, then pulled into a rough circle on Route 9 and laid down fifty and sixty fire in all directions. AKs cracked back at them. McCormack was firing his rifle when an RPG shrieked at the APC beside his. The track commander's head exploded and the driver, suddenly splattered with blood and bits of flesh, went into shock. Something boomed in front of McCormack's APC and shrapnel stung his face and head; a LRRP medic hastily wrapped a bandage around his forehead as he kept his M-16 in action. The firepower of the wagon-train circle did no good, so they hit Route 9 again, firing and taking fire until they were about a mile from the ambush site.

Bravo Troop halted on the roadside and it was pandemonium as the casualties were carried from the vehicles to be treated. McCormack was waiting for the medevac when the grunts around him began speaking incredulously of an order that had just been radioed to Captain Poveda; because the disabled command APC had a radio decipher code in it, Bravo Troop was to proceed back into the ambush zone to secure the wreck and the nearby downed helicopter. As it was not a matter of rescuing Americans, but of salvaging materiel, none of the GIs McCormack saw seemed willing to go back—for the sake of a radio. He himself was taken aback by the stupidity of such an order. If the gear's so important, he thought, why not just have a Cobra blow it apart so the enemy can't get to it. A medevac came in and Sergeant McCormack got on board, glad to get the hell out of the situation; the bird lifted off with three WIAs and two KIAs.

The MPs at a Route 9 checkpoint told Sgt. Frank Burnett that a cav unit was in trouble. The only cav folks he knew in the area was Bravo Troop. He'd helicoptered to them the day before, dispatched from Hq&Hq Troop to check on some complaints about the mail; when he'd left this morning to hitchhike back to the 1/1 Cav Rear in Chu Lai, Bravo had been laagered off the road with some artillery and ARVN units. His first thought now was that the grunts were in a shooting feud with the ARVN, but he decided to hop in the MP jeep going to the scene.

They halted a hundred feet from Bravo Troop, which was strung out along the side of Route 9. It was chaotic, some men milling around, others lying in the grass with medics bent over them. A helicopter arrived, a senior officer and an NCO hopped out, and Burnett watched the curious sight of the old sergeant running up and down the column, waving his arms and yelling at the men to get back on their vehicles and move out. The grunts ignored him.

Burnett was too far away to hear all of the dialogue.

Lieutenant Colonel Breeding, ten days in command of the squadron, had ordered Poveda to retrieve the APC and helicopter, and Bravo Troop had nonchalantly refused.* Now Breeding and the cavalry sergeant major had come on the scene and were arguing with the grunts who only snapped back with a list of complaints—they had only sixty men left, the NVA were obviously dug in deep and would ambush them again, night was coming, and the equipment just wasn't worth getting killed over. Unimpressed, Breeding said to get moving; one of the grunts guffawed in his face, "You must be out of your fucking mind!" With that the colonel had his sergeant major line up the enlisted men and take down the names of those refusing to go. Two men said they would go; fifty-three refused the order.

General Hill, monitoring the situation from Khe Sanh, got on the radio to calmly ask Poveda why his troop wasn't moving. After Poveda explained the situation, Hill informed him that he was no longer in command.

The GIs of Bravo Troop were disgruntled and when reporters arrived

---

*The actual refusal was covered by the press, including a *Time* magazine account (April 5, 1971) "Incident on Route 9" and an article in *Armed Forces Journal* (by Robert Heinl, May 3, 1971).

at Lang Vei to give the incident page one coverage, they found the grunts weary, filthy, and bitter. Sp4 Randy Thompson of Evansville, Indiana, was quoted in the press. He was one of the men who had volunteered to go back into the ambush to rescue Poveda, but when it came to Breeding's order, he commented, "The reason given wasn't a very good one. It was after a piece of machinery that could have been replaced. I didn't see any sense in risking any more lives."*

Five days later, Sp4 Thompson was killed in action.

The second day for Charlie Battery, cut off at Lao Bao, was a repeat of the first. Pfc Keeney sat hunched against the impact concussions in a bunker. He could hear no return fire and occupied his mind by counting the incoming rounds: 294. When the shelling finally stopped, the artillerymen ducked a few more harassing rounds to carry the wounded to their LZ, and Keeney stood atop his bunker to watch the Hueys come in. He saw an army chaplain, an older officer, waiting for a ride out. The chaplain had helicoptered in only the day before, saying he would ride out the siege with his boys; perhaps he'd been called back, but Keeney couldn't shake the feeling that he was running out on them. The Huey was lifting off with the chaplain aboard when the battery's ARVN interpretor suddenly bolted, jumping on a skid and hauling himself inside. The shelling started again.

All that Lieutenant Colonel Ganahl had on his mind was clearing the mess that blocked Route 9. He was the commander of the 2d Battalion, 94th Artillery; his men were trapped at Lao Bao. The situation was critical. Ganahl had been overhead in his C&C when they'd started the withdrawal: he'd been alerted that the road was open, had ordered Bravo Battery to move out, then had watched horrified as 122mm artillery had hit the column as soon as it had rolled onto Route 9. Ganahl was constantly helihopping along the road and it became obvious that the NVA were dug in to stay. Once he and a battery commander had the C&C land in a field outside Lao Bao to check it for use as a camp stop when they finally got out. Time was short, so instead of making a ground inspection, they just looked from the bird, then ordered the pilot up. At that point, AK-47

---

*As a result of this incident involving Bravo Troop, Lieutenant Colonel Ganahl requested a more reliable armor battalion and the 1/77 Armor was sent in.

tracers tore at them from two sides of the treeline and they just managed to veer away. Ganahl flew into Lao Bao and the GIs were tense; their ears were tuned to pick up the sound of incoming amid all of the camp noises, and he noticed they always seemed to be positioned two seconds from a foxhole. He was deeply impressed by the courage and tenacity the artillerymen were displaying, but he knew they were not invincible.

The 1/1 Cavalry had initially been responsible for the road, but they were not the most disciplined troops Ganahl had ever seen. More importantly, as he reported to General Hill, the cav did not have the equipment needed to dig out the NVA. Their Sheridans, for example, were not really tanks, but lightly armored reconnaissance vehicles. With this in mind on the evening of 20 March, General Hill radioed Lieutenant Colonel Meyer with orders to displace the 1/77 Armor with its heavily armored M48 main battle tanks, from Vandegrift to Lang Vei.

It was sunny and hot the next morning as Meyer conferred with Majors Wilson and Murphy; they were to organize the Scout Platoon, Mortar Platoon, the tanks in B and C Companies, and an attached mechanized infantry platoon from B/1/61, and dispatch them down Route 9 to establish the new battalion CP at Lang Vei. At the same time, they were to coordinate the arrival of 101st Airborne elements to take up 1/77's former area of operations. While the units were still gearing up, Meyer boarded a Loach to fly ahead for a briefing at Khe Sanh. He went alone, trusting Wilson and Murphy to get the battalion moving. He liked to lead from the front, unhindered by staff officers, able to shift quickly from unit to unit. As he took off, they were cleaning up the mess of the previous night's sapper probe on Vandegrift; two blivets of aviation fuel had been burned and one North Vietnamese body found.

At Khe Sanh, General Hill briefed Meyer on the current situation along Route 9. Because the heavy M48 tanks of 1/77 would eventually tear up the unpaved stretch of the highway, they had not maneuvered past Vandegrift in the previous fifty-two days of the operation, and Hill had to orient Meyer on the AO behind Khe Sanh. Lang Vei was more or less secure, but the four miles of road from there to the Laotian border had been nicknamed Ambush Alley by the troops. The Tchepone River, which formed the international boundary, looped north at two points where it was close and parallel to Route 9. It was at these two points that NVA fire was the most intense; the enemy units were able to slip back across the river, which U.S. troops were forbidden to cross, at will. From Lang Vei to a point just west of the first loop in the river, where NVA on the Co Roc could bring the road under fire, was the responsibility of 1/1 Cavalry (Lieutenant Colonel Breeding) with their CP at Lang Vei. From there to the border was the AO of the 1/11 Infantry (Lieutenant Colonel Farrar) with their CP at a point on the border called Ta Bat.

Hill explained that two artillery batteries of the 2/94 Artillery (Lieutenant Colonel Ganahl) were located in the 1/11 AO; the easternmost one was on the south side of the road in the Lao Bao pocket, and the other, an attached battery, was about a kilometer away on the north side of Route 9. The 1/11 CP was only short distance from that artillery position. Hill said that the two batteries had been cut off for three days now, under NVA shelling and probes, and noted that the initial moves into the area had ended with the disaster of the Bravo Troop refusal. A helicopter, some APCs, Sheridans, and 175mm SPs were disabled along Route 9, and General Hill taxed Lieutenant Colonel Meyer with five assignments:

1. reopen Route 9 from Lang Vei to Laos
2. establish effective control of the 1/11 Infantry companies and 1/1 Cavalry troops strung out along the road
3. evacuate the two stranded artillery batteries to the Lang Vei area
4. recover the vehicles and equipment in the area
5. hold the road open for the return of the ARVN 1st Armor Brigade

After his briefing with Hill, Meyer had the Loach pilot fly him to the 1/1 Cav CP at Lang Vei, where he was briefed by Col. James Townes (1/5 Mech Deputy Commander), Lieutenant Colonel Breeding, and Lieutenant Colonel Ganahl. Ganahl and he were friends from West Point, where both had been assistant math professors, and Ganahl wished Dick Meyer good luck, saying he was the man for the job.

While Meyer was being oriented on the situation, the 1/77 Armor task force was moving from Vandegrift with the APCs of the Scout Platoon in the lead. By the time Meyer had the Loach drop him at the front of his moving command, they were just west of Lang Vei. The scouts were linking up with the easternmost element of the 1/1 Cav—Bravo Troop. They were in the process of reorganizing and preparing to evacuate damaged vehicles. Meyer was taken aback at the sight of these Americal Division grunts; they were grubby, unshaven, sloppily dressed, many of the men stripped to the waist in the searing heat. He knew some of his troopers disliked him for forcing them to bake in helmets and flak jackets, but his main concern in enforcing such discipline was to get men home alive. You can't get buddy-buddy with the men, he judged, it only gets them killed in the long run. He talked briefly with the commander of Bravo Troop, told him that he was taking control of the highway, instructed him to get on the 1/77 radio net and to continue reorganizing with his Scout Platoon. He also told the commander to hold their position and secure the flanks for the return of his task force with the artillery.

The tanks and tracks of Charlie Company, which had been following the Scouts in the road march, rumbled in from the east. They halted and Meyer climbed onto the deck of the lead tank, told the staff sergeant to climb to the loader's seat, and took his place in the fifty cupola. The colonel slid the CVC helmet on, snapped the radio mike in front of his mouth, and ordered Charlie Company onward. They roared past the party on the road, churning red dust in the dry, torrid air.

Sergeant Major Nelson was at the 1/77 CP track at Lang Vei, getting things organized, when several tracks from Bravo Troop 1/1 Cav drove into the perimeter. They had four or five dead men in body bags laid across one of the APCs. Some of the tracks had battle damage, and the filthy grunts wearily climbed off, passively mumbling that they were through fighting. They sat down beside a bunker, turning their backs to everything. Nelson inspected the vehicles and discovered that the driving rods and bolts from all of the fifties and sixties were missing. When he asked a couple of Bravo sergeants why the weapons were disabled, they said that the men had done it to prove a point. Nelson asked what the hell was going on, but the young sergeants were long-haired, dusty, and in the same disgusted mood as the grunts; they said they didn't want to talk about it. Nelson, with some of his own NCOs, scrounged spare parts, and repaired the weapons. He called to the GIs about the body bags, but they ignored him, so he and his NCOs had to physically tag the bodies—unzip the bags, check dog tags and wallets on the corpses, and fill out casualty slips to tie to the bags.

Out on Route 9, the rest of Bravo Troop had formed on line, facing west, as 1/77 Armor moved past. Sp4 Spurgeon was walking through and stopped, shocked at the scene. About thirty Bravo grunts stood atop their APCs, many shirtless, six or eight of them yelling and flipping the bird at several officers standing before them. One or two officers shouted back, but Spurgeon could only catch bits of what was said through all of the vehicle noise.

"Fuck you! You wanna get it, get it yourself! You wanted to come here!"

"You'll go because you're a soldier in the United States Army, that's why!"

"Oh yeah, stick it up your ass!"

On the road, the tankers of 1/77 Armor hauled past, raising dust and a loud rumble. They ignored the verbal fighters. They were headed for combat.

Both sides of Route 9 were choked with tangled thickets of elephant grass, brush, and trees, much of it higher than the passing tanks. The column clanked noisily around the first curve west of the Scouts and Bravo and immediately were ambushed. The flash of an RPG being fired came from the left, the shell missed the rear of Meyer's helmet. The 90mm main gun rapidly traversed to roar shot into the brush, the driver accelerated, and Meyer gripped the butterfly handles of the fifty, putting out rounds until the barrel grew steamy, hot brass and links bouncing around his feet. The second tank in the column, with the commander of Charlie Company in the turret, roared in their dusty wake, also hosing down the left side of the road.

Meyer shouted into the intercom for the rest of the column not to fire up the countryside—U.S. troops were in the area.

At the next curve in the road, the NVA opened fire again, RPGs exploded in clouds of smoke and dust, AK rounds clanged against the tanks, and the brush shook in return from 90mm canister rounds and raking bursts from the TC hatches. The tanks never slowed down; their job was rescuing the artillerymen, not routing the entrenched NVA until later. Shortly after outrunning the second ambush, Meyer could see another cav unit on the road, Sheridans and APCs in a wagon-train circle as if expecting a ground attack. It was C/1/1 Cav, and Meyer radioed for their captain to get on the 1/77 net, secure the flanks, and hold the road open for their return. More troops appeared in the area. A company from the 1/11 Infantry was manning roadside foxholes and the battalion commander, Lieutenant Colonel Farrar, was riding in a cav track. Meyer quickly conferred with him on the exact location of the artillery and infantry posts.

Meyer and his tanks got moving again, then slowed down to maneuver around the scene of the Bravo Troop ambush. The burnt-out APC squatted on the side, the Huey, nearby, shot full of holes and the doors hanging open. Blackened rubble lay on the ground, smoke still curling from it. Meyer skirted the wrecks, but when the Charlie Company captain attempted to bypass, his tank lurched into a shell crater. The tank was relatively level, but the tread was down deep enough so only a recovery vehicle could winch it out.

The column came to a halt. The NVA opened up again.

The tanks raised a deafening roar as they fired back into the bushes. An RPG penetrated the command track of Charlie Company and it burst into flames, killing two GIs and wounding three. Mortars and rockets began impacting on the road and the staff sergeant in the turret of the third tank was hurled into the air.

Meyer was hesitant to leave the road, not knowing what obstacles of enemy or terrain might block his tanks. He decided they would just have to maneuver under fire past the wrecks. During a slack in the enemy fire, a lone medevac darted into the swirling road dust to take the casualties aboard. At the same time, a second company from the 1/11 Infantry swept in from the side of the road, and Meyer radioed their CO to stay put to secure the area around the ditched tank. He also ordered his Bravo Company tanks, which were bringing up the rear, to stay and disperse in the area while he proceeded towards the artillery with just Charlie Company.

Inside the artillery perimeter, Keeney could hear the shooting to the east, when they weren't ducking into their bunkers from all of the incoming. He was more than nervous. The treelines shimmered in the wilting heat, flies swarmed thickly over abandoned food and the rotting bodies of ARVN and NVA around the perimeter. The stench was terrible. They were short of ammunition and water. At around noon, he heard the blasts getting closer, heard the distinct roar of vehicle engines.

Keeney had a terrible thought about Soviet-made tanks.

The first U.S. M48 main battle tank roared into the center of camp, easily busting through the elephant grass and the flimsy perimeter of culvert bunkers and a single strand of concertina. Two other tanks drove to the opposite end of the perimeter to set up some kind of defense. Keeney stood near the lead tank and could see the man in the TC hatch from the waist up. He was buttoned up in a CVC helmet and flak jacket, a lieutenant colonel insignia on his collar, and had the 5th Mech Red Devil shoulder patch on his dusty sleeve.

Keeney had no idea who Lieutenant Colonel Meyer was.

Meyer surveyed the grimy artillerymen around the tank. "Are you boys ready to get out of here?"

"Hell yes, let's go!"

Meyer was impressed; the artillerymen looked tough and disciplined.

The link-up had been made with Lao Bao, but Meyer still had to get his tanks another kilometer or so further, to the 1/11 CP, and then double back to the other artillery position, both of which were on the north side of the road. They kept moving and found the infantry CP, which was only some foxholes in the low brush covered with culverts and sandbags. Meyer could see no tents, bunkers, or anything permanent. As the armor took up positions around the perimeter, the freight-train sound of incoming rumbled in. Fired from Laos, 122mm artillery accurately impacted inside the CP. The grunts scrambled for their foxholes and the tankers slammed shut the hatches of their big M48s.

The call for mech infantry support for the 1/77 run to the arty was relayed to Bravo Company 1/61. They mounted out of Charlie Two on the DMZ, packing onto their APCs, and hauled down Route 9. Coming around a bend in the road, the TC in the lead truck saw a lone NVA down the stretch, his back to them, burying a mine. The TC cut the North Vietnamese in half with a sweeping burst of his fifty. They stopped at Vandegrift, two of the platoons deploying on the perimeter, and the First Platoon continued full throttle down the dirt highway. Near Lang Vei, they took RPG fire, the third track hit from a hedgerow forty yards away. The rocket-propelled grenade shot a couple of feet over the track deck, and caught an M-60 gunner in the trunk, blowing his head off, and spraying the others with shrapnel. The first two tracks wheeled towards the ambush, laying down a wall of fire against the AK. The Delta on the second APC jumped enraged from his hatch, grabbed an M-60, and charged into the hedgerow, firing madly. The NVA fell back, leaving two bodies and blood trails in the brush.

The platoon continued its dusty race.

At the 1/11 CP, Lieutenant Colonel Meyer stayed hunkered in his tank turret as the NVA barrage continued. He monitored the various actions over the radio, then called Colonel Townes to update him on the situation. He and the tanks of C Company were in place with 1/11 at Ta Bat; he had radio communications with two companies of 1/11 and two troops of 1/1 Cav holding flanking positions on Route 9 with his Scout Platoon; B Company tanks were securing the area where the APC was burning and tracks of B/1/61 had linked up there. To add to the confusion, the single 1/11 company at Ta Bat and the battalion command group were scheduled to be helicoptered to Khe Sanh. Colonel Townes directed that the infantry withdrawal should continue when the shelling allowed, and for Meyer to put the 1/11 vehicles into his road force. Meyer requested permission to try to evacuate the artillery batteries at this point, and Townes gave him the go-ahead.

It was now around four in the afternoon.

When a lull came in the shelling, the helicopter Meyer had requested quickly darted into the Ta Bat LZ and he climbed in. The Kiowa Scout dropped him at the second artillery battery, located between Ta Bat and Lao Bao, and he ordered them to assemble their gear and their 175mm SPs in march order. The tanks of Bravo were ordered up to escort the battery. They were to hit Route 9 going east, link up with the battery at Lao Bao, and continue full throttle for Lang Vei.

It took an hour for Bravo 1/77 and Bravo 1/61 to arrive at the position. Meyer took command of a lieutenant's tank and led the mech-infantry tracks back to Ta Bat, where they joined Charlie Company and the assembled 1/11 vehicles, and prepared to run Ambush Alley all over again. Incoming artillery exploded every now and then as the column formed up.

They departed in a clanking, rumbling cacophony and Meyer stood to watch the dust rise as they disappeared down the road. At that point, he was in a hurry to get back to his forward CP at Lang Vei, and called for another helo. He had operational control of elements of five other battalions (1/11 Infantry, 1/61 Mech Infantry, 1/1 Cavalry, 1/44 Artillery, and 2/94 Artillery) and wanted to insure that they were all on the 1/77 radio net and had secured their assigned positions on the road. His task force was strung out along Route 9 from east of Lang Vei to the Laotian border. He knew Bravo 1/1 had been mauled in the area and hoped his one advantage would bring success—he had at least partial flank security on the highway.

The lead of the column was at Lao Bao and Charlie Battery scrambled to march order. Keeney could see the armor crewmen behind their guns and hatches, their body movements transmitting one message; Move! It felt good to see Dusters in the column; their rapid-fire 40mm cannons can tear up a hill in nothing flat, Keeney thought, as he hoisted himself on the back deck of an M48 tank with two other artillerymen. The column moved out and hit Route 9, gear and vehicles left abandoned.

The North Vietnamese response was immediate, and the convoy responded with a fury: fifties and sixties chattered along the line, 90mm cannons boomed, twin-forties shredded the brush with streams of flashing rounds. Keeney hung on tight to the fast moving, bumping tank, astonished to see NVA on the south side of the road. Fifty yards into the brushy tangle, North Vietnamese in green pith helmets popped up to empty AK-47 magazines. The two men sharing the ride with him were shooting back. Keeney dug into his own ammo bandoliers and burned off mag after mag from his M-16. He couldn't tell if he was hitting a thing, but the crack of AKs continued along the whole route and he kept his rifle working, not pausing to look back. Keep firing! Keep moving! An ambushed and riddled jeep was on the side of the road, wrecked, and the driver lay dead in the thick dust of Route 9. Keeney watched in anguished amazement as the tanks and tracks hurtled over him, some of the treads grinding the corpse even deeper into the road. No one was willing to stop for a dead man and, as they rumbled past, Keeney glanced down to see the insignia of a major on the dead man's jacket collar.

The enemy fire kept up, and the column levelled shattering doses of fire into the brush to keep the enemy down so they could keep moving. By the time they pulled off of Ambush Alley into the sanctuary of Lang Vei, Keeney was filled with one simple emotion—absolute joy at being alive. He hadn't thought he was going to make it. He was alive, he thought, only because other GIs had barrelled through all of that fire to pull them out, and he felt unspoken gratitude to those grimy armor troops climbing off of their machines. There was also a deeper feeling of sorrow at the sight of the blasted vehicles on the route. He knew what those burnt-out hulks meant in human terms. He hustled over to the Hq&Hq Battery where a buddy gave him a big grin and an exaggerated story of how the battalion had written them off and had been ready to send letters to their next of kin. He also repeated the rumor among the artillerymen that as soon as Charlie Battery had left, the NVA had swarmed over Lao Bao, waving communist flags. True or not, Keeney wasn't impressed, thinking, the gooks didn't try anything like that when we were still in place. Outside the command bunker, Keeney was amused to see Lieutenant Colonel Ganahl surveying them with a slack-jawed grin, seemingly astonished to see they'd made it back in one piece. The old chaplain was there too, and as Keeney remembered, "He couldn't even look at us, which I thought was pretty bad for a chaplain. We never did see any more of him after that. We were glad of it, and he was probably glad he didn't see us, too."

The tanks of Charlie Company roared into Lang Vei at dusk, putting a dust haze in the air, stopping so quickly that the giant machines rocked back and forth on their suspensions. Sp4 Spurgeon had served with Charlie before volunteering for the snipers and he jogged to them. The crew of one tank was climbing off, dragged out and dusty, and he saw an old buddy emerging from the driver's hatch. He was shirtless, completely covered with dirt and sweat, and was keyed up.

"Spurgeon, you want body count," he challenged, "If you want some body count, you'd better come with us! I swear to God the place is crawling with dinks, real live gooks, tons of 'em! You won't even have to use your scope!"

"Slow down," Spurgeon answered, unbelieving, and asked for details. "Not tons of 'em, dammit. Where'd you see 'em?"

"Both sides of the road."

"What were they wearing, fatigues, helmets, what?"

"They're NVA, goddammit! They're fully-uniformed NVA using us for target practice! They're dug in in bunkers. Some of 'em let us drive right past 'em, then suddenly appeared in our rears with RPGs. Some of the bastards just stood up in the middle of the road and faced us down with RPGs. Goddammit, Spurgeon, I'm telling you this is it! You ain't ever going to see action like this! Ever! They're firing RPGs at us like machine guns!"

"Hold on, I'll be right back."

"Better hurry up, dammit, we're getting ready to go out again!"

Spurgeon jogged over to battalion operations, but an officer there politely told him it would be crazy for a sniper to hang onto the outside of a tank in that fire: he'd just be blown off. Spurgeon was inwardly happy at the answer. Saying he wanted to go had only been a bit of bravado; he knew it was virtual suicide and thought, thank God for that officer. He walked back to the tank where his friend was standing in the driver's hatch putting his CVC back on. "Coming?"

"Can't," Spurgeon grinned weakly, feeling, for a moment, like a coward. "Battalion says we're too valuable."

His buddy smiled, waved goodbye, and drove his tank back towards the shooting on Route 9.

Sergeant Markle, of the Dusters with A/1/44 Artillery, had left Lao

Bao for Dong Ha to scrounge spare parts, when he heard about the fighting at the 2/94 base. He hitchhiked back to Lang Vei, catching up with his Duster section after they'd escorted the artillery back from the border. Then they were ordered to go back west to a little column of recovery vehicles. Heading west, they passed the shot-down Huey on Route 9, then came upon three M48 tanks stopped on the road, a lumpy body bag lying in front of one of their tanks. They appeared to be waiting for a medevac. The Dusters swerved on past, then slowed down at a dip in the road, crossed a culvert over a stream at the bottom, and gunned it up the steep opposite bank. Just as they got to the top, NVA ambushed them from the left, and they hauled through a din of AKs and RPGs. As the fire petered out, Markle noticed a cav Sheridan stopped to the right, two GIs standing on the turret. When suddenly the yellow smoke of an RPG streaked from the brush on the right, he watched, astonished as the two grunts on the Sheridan effortlessly disappeared down the hatches as if trap doors had been sprung beneath them. A second later, the RPG exploded above the tank. Markle shouted, "That sucker's behind us!" and the gunner spun the twin-forties to send a stream of shells after the RPG team. They kept moving through the occasional fire. That was Ambush Alley.

While the Americans were fighting and dying to open Route 9 on 21 March, the men for whom they were wrestling to hold it open were experiencing their own difficulties. The ARVN 1st Armor Brigade had made it to LZ Alpha the day before, regrouped and pushed on, still without the air cav to screen for ambushes. They ran through one particularly tough one, giving and taking casualties. On the 21st, they passed LZ Bravo and were three klicks east of it when another ambush erupted. They immediately requested air support.

Lieutenant Ferrell, of C/7/17 Air Cav, was in their troop tent at Khe Sanh at that time. His friend, WO Lancaster, had just received an anniversary card from his wife and was in good spirits. He showed her photo to Ferrell and bragged how pretty she was, and she really was. Word then came to mount up. Ferrell climbed aboard his Cobra with a big pilot whose flying abilities he did not trust, while Lancaster strapped into a second Cobra with a new warrant officer named Jim Manthei. Manthei had been in-country for a month, serving two weeks with another unit before the losses over Laos had prompted his transfer to Khe Sanh. Lancaster had flown with Ferrell for a month, teaching him the ropes, and now he was doing the same for Manthei.

The two gunships sped into Laos and found the ARVN armor stalled at a point where the road curved south like a horseshoe, a jungled hill in the pocket. The front of the column was under heavy fire east of the horseshoe, but the command vehicles were to the west and out of visual contact with the lead because of the hill. Ferrell dipped his Cobra low, as an English-speaking ARVN officer on the radio directed them in, and noticed the lead ARVN vehicles seemed hardly to be returning fire. Then he noticed NVA foot soldiers swarming in the trees on the north shoulder of the road and several RPGs streaked out with smoke trails to hit a tank and APC. The ammunition and fuel must have ignited because they went up in balls of fire, the tank turret spinning into the air.

Jesus, Ferrell thought, it was like watching a war movie.

Lancaster dove first, Ferrell close behind, strafing the hill from south to north. Three 12.7mm positions cut loose from the trees, the first burst slicing so close to Ferrell's ship that it seemed he could reach out and touch the tracers. He radioed Lancaster that he had three muzzle flashes east of the hill. They banked around and made three more passes, pumping rockets, automatic grenades, and minigun fire into the jungle. After Ferrell's third run, emptying his rocket tubes, only one NVA gun was still firing.

Ferrell, out of ammunition and short of fuel, radioed Lancaster that he was heading for Khe Sanh. Lancaster answered that he had a few more rockets in his tubes and was going in after the last gun position. Ferrell called for him not to—it was too risky without a wingman providing cover—but watched as his partner rolled down anyway and screamed in. Rockets exploded all around the NVA emplacement, Lancaster broke his dive veering left, his broadside to the enemy, and was hit by a torrent of tracers. He calmly reported his tail rotor was destroyed and requested Ferrell to cover while he made an emergency landing. He peeled off to the south, then dropped to a hundred feet over a field of elephant grass. Lancaster tried to bring the vibrating Cobra to a hover, but with the tail rotor gone it only began rotating out of control on its axis. Then it suddenly crashed hard to the ground. Their radio went dead. Ferrell had been calling for medevacs the whole time, so within moments a Huey dropped beside the crashed Cobra and other gunships converged on the field to provide cover. Ferrell departed station to refuel when the medevac crew reported they had both downed pilots aboard.

As it turned out, Lancaster and Manthei were dead. The force of the crash had snapped their necks against the "chicken plate" chest armor worn by pilots.

Lancaster had been Ferrell's best friend.

Meanwhile the ARVN armor was still being battered. USAF airstrikes were requested, but they did more harm than good—napalm canisters missed their mark, killing twelve ARVN and wounding almost a hundred more. Colonel Luat pulled his brigade west into the wake of their own retreat in order to regroup. An NVA prisoner said two regiments were waiting further east on Route 9 to demolish the ARVN armor and Luat radioed the information to airborne headquarters. General Dong, in response, airmobiled a paratrooper unit to clear out the NVA ambushers, but then did not alert Luat that the highway had been secured. Without this information, and only five kilometers from the border, Luat ordered his men off the road and they continued southwest, needlessly fighting the jungle and fording streams.

On 22 March, Lieutenant Colonel Meyer organized his command to retrieve the abandoned vehicles and equipment strewn along Route 9. It was the morning when the two Duster sections of Alpha Battery 1/44 Artillery got the word to escort another artillery run back to Lao Bao for some of the abandoned 175mm guns. It was a hairy idea, Sergeant Markle thought. He'd believed in stopping the Communists. But he'd never seen anything like the chaos on Route 9. They prepared to move out from Lang Vei, one Duster on point, the other at the end, an M48 tank and two M88s in the middle. The GIs had a guest with them that morning, a civilian reporter named Holger Jensen, who had showed up with a flak jacket and a note pad.

The Duster leader, Sgt. Kenny Osborne, said to mount up.

"Hell with it, sarge," a GI bitched, "We don't want to go back there."

Osborne ignored him and climbed onto the last Duster. The grunts followed him aboard. One of the GIs climbed in the driver's hatch on the front deck. The Duster had twin-40mm cannons behind a shield which encompassed them like a turret with no top. Sp4 Wooten dropped into the gunner's seat, and Staff Sergeant Osborne crouched beside him with a grenade launcher. Sergeant Markle stood behind the seat, he and Sgt. William Lore manning an extra M-60 they'd brought along. Sgt. Wayne Coons was behind the other pig. The reporter, Jensen, hung onto the back deck.

The five vehicles took off from Lang Vei and hit the highway, passing the first signs of wreckage, bomb craters on the road, and the wrecks of two APCs and three trucks. As they rounded the first big curve in the road, the 1/61 APC still smoking down the road from them, and all hell broke loose. AK-47s sprayed from the brush on the left, Osborne pumped rounds from his grenade launcher, and puffs of smoke from NVA mortars rose on the Co Roc. Osborne shouted, "Get 'em, dammit!" and Wooten spun the turret, hammering fire from the twin-forties. One GI grabbed shell clips from the turret ammo wells, Wooten worked the pedal firing button, and fifty rounds shrieked across the Tchepone River, each one a tracer flashing from bright green to red in flight and popping sparks at impact against the brushy ridgeline. Markle grabbed M-60 belts and fed Lore's pig, as he and Coons frantically fired up the left side of the road, all of them too keyed up consciously to notice the AK rounds ricocheting off of the Duster armor.

The mortar fire stopped. They roared past the ambush.

Osborne slumped down, mumbling bitterly to Jensen, "I think we got 'em. That makes four this week. Those damned ARVN sitting on top of the ridge have let the North Vietnamese move in right under them." The Duster crunched over some C ration boxes littering the road, and split a sleeping bag which whirled feathers in their wake. A line of APCs edged past them, on the way back to Lang Vei, and the grunts exchanged peace signs. At an infantry strongpoint in the bushes, the column abruptly halted. Markle glanced ahead and saw a roll of concertina which the grunts had thrown across the road. Aw shit, he cursed, we're sitting ducks stopped like this. Some of the GIs ran out to pull the wire away as the column sat idling, and one of the infantry officers came up to ask Osborne if his Duster could stay to give them fire support.

Mortars came in. The armor column quickly rumbled past the grunts.

The convoy dodged around the junked vehicles, artillery pieces, and helicopter. The ride was quick and bumpy and their extra M-60 bounced off of the Duster. Jensen tapped Markle on the shoulder to point it out, and Markle could only think, are you crazy? We're not stopping for some damned machine gun. It was hard enough just keeping up with the others. At best, on the way back they might run over it so that the NVA couldn't recover it.

They pulled into the abandoned 2/94 firebase at Lao Bao. A dirt trail split the perimeter and they stayed in the side where there were a couple of 175mm guns, a few trucks, and some ammunition and powder charges. A downed helicopter squatted in the elephant grass. The GIs dismounted from the five vehicles, hurriedly moving about as an occasional 122mm round or mortar shell exploded nearby. The crew of one of the M88s hooked a 175mm SP to the back of their track. Men began blowing up the ammunition pits while others rooted through the deserted bunkers for important papers. Markle and another grunt dragged two trailers full of 40mm ammunition and latched one behind their Duster. After thirty minutes, Staff Sergeant Osborne shouted that they were leaving and tossed a thermite grenade into the ammunition trailer that they couldn't drag with them. They hauled back to Route 9, not looking back as the rounds cooked off.

Heading east, Markle looked down into the lush ravine on their right; a 175mm SP was resting on its side down the slope, as if it had been hurriedly shoved off the road. They were coming back at a good clip, swerving in dusty curves around the wrecks on the road, when Markle looked up just in time to see an M48 tank stopped dead ahead of them. "You gotta turn the gun!" The guns were not locked forward because the locks sometimes jammed. A GI sitting in the chair, his hands on the crank to turn the twin-forties, began frantically spinning it. But the Duster hauled past the halted tank too soon. Markle watched the barrels crunch into some C rat cartons hanging on the tank turret and, suddenly, the Duster turret began spinning out of control. Their driver kept hauling. At each revolution, the crank smacked into the helmet of the GI now slumped in the seat, and Markle tried to grab the crank. It whipped painfully into his hand and then the GI grabbed the hand to let Markle know he was okay. Markle was in pain and pissed off: gooks are probably sitting in the bushes laughing their asses off at us stupid Americans.

Passing the smoking APC at the curve, it happened all over again— AK tracers and yellow trails of RPG smoke laced past the vehicles. Mortars impacted near the road. Fifties and sixties chattered furiously from the armor, the Dusters poured down forty mike-mike, and they outran the ambush again. No one was hit and they closed on Lang Vei where the treelines melted down to brushy plains. The men felt safer, even though a few departing mortar rounds exploded nearby. Coons fell asleep against his M-60. Lore said, "Man, I'm hungry," and broke out some Cs. Jensen noticed the back of his flak jacket was peppered with shrapnel. Markle fretted that he had forty-three days to go in-country and this was the worst he'd seen in Nam.

On the morning of 23 March, another patrol with 1/77 Armor

protection left Lang Vei to retrieve the last eight-inch gun from Lao Bao. Half of a mile west of the basecamp, the tanks, recovery vehicles, and Dusters passed a hundred Montagnards fleeing Laos after their village had been hit. A mile later, two RPGs whooshed from the brush; two men were slightly wounded, but the patrol kept moving. Two miles from Lao Bao, the lead tank hit a mine and two GIs on board were hurled into the dust, their feet blown off. Mortar fire began dropping around them. Soldiers dragged the casualties to the next vehicle in line as they tore on, grunts spraying the road almost nonstop. When they neared Lao Bao, they stopped on a rise overlooking the river and Laos. The first vehicles of the returning ARVN column were fording the river back to South Vietnam. The ARVN paratroopers on deck waved at the Americans. The grunts did not respond. The day before, Colonel Battreall and the other advisors at Kilo had spent a hard day slingloading fifty-five-gallon gasoline drums under Huey helicopters for transport to the 1st Armor Brigade. At that high altitude, the small slicks could only handle two drums a trip so not enough fuel was transported across the border for all of the vehicles. A small airborne bulldozer was also slingloaded to a Chinook, so it could accompany the returning column and cut the sheer banks of the Tchepone River at whatever point Colonel Luat decided to cross.

At midnight a column of NVA tanks following the ARVN armor was stopped by U.S. air and artillery. By early morning, Luat and the 1st Armor Brigade had finally endured the twelve miles from Aloui to the Tchepone River, and were crossing back into South Vietnam. The advisors constantly monitored the radios of their ARVN counterparts, and when they crossed the river, Battreall and the five brigade and squadron advisors boarded an unarmed Huey so they could link up with Luat on the border. They traced along Route 9 and Battreall, who had heard little about the bitter ambushing along the highway, was taken aback to see at least five tanks and APCs abandoned and still smoking on the road. He didn't know the details, but could picture a U.S. column, confident in its firepower and armor, going down the road fat, dumb, and happy, and getting mauled for its lack of attention to flank security. It was such a mess below them, he remarked to the majors in the cabin, "Christ, somebody really fucked up down there!"

The Co Roc ridge was just outside the left side door, and a concentration of 12.7mm machine guns suddenly cut loose from the crest. It was a long, continuous burst and Battreall could see the muzzle smoke. With no door-gunners, they could just hold tight as the pilot sent the ship into a wild evasive action, flying north and west and crossing the river into Laos. To the delight of the advisors, the pilot circled high, then flew back towards South Vietnam above the trail that the ARVN had followed. At a hundred-foot altitude, they had the chance to observe two or three kilometers of the armor's route of march. They could see only abandoned vehicles on the side of the jungle path.

Battreall was impressed with the scene. If the armor troops had panicked, as the media and others claimed, the men would have simply abandoned their vehicles when they ran out of gas and continued their headlong flight on foot. They would not have stood in line to refuel; yet, the refueling must have been carried out calmly because the only vehicles sitting abandoned with empty fuel tanks were noncombat M577 command tracks and M 548 tracked cargo carriers. Passing over the border, Battreall could see the tiny engineer dozer still working to cut the east bank as the last tanks and APCs splashed into the river from the west side. A pair of Phantoms could be seen making repeated passes about eight kilometers behind the armor column. Battreall scanned with binoculars from the Huey door and could just make out the burning hulk of a Soviet-made T54 tank.

When Battreall and the advisors caught up with the 1st Armor, they were in an open parade field at the dilapidated Lao Bao Jail near the abandoned artillery base. The men disembarked from the APC decks and Colonel Luat stood in the brush organizing for the Route 9 drive back to Kilo. They were still within small-arms range of Laos, Battreall noted with concern, but fortunately not a shot was fired at the milling crowd. None of the ARVN seemed to notice their vulnerability. The advisors broke up to find their respective counterparts and Battreall approached Luat, taking in the scene as the ARVN paratroopers with the armor began boarding a truck convoy. "Everyone was visibly pleased and relieved to be 'home,' " he said, "and I saw a great deal of grinning, shouting, back slapping, and hugging going on. I was struck by the very warm and cordial leave-taking between the infantry and armor troops. There was nothing hangdog or crestfallen about anyone on the scene; indeed, everyone seemed to anticipate a hero's welcome upon reaching Khe Sanh."

So did Colonel Luat. He stood in dusty fatigues, calm and cheerful, almost cocky, proud about what his brigade had endured in Laos. It took five hours for the tail end of the column to depart Laos. They finally pushed out with 22 M41 tanks, 54 APCs, and 22 other assorted vehicles. Left behind in Laos, destroyed or abandoned, were 21 tanks, 26 APCs, 13 bulldozers, 2 road graders, 2 trailers, and 51 assorted vehicles. One of the squadrons raised dust on point and Colonel Luat's three command tracks followed them, with Colonel Battreall aboard. The rest of the brigade spaced out behind them. The brush thick, the road rolled, and, before long, the head of the column was out of sight and stopped. The radio crackled back that an American officer had parked his helicopter smack in the middle of the road so he could inspect the blown-up equipment in one of the ambush zones.

A U.S. tank platoon from the 1/77 Armor had fallen in behind the CP APCs and, as soon as they halted, the lieutenant in the lead tank shouted, "Hey, you slopes, get the hell outta the way!" Battreall slid off the back of his APC, climbed up the front of the tank, looked the young lieutenant in the eyes, and said calmly, "You're yelling at the commander of the 1st Armor Brigade. He's been in Laos for six weeks. You haven't. Keep your mouth shut." The lieutenant then looked as if he were in a stranglehold. In a few minutes, after the column got moving, the U.S. tanks peeled off into the roadside brush.

They had only gone a few hundred more yards when shooting broke out from the point. Battreall, Luat, and the rest ducked inside their vehicles as the ARVN responded with standard procedure—accelerated speed and a sheet of machine gun and 76mm canister shot laid into the flanks. The vehicles hauled past, no one visible in the undergrowth, and the shooting evaporated. Luat ordered a cease fire, then pulled his three command tracks to the side of the road so they could watch the column pass. He waved at the troops, shouting, "Well done, I'm proud of you!" The little dozer was in the column, its engineer sergeant still chugging along and waving back. Battreall was surprised—he had expected the driver to abandon the dozer after the river crossing in exchange for a faster and safer tank or track—and Luat was impressed enough to send a staff officer to get the sergeant's name so that he could be decorated.

The rest of the movement to Kilo was without incident, but before long Battreall discovered that their brief firefight had been with Americans. He had been worried such an incident might take place—rearward passage of lines was a tricky maneuver and during NATO exercises he'd been in, with everyone wearing the same uniform and speaking the same language, there had always been cases of friendly fire or bridges blown up in the face of friendly units about to cross. Battreall had helicoptered to Khe Sanh several days before to discuss just this problem with General Hill. He had also assigned one of his advisor majors the job of coordinating routes, communications, and recognition signals between the ARVN and U.S. units.

He heard that a nervous GI had started the fray. Lieutenant Colonel Meyer was at his 1/77 CP at Lang Vei when the shooting broke out and he remembered not a trigger-happy GI, but the lead ARVN raking the brush as a precaution against ambush. One of his officers had shouted into the radio, "These idiots are shooting at me!" For all the advance preparations, Meyer had no communications with the ARVN and could only relay the problem to Hill and radio his unit commanders to keep their men under cover. When the scene of the accidental firefight was checked, GIs found an abandoned ARVN M41 tank and drove it back to Khe Sanh, jeering once again about their South Vietnamese allies.

After reorganizing at Kilo, Colonel Luat prepared to attend General Lam's briefing. Battreall declined to attend, not wanting to edge in on the credit he felt should go to Luat. With the brigade back in South Vietnam, Battreall's job was done. At the airstrip, he found the aide to General Weyand and asked if he could hitch a ride back to Saigon. When the briefing ended, Weyand and Battreall climbed into the USAF twin-engine executive jet and DEPCOMUSMACV remarked, "That armor commander's a real basket case, isn't he?"

"What?" Battreall almost shouted.

Weyand described how, at the briefing, officers from ARVN I Corps and U.S. XXIV Corps severely criticized Luat for the failures of the 1st Armor, going as far as to call him incompetent and a coward. Weyand said Luat had come unglued under the attacks. No wonder, Battreall thought, he'd come back expecting a hero's welcome and instead was made the scapegoat for whatever had gone wrong during the operation. He could have kicked himself for not going to the briefing where he could have spoken in Luat's defense. During the rest of the flight to Saigon, Battreall described his case to Weyand. Most of the problems lay not with Luat, a brave and fine gentleman, he said, but with General Dong who had been in control of the armor brigade. Dong lacked coherence under pressure and the armor had suffered accordingly, receiving little support or guidance. The debacle at Hill 31 occurred, he said, not because of the failure of the armor, but because of a conflict in orders. Once there, the

ARVN tankers had performed well. The brigade lost so many vehicles during the withdrawal, he explained, because the road was in bad repair, because Dong withdrew their air cav support, and because he did not keep them posted on the battlefield situation. There were credible witnesses who would have taken fierce argument with Battreall's explanations in defense of Luat. Weyand, though, seemed receptive and, as things turned out, Colonel Luat retained his command.

A few weeks later, Colonel Battreall flew to Quang Tri to present his after-action report to General Sutherland and to offer further defense for Luat. Battreall considered Sutherland, " . . . a cordial and intelligent gentleman. . . . I found him courteous and willing to listen, which is not all that common a trait among senior commanders." On the other hand, Sutherland was not impressed by Battreall's rationale of why the ARVN armor had failed and thought Battreall to be, ". . . one of those colonels who always tried to paint a picture rosier than reality, always had many reasons and excuses for ARVN armor failures to perform, always could present reasons why armor units should not be used, and was trigger quick to criticize higher headquarters." In the official accounts of the Laos operation, the ARVN 1st Armor Brigade has been described as having done a miserable job in Laos.

Four days after turning twenty on 21 March, Sp4 Spurgeon was in the bush on a sniper patrol. Actually the mission had first been detailed to Sgt. John Wondra and his partner, Felix, when an operations NCO dropped into the sniper bunker at Lang Vei and told them they were to hunt for NVA RPG teams hitting the highway.

Wondra liked Spurgeon and asked if he wanted to go.

"I don't want to break the team apart, if Felix wants to go."

Felix shrugged, "I don't give a fuck."

They geared up, Spurgeon feeling gung-ho again, slapping on a camouflage beret and gun gloves; he shouldered a rucksack and the radio, slung an LAW across his back, and stashed a couple of claymores in a pouch. Wondra wore a bush hat and they both carried M-14 sniper rifles, the scopes unhooked and hanging from their web gear. They joined a squad of grunts aboard a couple of APCs which took them about a mile down the road, east of Lang Vei. They walked fifty yards into the thick brush; then the squad leader said, "Here ya go," and began taking his men back towards their vehicles.

Spurgeon called nervously, "Where you going?"

"We're leaving you two in here." That was the plan the squad leader had been given.

Oh shit, Spurgeon thought, just us two alone—do I really want to do this? Spurgeon and Wondra walked off into the bush, feeling peaceful in the warm sunlight, Spurgeon thinking that it might be best to just screw around. A stunted palm tree in the brush contained a beehive high up, and he pulled out a grenade to frag the hive off so he could climb up and look around. Everybody else calls it fucking off, he laughed inside, I call it reconning by fire. But Sergeant Wondra whispered to knock it off and they kept patrolling, dropping their rucks under a tree and crossing a narrow stream about ten feet away.

Wondra found footprints in the mud of the opposite bank, and Spurgeon was interested again. They started down a path towards a treeline, Wondra disappearing into the brush thirty yards to the left.

Spurgeon glanced down for a moment as he crossed the field, but looking back up, his heart nearly stopped. He saw the shock of black hair first; then he focused on a chest, an arm, the wooden stock of a rifle, a faded shirt. A man was walking across his front, partially hidden among the trees forty yards ahead of him, moving east but looking north, away from Spurgeon. It was the first NVA he'd seen who was not dead, wounded, or a prisoner. He couldn't believe it, and thought for a second, what's an ARVN doing out here? Then he panicked, God, no, ARVN always wear helmets and no ARVN would have the balls to be out here alone. Oh shit, it's a dink! He stood exposed in the grass, M-14 to his shoulder, trying to line up the man's head in the peepsight as he walked in a slow crouch behind the trees. Spurgeon's mind was reeling; I'm in the open. What if he turns and sprays me? What if I lose him? Where are his buddies? His heart was pounding, his hands shaking so that he was unable to keep the NVA's head in his sights. From the corner of his eye he could see Wondra pushing through the brush, and he prayed for him not to make any more noise than he already was. He lined up the black hair one more time; then suddenly Spurgeon was firing, jerking the trigger uncontrollably, rapping off five shots so fast that he didn't know if his eyes were open or closed.

The North Vietnamese was nowhere in sight.

Spurgeon dropped in the grass, tugged off his gun gloves, and knocked off his beret as he frantically unslung the LAW. He extended the rocket to its firing position, put it over his shoulder as he kneeled, and plugged his ears with his left shoulder and hand. Just as Wondra ran up from behind, Spurgeon pressed the firing button. Wondra dove to avoid the backblast, and the 66mm projectile screamed to impact in the woodline. Spurgeon turned and suddenly noticed Wondra sprawled in the grass, his face drained, his eyes with a what-the-hell-are-you-doing expression. Spurgeon pointed to the trees and mouthed, "Gook . . . gook . . . gook."

A look of wonderment appeared on his face. "Oh."

Spurgeon and Wondra looked at each other, Spurgeon exulting in the moment—no one chicken, both ready to fight. They heaved grenades at the treeline, then started forward through the grass in an exaggerated crouch to keep low, M-14 rifles at the ready. Spurgeon saw the NVA in the trees and, thinking he was playing dead, walked quickly to him, firing from the shoulder. The man did not move. They stood over the body. The North Vietnamese was sprawled dead on his back, a tiny shrapnel hole in the back of his head, a trickle of blood from his nose drying in his hair. The man was young, wore sandals, had a faded uniform with a unit designation stitched over the left breast pocket. Spurgeon was still afraid that he might have killed an ARVN until he tugged an AK-47 rifle from under the body. He hefted the weapon, a three-sided bayonet folded against the stock. They were worried that more NVA might be in the area, so Spurgeon pointed the rifle in the direction the man had been coming from. It didn't fire. He flipped the safety, squeezed off a couple of rounds, then dropped it to full auto and emptied the AK's thirty-round banana clip. Then they looted the body for souvenirs.

They ran back across the stream, tripping and giggling with nervous excitement. They tossed a grenade and waited. It was a dud. Then, they grabbed their rucks, and scurried for Route 9. They were afraid of more NVA but felt like a million. They had a kill! They stood on the road, calming down and laughing at themselves for being so gleeful. They walked back to Lang Vei, popping a purple smoke grenade and waving at an American chopper that circled down to look them over. At the operations bunker, they were debriefed, an NCO taking notes as Spurgeon lied, saying he'd killed the NVA with a single head shot. They turned in the captured gear, then walked back to the sniper bunker and kicked back in some lawn chairs, breaking out the sodas and beer to celebrate the team's first victory.

For the artillerymen rescued by the armor, things soon shifted back to the lackadaisical style of the old days now that they no longer were in the real war zone. Pfc Rhodes and his buddies in A/2/94 were able to take quick showers at Khe Sanh on 25 March; then they packed up for Vandegrift where ammunition was being blown in place and things were being packed up. It was quiet there so they loaded aboard a truck to go swimming in a river about a mile down the road, while a couple of GIs kept watch aboard a quad-fifty guntruck. It was Rhodes's first thorough scrubbing in two months. At other times on the Vandegrift perimeter, the Dusters and quad-fifties did extended Mad Minutes and the artillerymen joined the noise, Rhodes popping a few mags on his M-16 and pitching several grenades. It was great fun. From Vandegrift they rejoined the rest of the battalion at Mai Loc, south of Cam Lo.

They were put right on the perimeter line with the ARVN, a situation which gave the battalion commander, Lieutenant Colonel Ganahl, nightmares about night attacks. They built culvert-and-sandbag shelters and got down to scrubbing the caked red dust off of the gun tubes and commo gear. The artillerymen kept up their guard because they knew their position was insecure, but it wasn't the same as Lao Bao and it screeched on their nerves when the lifers began howling about police calls, haircuts, and mustache trims. Someone tossed a frag into the battery first sergeant's tent when he wasn't there, to scare him off their backs. It worked. The captain's jeep driver drilled another unpopular sergeant through the leg with his M-16 one night and was hauled away by the MPs. At night the Dusters and quad-fifties lit the sky with torrents of red tracers, while the searchlight teams and artillery illumination rounds turned the black to white. There was never any return fire. During the day, the mama-sans from a local ville swarmed the perimeter wire to sell beads, headbands, clothes, trinkets, and dope. Rhodes and his buddies hadn't done any pot in a long time; they'd gone dry during the border fighting, but now they could get obestol again. Lieutenant Colonel Ganahl had his suspicions about what was going on and they were confirmed one night when a quad-fifty gunner opened up without warning, managing to riddle the tent of the ARVN base commander with bullets. It turned out he'd been shooting for fun. The ARVN commander had not been in the tent at the time and politely accepted Ganahl's apologies. The next night, an explosion rocked the 2/94 line. Inspecting the crater, which was just far enough away from their bunkers not to hurt anyone, Ganahl discovered fragments from a U.S. 105mm shell and noted that the angle of impact was from the ARVN encampment. The South Vietnamese were just providing a friendly payback.

On the morning of 26 March, Lieutenant Colonel Meyer and Sergeant Major Nelson prepared to make an inspection trip to Charlie Company on the Laotian border. As they were boarding their vehicles at Lang Vei, Meyer noticed Nelson taking extra precaution in lacing and snapping his flak jacket tightly. Early in the operation, the sergeant major had been wounded by a 122mm rocket fragment when in a jeep on Route 9 near the Rockpile, and had spent fifteen days in the hospital.

They pushed west on Route 9, Meyer in the lead tank, followed by a Scout track. Nelson was in the loader's hatch of the second tank, and another track brought up the rear. They were cutting down the road when Nelson saw the flash of an RPG in the roadside brush to the left, then watched the projectile shriek over the back deck of Meyer's tank, barely missing it. They kept hauling, laying down suppressive fire. The TC beside Nelson was simultaneously firing his fifty and traversing the 90mm main gun to the left. Nelson was reaching down to pull the charging handle to cock the coaxial 7.62mm machine gun when a second RPG suddenly shuddered the tank with a terrific clang. The round penetrated the track blocks hanging as extra armor, punched through the side of the turret, and burst on the ammo feed tray of the coaxial gun, shooting a blizzard of shrapnel, ammo, and pieces of the tank into Nelson. A small grease fire started inside the turret, but the gunner quickly put it out. The front of Nelson's flak jacket was shredded, his right leg ripped, bleeding, and broken, both hands painfully lacerated. The flak jacket had absorbed most of the blast and saved his life.

They kept moving until they reached Charlie Company on a ridgeline off the road overlooking Laos. Meyer got there first, remaining behind the fifty mount of his tank as the gunner traversed the long 90mm cannon and carved out sections of the brush around them with roaring canister shot to discourage any more RPG teams. Nelson painfully climbed down from his tank, limped over, and called to Meyer. The colonel turned to see his old friend standing helpless, bloody, flak jacket hanging in rags, his hands too cut up to unfasten the armor jacket. Nelson shouted in jest, "Why me again?" Within ten minutes a Huey picked him up. After the medevac, the tankers buttoned up inside their machines and Meyer directed airstrikes and artillery along the southern side of the dirt road. Charlie Company swept the burnt-out area and found one dead NVA, remarkably intact for all of the firepower poured in at him.

CHAPTER SIXTEEN:
Skirmishes for Khe Sanh

The North Vietnamese counterattack also hit the main base at Khe Sanh. The airfield had taken occasional rocket and mortar raids, but in mid-March the shelling became almost constant and included artillery. The main area of bombardment was the section of the perimeter manned by D Troop, 2d Squadron, 17th Air Cavalry, 101st Airborne Division. Dug between the bunkers of 3/187 Infantry and 4/77 Aerial Field Artillery, the Delta bunker line had gone up at the beginning of the operation to watch for NVA infiltrators. They had seen none, but were now taking up to two hundred rounds a day. Pfc Bill Warren, the troop RTO, spent a lot of time crouched in those bunkers, listening to his heart pound as the NVA artillery erupted at ground level. Many were duds—left over from the marine siege, he guessed—and, when they impacted with the hard red clay, the bunker shook and Warren would mutter nervously, "Man, that was close . . . what would have happened if it went off?"

Sometimes Warren could only wonder what he was doing there. In his own mind, he made a conscious effort to remember that he was just a draftee doing his time in this useless war, and not to get too close to his buddies because he didn't think he could take it if one were killed. But that didn't mean he didn't feel a bond with the men beside him and, in the back of his mind, he knew he had to be in Vietnam. He had been twenty and driving a cab in the Bronx when the draft notice had arrived. He was from a traditional family whose members always served, and his only strong impulse was to go with the program. He'd arrived in Nam in January 1971. He'd been almost surprised at how professional Delta Troop was: he saw men smoke grass and opium at Camp Eagle, but never on missions; and not only did the grunts stick together, but they were damned good at their jobs. Warren even liked their CO; a small, wiry captain named Thomas who always looked out for his troopers and got the job done with no petty harassment.

Most of the Delta troopers took the shelling in stride. It started in earnest on 15 March when nearly two hundred 122mm rounds hit the base at a cost of three GIs wounded and five ARVN killed—plus fourteen damaged helicopters and trucks. The following evening, a salvo of sixty mortar rounds wounded four GIs, blew up a helo and a truck, and damaged four more vehicles. The next night, 17 March, the first rounds hit the airstrip and the men of D/27th Engineers left their bunkers to begin repair. And so it went. It was a tense time, but only a few of their comrades were hit and the Delta cavalrymen tried to laugh it off. Warren provided some comic relief the morning he ran naked from his cot to a bunker during a shelling and found himself squatting beside a 101st chaplain in his undershorts. One of the platoon leaders provided most of the laughs; it seemed that every time he went to the latrine they took incoming, and he would scurry for a bunker holding up his trousers. He varied his times but it did no good, and finally the command-bunker radiomen took to kidding him to hold it for their sakes. One of the wilder grunts refused to climb inside a bunker, even when directly ordered to, saying the only thing he wanted from Nam was a Purple Heart. Yeah, it was tough, Warren reckoned, but everyone was making the best of it.

On 19 March, the NVA shelling picked up in tempo, roughly twenty rounds an hour all day, and the Delta grunts spent most of their time underground.

To combat the increased enemy activity around Khe Sanh, Lieutenant Colonel Sutton's 3/187 Infantry was shifted from the Rockpile to the mountains northwest of the base. The CP was relocated to the airfield on 15 March, and the rifle companies continued what they'd been doing since the first day of the campaign—humping the hills for the North Vietnamese Army. For the grunts, the days seemed to merge together until time meant nothing but another day marked off DEROS calendars. At night they lived in the jungle, and at daybreak they started out again. It was always the same—point man up front, gut tight as he silently snaked through the trees, the rest of the company filing behind, sweat towels soaked around necks, moving under hundred-pound rucks. It was like being in an oven-hot green tunnel. Minute by minute, the landscape and sun were more of an enemy than any Vietnamese who might be lurking; wait-a-minute vines coiled around legs and canteen tops, thorns tore at arms and faces, jungle rot spread, clothes rotted in the humidity, mouths burned from thirst and bile, and leeches appeared seemingly from nowhere to attach themselves.

The grunts humping the Laotian border jungle rarely had any idea of what was going on; it seemed to be useless wanderings. But at a time when many units were just going through the motions the 3d of the 187th could take some pride in exhausting, meandering patrols. They were not searching and evading; they were hunting for the enemy. And when sometimes they did bump into the Communists, men on both sides died. The 3/187 Infantry was credited with killing forty-eight NVA, but nineteen of their own were killed during the operation: two from Hq&Hq; seven from Charlie; three from Delta; five from Echo Recon. Also counted on the list of the dead were the battalion commander and his operations officer. They died on 17 March 1971.

In accordance with their usual policy of getting on the ground with the troops, Lieutenant Colonel Sutton and Major Scharnberg called for a helo to transport them that day. Scharnberg had just returned to the battalion the day before. After being wounded on Purple Heart Hill, he was only in the hospital a few days before he returned; Sutton, knowing the young major was gung-ho enough to head back into combat not fully recovered, radioed Major White at the 3/187 Rear to make sure he was sent home on leave. Against Scharnberg's protests, White did just that. Upon his return, Scharnberg spent one night at Camp Evans, then made it to the Khe Sanh CP on 17 March. The chopper that arrived for them was a Kiowa Scout from the 5th Mech. Sutton had drawn the same pilot and bird for several days and commented to White that he trusted neither; the Scout was too small and frail for his tastes, the pilot too young and reckless—he flew low and fast, hopping hills with the skids barely clearing the trees.

They left for the field but never made it. The bodies of Sutton, Scharnberg, and the pilot were later recovered from the wreck. There is a possibility they were shot down, but a distraught White thought it was probably due to pilot error—flying too low and being smacked to earth by a down draft. Bravo Company was NDP'd atop a hill on the border when news of the colonel's death reached them via the radio. Some of Sp4 Kucera's buddies mockingly put up a cross and told jokes until their lieutenant interrupted sharply with, "You better not let the CO see that." They disliked Sutton because he drove them hard and was willing to take chances to get body count. But on many occasions, Sutton had left his C&C to join his grunts in a firefight on the ground. Kucera decided it was a Patton thing: any fiercely aggressive commander was bound to be disliked by his men. Sutton had balls, Kucera thought. But he, too, did not mourn his death.

The day of the crash, General Hill immediately transferred one of his mech officers, Lt. Col. Robert Steverson, to assume command of the 3/187. Maj. Chester Garrett was sent from the battalion's parent brigade (3d Brigade, 101st ABD) to take over as the S3. The two were a mixed blessing. Steverson had been the 1/5 operations officer and was well qualified to take over, his previous position having made him intimately aware of the daily goings on of all of the units in the AO. He was tactically proficient and doggedly determined; he also had an uncanny ability to look at maps and terrain from his C&C and instantly visualize the whole scheme of where and how his battalion should move. His only weakness was being a workaholic, sometimes pushing himself to exhaustion and suffering from lack of sleep. It wasn't long before the battalion officers thought Major Garrett had been transferred to them simply to get him out of the hair of brigade. He was gung-ho to a fault, stubborn, and refused to take advice; it got to the point, for example, that the 3d Brigade S3 had to call Major White to coordinate because Garrett refused to talk to him.

The new commander's test came on 20 March, when Bravo, Delta, and Echo Recon all had contact in the mountains around Khe Sanh.

Bravo Company had been CA'd into the area the day before in response to recon patrols who could hear NVA artillery firing from smack on the border, several miles north of Route 9. The area was semipinpointed in the jungle. Bravo was to locate the arty and, if found on the RVN side of the blue line, knock it out. When they helicoptered in, some 12.7mm fire cracked at the birds and the door-gunner in Kucera's slick shouted, "Hot LZ!" Kucera frantically tried to untie his helmet hanging from his ruck, finally getting it on just as they touched down atop a hill.

Kucera jumped out and dove into a bomb crater. Then he noticed everyone was looking at him as if he were nuts. The grunts in the first couple of lifts had already secured the hill, and only the helos were still taking fire. They patrolled west toward the border through a valley of rolling elephant grass, and NDP'd in a bamboo thicket. They called in artillery and airstrikes on two NVA mortars that they could hear just west of them on the border; there were three secondary explosions. That night two rounds exploded near them, and NVA artillery could be heard firing all night long. On the morning of the 20th, two more rounds exploded close enough to pelt shrapnel over them. They packed up and continued the hump towards Laos, so close to the NVA guns they could feel the ground vibrate from each round being fired and could hear them whistle towards Khe Sanh. The Bravo captain radioed Steverson that he could definitely hear one tube working on the border, firing every fifteen to twenty seconds.

Meanwhile, teams from Echo Recon worked their way to the border. By half past nine, the leader of Recon Team One reported taking AK-47 fire from an NVA squad and called in arty. The leader suspected that more NVA were in the jungle and requested helicopter extraction before his seven man team was cut off. Lieutenant Colonel Steverson, in his C&C orbit, replied that an emergency resupply of ammo could be made, but that Recon Team One was to remain on the ground and aggressively seek and engage the enemy. Another recon team made contact with a small group of NVA; they too were denied permission to extract, which was standard reconnaissance procedure.

Steverson was intent on ferreting out the NVA.

By noon Bravo Company was almost on the border, moving towards the sound. They were walking single file through thick brush when they suddenly noticed they were in an NVA bunker complex, bunkers stretching all around, commo wire strung between them. Kucera was next to the lieutenant and RTO when shooting broke out along their strung-out file. Everyone dropped in place, Kucera clutching his M-16 and scanning the brush, holding his fire because he couldn't find a target. He felt damned glad that the lieutenant and the captain knew what to do. A staff sergeant down the line sprang up firing his rifle—drilling an NVA with three rounds through the throat. Another burst of AK cracked and was answered by an M-16. Kucera rolled over to look. A kid three days with the company, had been hit in the leg, but had dropped the NVA who'd shot him with his return burst.

The kid started going into shock.

"Hey man," a grunt joked to keep him awake, "You're going back to the World."

The kid snapped out of it and grinned.

The firing kept rippling along the line, Bravo killing eleven NVA.

Kucera could hear the captain over the RTO's hand mike, arguing with Steverson that he needed AFA, not just arty because the target was too close. Before long two Cobras came in and the pilots told them it looked like an anthill with all of the NVA coming out of the bunkers. They said that the company was surrounded, and just to sit tight. Then the gunships began strafing, expertly putting rockets and minigun fire around the grunts. The pilots had a great time picking off NVA. The lieutenant's RTO tried to contact one of the pilots, but he said, "Wait one, I'm inbound on a gook," and flashed over Kucera's head, pumping rockets and laughing "Got 'em!" The Cobras went back to Khe Sanh three times to refuel and rearm. Phantoms dropped nape; Kucera could not see the explosions for all the vegetation; but he could hear the canisters burst and a second later the wind would be sucked from his lungs. The firepower gave Bravo the breather they needed to pull out of the NVA basecamp. U.S. artillery roared in behind them to cover their movement.

Bravo made it to their NDP in the bamboo, and the captain hurriedly organized a defense, passing LAWs along the line. But nothing happened. The NVA artillery for which they'd been searching was confirmed to be on the Laotian side of the border, and thus immune to U.S. ground attack. But Kucera's platoon leader and another lieutenant, both ex-SF, didn't care about the rules and asked for volunteers to conduct a night raid on the guns. Kucera thought it was suicide, but he was impressed to see many others step forward. They were draftees second, he thought, Screaming Eagles first. It was a great feeling. Steverson, of course, denied them permission to go, and turned his attention back to the mountains. The fight was not over yet.

The seven men of Recon Team One were still running, pursued by the North Vietnamese. The recon platoon leader, a lieutenant named Sloan, was on the ground with them. They could only find clearings in the jungle big enough for one Huey, which would only take five men, and Sloan was not willing to separate the team and risk having two men cut off. At dusk they made a tight position atop a jungled hill and called for reinforcements.

At that time, Lieutenant Stephen's platoon of Delta Company was waiting on the Khe Sanh airfield, preparing to return to the field after a night of pulling security at the 101st ABD TOC. Word came that recon was in trouble and that Second Platoon was going in. It was six in the evening when they CA'd into a clearing on the side of recon's hill, Stephen unaware that it was a hot LZ until he saw green AK tracers zipping up from the treetops, silent under the noise of the rotors and the door-gunners' M-60s. The Hueys hovered, the twenty grunts jumped out, and the firing stopped as soon as the choppers banked away.

A few men from recon came down the hillside and led the platoon up to their NDP. The recon team was out of food and water, three men had collapsed from exhaustion, and Lieutenant Sloan asked that they not be required to pull night guard. The infantrymen were still setting up around them when AK-47 fire shattered the dusk, twenty-five yards from where Stephen was sitting. A magazine or two was emptied, then silence; then one of Stephen's men, a GI nicknamed Tex, started crying out for help.

Lieutenant Stephen immediately took point, followed by Lieutenant Sloan, Sp4 Ken Irons, his new RTO, Sp4 Ronny Wilson, his medic, and six other grunts.

Tex nervously shouted at their approach, "You better speak English or you're dead!"

Stephen yelled, "Tex, it's me!"

It was pitch-black in the jungle as they formed another tight perimeter. The story was that Tex, two recon sergeants, and their Kit Carson Scout had left the NDP to place an MA on a jungle trail. Stephen had not ordered them out, and figured the recon men were still nervous. The NVA had ambushed them. One sergeant was killed instantly and the other had four or five AK rounds in him. They called a medevac and organized for the night. They could hear NVA moving around the hill in the dark, so Stephen radioed to his platoon sergeant to sit tight in the original NDP, while his little group similarly stayed in position. No one was to move, make noise, sleep, or give away his location by shooting in the dark.

Doc Wilson, a young Southerner and a fantastic medic, worked to keep the recon sergeant alive on the jungle floor. Fog had rolled in, delaying the medevac for hours. The North Vietnamese were all around, the moon and stars exposed silhouettes in the dark; but, for those long hours, Doc Wilson kept working, drawing attention to himself by holding an IV bottle high over the wounded man. Doc Wilson was absolutely fearless that night, but it was all in vain. A helo was inbound from Quang Tri with a jungle penetrator basket when the sergeant silently succumbed to his wounds. The medevac was cancelled. Wilson crawled over to Stephen and Sloan and passed out from exhaustion.

Stephen put the young medic in for the Silver Star, but higher downgraded it to a Bronze Star for Valor.

In the morning, helicopters came for the bodies and recon survivors, leaving Second Platoon in place. Fifteen minutes later, Stephen was checking his map when M-16s cut loose. He crawled to an old bomb crater and the three grunts inside said they'd fired up three NVA who were walking right toward them. They pointed at a body several yards away. Stephen couldn't see anything through the foliage so he told them to throw some frags and use the M-60. This done, they yelled, "Chieu hoi!" There was no response, so Stephen crawled toward the spot at which his men were pointing, a black sergeant following him.

The wounded NVA sprang up when he had gotten five feet away, his AK-47 chattering.

Stephen emptied his M-16 into the man.

They counted twenty-one bullet holes in the North Vietnamese, and could see another dead NVA lying further out. Battalion wanted evidence before a kill was claimed, usually items of clothing, but Stephen was too wrung out. He didn't want to risk himself or his men for a body count, so he only radioed in one confirmed kill.

On 22 March, the weather had been foul all day. Charlie Company 3/187, under Capt. Thomas A. Rodgers, continued its patrols northwest of Khe Sanh in search of NVA firing positions. They had not had a contact in about a week and, as the platoon slogged through the rainy jungle, this was more of the same. At noon Second Platoon found a deserted complex of twenty NVA bunkers in the undergrowth. They were empty save for some old tennis shoes and U.S. batteries. About ten minutes later, First Platoon found five small bunkers and destroyed them. The platoons regrouped by dusk and NDP'd in a spot of wet elephant grass.

The weather got worse that night, rain and wind slapping through the brush so that speaking voices were drowned out, and a blanket of fog cutting visibility down to zero. It was half an hour before ten that night, and the grunts were shivering miserably under ponchos in their mud holes, when a burst of fire broke out from the Second Platoon side of the line.

About a dozen North Vietnamese had crept up through the wind, rain, and fog to assault the platoon's M-60 position.

They must have watched the Americans set up.

Sp4 Steve Wheeler and Pfc Roger Stahl were two of the first to move. Wheeler was a medic from Florida, a brave man in the bush but a rebel in the rear. Stahl was a draftee from Pennsylvania who had turned twenty-one during his five months in Nam; he was a very quiet, blond kid who'd gone off without question because he thought it was his duty. Stahl and Wheeler were close, the medic feeling that, in the free-for-all of contact, he could count on Stahl to watch out for him. The shy, unassuming kid always did his best and was well liked in the platoon.

When the NVA moved on the M-60 foxhole, Stahl and another grunt crawled from their holes towards the shooting, Stahl shouting back, "Doc, someone is hurt over here!" Wheeler pushed through the elephant grass on his stomach, whispering that he was coming. He was five feet from them when the NVA suddenly flung satchel charges and grenades around the M-60. Everything went off at once. Mud and shrapnel sprayed all around Wheeler, as Stahl and his companion collapsed. Wheeler rolled to them. Stahl had been hit in the chest by shrapnel. Both men had been killed instantly.

Blind firing erupted from the foxholes, as Captain Rodgers got on the radio to battalion at Khe Sanh, requesting a flareship; he was told it would take too long to get the bird on station. The enemy tormented Charlie Company for the rest of the night, moving unseen through the brush. They even snatched the M-60 from the perimeter. At each rustle around them, the grunts threw hand frags and fired LAWs and M-79 grenade launchers. Artillery illumination burst overhead, serving only to reveal company positions to the enemy who stayed hidden in the thick undergrowth. Each time the flares burned out, the NVA tossed more grenades into the lines. Major Garrett at the 3/187 CP monitoring the radios, ordered mortar fire to be placed around C Company's NDP for the rest of the night, and told them to set fire to the grass near their position so aircraft could find them in the fog. The grenade duel continued through the night, even when a plane circled dropping parachute flares.

Five GIs were dead, four wounded.

The one-sided skirmish was still sputtering when the battalion command post began taking mortar fire, then the crack of automatic weapons could be heard. Khe Sanh itself was under attack.

Captain Thomas and the platoon leaders of Delta Troop were all in the CP bunker with a few RTOs and riflemen. At two in the morning, they were hit by artillery and mortars, and a U.S. artillery battery was alerted to fire illum in case of ground attack. After less than an hour, the artillery barrage stopped, but mortars kept dropping in from the vicinity of the Khe Sanh waterfall.

At 3:15 A.M., the bunker guards suddenly started shooting.

North Vietnamese sappers streamed in behind the mortar rounds, avoiding the claymores in the perimeter wire and disappearing behind the bunker line. Pfc Warren was sleeping on a cot in the CP bunker when someone kicked him and screamed, "Sappers!" He quickly laced up his jungle boots, grabbed his M-16 and bandoliers, and jogged to his preassigned position in a ditch that ran from the bunker to the airstrip. Warren had never been in a firefight before and cringed in his open, solitary spot, flat in the dirt. He looked around apprehensively, but could see no one moving, even though red and green tracers burned in all directions. Time seemed to drag by until a lieutenant finally emerged from the bunker and shouted to get to the airstrip. He ran there alone and went prone in the strip of elephant grass bordering the runway. He could see other GIs on either side of him, fifteen yards away, also down in the grass, rifles ready. He did not call to them, afraid of giving his position away. He had been there for five minutes when an RPG exploded in a white flash against the CP bunker, spraying fragments into the ditch he'd just vacated. Oh shit, Warren thought, the shock of what was really happening beginning to sink in.

A sapper sprinted to the strip to the refuel/rearm point manned by DISCOM, 101st Airborne and hurled in a satchel charge. Then the whole world seemed to explode around Warren, as a ten-thousand-gallon fuel blivet and a store of 2.75-inch rockets went up. Everything was sound and flash. He covered his head with his hands, as rockets tore into the night sky like Roman candles. The berm roared with fire, shrapnel whipped loudly overhead. More RPGs began shrieking in and tracers tore a light show among the bunkers. Grunts from the perimeter appeared out of the shadows, dragging dead sappers. They dropped them on the strip, intent on keeping the NVA from dragging them away. Warren stared at the corpses, the first of the enemy he had ever seen. There were four or five of them, skinny little men with short black hair and dirt smeared on them for camouflage.

Five of the sappers slipped between the 2/17 Air Cav and 4/77 AFA bunkers, then dropped into the communications trench between them. They ran down it, screaming and pitching grenades and satchel charges into the Delta Troop bunkers. Sp4 Michael J. Fitzmaurice, a shy enlistee from South Dakota, and three other GIs were in a bunker when three satchel charges were tossed in. Fitzmaurice scrambled, managed to toss two back out, then dove atop the third with his flak jacket outstretched. The explosion threw him back, riddled with shrapnel. A piece had torn his eye and blood poured down his face. Fitzmaurice stumbled into the trench line, firing his M-16, gunning down two of the sappers. He dropped the empty rifle, grabbed a machete, and stormed down the trench. He ran into three other sappers and hacked them all to death in furious, hand-to-hand combat. Fitzmaurice, the quiet kid, was bleeding badly and out of his mind from adrenaline. Some GIs had to physically drag him back to cover.

The firefight was intense until about four in the morning, when only a few sappers survived to fire back. At around five, the NVA reappeared in the fog outside the wire in what appeared to be an effort to recover their dead. More shooting broke out. The refuel/rearm point continued to explode. In the 4/77 AFA area, a captain, checking bunker to bunker, stepped into one damaged dugout just in time to see a wounded sapper bolt from a cot and run out the side port. The captain chased him down the trench and shot him with his .45 pistol.

While a medic bandaged the prisoner, U.S. and ARVN officers conducted a quick field interrogation. The sapper said he was a member of the 15th Sapper Battalion, only recently dispatched down the Ho Chi Minh Trail to destroy the Cobra gunship and command facilities at Khe Sanh. This was their first mission after extensive training. The prisoner said they had thoroughly reconnoitered the perimeter for two weeks, and had even used the night fog as cover to stage rehearsal attacks. Forty sappers had made the actual assault and most of them had gotten through the wire before anyone had spotted them.

With the sun up and the shooting petering out, Warren rose from his position and trudged back to the CP bunker. Men were moving and scrambling, and he got back on the radio as Captain Thomas called in immediate medevacs for his wounded. The wounded were evacked; the grunts were talking. Warren listened, picking up on what happened. One GI said he'd turned a corner in the trench, had seen a sapper bandaging a wounded comrade and had blown them both away. He'd taken a beautiful 9mm pistol from the one doing the bandaging. Others were talking about the man who'd refused to come in a bunker during the shelling; they said an RPG had exploded near him and he'd freaked out, dropping his rifle and screaming nonsense. He was sent out with the wounded. Some of the GIs said that a woman reporter, strolling into the area when they were cleaning out the last of the NVA, had pissed everybody off by shouting that she would bring the captain up on mutilation charges. The bodies of the sappers had not been mutilated; the effects of a magazine of 5.56mm from an M-16 or of a hacking machete on a naked body at close range were just gruesomely effective.

Most of the talk centered around Mike Fitzmaurice, who had been placed aboard one of the first evacuation helicopters. Warren recalled him as a quiet kid who drank beer and listened to C&W; no one could believe what he'd done. But to his fellow grunts he was a hero and the captain collected witnesses' statements to write up a citation for the Medal of Honor. The cost of the melee was counted up—three GIs killed and fourteen wounded, against fourteen dead NVA, one prisoner, and numerous blood trails in the brush outside the bunker line. Warren looked at the fourteen NVA bodies laid shoulder-to-shoulder on the airstrip, clad only in black briefs, ammunition and explosives strapped to them. When you run into a perimeter, he thought, you know you're not coming out. The courage of the NVA amazed him. Later, in a firefight in the A Shau Valley, he saw them stand in their spider holes on a hillside to duel with AKs against strafing Phantoms. Not a smart idea, he figured, but it took a lot of nerve. Warren was struck by the differences between the American and North Vietnamese troops. The good morale in Delta Troop didn't come from any belief in the war, but from camaraderie and good leaders. When it came to a solid firefight, he thought the grunts were equal to or superior to the NVA. But they didn't measure up when it came to motivation and dedication. By that stage of the game, the war seemed useless to them, and he couldn't help but respect these young Vietnamese who died for their country. The enemy seemed like a stubborn boxer; no matter how many times the Americans pummelled him, he kept coming back.

The action around Khe Sanh did not end with the dramatic sapper raid; the shellings continued and the 3/187 Infantry continued beating the bush. The day after the raid, two helicopters were shot down in the hills on the border, and Delta Company went to get them. The birds were ablaze in a small valley, three NVA 12.7mm postitions set up like a horse-shoe on the ridges above them. Lieutenant Colonel Steverson planned to insert half of Delta on one side of the ridge, the rest on the other side, and have them sweep to the top. From there they could medevac any survivors. If Delta were halted, elements of B and C Companies, with mortar teams, were readied to CA into the area at the colonel's discretion.

Sp4 Daugherty, sitting in a Huey with Captain Edwards, knew none of the details. They'd suddenly been picked up from their hilltop position, and now he sat beside a buddy named Craig, his feet hanging from the cabin door, cradling his M-16 and feeling tense. They came in low over the LZ, a small plateau on the ridgeline, and Daugherty looked down in horror. The fire from the crash site had spread up the hill and flames now shot up around the landing zone. Their slick went in, the prop wash sending smoke, fire, and ash up in a whirlwind around them. The skids hovered six feet off of the ground, the door-gunner screamed to jump. Daugherty tumbled out, and quickly ran uphill with the rest, cursing the lifers for dropping them in the middle of a brush fire. He noticed then that his plastic canteen had started to melt.

Lieutenant Stephen's Second Platoon was CA'd onto the opposite side of the ridge. Stephen was in the lead bird, Steverson telling him on the radio that his LZ was hot. Because he declined to give Stephen coordinates, Stephen was convinced that the crash site must be in Laos. Fire poured at the Hueys as they came in, the lead ship taking hits, Stephen choked with a sense of helplessness as one or two green tracers zipped through the open cabin. The bird hovered at ten feet and they jumped into tall elephant grass. The second bird also dropped off its troops, but the third took hits on the approach, pulled away over the LZ, and—either because they panicked or had guts—two GIs jumped from it at twenty feet. Only ten men were on the ground with Stephen and they crouched in the elephant grass as AKs and the 12.7mms tore holes in the air. The noise was incredible, the NVA seemed to be everywhere. They could even see them darting among the trees.

Lieutenant Colonel Steverson, above in his C&C, radioed that the downed helos were a hundred meters to the southwest. Lieutenant Stephen refused to move until he had map coordinates.

The colonel angrily read off the digits; they were only a hundred yards from Laos. The NVA kept firing; U.S. artillery pounded in. The next thing Stephen knew, M-79 rounds were lobbing from over the crest where the rest of Delta was setting up. North Vietnamese were spotted between the two groups. Stephen insisted over the radio that grenades were exploding within fifty yards, but Steverson said that the NVA must have a launcher. Stephen had no idea that the rest of Delta Company was even in the area.

On the other side of the ridge, Daugherty could also see NVA among the trees. An FAC plane circled overhead, on the radio with him; the pilot said air was on the way, then sailed low and fired a white-phosphorus rocket. It exploded brightly in the jungle down the slope from them, and Daugherty reported that the marking round was right on the NVA. He read the grid coordinates that they were holding, and the FAC answered that he couldn't bring jets in that close to U.S. troops. Daugherty asked the pilot if he could guarantee that they would put their ordnance on the target. When the FAC answered yes, Daugherty said there'd been a mistake; they were really a klick away from the marking round.

The pilot answered conspiratorially, "That's all I wanted to know."

And then the jets came in. The grunts couldn't even see them from where they hugged earth and curled up. They held their ears and helmets as the sky broke with earsplitting shrieks, the valley erupted in geysers of smoke, splintered trees, and hot shrapnel, and the hill under them shook with concussion waves.

The first airstrike hit a quarter-mile to one side of Stephen's platoon. When the second pass hit on the opposite side, he radioed the colonel that he was bracketed by their own firepower.

Under heavy fire, Steverson took his C&C down on a low-level pass over the jungle, marking the exact NVA positions with red smoke grenades.

After the bombing, Stephen took point as his platoon worked its way towards the wrecks. They exchanged fire with some NVA who disappeared back into the jungle, then found the first crash. The helicopter was still smoking, but the fire was burning itself out. They dragged two bodies from the first bird; at the second, they found three dead but two survivors. The platoon humped back up the ridge and Hueys dropped into the LZ, under fire, to get the five burnt bodies. The slicks started to skim away when, on the other side of the mountain, Daugherty heard someone shout. He jerked his head up in time to see a body falling from one of the choppers. It disappeared behind the treeline. Gunships began darting low, trying to get a fix on where the body had landed, but they couldn't and Lieutenant Colonel Steverson decided to abandon it. It would have been too risky a game of finding a needle in a haystack, considering the NVA presence. The grunts were disgusted; all of this work and danger, and they had just let a body get lost; the door-gunner was too chicken, according to the rumor, to grab the roasted body when the chopper banked away. Daugherty, for one, felt sad that a fellow American soldier, dead or alive, had to be left behind in that stinking jungle.

The LZ was too hot to extract Second Platoon, so Stephen was ordered to hump to the top of the ridgeline. He again took point and, coming to the crest, saw a rifle barrel ahead in the foliage. He instantly shouldered his M-16 and dropped the sights to the man's forehead, ten feet away.

He was about to pull the trigger when he noticed the man was wearing a GI pot.

A grunt from one of the other platoons was lying flat, waiting for them, and only then did Stephen realize his was not the only platoon there. He lowered his M-16 but, still keyed-up from the fire, shouted, "You better speak English, motherfucker, or you're dead!"

Mission accomplished, it was time to get out.

They were waiting for the slicks to arrive when a volley of AKs suddenly burst from the brush forty meters ahead of Daugherty. He scrambled for cover with the others, dropping to the prone in the tall grass and shouldering his M-16. There was nothing to see but a wall of elephant grass and scrub brush ten feet in front of his face. More fire cut overhead and his radio crackled; the RTO on the right flank was taking fire from a ridge, while the RTO on his left said they were taking fire from the left. Daugherty and the rest just fired blind bursts back into the vegetation.

The NVA fire slackened off, the grunts popped smoke, and the choppers began coming in. The infantrymen on the fringe fired furiously while others jogged for the birds. Daugherty looked from his bed of elephant grass at the fourth from last helicopter twenty feet up, smoking from a burst of AK. It caught fire, shuddered as the pilot struggled to control it, and careened towards the grunts. Daugherty frantically grabbed Craig, lying beside him, and they dropped their rucks, grabbed their rifles, and bolted into the grass, stumbling and falling in the thick brush. He fell down, Craig leaped over him, and he scrambled back up, plunging into the wall of elephant grass. The Huey hit the ground hard behind them and burst into flames. Another slick sped into the smoky LZ, got the crew and some grunts aboard, and departed amidst the AK-47 fire.

Only two helicopters were still orbiting and Daugherty was worried; with the shoot-down and the crew evack, that much less space went to the infantrymen. They would have to double up on the last two birds. The Hueys came into the LZ, and the last grunts fired a couple of bursts into the brush and made a dash for them. Daugherty stepped on a skid as the helicopter began lifting off. He swung his other leg into the cabin and a grunt inside grabbed his web gear just as a burst of green AK tracers flew through the open cabin. He fell exhausted to the chopper floor as they gained altitude. The last slick came out of the LZ behind them, rounds punching through the aluminum floor, slightly wounding two grunts.

They set down on the Khe Sanh airstrip and began jumping out, TV crew filming them. The rest of the company gathered around. Buddies, who had before been concerned that they might not get out because of the chopper backup, were now slapping arms and laughing. A friend of Daugherty's from Rhode Island met him on the strip. The TV people had their camera on Daugherty and he didn't know why until his buddy laughed and pointed at his helmet. In the helmet band was the insignia of a lieutenant colonel he had found on the floor of a helicopter and jokingly stuck there.

Delta Company had been in contact for seven hours, and Daugherty wandered off the strip, still numb and shaken. He walked aimlessly and took off his helmet; then a captain he'd never seen before stuck his face in his and screamed, "Just where the hell do you think you are! Put your helmet back on!"

Daugherty went blank.

When he came back to his senses, he was sitting in a bomb crater. It seemed like a safe place. He had no idea what had happened to the captain. By dusk more Hueys had come for them and Delta Company was back in the mountain jungles.

The next day, another fierce firefight broke out in the Khe Sanh mountains, this one fought by Lieutenant Johnson's platoon of Alpha 3/5 Cav in the Punchbowl. Following the debacle of Bravo 1/1 Cav, General Hill had detached some of the reluctant cavalrymen to Johnson because of his good reputation. After some in-the-field retraining, he decided to take them on a daylight foot patrol. They organized at Emerald City, Sergeant White watching from his tank as the 1/1 Cav GIs milled around as if they wished they were anyplace else.

The patrol filed through a narrow valley pass, virtually cut off from one another in the thick foliage; then the NVA cut loose from spider holes flanking the pass. The three GIs in the lead disappeared in the sudden blast of AK-47s; a crossfire tore into the main body of the patrol, and the grunts hit the dirt as Lieutenant Johnson crawled forward. He found two men dead, the other mortally wounded, and then he too was hit, an AK round drilling his leg. Terrified and disorganized, the patrol inched away under the crossfire, abandoning Johnson. The lieutenant, seeing an NVA rise from a spider hole, gunned him down with his M-16.

He scurried into the dead man's dugout to hide.

That, at least is the story the Bravo grunts gave as they straggled back. At Emerald City, the platoon sergeant quickly organized a rescue patrol. He told White to send a volunteer from his tank, so the crew drew high card to see who would go. White pulled the Queen of Spades from the deck. He joined a dozen GIs as they hauled ass toward the shooting aboard a couple of tracks. They dismounted and moved into the thick brush. White was the fourth man in line as they walked downhill on a narrow trail—and it happened all over again. From hidden spider holes, a scythe of AK-47 fire cut down the lead three men, and White dove terrified under a large boulder, cropping from the side of the jungled draw. The sergeant, lying prone ahead of him had two LAWs slung over his shoulder, so White grabbed his web gear and hauled him to the boulder. He suddenly realized the man was dead, stitched across the torso by AK rounds. The rest of the patrol had ducked behind the other side of the giant boulder, and were discussing pulling back. White screamed that he was still there. They set up an M-60 to cover his retreat but every time he tried to move from the boulder AKs opened up. He started tossing grenades downhill at the phantoms in the jungle until the firing died down. He put his bush hat on his M-16 and stuck it out. When it drew no fire, he rolled out and ran like hell back to the patrol. They all pulled back then, leaving the bodies.

White had painfully wrenched his ankle scurrying under the boulder, and a medevac deposited him and a grunt from the patrol with a graze wound at the squadron aid station.

Back in the draw, they could still hear Johnson crying out so a platoon from Bravo 3/5 Cav tried to move in from a different direction. They too were halted by the intense fire. Johnson tried to crawl back, but another burst hit his wounded leg and he shouted that he couldn't move. No one could see him or the North Vietnamese for all the foliage and

Lieutenant Colonel Osborn, monitoring the action from Emerald City radioed for the platoons to fall back. He sent in F4s to dislodge the NVA. The Phantoms dropped 250-pound bombs, and no one could be sure that they wouldn't blow up Lieutenant Johnson along with the enemy. Lieutenant Christian, with Osborn at the TOC APC, saw tears in the colonel's eyes after he gave the order.

But it worked. The shooting petered out after the airstrike and a Huey was able to go in for Johnson and the dead men. Sergeant White watched as they carried Lieutenant Johnson into the aid station on a litter. He'd been cut off, all alone, under intense fire, for hours; he faded in and out, his face was ashen, his trousers bloody and stinking. As the doctor cut away the frayed trousers, he mumbled, embarrassed, "I messed myself, I messed myself."

"Looks like you're going home," White said.

"Yeah," Johnson grunted, "I'm not going to have to put up with this bullshit anymore."

White was glad that Johnson had made it out okay; he was good in combat and was the kind of officer, he thought with approval, who wouldn't tolerate heroin, but would look the other way if a dude lit up a little grass.

The official assessment of the contact was six U.S. KIA and five WIA, against thirty-six NVA killed. That sounded good on paper, but did not prevent General Hill from sending the Bravo GIs back to the 1/1 Cav, dissatisfied with their reaction to the ambush. Besides the official repercussions, the incident convinced the 3/5 Cav grunts that 1/1 Cav was flaky. When they finally headed back for Dong Ha, White and his crew were intent on the cold beer and good pot in the rear. They shut down in the motor pool, cleaned the expended brass out of their vehicles, refueled, rearmed; then they wandered back to their hootches only to discover that elements of 1/1 Cav had moved in, laid claim to the barracks and hootch maids, and refused to budge. There were shouts, a few punches, and one of White's buddies started a Sheridan in the 1/1 motor pool, aimed it at the hootches, and jumped out. They laughed like hell as GIs chased after it. First Sergeant Bradley finally broke up the fight and returned their hootches to them. That was a good old army story of unit loyalty, but as the stress of combat wore off, the 3/5 Cav even fell upon itself. It was White's first long standdown and it shocked him to see black troopers who'd fought beside him suddenly band together and travel in groups. They picked fights with whites, and the undercurrent of hate disturbed White enormously. It made him want to get back in the bush just to be away from the rear. Sergeant Keefer's platoon withdrew to the main base at Khe Sanh. He thought it would offer some relief from the punishment they had suffered in the bush, but he soon found that Khe Sanh was just one more bad scene tacked to the end of an operation he thought was a mess from start to finish.

The shelling continued as Keefer noted in his diary:

March 27. We're on our way back down south now. We are stopped at Khe Sanh. We are taking 140 and 122mm rockets and 152 artillery from across the border.

March 28. We've been taking more rockets. There's just no place to hide. One of our APCs was hit right on top. Three guys died.

March 29. Didn't take any rockets today.

March 30–31. Took about 10 rockets yesterday and about 23 today.

April 1. Took 5 rockets this morning and 8 tonite.

April 2. We were told we'd be leaving today. But now they come telling us we'll be here for another 3 to 10 days. Sure will be glad to leave this place.

Ray Keefer was twenty-one years old, but his face no longer looked as boyish as it had when he'd arrived in Vietnam. Gray hair peppered his blond shag and he felt like a tired old man. The very last note in his Vietnam diary read, "Only God knows how much I miss my home and want to be back home with my family. Just 59 more days left in the Army and I'll be out."

CHAPTER SEVENTEEN:
Standdown

The South Vietnamese were in Laos for forty-five days, and the last ones out were the Vietnamese Marines. Initially serving as the I Corps reserve force, they had been committed in early March to occupy the firebases that the 1st Division had abandoned for the drive to Tchepone. As the withdrawals continued, the marines came under increasing pressure. By the time they were the last South Vietnamese in Laos, this was their deployment: the 2d, 4th, and 7th Infantry Battalions, 147th VNMC Brigade on LZ delta; the 1st, 3rd and 8th infantry battalions, 258th VNMC Brigade on LZ hotel; the 369th VNMC Brigade in reserve.

Their formidable task was to blunt the NVA counterattack. The U.S. Marine advisors chafed at their own inability to fight alongside their counterparts in Laos. Headed by Colonels Frank Tief and Pat McMillan, the advisors endured numerous artillery attacks at the rear command post; four of them, Majors Pat Carlisle, Bill Dabney, Bob Martin, and Fred Tolleson, were even allowed to overfly the VNMC AO (these flights were made in the face of heavy fire from radar-controlled 37mm flak guns, for which Carlisle, Martin, and Tolleson won Silver Stars, probably the only advisors decorated for heroism during Laos. For unexplained reasons, Dabney was not decorated, perhaps because, of the four, he was not aerial-observer qualified). But even the flights weren't enough. The marine advisors thought of themselves as a breed apart, all second-tour vets who attacked their new responsibilities as fiercely as they did any enemy hill. They spoke Vietnamese, wore the VNMC uniform, ate their food, lived with them in the field, fought beside them. They usually worked alone or in pairs, and often sneered at some of the U.S. Army advisors, at least the ones whose hootches were little replicas of America with real beds, pinups on the wall, refrigerators full of beer, and a stereo playing in the corner.

They wanted to fight with their comrades in Laos. The Vietnamese Marines were brave, sometimes almost suicidal in their acceptance of the never-ending war. Many of their officers had received training in the United States, and they emulated the training and tactics of the U.S. Marine Corps. They had proven their combat worth in the Mekong Delta and Cambodia. But Laos was a new test. The terrain of unfamiliar, rugged mountains was nothing like the tabletop Delta paddies to which they were accustomed; and they were facing a numerically superior, well-equipped, well-motivated NVA force that knew the area.

A lesser unit would have been destroyed doing the job handed the Vietnamese Marines in Laos. As it was, they were seriously bloodied.

With the 1st Infantry and 1st Airborne Divisions airlifted out, and the 1st Armor Brigade racing for the border, the full weight of the NVA counterattack fell upon the single VNMC brigade at LZ Delta. The North Vietnamese soldiers hugged the perimeter and kept the U.S. helicopters away with heavy small-arms fire. Supply drops to the hilltop missed. The marines were almost out of ammunition and on 20 March, the brigade prepared to pull out. But the NVA attacked that day and penetrated the wire. It was a horrific meatgrinder, but the Vietnamese Marines held. The next day, they were directed to spike their artillery pieces in preparation for helicopter extraction; but the helicopters could not get through, and the NVA shelled them without reprisal.

Men shot across the divided perimeter, and shouted across each other's radio frequencies. The NVA calls were always for surrender.

"You realize too well that we are all around you, and can move in at any time, not because you are bad soldiers, but because you are so few, so lonely, and a little frightened. We are Vietnamese, why do you fight for the American imperialists? You should be fighting for your own country, the Vietnamese people."

One South Vietnamese shouted back on the radio, "Sons of bitches, you are working like dogs for the Chinese, for the Russians, you are selling the country to them."

On 22 March, the NVA shelled LZ Delta all day and, in the late afternoon, the assault came. Ten Soviet-made tanks mounted with flame-throwers spearheaded the attack, infantrymen rushing with them. The marines poured fire from their bunkers, halting the attack. They blew up two tanks with LAWs. Another tank hit a mine and exploded. A Phantom strafed the NVA, blowing up a fourth tank. The NVA simply shelled again, then launched another assault. They ran straight at the marine line, screaming, "Assault, assault!" and they died en masse. But there were too many of them. The marines ran low on ammunition, and their casualties were heavy. All three VNMC battalion commanders on the hill had been wounded. The line began to break.

The order came to retreat to LZ Hotel.

The weather had turned misty and rainy, and the helicopters could not get in to evacuate the marine wounded. Over a hundred who could not walk would have to be left behind. They watched, terrified, as their comrades prepared to pull out, afraid of what the Communists would do to them, knowing that, even if they survived, the American B52s would be coming to bomb the victors. Men pleaded with their friends to shoot them. No one could.

A private named Binh in the 2d Battalion was getting ready to leave when a friend called him over. The man was wounded and could not walk.

He whispered for a grenade.

Binh gave one to his friend and ran away.

Seconds later there was an explosion.

The North Vietnamese surged over the abandoned bunkers, with tanks and infantry, and the marines retreated down the eastern slopes of LZ Delta. The wounded tried to hobble after them, but stumbled and were swallowed up. Tank and artillery fire burst among the survivors; NVA charged after them with the blood-curdling cry, "Assault!" and the retreat disintegrated. In the chaos, commanders lost control of their men, with every man for himself fleeing into the valley. There was no relief—the NVA outnumbered them and were everywhere.

Private Binh found himself with a hundred other marines. They moved through the black jungle, terrified of ambush. North Vietnamese running through the area paused a few times to shoot towards them. Confused and frightened marines also opened up on them in the dark. Some of the men were gripped with panic, and threw away their rifles and gear to run faster.

A captain named Tien finally stopped the group and shouted angrily at them to get their heads together and follow him.

The marines hesitated.

The captain drew his pistol, jogged uphill, and frightened men followed him. Private Binh's group made it to safety.

With daylight and better weather, helicopters were able to come in for some of the survivors, while others kept walking towards the border in small groups, evading the NVA. The brigade reported thirty-seven men missing and hundreds more killed or wounded, but two thousand NVA had died in the overrunning of LZ Delta. Nevertheless, on the morning of 24 March, the hammer fell on the last South Vietnamese in Laos—the 258th VNMC Brigade on Hotel. In two hours before noon, U.S. Air Cavalry teams spotted at least five groupings of Soviet-made tanks on the border, and blew up ten of them. Meanwhile, North Vietnamese probes were launched at the wire around LZ Hotel.

Back in Saigon, Lieutenant General Khang, Commandant of the VNMC, received the situation reports. He had never joined the command post on the Laotian front, presumably because he was miffed at having been relegated to being under Lam's command (no clear reason emerged, however, from within the politics of the Vietnamese hierarchy). In order to minimize casualties among his remaining units, Khang ordered Colonel Lan—without consulting with Lam to weigh the consequences—to evacuate LZ Hotel. An orderly helicopter withdrawal of the troops and artillery pieces on the Co Roc was conducted. The next day, an angry General Lam ordered two VNMC reconnaissance teams back to the high ground of the Co Roc to monitor the counterattack. They had little to report; the Communists' fury did not reach across the border. Perhaps they did not want to risk further heavy casualties and were content to hit-and-run and shell along the Quang Tri front. Most likely, they were too busy licking their wounds after having taken tremendous casualties in wreaking havoc on the ARVN withdrawal. No Americans or South Vietnamese could say for sure.

The last South Vietnamese, the recon teams, were out of Laos on 24 March 1971.* Commented a marine corporal from the 147th Brigade,

---

*At least that is the official version. One marine advisor saw Colonel Lan talk to the team leaders he was supposed to send to the Co Roc; he seemed distressed

"The papers and the radio kept on saying there was a Laos victory, I have learned now, but what a joke. We ran out like wounded dogs."

The view was not so bleak at the command level. The 147th Brigade had been mauled, but had survived, was regrouping, and was still combat ready; the 258th had been bloodied; the 369th Brigade had not even been touched. No battle is without its moments of tragedy and panic, but the marines had met the challenge of their first division-sized fight. The North Vietnamese had been halted at the border.

Major Dabney, USMC, senior advisor to the 3d Battalion, 258th VNMC Brigade, was more cautious about claiming victory. He had no doubt that the individual South Vietnamese had soldiered bravely in Laos; but that wasn't enough to salvage the operation and he considered Laos a disaster. Dabney was an ex-sergeant, a graduate of VMI, a tough, blunt man on his second voluntary tour. His first year had conditioned him to the realities of Vietnam. He'd been a rifle company commander with the 26th Marines then, in exactly the same area that he was in now. The only fond memory he had from that experience was the stunning spirit of his marines.

Khe Sanh had ended in victory and Dabney had never been prouder of the marine team. But numerous problems had cropped up, some of which reappeared during Lam Son 719. The worst was the lack of turnover of information between units. He'd seen time after time when marine companies would walk into the same NVA ambush spots at different times, because no one had warned them. Battalions and regiments often did not pass on information, and Dabney cynically described intelligence in Vietnam as a few filthy grunts watching another outfit patrolling towards a valley where they'd been mauled and muttering, "Geez, I wish they wouldn't do that." That was a major problem as he saw it with Operation Lam Son 719. The U.S. Marines had been fighting in the area for five years and, in 1969, had even made a raid into Laos. They knew the terrain and disposition of NVA artillery; many of the command and staff officers who had successfully defended Khe Sanh in '68 were readily available for advice, but Dabney knew of no time when the U.S. Army turned to them when planning and executing Lam Son 719. It was wearisome to keep reinventing the wheel.

at ordering them to almost certain death, and the impression was that he instead had quietly ignored the directive.

Dabney had been wary of the operation since first he had been briefed two months earlier at 3d Battalion Headquarters at Quang Tri. He had, in fact, been appalled, thinking the plan invited disaster. If Tchepone was a legitimate target, he thought, why not simply take the divisions and brigades allotted to I Corps and march them en masse to the target and back? That way, he surmised, the Communists could never obtain any substantial victories because they couldn't successfully challenge the size of such a force. In addition, the helicopter LZs would not have been covered with AA fire since they would have been deep in allied lines; bloodied units could have been rotated easily within the moving battle group; and communications would have been similarly simplified, instead of strung out among various firebases and HQ elements all the way back to Dong Ha.

As he saw it, the plan for mutually-supporting firebases called for an adeptness and experience at fire coordination, resupply, and communications that the ARVN simply did not yet possess. The firebases, dropped like islands in an enemy sea, did nothing but allow the NVA to encircle and attack at will, one at a time. The ARVN had never been involved in such a complex operation, and the only way he saw that they might be able to hold their ground was with expertly orchestrated air and artillery support, such as that which the marines had been able to achieve at Khe Sanh. Dabney knew very well, though, that the USMC air-ground team had been in the making for thirty years, and the South Vietnamese had always relied upon their advisors to handle such matters. Now the advisors were removed from the field of battle.

The ARVN advantage in Laos was firepower; but the mere presence of might was meaningless, only its application mattered. The case of the awesome B52 bomber illustrates this. As they had done during the seige of Khe Sanh, the North Vietnamese encircled the firebases in Laos. In 1968 the problem had been that the Marines could not use air and arty against targets so close to their own perimeters without observation and control which could not be achieved in the dark. This scenario was even worse for the firebases in Laos; Dabney suspected that the NVA were in close around-the-clock. Arc Lights would have eliminated them, but the USAF was not given accurate reporting on the disposition of friendly patrols around the firebases. This meant that they were forced to place their bomb loads at least four thousand meters away, well beyond likely NVA locations. So for all of the thousands of tons of ordnance dropped in support of the ARVN firebases, it was logical to assume that it had little effect.

The North Vietnamese, on the other hand, were given a great opportunity by the ARVN firebase plan. Although the NVA had relatively poor communications and could never hope to match the allies in raw firepower, the presence of fixed ARVN positions allowed them to use their limited resources to the greatest effect. The NVA sited their artillery and mortars in scattered, single-gun positions, and ranged the tubes individually at the various South Vietnamese posts. Since they never moved, the NVA could fire without observation, night and day, accurately hitting any targets of opportunity (medevac and resupply helos, for example) on the fixed positions, without going through a lengthy fire-registration process.

That was nothing new, Dabney knew; the NVA had used that tactic against his regiment in '68, but the USMC knew how to use firepower. It was difficult to pinpoint and neutralize single-gun positions in the jungled mountains, but with Marine infantrymen directing Marine aircraft (with one overall Marine commander) they had succeeded. The tools were available to the South Vietnamese in Laos, but the experience and cohesion were missing. To begin with, the Vietnamese Marines were operating as a division when before they had rarely even worked in multibattalion campaigns. So the three brigades headquarters had no firesupport-coordination experience, the battalion commanders having usually left such matters to their U.S. Marine advisors. Now, in Laos, the situation involved South Vietnamese without advisors relying on U.S. Army helicopters, Air Force jets, and U.S. and ARVN artillery. This was a tangle; Dabney was not particularly surprised to learn that when the 147th was being overrun on LZ Delta, the 258th on LZ Hotel had 155mm guns in range but was not alerted to fire in support.

He had seen only a rare VNMC unit with the training and experience to, when in contact, coordinate between squad, platoon, and company leaders on the radio, pinpoint the enemy with spotter rounds, then further coordinate with the battalion commander to place U.S. firepower from different services on the enemy. Even his helicopter flights over Laos did little good because the VNMC mortar crews did not have the capability of accurately marking the NVA with white phosphorus shells; and B52s could not be employed in a carpeting manner since, because of the scattered command posts, it was difficult to locate friendly patrols around the firebases.

The result was that the South Vietnamese trump card over the numerically superior NVA—massive firepower—was negated because of inexperience. In fact the NVA could even outgun the firebases.

Most matters seemed similarly bungled. The logistics officer in Dabney's battalion was an uncaring character who responded to the overwhelming logistics of the operation by adhering to a strict schedule: the battalions were resupplied in turn, not when they specifically needed it. Thus, units were overrun because they had practically no ammunition while others had stockpiles of the stuff which was left behind when they retrograded back to South Vietnam.

Dabney's concerns were so great that, before the withdrawal from Tchepone began, he hopped a helo ride to the U.S. 1st Marines CP at Da Nang. He talked with two old acquaintances, Col. P. X. Kelley* the regimental commander, and Col. Al Smith, G2 of the 1st Marine Division. He explained the problems that he saw and predicted that Lam Son 719 was a disaster in the making. Kelley and Smith seemed impressed and arranged a meeting with Lt. Gen. Donn Robertson, commander of III MAF.

When the ARVN began pulling out, the NVA began isolating and overrunning positions. It wasn't the fault of the South Vietnamese, Dabney thought, it was MACV's plan. Without the bravery of the marine and army aviators going in to pull out the men, he surmised that Lam Son 719 could have been annihilation, instead of merely a disaster. Dabney could only thank God that the weather hadn't turned foul and trapped the South Vietnamese inside Laos.

The withdrawal of U.S. troops and installations from the Khe Sanh area went at a steady pace, beginning when the ARVN started pulling out of Laos and heading back south themselves, and was marked by a final few casualties in the rocket raids and convoy ambushes. On 25 March, the 27th Engineers began taking up the assault runway matting at Khe Sanh and, by 1 April, the removal of the airstrip was completed. In the sky, Chinooks could be seen headed east with slingloads of materiel, engineer equipment, bridges, and artillery pieces. Along Route 9, long convoys streamed for Dong Ha and then Quang Tri, stacked with salvaged gear. The man detailed to supervise the evacuation of Khe Sanh, Colonel Rosenblum of the 101st DISCOM, watched impressed as the base perimeter quickly shrank; they had been able to go in, set up a giant logistical

*Now the Commandant, U.S. Marine Corps.

center, then pull out leaving nothing behind, the NVA responding with only a few departing rocket raids. The North Vietnamese simply couldn't react to fast-moving situations, Rosenblum thought, and if he were the NVA general he imagined he would court-martial the NVA commander of the Khe Sanh AO for incompetence.

FSA-I at the Vandegrift Combat Base was officially closed on 4 April. By 6 April, FSA-II at the Khe Sanh Combat Base was a desolate ghost town; the last convoys left on Route 9 and the Yellow Brick Road, a small detachment staying long enough to fire tear gas canisters into the U.S. bunkers. The gas crystals would make the shelters unlivable for two years. With gunships and M48 tanks guarding the route, Khe Sanh was evacuated without a major hitch. Also on 6 April, the last elements of the 1/11 Infantry (D Company and the battalion command group) were airlifted from Khe Sanh to Quang Tri. On Route 9, the 1/77 Armor began a leapfrogging, retrograde action back east from Lang Vei, attached engineer elements removing all of the AVLB bridges installed west of Vandegrift. The 1/1 and 3/5 Cavalry, and the 1/61 Mech Infantry also joined the pullout. On the evening of 8 April, Pfc DeAngelis watched as his old friends in Bravo Company rolled back into Quang Tri. He could see them coming a mile away, the dusty, battered caravan of APCs looking like a Fourth of July celebration as the grunts fired flares, pitched smoke grenades, and raised general hell in their joy to be heading back. DeAngelis joined them in the EM Club to down some beers, and later wrote to his parents, "They were out for 75 days and never got mail or clean clothes the whole time. There fatigues were literally rotted on there backs and they were all caked with dirt and very pooped too. (But happy to be back). . . . They lost 15 men 6 from my old platoon and I think everybody got some small kind of wound at one time or other. Anything that could ever happen to a bunch of grunts happened to them. Believe me, there is now no one left from my old squad. Two of the guys got killed. I've got pictures of them at home someplace. What can I say to tell you how I feel right now."

On 8 April, the 14th Engineers removed the last of the bridges placed for the operation and on 9 April, the last pullout was set in action. Trash fires rose at various points in the jungled hills where the grunts of the Americal and 101st Airborne cleaned up their last NDPs. A flight of Hueys dropped into the jungle home of Bravo 3/187 and the men packed their gear and themselves aboard. They were deposited first in another LZ where they boarded a Chinook, and finally touched down at Camp Evans. The Screaming Eagles' brass band was on the runway playing for the filthy grunts as they trudged off the strip. How hokey, Sp4 Kucera thought, who cares? Shortly thereafter, the battalion held a memorial service formation. Nineteen ponchos were laid out before an altar with nineteen pairs of empty jungle boots. A pet dog of Bravo Company named Yo-Yo wandered out during the ceremony and voided on the late Lieutenant Colonel Sutton's poncho. The grunts collapsed with laughter.

On the last morning, Captain Downey of Charlie 2/1 Infantry received a radio call from the 4/3 CP that they were to be extracted from their hilltop. They were ordered to fire a Mad Minute around their perimeter, expend whatever mortar ammunition they still had, bury their garbage, police the area, and be prepared to leave aboard helicopters at 1130 hours.

That was at around half past seven in the morning; by eleven they were packed and ready to go. Downey was called by the battalion operations officer, who was in his C&C helicopter. The major said that there were some delays and the pickup would probably not be until 1300 hours. It was a little after noon when they heard the first popping thunks of 82mm mortar rounds leaving their tube. Explosions began walking across Charlie Company's position and the grunts jumped into foxholes, unable to fire back because they had used up all of their mortar ammunition that morning. One GI was slightly wounded, but the company RTO could raise no one on the medevac channel. Downey got on the radio and finally convinced the major to leave his C&C orbit to get the wounded trooper. The mortaring stopped as soon as the helicopter came into view; as the C&C was lifting off with the injured man, the major radioed, "Your birds are on the way, be ready in five minutes!"

Downey shouted for his men to get organized. They waited. Thirty minutes passed. No helicopters appeared and his RTO could raise no one on the radio. On nearby hills, they watched other choppers going in to pick up other units. After another twenty minutes, Downey noticed with apprehension that everything was perfectly quiet. No helicopters were overhead, no traffic was on the highway below; so still he could hear the jungle birds.

The North Vietnamese mortar crew opened fire again, and the men dropped back in their holes. It was a heavy, accurate shelling, and the young FO lieutenant crouched beside Downey, shouting into the radio, calling the artillery frequencies at Khe Sanh and Vandegrift. No one answered. The lieutenant and the company's ARVN interpreter just managed to make contact with an ARVN 155mm howitzer outfit on a small firebase barely within range; then the NVA began jamming the radio. They must have been close because their voices were loud and clear through the receiver, effectively blocking transmissions with loud screams and laughs. Downey would have laughed too, if he hadn't been so nervous, when the NVA began shouting corn such as, "You die now, GI!" It was like being in some WWII movie, he thought.

The mortaring continued at a steady pace.

Finally, twenty Huey slicks appeared in the sky above Charlie Company, coming from the direction of Dong Ha, and four Cobra gunships darted down, circling the perimeter in search of a flash from the NVA mortar. The enemy's response was to put a second tube into action; the new one was much closer, Downey noted, the time between the thunk and the explosion being shorter than before. Dodging the mortar attack, the Hueys began coming in, three at a time. They landed on the crest of the hill, above the infantrymen's foxholes, and the grunts dashed for them. Captain Downey's five-man command group was the last out. Their Huey settled down, another mortar round exploding next to their hole; Downey yelled, "Run!" and they bolted uphill. Downey flung himself and his rucksack aboard, his RTO clambered on behind him, and the bird bolted out of the jungle landing zone.

At Dong Ha, the operations officer of 4/3 came over to Captain Downey to tell him that his C Company, 2d Battalion, 1st Infantry, 196th Infantry Brigade, Americal Division had the distinction of being the last U.S. infantry unit withdrawn from Operation Lam Son 719.

Coming in last was Lieutenant Colonel Meyer's 1st Battalion, 77th Armor. The day before, they had camped outside Khe Sanh after departing Lang Vei under mortar fire. As they blew up extra equipment and ammunition, a resupply bird dropped in. The battalion sniper squad brusquely greeted an FNG who hopped out; then they climbed aboard to get back to Quang Tri. Only Sp4 Spurgeon decided to stay with the tank column, hopped up about his kill and hoping for more action. The next morning, 9 April, he was sitting atop a tank with a smoke and a cup of C rat coffee, when a APC from the 3/5 Cav roared into their perimeter, coming to a quick dusty stop. A filthy crewman spotted Spurgeon and hustled over.

"You a sniper?"

"Yeah."

"Well, one of your snipers was killed last night, and another wounded pretty bad. We picked 'em up last night after they called for help."

"My snipers are in Quick Town, they were lifted into the PX for some supplies last night!"

Confused and agitated, Spurgeon jumped on the tank of the Bravo Company captain and asked him to check higher about two snipers being hit the night before. The captain nodded from inside the turret, spoke into the radio, then pulled his helmet off and said, "Yes." Before long they hit Route 9 and it was well after dark when this last group rolled past the Quang Tri perimeter gate. Spurgeon rode on the back deck of one of the tanks, surprised to see an Australian floor show grinding away on a plywood stage in the battalion area. The GI audience greeted the last column with enthusiastic cheers and smiles. The tanks had to slow down because of the applauding soldiers crowded around, and Spurgeon noticed Sergeant Wondra smiling up at him from the crowd, in new fatigues, a bandage taped to the top of his partially-shaved head.

He hopped off the tank and Wondra gave him a big bear hug.

In the sniper hootch, the men were clean shaven, in clean clothes, and cheerful as they passed beers and sodas. Spurgeon asked about what the cavalryman had told him—two snipers shot up—and the story started coming out. The helo taking them to Quang Tri had been diverted to a 3/5 Cav hill outpost, where they joined two 101st snipers, and had dug in for the night. Having been forced to set up in broad daylight on an open hill, the men were nervous. At around midnight they saw flashlights in the hills to the north. Attention focused in that direction when RPGs and AKs suddenly opened up from their rear. The snipers burrowed into their holes, except for the team of Wondra and Felix who returned fire despite shrapnel wounds. The 101st staff sergeant in charge froze, according to the snipers. One of them had to wrestle the radio from him, and he had just contacted the cav at the bottom of the hill, when an NVA sprang into the perimeter. From three feet away he shot Felix through the head with his AK-47, the body bouncing against Wondra who spun to see the North Vietnamese crouched at the rim of the foxhole. They fired at the same time. The M-14 round hit the NVA in the chest, killing him, while the AK round hit Wondra on the top of his head, knocking him down. Blinded by blood, he heaved grenades at the NVA. Flares burst overhead, the cav tracks rumbled quickly up the hill, and the enemy disappeared back into the night.

Felix was probably the last KIA in the 1/77 Armor, and possibly the last in the operation. The armor battalion had been in the field for seventy days for the Laotian campaign, the first out and the last back in.

CHAPTER EIGHTEEN:
Where Victory Lies

T he time chosen officially to close the log on Operation Dewey Cunyon II/Lam Son 719 was 5:08 P.M., 6 April 1971. No ground troops remained in Laos or in the Khe Sanh area, as the effort had been a spoiling attack, not a land seizure operation. As always in the Vietnam War, a tableau of statistics was presented to determine success or failure. The XXIV Corps After-Action Report gives this breakdown of U.S. casualties during the battle:

101st Airborne Division:	68 KIA	261 WIA	17 MIA
1st Brigade, 5th Division:	55 KIA	431 WIA	3 MIA
Americal Division:	47 KIA	256 WIA	7 MIA
223d Combat Aviation Battalion:	19 KIA	59 WIA	11 MIA
XXIV Corps Artillery:	9 KIA	76 WIA	0 MIA
U.S. Army Support Command:	8 KIA	40 WIA	0 MIA
45th Engineer Group:	6 KIA	11 WIA	0 MIA
7th U.S. Air Force:	4 KIA	N/A WIA	0 MIA
504th MP Battalion:	3 KIA	15 WIA	0 MIA

While according to XXIV Corps, 219 Americans were officially listed as killed in the Laotian campaign, the figure released for publication—to *Newsweek* for example—was 102 KIA (roughly the number killed in aerial combat over Laos). But the rules of the game dictated that even the higher figure be slightly lower than reality. For example, the total did not take into account various support units which served only sporadically and briefly during the operation (MP detachments, small USMC units, 1st Signal Brigade radio outposts on the battlefield, and others). Also, the mortally wounded were counted as WIA instead of KIA since they died in a hospital or aboard a helicopter, not in the field. Similarly, nonhostile deaths were not tabulated (for instance ten aircrewmen were killed and four missing in mishaps; SUPCOM reported fourteen fatal traffic accidents during the campaign; nine U.S. Marines were killed in a CH53 crash in South Vietnam after nursing their ship out of Laos, apparently with battle damage).

The same type of gerrymandering occurred in the listing of U.S. battle damage. For, example 107 helicopters were reported lost during the operation (fifty-three Hueys, twenty-six Cobras, 9 Loaches, 8 UN1C gunships, 6 Kiowa Scouts, 3 Chinooks, and 2 Sea Stallions); this does not include 5 destroyed in accidents. In addition, a helicopter retrieved from the battlefield, even if it were burnt-out junk, was not counted as lost; thus, although an additional 618 helicopters were reported as damaged, it would be impossible to determine how many had been shot down in combat and then slingloaded out by Chinooks after the shooting was over, or how many made controlled crashes in friendly territory.

The South Vietnamese suffered severe losses, up to 50 percent in some units, with the breakdown as follows:

1st Infantry Division:	537 KIA	1,607 WIA	537 MIA
1st Airborne Division:	455 KIA	1,992 WIA	0 MIA*
VNMC Division:	335 KIA	768 WIA	37 MIA
1st Ranger Group:	93 KIA	435 WIA	27 MIA
I Corps units:	55 KIA	314 WIA	24 MIA
1st Armor Brigade:	54 KIA	367 WIA	0 MIA
	1,529 KIA	5,483 WIA	625 MIA

---

*A false figure; Colonel Tho, CO, 3d Airborne Brigade, was captured on Hill 31 along with numerous other ARVN paratroopers.

Compared to the recorded deaths of 219 Americans (and 38 MIA), and 1,529 South Vietnamese (and 625 MIA), the North Vietnamese suffered grievously. The official count was 19,360 killed and 57 captured (of this, the U.S. was credited with 4,795 kills and 8 captures, while those killed by U.S. tac air and bomber missions were included in the ARVN total). Thus, according to the allied figures, perhaps one-half of the NVA committed to Laos were killed.

The Laotian operation had not been merely a body-count exercise but, more importantly, an attempt to disrupt the NVA buildup to preempt their invasion of MR1. In this endeavor, the statistics of destruction were these: 5,170 individual weapons; 1,963 crew-served weapons; 2,001 vehicles; 11 combat vehicles; 106 tanks (88 confirmed by U.S. aerial recon); 13 artillery pieces; 93 mortars; 98 radios; 1,250 tons of rice; 170,346 tons of ammunition (20,000 tons verified by the U.S.).

The reading of success or failure into these numbers was a tricky and controversial business. The very nature of the plan—calling for a withdrawal from enemy territory under fire—brought about the specter of disaster; coupled with the ferocious NVA resistance to the operation, a surface examination could easily read failure. As it was all in the eye of the beholder, claims of success by the military quickly conflicted with more pessimistic reports from the press. The world press—and, thus, the American people—were generally convinced that the operation had been ill-planned with too much emphasis on U.S. firepower, the invasion halted, the withdrawal a chaotic rout. By 1971 the press corps generally had become an antiwar body and, to the detriment of unemotional analysis, their commentary on Lam Son 719 most often came from keyed-up sources—exhausted ARVN just off the helicopters from heavy combat in Laos, and bitter American pilots just back from the air war over Laos who spoke vindictively of the ARVN "getting their asses kicked."

The prevailing frame of mind can be understood by media reaction to certain events during the campaign. When General Abrams imposed a news embargo during the buildup in MR1 and during the first days of Dewey Canyon II, his reasoning was for security. Accordingly, he also embargoed the news of the embargo to prevent communist speculation. The press ignored this second constraint and informed home offices of the general facts so that stories could be published in the United States; they hinted without restraint that the troop buildup pointed to an invasion of Laos (blow to the allied ruse-operations aimed at worrying Hanoi about an invasion of North Vietnam); and they implied that the embargo was really a sinister cover-up. Suspicious of the ban on U.S. ground troops in Laos, many reporters turned their attention to trying to find some. They could not, but still managed to leave the impression that U.S. advisors and pathfinders were indeed in Laos. They also indicated that U.S. advisors in ARVN command posts were proof that the South Vietnamese were, in fact, puppets to U.S. commands; the advisors were merely doing what they always did, giving advice which was not always taken.

To accuse the press of going out of its way to show Lam Son 719 in the worst possible light does not, however, necessarily mean that the Laotian campaign was a stunning success. On this subject, even the opinions of military men were mixed. General Westmoreland, Army Chief of Staff, wrote of the problems: "Command arrangements at the top were unsound, and the plan had been developed too quickly for adequate provision for close co-ordination between the ARVN troops and their American support. Long accustomed to working with American advisors, subordinate ARVN commanders had difficulty without them in arranging fire support and resupply. The senior American advisor and the over-all ARVN commander were operating from different bases. Several senior ARVN commanders folded, prompting President Thieu to intervene and start issuing orders himself as far down as regiments, in many cases without General Abrams' knowledge."

The catalogue of disasters could continue. Intelligence had underestimated the speed and fury of the NVA counterattack, and this contributed to the loss of several ARVN firebases; the allies had indeed been defeated in some of the Laotian battles. General Dong and his relation (or lack of) with Colonel Luat of the 1st Armor caused needless problems. The response of some soldiers was cowardly: not merely grabbing a skid during a unit pullout, but shoving wounded aside to desert on medevac choppers. Because of the intelligence failure, the ARVN forces in Laos were too small to defend themselves adequately against the massed NVA units; given the option of beefing up their invasion force and staying longer in Laos, the ARVN commanders opted for a withdrawal, before the Communists closed them off and destroyed them piecemeal. The smaller of the two targeted base areas, BA 611, was untouched, except for a few Hoc Bao commando raids during the withdrawal sequence.

Despite these setbacks, the judgement of the command was expressed by General Sutherland, who called Lam Son 719 a victory in that

U.S. and ARVN successes outweighed their mistakes. A few facts were evident, the most important being that the assigned mission to reach Tchepone and destroy BA 604 had been accomplished by the ARVN task force. Some units were badly mauled (the 3d Airborne and 39th Ranger Battalions, for example, were withdrawn as combat ineffective due to casualties), but the NVA plans of invading MR1 had been set back a full year, as the planners had hoped. All of this had been accomplished in the face of grave odds. Outnumbered two-to-one on the ground, the ARVN soldiers (with massive, but not always responsive, U.S. firepower) had inflicted ten casualties on the NVA for every one that they suffered. I Corps had never previously controlled such a large operation and, except for the 1st Infantry Division, none of the ARVN divisions had worked as an entity before; yet, they had successfully disrupted BA 604 and the Ho Chi Minh Trail. Even though the withdrawal was executed under intense counterattack, most ARVN units pulled out in good military fashion ("They had to have damn good small unit leadership," a U.S. general was quoted in *Time*, "or they wouldn't have got out of there.").

The objectives of the operation had been down-scaled once the strength of the NVA became fully known, but it had nonetheless been a stinging blow to the Communists. There was no NVA invasion of MR1 that year. Vietnamization had been tested, had strained but had not cracked, and now had continued room to grow. Many, especially advisors, rejected the theory that ARVN failed so miserably in Laos that the final communist invasion of 1975 was a foregone conclusion. They blamed that capitulation on the total withdrawal of U.S. air support, the cutoff of U.S. supplies to the ARVN, and a botched attempt by the ARVN to fall back and regroup in the face of numerically overwhelming and well-supplied NVA troops. They point instead to March 1972. It took North Vietnam until then (even with massive Soviet aid and the stripping of many villages of every able-bodied man for the army) to recover from Lam Son 719 and to launch their invasion of MR1. They came across the DMZ in a conventional infantry assault supported by hundreds of Russian-made tanks, quickly defeating an inexperienced ARVN division and seizing the border firebases, as well as Dong Ha and Quang Tri. The ARVN finally recovered and in brutal battles involving house-to-house combat, artillery duels, and tank engagements, the ARVN and VNMC—many of whom were veterans of Laos—drove the NVA invaders back to the DMZ.

After Lam Son 719, the media quoted an American commander who said, "The success or failure of the operation will not be apparent until well into the fall. If there is no serious communist military activity in South Vietnam before then, it will have been well worth its cost." By that measure, Operation Lam Son 719 was a victory.

The average American soldier in Operation Lam Son 719 knew nothing of the big picture. His view was limited to a platoon, and a patch of jungle or a stretch of road. Some in the rear recalled the drugs and the sense of abandonment, while some in the infantry experienced the misery of the elements, occasional stabs of fear, and the sustaining element of comradeship. What they knew about the invasion came from tattered newspapers; they saw the photographs of ARVN clutching skids and read horrid accounts of disaster. Most thought the ARVN had been defeated in Laos.

The U.S. Army, however, accomplished every mission it had been assigned during Lam Son 719. For all of its morale problems, it had been successful in the field. But, by 1971, the glory of victory meant very little to the average GI who saw it as just another operation in an unending war. The fact that they once again pulled out and abandoned Lang Vei, Khe Sanh, and the rest, made hollow the sacrifices put into the campaign. What they had were their buddies, their pride, and even their patriotism, but little sense of accomplishment. In the eyes of the grunts, Nam was just as hopeless after Lam Son 719 as it had been before.

Operation Lam Son 719 turned out to be the last major operation the U.S. Army executed in Vietnam. The withdrawals continued, the long, dirty war ebbed and flowed. Two more statistics explained the foot soldiers' weariness with the situation: even though Laos was the last big campaign, it was seventeen months before the last U.S. infantrymen were pulled out, and another three years after that before the last American was killed-in-action in Vietnam.

Sergeant Keefer rotated home in August 1971, with a routine Bronze Star and a head full of things he'd rather forget. His homecoming was typical of the time. The jet from Tan Son Nhut took him from the war zone to the state of Washington in under twenty-four hours. He signed some papers, then was on the street with his discharge and a ticket back to Maryland. He had a military standby seat on a civilian airliner, but someone else got it. Keefer approached the man, explaining that he was just back from Vietnam, just out of the service, and hadn't seen his family in a year. He was wearing his uniform with the Bronze Star, Army Commendation Medal, and Purple Heart with four oak-leaf clusters. The man looked at the uniform, said he wouldn't give up his seat to trash, and turned his back. And Keefer wondered why he'd spent eighteen months with his life on the line.

Many, too many, veterans of Operation Lam Son 719 have told the same type of stories about their homecomings.

EPILOGUE

General Abrams (COMUSMACV) became Chief of Staff in 1972, and died in office of cancer after thirty-eight years of distinguished service. General Weyand (DEPCOMUSMACV) followed Abrams as commander in Vietnam, 1972-73, then as Chief of Staff from 1974 to his retirement in 1976. Lieutenant General Sutherland (CG, XXIV Corps) was awarded the DSM* for his corps command, having earned two Silver Stars, a Bronze Star, two Army Commendation Medals, and two Purple Hearts in WWII. He retired to Beaufort, South Carolina. Brigadier General Jackson (Deputy SA, XXIV Corps) retired to Hartsville, South Carolina.

General Vien (Chief of JGS) escaped to the United States when South Vietnam fell in 1975. Lieutenant General Lam (CG, I Corps) was relieved of command during the 1972 Easter Invasion; he too escaped the communist takeover and lives in California. Colonel Luat (CO, 1st Armor Bde.) was wounded during the Easter Invasion; as a province chief during the 1975 takeover, his helo was downed over communist lines and

*During unpopular wars, medals are given out liberally as a morale booster and Vietnam was no exception. Consequently, medals earned for specific deeds of valor will be indicated here by writing the full name of the award. Medals for service or end-of-tour awards will be indicated by their abbreviations.

he was never heard from again (a former ARVN regimental commander recently released by Hanoi reported seeing Luat and Lieutenant Colonel Dung of the 11th Cav in a communist "reeducation" camp). Colonel Hiep (Armor Cmd.) made brigadier general; he and his family escaped Saigon and, after working as Refugee Coordinator for Catholic Relief in Florida, he took a job with an aerospace corporation. Colonel Battreall (SA, Armor Cmd.) was shot in the leg by an AK-47 aboard Luat's APC in the Easter Invasion, then returned for a third Vietnam tour. He retired in 1979 with four LMs, three BSMs, three MSMs, AM, ARCOM, and a Purple Heart; he presently lives with his wife at Sierra Vista, Arizona, and teaches writing improvement to officers at a local army base. Colonel Harrison (SA, 1st Inf. Div.) received two Silver Stars, two LMs, two Distinguished Flying Crosses, a Soldiers Medal, two MSMs, thirty-nine AMs, two JSCMs, and two ARCOMs after two tours in Vietnam; he retired as a major general and now is a businessman in Belton, Texas. Colonel Pence (SA, 1st Airborne Div.) retired as a disabled veteran in 1972, and died of cancer two years later. Major Dabney (SA, 3d Bn., 258th VNMC Bde.) is presently a colonel.

Major General Tarpley (CO, 101st ABD) retired to Columbus, Georgia. Brigadier General Berry (ADC) was Superintendent of the Military Academy at West Point, 1974–77; he later commanded a corps in Europe and retired in 1980 with three stars. After four years as Commissioner of Public Safety in his native state of Mississippi, he retired again and lives with his wife in Falls Church, Virginia. Colonel Rosenblum (CO, DISCOM) received the Bronze Star, Air Medal, and Army Commendation Medal for Valor and retired as a lieutenant general in 1984. Colonel Davis (CO, 101st Aviation Grp.) won the Silver Star, two LMs, two Distinguished Flying Crosses, MSM, and twenty-three AMs. He retired to Stratford, Connecticut, where he is with a defense contractor. Lieutenant Garwood (Pathfinders, 101st Aviation Grp.) won the Soldiers Medal for the minefield rescue, two BSMs, two AMs, and an ARCOM; commander of the Golden Knights Parachute Team, he was recently selected for lieutenant colonel. Corporal Fearn (Pathfinders, 101st Aviation Grp.) was KIA in May 1971, during a CA into a hot LZ. Captain Brandt (D/101st Aviation Bn.) was reportedly given only posthumous awards of the BSM, twenty-seven AMs, and the Purple Heart. Lieutenant Updyke (C/158th) was discharged as a captain in 1972 with the Distinguished Flying Cross, several AMs, and a ARCOM. He was divorced within a year. He is now remarried, has two more children, and lives in Evansville, Indiana. WO Smith (A/158th) won the Distinguished Flying Cross for his first day in Laos, a second for his last day, and was medically retired in 1972 with the BSM, thirty-six AMs, ARCOM, and Purple Heart. His wounds left him in a wheel chair and he was married and divorced within a year of getting out of the VA hospital. He remarried in 1975, lives in Fayetteville, Pennsylvania, and continues his flying with a modified airplane. Lieutenant Colonel Steverson (CO, 3/187 Inf.) retained command until the battalion was withdrawn in December 1971; he retired as a colonel in 1979. Major White (XO, 3/187) retired in 1972 with two Bronze Stars for Valor, two BSMs, MSM, ARCOM, and two Purple Hearts. He has since gone to bible college to earn a Master of Theology and lives with his wife in Florence, Alabama, where he is a minister. Lieutenant Daltan (D/3/187) was KIA in June 1971. Lieutenant Stephen (D/3/187) won the Bronze Star for Valor for the body-recovery mission, plus two BSMs and an AM. He has remarried, has two stepsons and a daughter, and is a farmer in Martinsville, Illinois; he also serves on the board of directors of the State Farm Bureau and makes public appearances to speak for Vietnam veterans. Sp4 Daugherty (D/3/187) was wounded again in May 1971, when noises on the perimeter resulted in a buddy squeezing off a poorly-aimed M-79 round. He rotated home in September as a sergeant, and was discharged the same day with the BSM, AM, two ARCOMs, and two Purple Hearts. He was divorced from his wife within a year of getting back from the war; he is now remarried and works as an industrial engineer in Windsor, Connecticut. Sp4 Kucera (B/3/187) made sergeant, left Vietnam in September 1971, and was mustered out in December with the BSM, AM, and two ARCOMs. He is in his second marriage, lives in Cudahy, Wisconsin, and is a troubleshooter for a hydraulics maintenance service.

Brigadier General Hill (CG, 1/5 Mech Div.) served in Vietnam until June 1972, and retired as a major general in 1978. He lives in Austin, Texas, and is a practicing attorney. Lieutenant Colonel Meyer (CO, 1/77 Armor) earned the Silver Star for the artillery rescue and retired in 1979 as colonel with the DSSM, two LMs, MSM, four BSMs, twelve AMs, and an ARCOM. He lives with his wife in Pebble Beach, California, and teaches computer science at a local junior college. Sergeant Major Nelson (CSM, 1/77) retired in 1973 with the Bronze Star for Valor, BSM, MSM, twelve AMs, three ARCOMs, and six Purple Hearts. He finished college, lives with his German-born wife in Severn, Maryland, and is an industrial safety consultant in business for himself. Sergeant Wondra (HHC/l/77) is a police officer and a helicopter pilot in the Minnesota National Guard. Sp4 Spurgeon (HHC/l/77) extended to C/3/5 Cav after the brigade withdrew from Vietnam in August 1971, and was discharged in 1972 with the Army Commendation Medal for Valor, ARCOM, and Purple Heart. He is in his second marriage, and is a federal correctional officer and a captain in the California National Guard. Captain Bodenhorn (CO, A/1/11 Inf.) won the Bronze Star for Valor in Laos, plus two BSMs and six Purple Hearts; he was recently promoted to lieutenant colonel after a stint with the U.S. Military Assistance Group, El Salvador. Lieutenant Clark (A/1/11) is a professional comedian in California. Sp4 Castro (A/l/ll) spent three months with the 101st Airborne after the brigade was withdrawn and was discharged in 1972; after a ten-year fight with the VA, he is drawing a 10 percent disability for his back injury. He is still married, has two children, and is a produce grocery clerk. Lieutenant Colonel Stallman (CO, 1/61 Mech. Inf.) retired as a colonel to Cocoa Beach, Florida. Private First Class DeAngelis (D/1/61) was transferred as a line grunt to A/3/5 Cav, and was discharged Christmas Eve 1971 as a Sp4. He is now married, has a daughter, and is a mechanical engineer in Torrington, Connecticut. Lieutenant Colonel Osborn (CO, 3/5 Cav) retired as a colonel. Captain Stewart (CO, A/3/5) won the Bronze Star for Valor, BSM, Army Commendation Medal for Valor, and two Purple Hearts. He retired for health reasons as a lieutenant colonel in 1984, and lives with his wife and children in Puyallup, Washington. Lieutenant Christian (XO, B/3/5) made captain on his second tour, married, has two children, and is now a major. Sergeant McKenzie (HHT/315) was discharged with a BSM, and lives in Salem, Ohio. Sergeant White (A/3/5) was seriously wounded and medevacked in July 1971, earning the Silver Star, BSM, ARCOM, and two Purple Hearts. His first day home, somebody who didn't know him but hated his uniform, beat him up; that capstoned his bitterness about the war and America, and since then his life has been downhill. He was discharged in 1972, busted to private, and has been arrested twenty-seven times for public drunkenness, disorderly conduct, assaulting a police officer, and other antisocial behavior. He now lives in Owensboro, Kentucky, is in his fifth marriage, and has no job; he receives twenty percent disability from the VA for wounds, and 100 percent for Post-traumatic Stress Disorder. Sergeant McCormack (Brigade LRRP) was discharged in December 1971, with a BSM, ten AMs, Army

Commendation Medal for Valor, and two Purple Hearts. He has married, finished college, and is an office manager in Bristol, Connecticut. Sp4 Walters (P/75th Rangers) completed his tour with the 1st Air Cav; he was discharged in 1973 with the standard combat infantryman's complement of BSM, AM, and ARCOM. He was married and divorced, has full custody of his son, and is a lieutenant on full-time status with the Alaska National Guard.

Lieutenant Colonel Burnett (CO, 1/1 Cav, Americal) was carried as MIA until 1979 when his status was changed to Presumed Killed In Action and he was posthumously promoted to colonel. Lieutenant Colonel Breeding (CO, 1/1) left Vietnam with a BSM and a Purple Heart; he died at Fort Knox in 1975. Sergeant Burnett (HHT/1/1) lives in Metairie, Louisiana; he is a purchasing agent with an alarm service and he and his wife rent a catering service. Sergeant Keefer (A/1/1) was mustered out in 1971 with the BSM, ARCOM, and five Purple Hearts; he has been in VA counselling since 1973. He was recently divorced and shares custody of his two sons. Since the war, he has bounced from job to job and is now a security guard and a crab fisherman in Ridgely, Maryland. Sp4 Smith (A/1/1) rotated home with an ARCOM and now works for the civil service in Long Beach, California. Private First Class Ollie (A/1/1) lives in Maryland with his wife. Private First Class Robinson (A/1/1) died outside Da Nang. Bathing in a stream, he stumbled into a deep hole and drowned. Private First Class Wolf (A/1/1) was reportedly killed soon after leaving Vietnam while driving on drugs. Lieutenant Colonel Coast (CO, 4/3 Inf.) was killed on 20 April 1971 when the main blade of a Loach hit him in the head; he was sorely missed by his battalion. Lieutenant Dewing (A/4/3) was discharged with the Silver Star, two BSMs, AM, and a Purple Heart; he is now married, a major in the reserves, and is a Department of Defense management analyst for an infantry brigade at Fort Richardson, Alaska. Private Morse (A/4/3) spent eighteen months in the hospital and was discharged an Sp4 in 1972 with two Purple Hearts and a 100 percent disability—plus, bullet shrapnel in his spine, impotency problems, a colostomy bag, a paralyzed right leg, and an addiction to painkilling drugs. He left the hospital a junkie, continued using drugs to forget his physical and mental pain, then began robbing drugstores in Massachusetts for narcotics. One night he was asleep, stoned, when the police broke in: he sat up, saw the guns, hit the floor Nam-style and came up shooting. He was charged with four counts of armed robbery, attempted murder, and ended up getting a divorce from his new wife. He was in prison 1976–1980; after two years on parole, he was arrested for drug use and sent back to jail. Three days before he was to be paroled to a VA hospital, two cons looted his cell. Morse confronted them and it came down to him, small and disabled, against two big men in a heated confrontation; Morse moved first. He stabbed them both, and wound up in solitary confinement for seventeen months. He was released in 1984 and immediately joined former platoon buddies, Dewing and Barnhart, at the Vietnam Veterans Memorial in Washington, D.C., where they laid a wreath and unit insignia below the names of their friends killed in Operation Lam Son 719. He now lives with his sister in Sherman, Texas. Captain Downey (CO, C/2/1 Inf.) left the army in 1973, dissatisfied with the service and the direction of the war; he is presently married and manager for personnel security at a large defense contractor in Los Angeles, California.

Lieutenant Colonel Kirklighter (CO, 223d CAB, 1st Aviation Bde.) won the Silver Star at LZ Blue and Distinguished Flying Cross at LZ Hotel Two; he retired as a colonel and lives with his family in Ballwin, Maryland. Major Klose (S3, 223d) received his second Silver Star for LZ Hotel Two and retired as a colonel in 1985; he lives with his wife and children in San Francisco, California. Major Bunting (CO, 48th AHC) is now a colonel. Captain Johnson (173d AHC) is still a captain and continues flying. Lieutenant Smith (48th AHC) won the Distinguished Flying Cross for LZ Hotel Two; in combat after Laos, he earned the Silver Star, BSM, twenty-nine AMs, ARCOM, and two Purple Hearts. He is now a country veterinarian in Griffin, Georgia, and is in the National Guard to continue his flying. Sp5 Lundstrom (173d AHC) was discharged in 1972 with the Distinguished Flying Cross and several AMs; he now has a family and works for the post office in Canton, South Dakota. Lieutenant Colonel Pitman (CO, HQ & Maintenance Sqd., 1st MAW) is presently a brigadier general commanding the 3d Marine Air Wing. CW3 Hawk (165th Aviation Grp.) is now a CW4 with two BSMs, three MSMs, thirty-five AMs, and two ARCOMs. Sp5 Fujii (237th Med. Detachment) was awarded DSC for his four days in Laos (reportedly after being recommended for the Medal of Honor); and later he won the Silver Star, several Bronze Stars and Air Medals, and the Purple Heart. He is now a telephone repairman in Hawaii. Sp5 Wilder (174th AHC, Americal) won the Distinguished Flying Cross for LZ Lolo, and was discharged in 1973 with two Air Medals and an Army Commendation

Medal for Valor, plus two Purple Hearts; he is with his third wife in Jonesville, Virginia, and is a hairstylist.

Lieutenant Colonel Molinelli (CO, 2/17 Air Cav, 101st ABD) is presently a major general. Lieutenant Colonel Rider (CO, 2/17) is now a colonel. Sp4 Fitzmaurice (D/2/17) was awarded the Medal of Honor and a Purple Heart for the sapper attack, an event he does not like to discuss. He is married, has two sons, and works for a packing company in Yale, South Dakota. Private First Class Warren (D/2/17) was wounded twice in a firefight in the A Shau Valley in April 1971, and was medically discharged with the Purple Heart. He now lives with his wife and five children in the Bronx, and works for the Department of Environmental Protection. Captain Mercadante (B/7/1) won the Distinguished Flying Cross for the photo recon mission, and an Air Medal for Valor in the Mekong Delta; he also has the BSM, thirteen AMs, four ARCOMs, and is on the list for lieutenant colonel. Lieutenant Cannon (B/7/1) was KIA in the Mekong Delta. WO Beck (B/7/1) flies for Continental Airlines. Wo Borders (B/7/1) won the Air Medal for Valor in Laos; in subsequent action in the Mekong Delta, he earned two Distinguished Flying Crosses, fourteen AMs, a Purple Heart, and suffered an amputated leg. He was medically retired in 1972 and now lives in Longmont, Colorado, with his wife and two children; despite his injuries, he works as a commercial helicopter pilot. Lieutenant Ferrell (C/7/17) won the BSM, three Air Medals for Valor, and thirty-one AMs; he and his wife now have two children and he is a major.

Lieutenant Colonel Ganahl (CO, 2/94 Artillery) received the LM and BSM for his nine months as battalion commander, and retired as a colonel to Great Falls, Virginia. He is now a programs manager and systems engineer with IBM. Private First Class Keeney (C/2/94) was discharged in 1972 as an Sp4 with an ARCOM; he lives in his hometown of Chillicothe, Missouri, and runs a restaurant with his wife and five children. Private First Class Rhodes (A/2/94) was mustered out as an Sp4 and lives in Elk River, Minnesota, with his wife and child, where he is a sheet-metal fabricator and welder. Sergeant First Class Hatfield (HHB/8/4) retired with the Bronze Star for Valor, three BSMs, the Army Commendation Medal for Valor, and four ARCOMs; he lives in Babbitt, Nevada, and works for the army as a quality assurance specialist with ammunition surveillance. Sp4 Hallman (B/8/4) lives in Lolo, Montana, and receives a 100 percent disability for Post-traumatic Stress Disorder; "I'm kind of a recluse," he said,

"I spend a lot of time getting drunk and wondering why." Sergeant Markle (A/1/44) was awarded a BSM, ARCOM, and an Army Commendation Medal for Valor for the recovery missions. He lives in Orem, Utah, is married and has adopted a son; he is a captain in the Army Reserve and a junior high school teacher.

Brigadier General Sweeney (CG, Da Nang SUPCOM) retired as a major general to Virginia. Colonel Morton (CO, 8th Trans. Grp.) received the LM and BSM for the operation and retired as a brigadier general; he is presently a military consultant for a civilian firm in Pennsylvania. Major Chase (IO, SUPCOM) retired as a colonel with an LM, two BSMs, DMSM, two MSMs, and three ARCOMs; he lives with his wife in Alexandria, Virginia. Lieutenant Malmstrom (Cam Ranh Bay SUPCOM) won a BSM for Khe Sanh, and an end-of-tour ARCOM before being discharged in 1971; he is presently a bachelor in Saratoga, California, where he owns a retail store that specializes in stained-glass windows. Sergeant Michalak (USAF) was discharged in 1972 after two Vietnam tours; he has since married, has children, and works in Chicago as an overhead crane operator. Corporal Bartels (H&S/11th MTB) was mustered out in 1971, is married, has two children, and is an instructor in graphic arts at the University of Northern Iowa. Sp4 Brock (23d MP Co., Americal) volunteered for a second tour, 1971–1972, with the 504th MP Battalion, where he won the Silver Star for dragging two men from a disabled V100 during an ambush, although himself wounded and under fire. He quit the army as a sergeant in 1973, dissatisfied with the erosion of discipline he saw in the all-volunteer army. He is now in his third marriage and is a police sergeant in McCrory, Arkansas. Sp4 Carney (HHC/39th Trans. Bn.) was discharged in 1972 with an ARCOM and now works for the post office in Hull, Massachusetts; he was recently divorced and is in counselling for war-related psychological problems.

END NOTE

During the writing of this book, I received a plaque from one of the veterans whom I had interviewed by telephone. It certainly took me by surprise, but was a much appreciated gesture, and I'd like to publicly thank Frank Burnett. The inscription reads:

Keith William Nolan
is awarded
"Honorary Membership"
in
The 1st Squadron, 1st Cavalry
First Regiment of Dragoons
For his outstanding and caring
work in telling the truth about "Lam Son 719"
Given by
Trooper F. A. Burnett
1st Squadron, 1st Cavalry
Vietnam 70–71 "Blackhawk"

Needless to say, researching and writing a book has its discouraging moments, but such encouragement from the veterans makes it all worthwhile. Virtually every Vietnam veteran whom I had the opportunity of contacting was most helpful and this work would never have gotten off the ground without their great input. Thanks again, friends.

Glossary

AA: Anti-aircraft fire.

AFA: Aerial Field Artillery.

AK-47 or AK: standard communist 7.62 automatic rifle.

ALO: Air Liaison Officer.

AO: Area of Operations.

APC: Armored Personnel Carrier.

Article 15: Nonjudicial punishment for relatively minor offenses.

ARVN: Army of the Republic of Vietnam; individual South Vietnamese soldier.

AVLB: Armored Vehicle Launch Bridge.

BA: Base area.

Brother: Common form of address between black soldiers.

Bush: Anyplace outside a base where combat is a real prospect.

CA: Combat Assault, helicopter insertion of troops to the field.

CAB: Combat Aviation Battalion.

C&C: Command and Control helicopter used by commanders to super-vise units.

C4: Plastic explosive compound.

Chalk: Indicator of a helicopter's position in line (chalk two is the second ship).

Charlie: Nickname for the communist soldiers.

Chinook: Nickname for the CH47 transport helicopter.

Claymore: Above ground, antipersonnel mine used by U.S. forces.

CO: Commanding Officer.

Cobra: Nickname for the AH1G gunship helicopter.

COMUSMACV: Commander, U.S. Military Assistance Command-Vietnam.

Concertina: Barbed wire used by U.S. forces.

CP: Command Post.

C rations, C rats, or Cs: Combat field meals packed in tin cans.

CVC: Radio helmet worn by armor crews.

Dap: Ritualized handshake greeting performed between black soldiers.

DEPCOMUSMACV: Deputy Commander, U.S. Military Assistance Command Vietnam.

DEROS: Date of Estimated Return Overseas.

Dew: Nickname for marijuana.

Dink: Derogatory nickname for Vietnamese.

DISCOM: Division Support Command.

DMZ: Demilitarized Zone, dividing line of the two Vietnams on the 17th
    parallel.

Duster: Nickname for the M42 combat vehicle mounted with two 40mm
    cannons.

E-tool: Entrenching tool, military term for shovel.

FAC: Forward Air Controller.

Field: Anyplace outside a base where combat is a real prospect.

Flak jacket: Sleeveless armored vest designed to stop shrapnel.

FNG: Fucking New Guy.

FO: Forward Observer, an artilleryman attached to the infantry to direct
    support fire.

.45: Standard U.S. combat pistol.

Frag: A fragmentation grenade; to destroy something with a grenade; to
    purposely attempt to kill or wound officers or NCOs over personal
    grievances or for revenge.

FSA: Forward Support Area.

FSB: Fire Support Base.

GI: Government Issue, popular name for the American soldier.

Gook: Derogatory name for Vietnamese.

Grunt: Affectionate nickname for the combat infantryman

GSG: General Support Group.

Head: Nickname for drug user.

Head smack: To snort heroin through the nose.

Hootch: Any small shelter.

HQ: Headquarters.

Huey: Nickname for the UH1 series of helicopters.

Incoming: Enemy fire, usually meaning mortar, rocket, or artillery
    attack.

In-country: To be in Vietnam.

Juicer: Nickname for drinkers.

JP4: Aviation fuel.

KIA: Killed In Action.

Kiowa Scout: Nickname for the OH58 helicopter.

Kit Carson Scout: Communist soldiers who defected to the allies and volun-
    teered to serve with U.S. units as scouts and interpreters.

Laager: Nickname for assembly positions held by armor units.

LAW: Light Antitank Weapon, 66mm rocket, usually shoulder-fired against bunkers.

Lifer: Derogatory term for career soldiers.

Loach: Nickname for the OH6 helicopter.

LOC: Line of Communications.

LP: Listening Post.

LRRP: Long Range Reconnaissance Patrol.

LZ: Landing Zone.

M-14: A 7.62mm rifle generally phased out by U.S. forces in 1967.

M-16: Standard U.S. 5.56mm automatic rifle.

M-60: Standard U.S. 7.62mm machine gun.

M-79: Standard U.S. 40mm grenade launcher.

MA: Mechanical Ambush, euphemism for U.S. booby traps.

MACV: Military Assistance Command-Vietnam.

Mad Minute: Practice of placing heavy fire around a defensive position, usually at night, without warning or apparent reason, to dissuade enemy troops in the area.

Medevac: Medical evacuation helicopter; the act of being evacuated.

MIA: Missing In Action.

Minigun: Gatling guns capable of firing six thousand rounds per minute.

MOS: Military Occupational Specialty.

MP: Military Police.

MPC: Military Pay Currency.

MR: Military Region.

NCO: Noncommissioned Officer.

NVA: North Vietnamese Army; individual North Vietnamese soldier.

OJ: Opium Joint.

Phantom: Nickname for the F4 jet.

Pig: Nickname for the M-60 machine gun.

Point: Lead man on a patrol.

POL: Petroleum Oil Lubricants.

Pot: Nickname for marijuana.

PSP: Pierced Steel Planking.

PZ: Pickup Zone.

Quad-fifty: Truck mounted with four .50-caliber machine guns.

R&R: Rest and Relaxation, one-week leave granted to servicemen in Vietnam.

Reefer: Nickname for marijuana.

REMF: Rear Echelon Motherfucker.

RIF: Reconnaissance In Force.

Rock'n'roll: Nickname for firing a weapon on full auto.

ROK: Republic of Korea.

RPG: Rocket Propelled Grenade, standard communist shoulder-fired projectile.

RPG Screen: Chain-link fence placed around vehicles to absorb the blast of an RPG.

RTO: Radio Telephone Operator, a radioman.

Ruck: Nickname for rucksack or backpack.

S&D: Search and Destroy.

S&S: Supply and Service.

Sea Stallion: Nickname for the H53 helicopter used by the U.S. Marine Corps.

Sheridan: The M551 armored reconnaissance assault vehicle.

Short: Nearly to have completed one's 365-day tour of duty in Vietnam.

Skag: Nickname for heroin.

Sky Crane: Nickname for the CH54 equipment-moving helicopter.

Slack: The second man in a patrol file who covered the pointman.

Slick: Nickname for Huey transport helicopters.

Smack: Nickname for heroin.

SP: Self-Propelled artillery piece.

SUPCOM: Support Command.

Tac Air: Tactical Air Support.

TAOR: Tactical Area of Responsibility.

TC: Tank or Track Commander.

TOC: Tactical Operations Center.

Track: Nickname for the tracked armored personnel carrier.

USAF: United States Air Force.

USARV: United States Army, Vietnam.

USMC: United States Marine Corps.

VC: Viet Cong.

Ville: Village.

VNMC: Vietnamese Marine Corps.

V100: Armored vehicle used by the military police, mounted with machine guns.

WIA: Wounded In Action.

Willy Peter: White Phosphorus.
WO: Warrant Officer.
World, the: Anyplace but Vietnam, usually referring to the United States.

Bibliography

Books

Brown, Corninne. *Body Shop: Recuperating from Vietnam.* Stein and Day, 1973.

Drendel, Loua. *Gunslingers in Action.* Warren, Michigan: Squadron/ Signal Publications, 1974.

Emerson, Gloria. *Winners & Losers.* New York: Random House, 1976.

Esper, George. *The Eyewitness History of the Vietnam War, 1961-1975.* New York: Ballantine Books, 1983.

Graves, Ralph, ed. *Larry Burrows: Compassionate Photographer.* New York: Time, Inc., 1972.

Hauser, William, Lt. Col. *America's Army in Crisis.* Baltimore, Maryland: The Johns Hopkins University Press, 1973.

Hinh, Nguyen Duy, Maj. Gen. *Lam Son 719.* Washington, D.C.: U.S. Army Center of Military History, 1979.

Jason, Alexander. *Heroes: The True Accounts of the Medal of Honor Winners Southeast Asia 1964-1975.* Pinole, California: The Anite Press, 1979.

Kirk, Donald. *Tell it to the Dead: Memories of a War.* Chicago: Nelson-Hall Publishers, 1975.

Kissinger, Henry. *White House Years.* Boston: Little, Brown and Company, 1979.

Lewy, Guenter. *America in Vietnam.* New York: Random House, 1978.

Palmer, Dave Richard. *Summons of the Trumpet: A History of the Vietnam War from a Military Man's Viewpoint.* Novato, California: Presidio Press, 1978.

Shore, Moyers S., Capt. *The Battle for Khe Sanh.* Washington D.C.: Historical Branch. G-3 Division, Headquarters, U.S. Marine Corps, 1969.

Simmons, E. H., Brig. Gen. *The Marines in Vietnam 1954-1973*. Washington, D.C.: History and Museums Division, Headquarters, U.S. Marine Corps, 1974.

Starry, Donn A., Gen. *Mounted Combat in Vietnam*. Washington, D.C.: Department of the Army, 1978.

Tolson, John J., Gen. *Airmobility, 1961-1971*. Washington, D.C.: Department of the Army, 1973.

Vien, Cao Van, Gen. *Leadership*. Washington, D.C.: U.S. Army Center of Military History, 1980.

Westmoreland, William C., Gen. *A Soldier Reports*. Garden City, New York: Doubleday and Company, Inc., 1976.

Willwerth, James. *Eye in the Last Storm: A Reporter's Journal of One Year in South East Asia*. New York: Grossman Publishers, 1972.

Periodicals

"As Common as Chewing Gum," *Time*, March 1, 1971.

Downey, Gerald. "Christmas Truce," *Leatherneck*, December 1983.

"GI's Other Enemy: Heroin," *Newsweek*, May 24, 1971.

"How the Invasion was Planned," *Newsweek*, February 22, 1971.

"Incident on Route 9," *Time*, April 5, 1971.

"Indispensable Lifeline," *Time*, February 15, 1971.

"Invasion Ends," *Time*, April 5, 1971.

"Just say it was the Commancheros," *Newsweek*, March 15, 1971.

"Last Big Push—Or a Wider War," *Newsweek*, February 15, 1971.

Linden, Eugene. "Fragging and Other Withdrawal Symptoms," *Saturday Review*, January 8, 1972.

McCaffery, Barry, Capt. "The American Soldier in Vietnam," *Soldiers*, July 1972.

McCaffery, William, Lt. Gen. "A Fighting Army Heads for Home," *Army*, October 1971.

Meyer, Richard, Lt. Col. "The Road to Laos," *Armor*, March-April 1972.

Morgenstern, Joseph. "Two Soldiers," *Newsweek*, March 15, 1971.

Okamura, Akihiko. "Crossroads at Tchepone," *Life*, March 26, 1971.

___. "The War in Laos," *Life*, March 12, 1971.

Saar, John. "A Frantic Night on the Edge of Laos," *Life*, February 19, 1971.

___. "You Just Can't Hand Out Orders," *Life*, October 23, 1970.

___. "Scramble for Safety." *Life*, April 2, 1971.

"Shootout at Quang Tri." *Newsweek*, January 25, 1971.

"Troubled U.S. Army in Vietnam." *Newsweek*, January 11, 1971.

"War Within the War." *Time*, January 25, 1971.

Warner, Steve, Sp4. "Darkness is Deadly," *Army Digest*, April 1971.

Weiss, George. "Battle for Control of Ho Chi Minh Trail," *Armed Forces Journal*, February 15, 1971.

___. "CO 2/17 AirCav: 'Gunships Took Tanks. Survived Flak,' in Laos," *Armed Forces Journal*, April 19, 1971.

"Withdrawal Pains." *Newsweek*, June 7, 1971.

Documents

Berry, Sidney, Maj. Gen., "Lamson 719—The Assault Into Laos 8 February–6 April 1971."

"Daily Staff Journal or Duty Officer's Log, 3d Bn, 187th Inf, 101st Abn Div, 19–24 Mar 71."

"Department of the Army. Headquarters, 1st Calvary Division (Airmobile). APO San Francisco 96490, Combat Operations After Action Report. 11 July, 1970. Operation Toan Thang."

"101st Airborne Division (Airmobile). Final Report, Airmobile Operations in Support of Operation Lamson 719, 8 February–6 April 1971. Volumes I and II."

"Operational Report—Lessons Learned, Headquarters, 57th Transportation Bn, Period Ending 31 October 1971 (U)."

"Operational Report—Lessons Learned, 1st Inf Bde, 5th Inf Div (Mech). Period Ending 30 April 1971, RCS CSFOR-65 (R3)(U)."

"Operation Lam Son 719, 8 February 1971 to March 1971. A Narrative Description."

"XXIV Corps, Lam Son 719. After Action Report, 30 Jan–6 Apr 1971."

"U.S. Marine Corps Oral History Program/Interviewee: Col. William H. Dabney, 20 May 1982."

INDEX

387